A MONTH IN THE COUNTRY
STONY BROKE
ONE OF THE FAMILY
THE BACHELOR
LUNCH AT HIS EXCELLENCY'S
A PROVINCIAL LADY

Ivan Sergeevich Turgenev

PLAYS

A MONTH IN THE COUNTRY
STONY BROKE
ONE OF THE FAMILY
THE BACHELOR
LUNCH AT HIS EXCELLENCY'S
A PROVINCIAL LADY

translated by

Stephen Mulrine

OBERON BOOKS
LONDON

First published in 1999 by Oberon Books Ltd.
(incorporating Absolute Classics)
521 Caledonian Road, London N7 9RH
Tel: 0171 607 3637 / Fax: 0171 607 3629
e-mail: oberon.books@btinternet.com

British Library Cataloguing-in-Publication Data
A catalogue record for this book is available from the British
Library.

ISBN 1 84002 048 2

Cover Design: Andrzej Klimowski
Typography: Richard Doust

Printed in Great Britain by MPG Ltd., Bodmin.

Contents

Ivan Sergeevich Turgenev, 1818-83

Stephen Mulrine

Ivan Sergeevich Turgenev was born on the 28th of October, 1818, in the regional capital of Orel, about 200 miles south of Moscow. His father was a lieutenant-colonel, decorated for bravery at the battle of Borodino, and a member of the minor Russian aristocracy, with a pedigree that included the court jester of Peter the Great. Not long after Turgenev's birth, the family moved to his mother's estate at Spasskoe, where he spent his childhood.

Turgenev's father seems to have taken little interest in domestic matters, but his mother, Varvara Petrovna, ruled with a rod of iron, earning a reputation for capricious cruelty, visited on her serfs and children alike. The young Turgenev witnessed sufficient casual brutality within his own family circle, and the local gentry, to confirm him in determined opposition to serfdom, and it is significant that his first real success, as a writer, was his *Sportsman's Sketches*, (1847-51), a series of anecdotes and impressions remarkable for their searching analysis of the peasants' plight.

Turgenev was educated at the universities of both Moscow and St. Petersburg, before leaving Russia in 1838, at the age of nineteen, to continue his studies in Berlin. By the time he returned to St. Petersburg, three years later, Turgenev's views on the perennial conflict between 'Slavophiles' and 'Westernizers' were already well formed, though his instinctive revulsion to any kind of dogma would make him enemies, throughout his life, among extremists of either party.

Turgenev began his literary career in 1843 with the publication of a narrative poem, *Parasha*, showing the influence of Pushkin's *Yevgeny Onegin*, and in that same year he met and fell in love with a Spanish opera singer, Pauline Viardot, who was to dominate his emotional life until his dying day. At the time of their meeting, she was twenty-two, three years younger than Turgenev, and almost half the age of her husband, Louis

Viardot. Despite his infatuation, Turgenev became a family friend, of such a degree of intimacy that he even sent his daughter Pelageya, the product of a liaison with a maidservant, to be brought up in the Viardot household.

In 1852, following the publication in full of his *Sportsman's Sketches*, and an ill-advised obituary in praise of Gogol, Turgenev was arrested and briefly imprisoned, before being exiled to Spasskoe. As a measure of the difficult circumstances in which all Russian writers worked, it should be noted that the very fact of his arrest was officially censored, and Turgenev was forced to plead with his friends not even to mention it in print. It was during this time, however, that he began work on the great novels of his maturity: *Rudin* (1856), *A Nest of Gentlefolk* (1859), *On the Eve* (1860), and *Fathers and Sons* (1862).

In the same year as *Fathers and Sons* was published, Turgenev began his effective exile from Russia, moving to the fashionable spa town of Baden-Baden, partly for health reasons, but chiefly to be near the Viardots. While his later novels, *Smoke* (1867), and *Virgin Soil* (1877), disappointed the extremist press, Turgenev made a triumphant return visit to Russia in 1879, and international acclaim included an honorary doctorate from the University of Oxford.

In 1880, Turgenev was an invited guest at the unveiling of the Pushkin memorial in Moscow, and although his speech was indifferently received, his latter years, marked by increasing ill-health, were made bearable by the genuine respect and affection of his countrymen. Old enmities, with Tolstoy and Dostoevsky notably, were resolved, and Turgenev could take his place unchallenged among the giants of Russian literature. In 1882, living with the Viardot family near Paris, Turgenev developed cancer of the spine, and died after a long illness on September 3rd, 1883. His body was returned to Russia, and buried in St. Petersburg, at the Volkovo cemetery.

Turgenev the Dramatist

Though his reputation rests mainly on his prose fiction, the ten plays Turgenev wrote between 1843 and 1852 represent a very concentrated phase of work, and when it is remembered that the best of these, *A Month in the Country* (1850), pre-dates Chekhov's great plays by almost a half-century, then it will be clear that this was work to some purpose. Unfortunately, Turgenev the dramatist tends to be seen in Chekhov's shadow, and the fact that his plays are virtually unknown to English readers, perpetuates an injustice.

Turgenev is admitted to the company of world dramatists on the strength of *A Month in the Country* alone, but his other plays have considerable merit. They are well crafted, highly performable pieces, ranging from what he himself describes as a 'scene', to comedies at one, two, and three-act length, and they are not only the true measure of Turgenev's achievement in the genre, but also shed an interesting light on the great novels which followed. This collection accordingly samples the best of Turgenev's drama, and in addition to *A Month in the Country*, these include *Stony Broke, One of the Family, The Bachelor, Lunch at His Excellency's*, and *A Provincial Lady*.

Turgenev's first play, *Indiscretion* (1843), might almost have been a dry run for *A Month in the Country*, with its triangular relationship of husband, wife, and young admirer, not to mention a proto-Rakitin, the husband's close friend who nurses a secret passion for the wife. However, it is by comparison crudely melodramatic, and his second play, the one-act *Stony Broke* (1845), shows Turgenev still learning his craft, very much at the feet of Gogol. That is no bad thing, and what might be regarded as Turgenev's first realist play incurred the wrath of the censorship, for its sharply satirical portrayal of the Tsarist nobility.

Stony Broke bears the clear imprint of *The Government Inspector*, and is in effect a development of the scene in which Khlestakov, and his valet Osip are at their wits' end, penniless and desperate in a run-down provincial hotel. Turgenev's variation on a theme of Gogol is an engaging little play, with a large cast of characters, many of whom appear only as off-stage voices, demanding money with a variety of menaces. His profligate young nobleman, Zhazikov, in his St Petersburg lodgings, is up to his ears in debt, and besieged by creditors, kept at bay by his old manservant, Matvei, in a series of comic exchanges. Zhazikov has of course been living well beyond his means, though he is heir to a substantial country estate, and when an attempt to borrow money from a wealthy acquaintance fails, Matvei finally persuades him of the benefits of country life, and he resolves to leave the city. Alas, at this point another of his own sort arrives from their home village, still solvent, and lends him enough money to re-launch his career of high-spending debauchery. Country life, needless to say, instantly loses its appeal.

Turgenev's third play, *A Fine Thread* (1848), is in arguably more typical vein, a contest between two suitors, one feckless and indecisive, the other solid and worthy, for the affections of a pretty girl, a theme he was to revisit, to some degree, in *The Bachelor*. Later that same year, however, social criticism was again uppermost in his two-act comedy *One of the Family* (1848), which exhibits more than a trace of Gogolian caricature in its indictment of upper-class modes and manners. Turgenev's targets here are social climbing St. Petersburg careerists, and the boorish provincial landed gentry, a combination lethal enough to ensure the play being banned until 1861.

The Russian title of *One of the Family* literally denotes a person living at someone else's expense, often an impoverished relative, of a type not unfamiliar in the country houses of the aristocracy – Telegin, in Chekhov's *Uncle Vanya*, is a good example. Turgenev's two-act comedy is set on a wealthy provincial estate, which provides free bed and board for a certain Kuzovkin. The young lady owner, Olga Petrovna, has been absent in St Petersburg for several years, and is now returning home with her new husband, Yeletsky, a rather superior and chilly civil servant.

Kuzovkin is ostensibly a dependant, but is in fact a minor nobleman who has been cheated out of his own inherited property, and is unable to afford the litigation fees to retrieve it. During lunch, he is plied with drink by the other guests, local landed gentry, and made to recount his long, confused story to the new master of the house. The wretched Kuzovkin is eventually insulted beyond endurance, and announces that while he may appear to be of no account, he is in fact Olga's real father. Yeletsky is horrified, and Kuzovkin vows to leave the house forever. Olga later presses Kuzovkin to tell her the full story, however, and he discloses some unpalatable truths about her late father's treatment of her mother, before his own liaison with her, which resulted in Olga's birth.

Thereafter, the action turns and twists as Yeletsky tries to buy Kuzovkin off – though the latter wishes only to be allowed to leave, and conceal the disgrace for his daughter's sake. Finally, a solution is found in that Yeletsky and Olga offer to redeem Kuzovkin's estate – he will take up residence there once more, and Olga can visit her real father in private. Those who had previously baited Kuzovkin are now forced to congratulate him on winning back his property.

It is not difficult to see why the Tsarist censorship took exception to the play, and even when it was produced in 1861, only the first act could be staged. Technically a comedy, *One of the Family* has its share of humorous passages, but like the best of Turgenev's work it sounds a sombre note, with considerable emotional power, developed at some length.

The three-act comedy Turgenev wrote the following year, *The Bachelor* (1849), is the longest of all his plays, apart from *A Month in the Country*, and again an apparently simple narrative is made to carry the complex emotional burden characteristic of his mature work. The plot centres on two bachelors, in fact, and Moshkin, a St Petersburg official in his late forties, the guardian and benefactor of Masha, is about to marry her off to the second bachelor of the story, Vilitsky, a handsome young civil servant with whom she is deeply in love.

During the final preparations for the wedding, however, Vilitsky begins to have second thoughts – Masha is neither rich nor clever enough for his career ambitions, he fears, and when his superior German friend Fonk expresses disapproval, Vilitsky attempts to back out of the marriage. Masha of course suspects that Vilitsky has gone cold on her, but he is too pusillanimous to tell her in person, and Moshkin eventually confronts him, to force him to admit the truth, and call off the engagement. The situation then takes a not-unexpected turn, however, when Moshkin realises that he himself is in love with Masha, and the play ends with a wedding once more in prospect, albeit with a different groom.

Turgenev wrote *The Bachelor* at the behest of the great actor-manager Shchepkin, and it became one of his few successes during this decade of work, perhaps because its criticism of the St. Petersburg managerial class was too restrained to excite controversy. Its three acts are basically detailed explorations of the characters' emotional state at each stage, and the plotting, which includes some well-observed secondary roles, is richly textured.

The influence of Gogol is again to the fore in *Lunch at His Excellency's* (1849), a one-act comedy basically cumulative in structure, as various invited and uninvited guests arrive at a certain Balagalaev's house. The latter's official title is in fact Marshal of the Nobility, a provincial elected office of considerable prestige, and he has organised a working lunch in order to settle a dispute between two local landowners, Bespandin, and his widowed sister, Kaurova. Other callers, Gogolian eccentrics to a man, include the former Marshal, still resentful over the loss of his position, and itching to interfere.

As the arbitration proceeds, the widow Kaurova proves so obdurate, all the while playing the victim, that the dispute not only proves impossible to resolve, but also draws all the other guests into the fray. Eventually, the issues become so entangled that the wretched Marshal abandons his guests and retires to his bed, in a state of nervous collapse. Turgenev's mockery of the philistine landed gentry guaranteed the play a rough passage through the censors, but it was nonetheless licensed for performance, and became only the second of his six completed plays to be staged.

Turgenev's most successful play, during his lifetime, was *A Provincial Lady* (1850), one of three short plays which followed *A Month in the Country*. Of the other two, *An Evening in Sorrento* (1852) is a romantic comedy in a suitably romantic setting, played out by a quartet of Russian tourists, pursuing their amorous inclinations in between complaining about the hotel service. *Conversation on the Highway* (1851), described by

Turgenev as a 'scene', and perfectly summed up by its title, is a rambling dialogue among three coach travellers, distinguished by some vigour of peasant speech, but no real shape.

Despite its condemnation as frivolous, by Turgenev's more sober-sided critics, *A Provincial Lady* was enthusiastically received by audiences, and indeed it is surprising that this elegant and witty comedy is so rarely performed in English. It is masterfully plotted, the tale of a clever young wife, Darya Ivanovna, who learns that an old flame of sorts, Count Lyubin, now an influential St Petersburg official, is revisiting the provincial backwater in which he spent his youth.

Darya's husband, Stupendiev, has a business appointment with him, and she adroitly manipulates events to get rid of her husband, in order to deploy her wiles on the Count. She then more or less fabricates a romantic past for herself and the now elderly Count, and in an accelerating sequence of events, including comic interruptions by her suspicious husband, brings the Count literally to his knees, in a declaration of undying love. At this point, Darya's husband catches them in the act, and she achieves her real ambition   a promise from the thoroughly compromised Count to find her husband a position in St Petersburg, and rescue them both from the tedium of provincial life.

Turgenev's substantial one-act play has a lively supporting cast, but is especially notable for the character of Darya Ivanovna, whose distinctly un-provincial accomplishments include music (so that she can accompany the smitten Count in the operatic duet he just happens to have composed), much better French than His Excellency himself, and an infinitely sharper wit.

Turgenev frequently disparaged his talents as a dramatist, going so far on one occasion as to call *A Month in the Country* a 'short story in dramatic form', quite unsuited to the stage. While that says more, perhaps, about Russian theatre in Turgenev's day, half a century before Stanislavsky's seminal production of Chekhov's *Seagull*, it is true that his shorter plays are derivative, and of uneven quality. They are very far from negligible, however, and the best features of his great contribution to the classic repertoire are all to be found there, in some measure.

A Month in the Country

Turgenev's troubles with the Tsarist censorship are well documented, and by no means unique: Pushkin's death was the consequence of a pistol shot, but his life was made intolerable by that same institution, and Ostrovsky, Turgenev's contemporary, was forced to wait almost a decade to see his first play performed in public – during which time he nevertheless established a reputation as the country's leading dramatist.

A Month in the Country, Turgenev's seventh play, had a particularly chequered history in that respect. Following its submission to the censors, titled *The Student*, in 1850, Turgenev was instructed to make Natalya Petrovna a widow, and remove completely the character of her husband Islaev. Natalya Petrovna's situation, courted on the one hand by her husband's friend, and infatuated on the other with her son's tutor, presumably cast an unacceptable shadow on Russian womanhood. Turgenev made the necessary revisions, which included blunting the political edge of the play, implicit in its first title, but the censors again refused him permission to publish. Not until 1855 was *A Month in the Country* finally printed, with the various cuts and changes demanded by the censor, and the play was only restored to something like his original conception, with the publication of his Collected Works in 1869.

Now regarded as one of the greatest plays in the European canon, *A Month in the Country* was first performed in Moscow on January 13th, 1872, more than two decades after it was written, and the failure of that production seemed to confirm Turgenev's own low estimate of his talents. Indeed, another seven years were to pass before the actress Maria Savina chose it for her benefit performance in St. Petersburg in 1879, playing the part of Vera, and won for *A Month in the Country* the recognition it merited.

As already noted, much of Turgenev's drama is derivative, and *A Month in the Country* is no exception. Turgenev was resident in Paris during the turbulent events of 1848, and almost certainly saw Balzac's melodrama *La marâtre* (*The Stepmother*) which was premièred in the city that same year. The plot and character echoes are too strong to be coincidental, and Balzac provides Turgenev with a model not only for the triangle of Natalya Petrovna, Vera, and Belyaev, but also most of the supporting cast. However, Balzac assigns a more active role to the Islaev figure, the infatuated stepmother's husband, and there is no equivalent to Turgenev's Rakitin.

Of course, Turgenev needed no model for Rakitin – his own infatuation with Pauline Viardot is the obvious source, as indeed he later admitted to Maria Savina. It is also the well-spring of much of the play's emotional power, and as a study in unfulfilled yearnings, and repressed passion, *A Month in the Country* must surely have acted as a beacon, to light Chekhov's path. Ironically, however, it was the latter's work, through which the Moscow Art Theatre developed the psychologically complex ensemble that became their trademark, that paved the way for a genuinely sensitive reading of the play, in Stanislavsky's production of 1909.

Stanislavsky himself took the part of Rakitin, and his own account of the experience focuses on the tensions underlying Turgenev's civilised table-talk, between youth and age, nature and nurture, freedom and constraint. Natalya Petrovna's inner turmoil is externalised in the characters of Rakitin and Belyaev – the one introspective, sophisticated, emotionally inert, the other fresh, spontaneous, uninhibited – and in reaching out to the latter, the 'hot-house rose', in Stanislavsky's phrase, yearns to become a field flower. The authentic field flower, however, in the person of Vera, is not only a rival, to be callously disposed of in a loveless marriage, but also a reminder of the futility of her desire.

All of Turgenev's work embodies social criticism to a greater or lesser degree, and his original title for the play, *The Student*, indicated a more significant role for Belyaev, the classless 'new man' who would shape Russia's future. In *A Month in the*

Country, radical ideas of that kind are to be inferred, rather than openly discussed, and Turgenev's political leanings are perhaps best shown in his negative treatment of the weak-minded Bolshintsov, and the unprincipled Shpigelsky. Indeed, by the end of the play, the latter is the only character who can truthfully be said to have achieved his heart's desire – if a team of horses, and a docile wife-cum-housekeeper merit that description. Shpigelsky also functions as the detached observer, of course, but his own moral and emotional vacuity makes him incapable of comprehending the passions he witnesses. Not so Turgenev's other observer, and *alter ego*, Rakitin, whose advice to his rival on the subject of love – a word that appears on almost every page of Turgenev's text – fairly chills the blood:

> In my opinion, Belyaev, any kind of love, happy or unhappy, it doesn't matter which, is an absolute disaster if you surrender to it completely. You wait and see! You've perhaps still to discover how those gentle hands can torture a man, with what tender solicitude they can tear your heart to pieces. Yes, you wait! You'll find out how much burning hatred lies hidden beneath that ardent love! And you'll remember me, when you long for peace, as a sick man longs for health – the most mindless, common-or-garden peace, when you'll envy any free, untroubled soul. You wait and see! You'll find out what it means to hang on a woman's skirts, what it means to be enslaved, intoxicated – and how humiliating and tiresome that slavery can be!

Turgenev's difficulties with the censor have already been noted, and it is significant that this speech of Rakitin's is the only one he restored, from the first round of enforced cuts, as soon as the opportunity arose, with the 1869 publication. No doubt the censor was again defending the honour of Russian womanhood, but the destructive power of love, asserted so unequivocally here, is experienced by both sexes, and Natalya Petrovna's self-lacerating soliloquies, as she tries to rationalise her obsession with Belyaev, indirectly echo Rakitin's sentiments.

Soliloquy is an important device in *A Month in the Country* – it has often been remarked that very little happens in the play, in terms of action, and indeed the climax, in which everyone goes his or her separate way, pretty much as before, is less resounding even than Chekhov, at his most understated. And Turgenev's dialogue is correspondingly muted – the electricity of charge and counter-charge is low-voltage, conducted for the most part between Rakitin and Natalya Petrovna, and later the disillusioned Vera – always within the bounds of propriety.

Despite Turgenev's protestations, *A Month in the Country* is not a novel in dramatic form. Certainly it exhibits many of the characteristics of his later prose, and in comparison with the plays of Chekhov, say, it is occasionally unfocused and lacking in pace. It might also be argued that the key monologues, so crucial to our understanding of the characters, are evidence of Turgenev's impatience with the restrictions of the form. Again, for a play with so little movement, Turgenev's stage directions are remarkably detailed, but that is perhaps an indication of anxiety, well-founded as it turned out, rather than an attempt to introduce narrative by the back door.

In truth, Turgenev's masterpiece needs no apology, and ever since Stanislavsky sought and found its inner dynamic, in the shifting moods and private agonies of these charming, intelligent people – 'making lace', as Natalya Petrovna puts it, in their stuffy rooms, rarely moving from the spot – *A Month in the Country* has continued to touch the hearts of audiences the world over.

Stephen Mulrine
January 1998

A MONTH IN THE COUNTRY

Characters

ISLAEV (ARKADY SERGEYICH)
a wealthy landowner, aged 36

NATALYA PETROVNA
his wife, 29

KOLYA
their son, 10

VERA (ALEKSANDROVNA)
Natalya Petrovna's ward, 17

ANNA (SEMYONOVNA)
Islaev's mother, 58

LIZAVETA (BOGDANOVNA)
Her companion, 37

SCHAAF
A German tutor, 45

RAKITIN (MIKHAILO ALEKSANDROVICH)
A friend of the family, 30

BELYAEV (ALEKSEI NIKOLAEVICH)
A student, Kolya's tutor, 21

BOLSHINTSOV (AFANASY IVANOVICH)
A neighbour, 48

SHPIGELSKY (IGNATY ILYICH)
A doctor, 40

MATVEI
A servant, 40

KATYA
A maid, 20

The action takes place on Islaev's estate at the beginning of
the 1840s. Between Acts I and II, Acts II and III, and Acts
IV and V there are intervals of a day.

ACT ONE

The curtain opens on a drawingroom. To the right is a card table, and a door leading to the study; at centre is a door into the ballroom; on the left are two windows and a round table, and there are settees in the corners. ANNA SEMYONOVNA, LIZAVETA BOGDANOVNA and SCHAAF are playing whist at the card-table, while NATALYA PETROVNA and RAKITIN are sitting at the round table. NATALYA PETROVNA is embroidering on a canvas, and RAKITIN is holding a book. The wall clock shows three o'clock.

SCHAAF: (*He speaks with a heavy German accent.*) Hearts...

ANNA S: Again? My dear sir, you're beating us all ends up!

SCHAAF: Eight hearts...

ANNA S: What? Honestly, the man's impossible.
    (*LIZAVETA BOGDANOVNA laughs.*)

NATALYA PETROVNA: (*To RAKITIN.*) Why have you stopped? Read on.

RAKITIN: *"Monte-Cristo se redressa haletant..."* Natasha, are you really interested in this?

NATALYA PETROVNA: Not in the slightest.

RAKITIN: Then why are we reading it?

NATALYA PETROVNA: I'll tell you why. A few days ago one of the ladies said: "You haven't read 'The Count of Monte-Cristo'? Oh, do read it – it's simply divine!"
    I didn't say anything at the time, but now I'll be able to tell her I've read it, and found nothing divine in it.

RAKITIN: Well, if you've made up your mind already...

NATALYA PETROVNA: Really, you're so lazy!

RAKITIN: Oh, all right, for goodness' sake! "*Se redressa haletant, et...*"

NATALYA PETROVNA: Have you seen Arkady today?

RAKITIN: I bumped into him down at the weir. It's being repaired, apparently. He was explaining something to the workmen, wading in up to his knees in sand, to make his point.

NATALYA PETROVNA: He gets carried away – tries too hard. That's a fault, don't you think?

RAKITIN: Yes, I agree.

NATALYA PETROVNA: What a bore! You're always agreeing with me. Now, read on.

RAKITIN: I see – you want me to argue with you, is that it?

NATALYA PETROVNA: I want... I want... I want *you* to want... Now, come on, read!

RAKITIN: Yes, ma'am.

SCHAAF: Hearts!

ANNA S: What, again? This is intolerable! Natasha! Natasha!

NATALYA PETROVNA: Yes?

ANNA S: Would you believe it, Schaaf's absolutely trounced us. Seven hearts, eight hearts, every time!

SCHAAF: And now again, seven!

ANNA S: You hear that? It's frightful!

NATALYA PETROVNA: Yes, it is.

ANNA S: That's whist for you! Where's Kolya?

NATALYA PETROVNA: He's gone for a walk with his new tutor.

ANNA S: Ah, yes. Lizaveta, will you partner me?

RAKITIN: Which tutor is this?

NATALYA PETROVNA: Oh, of course – I forgot to tell you – we engaged a new tutor while you were away.

RAKITIN: In place of Dufour?

NATALYA PETROVNA: No – a Russian tutor. The Princess is sending us a French tutor from Moscow.

RAKITIN: So what's he like, this Russian? Is he old?

NATALYA PETROVNA: No, he's quite young. Anyway, we're only taking him for the summer months.

RAKITIN: I see. A vacation job.

NATALYA PETROVNA: Yes, I think that's what it's called. Shall I tell you something, Rakitin? You enjoy observing people, analysing them, delving into them...

RAKITIN: What makes you think that?

NATALYA PETROVNA: Anyway – see what you make of him. I like him. He's quite slim, but well-built, rather jolly, with a bold look about him – you'll see for yourself. Of course, he's a bit gauche, and you can't stand that.

RAKITIN: You're being terribly hard on me today.

NATALYA PETROVNA: No, joking apart, keep an eye on him. I think he might turn out a real find. On the other hand, who knows!

RAKITIN: You're making me very curious.

NATALYA PETROVNA: Am I? (*Thoughtfully.*) Read on.

RAKITIN: *"Se redressa haletant, et..."*

NATALYA PETROVNA: Where's Vera? I haven't seen her since morning. Oh, put that thing down – I can see we'll do no reading today. Talk to me, that'll be better.

RAKITIN: By all means. What shall I talk about? You know I spent a few days at the Krinitsyns' place, and would you believe, our young lovers are bored already.

NATALYA PETROVNA: How could you tell?

RAKITIN: You can't hide boredom, can you. You can hide everything else, but not boredom.

NATALYA PETROVNA: Everything else?

RAKITIN: I think so.

NATALYA PETROVNA: So what were you doing at the Krinitsyns'?

RAKITIN: Nothing. It's a terrible thing, being bored among friends. You feel at ease with them, you're not uncomfortable – you're fond of them, there's nothing annoying you, but the boredom wears you down nevertheless, and your heart aches, a dull ache, a kind of hunger.

NATALYA PETROVNA: You must be bored with your friends often.

RAKITIN: Oh come, as if you've never been with someone you love, who bores you stiff!

NATALYA PETROVNA: (*Slowly.*) Someone you love... that's a strong word. You're too subtle for me.

RAKITIN: Subtle? What do you mean?

NATALYA PETROVNA: Yes, that's one of your faults. You know, Rakitin, you're very clever, of course, but... well, sometimes when we talk it's as if we're making lace. Have you seen how they make lace? They sit in stuffy rooms, never moving from the spot. It's a beautiful thing, lace, but a drink of cold water on a hot day's much better.

RAKITIN: Natasha, it's obvious you're...

NATALYA PETROVNA: I'm what?

RAKITIN: You're angry with me today for some reason.

NATALYA PETROVNA: Oh, you clever people – you've so little insight, for all your cleverness! Of course I'm not angry with you.

ANNA S: Ooh! At last, he's revoked! He's dropped a trick! Natasha, the scoundrel's revoked, he'll have to pay up.

SCHAAF: It's Lizaveta Bogdanovna's fault...

LIZAVETA B: Well, I'm sorry, but how was I to know Anna Semyonovna had no hearts?

SCHAAF: In future I shall not partner Lizaveta Bogdanovna.

ANNA S: What do you mean, it was her fault?

SCHAAF: In future I shall not partner Lizaveta Bogdanovna.

LIZAVETA B: As if I care! What a cheek!

RAKITIN: You know, Natasha – the more I look at you today, the less I recognise you.

NATALYA PETROVNA: Really?

RAKITIN: Yes, truly. I find a sort of change in you.

NATALYA PETROVNA: Oh? Well, in that case, you must do me the honour – since you seem to know me. Make a guess at what it is, this change that's taken place in me, go on.

RAKITIN: You'll have to wait...

(*KOLYA rushes in from the ballroom, holding a toy bow and arrows.*)

KOLYA: Granny! Granny! Look what I've got! Look! See!

ANNA S: Let me see it, dearest. Oh, what a lovely bow! Who made that for you?

KOLYA: He did... he made it... (*Points to BELYAEV, standing at the ballroom door.*)

ANNA S: And it's so well made too!

KOLYA: I've fired at a tree already, Granny, and I've hit it twice!

NATALYA PETROVNA: Show me, Kolya.

KOLYA: Mama, mama, you should see how Aleksei Nikolaich can climb trees! He's going to teach me, and he'll show me how to swim too! He's going to teach me all kinds of things!

NATALYA PETROVNA: (*To BELYAEV*) I'm most grateful to you for looking after Kolya.

KOLYA: I like him, mama, I really do!

NATALYA PETROVNA: I've mollycoddled him, I'm afraid. You must make a real little boy out of him, full of life. (*BELYAEV bows.*)

KOLYA: Let's go to the stables, Aleksei Nikolaich – we'll take some bread for my pony!

BELYAEV: All right, let's go.

ANNA S: (*To KOLYA.*) Come and give me a kiss first!

KOLYA: Not just now, Granny, later!

(*He runs into the ballroom; BELYAEV follows him.*)

ANNA S: What a sweet child! Isn't he?

LIZAVETA B: He is indeed.

SCHAAF: I pass.

NATALYA PETROVNA: Well, what do you make of him?

RAKITIN: Who?

NATALYA PETROVNA: Him... this Russian tutor.

RAKITIN: Oh, I'm sorry – I forgot. My mind was so taken up with this poser you've set me. Anyway, his appearance, yes... Actually, he's quite good-looking. I like him. He seems rather shy, that's all.

NATALYA PETROVNA: Yes.

RAKITIN: Still, I can't make up my mind.

NATALYA PETROVNA: Rakitin, why don't you and I take him in hand? Mm? What d'you think? We'll complete his education. It's an excellent opportunity for sensible, level-headed people like us. We are terribly level-headed, aren't we?

RAKITIN: This young man obviously interests you. He'd be flattered if he knew.

NATALYA PETROVNA: Oh, not at all, believe me! You can't judge him by... by what our sort would feel in his place. I mean, he's not in the least like us. That's the trouble, isn't it – we study ourselves intently, and then imagine we know other people.

RAKITIN: Yes, they're a closed book, and so forth. But what are you hinting at? Why do you keep taunting me?

NATALYA PETROVNA: You're my friend – who else would I taunt? You are my friend, you do know that. (*Squeezes his hand.*) My old friend.

RAKITIN: I'm afraid this old friend might have outstayed his welcome.

NATALYA PETROVNA: Well, you can only have too much of a good thing.

RAKITIN: Maybe so. But that doesn't make it easier.

NATALYA PETROVNA: Oh, come now. (*Lowering her voice.*) As if you don't know... *ce que vous êtes pour moi.*

RAKITIN: Natasha, you're toying with me, playing cat and mouse. But the mouse isn't complaining.

NATALYA PETROVNA: Oh, the poor little mouse!

ANNA S: Aha! That's twenty you owe me, Herr Schaaf!

SCHAAF: In future Lizaveta Bogdanovna shall not be my partner.

MATVEI: (*Entering from the ballroom.*) Doctor Shpigelsky has arrived, ma'am.

SHPIGELSKY: You don't announce doctors.
(*MATVEI exits.*)
My most humble respects to all the family. (*Kisses ANNA SEMYONOVNA's hand.*) Good afternoon, dear lady. You're winning, I've no doubt.

ANNA S: Winning? I'm just about breaking even, thank God! And that's the culprit there.

SHPIGELSKY: Herr Schaaf, with the ladies, too! That's not nice, I'm surprised at you.

SCHAAF: With the ladies, with the ladies...

SHPIGELSKY: Good afternoon, Natalya Petrovna, good afternoon, sir!

NATALYA PETROVNA: Good afternoon, Doctor. How are you keeping?

SHPIGELSKY: I'm pleased by that question – that means
you are well. And how am I? No decent doctor ever gets
sick – he just ups and dies... ha-ha!

NATALYA PETROVNA: Do sit down. Yes, I'm well, but
I'm not in good spirits. I suppose that's an illness, too.

SHPIGELSKY: Let me take your pulse. Oh dear, these
nerves of yours... You don't get enough exercise, Natalya
Petrovna, and you don't laugh enough. Yes, that's the
problem. Now, sir, why are you looking at me like that?
Anyway, I can prescribe you some of my white drops.

NATALYA PETROVNA: I have nothing against laughing.
I mean, take you, Doctor – you have a wicked tongue,
and I admire that, I really do, that's why I like you. So
tell me a funny story, Rakitin has been philosophising
non-stop today.

SHPIGELSKY: Yes, obviously it's not just nerves, you're
suffering from a little excess of bile, too.

NATALYA PETROVNA: Oh, not you as well! You can say
what you like about me, Doctor, but not out loud. We all
know how terribly perceptive you are. You're both
extremely acute.

SHPIGELSKY: I'm at your service, ma'am.

NATALYA PETROVNA: Now, tell us a funny story.

SHPIGELSKY: All right. But I've had no time to think,
I haven't an idea, and suddenly out of the blue, it's 'Tell
us a funny story...' You'll allow me a pinch of snuff first?

NATALYA PETROVNA: Honestly, what a palaver!

SHPIGELSKY: And you must admit, my dear lady, that
people have different tastes. What one person finds
funny, another won't. For instance, your neighbour
Khlopushkin – I've only got to pull a face at him, and he
goes into a fit of laughter, wheezing, tears running down
his cheeks. But as for you... Well, anyway, I'll try. Do you
know Verenitsyn? Platon Vasilyevich?

NATALYA PETROVNA: I think I do. Or I know of him.

SHPIGELSKY: He has a sister, she's quite mad. Actually,
I think they're either both crazy, or else both quite sane,
because there's absolutely no difference between them, but

that's beside the point. It's Fate, as they say, the destiny that shapes our ends. Anyway, Verenitsyn has a daughter, somewhat green, if you follow me, with pale eyes, and a little red nose, and yellowish teeth – in short, a thoroughly personable young lady; she plays the piano, and speaks with a lisp, moreover, so everything is *comme il faut*. She owns two hundred serfs, plus another hundred and fifty from her aunt. Auntie's still alive, in fact, she'll go on for ages, as crazy people do – there's always some compensation for our afflictions. She's made out her will in her niece's favour, and the night before, I personally poured cold water over her head, to no purpose whatsoever, as it happens, since there isn't the slightest possibility of a cure. Well, anyway, Verenitsyn's daughter isn't exactly a bad catch. He started showing her around, suitors began to appear, and among these was a certain Perekuzov, a rather weedy young chap, very timid, but with impeccable credentials. So, the father liked this Perekuzov, and so did the daughter... Why should there be any hold-up, then? To the altar, and God speed! And indeed, everything was going along swimmingly: Verenitsyn had already started prodding this Perekuzov in the tummy – you know what I mean – and slapping him on the back, when suddenly out of nowhere, just passing through, a young officer turns up, one Ardalion Protobekasov! He catches sight of Verenitsyn's daughter at the Governor's ball, dances three polkas with her, and no doubt says to her, rolling his eyes, "Oh, I'm so unhappy!" – at which my lady goes wild on the spot! Tears, sighs, groans... she won't look at Perekuzov, won't talk about him, the very word 'wedding' sends her into convulsions... dear God in Heaven, what a pantomime! Oh well, thinks Verenitsyn, if it's Protobekasov she wants, so be it. Fortunately, he's also a man of some substance. So Protobekasov's duly invited – you may do us the honour, he says... And Protobekasov does. Protobekasov comes calling, trails around after her, falls in love, and eventually asks for her hand and heart. And what do you think? Does

the Verenitsyn girl accept instantly, filled with joy? Not a
bit of it! God save us, it's more tears, more sighs, more
fainting fits. Her father's at his wits' end. What next? What
does she want? And what do you think she says to him?
"Oh, Papa," she says, "I don't know which of them
I love!" "What?" "As God's my judge," she says, "I don't
know, so I'd better not marry anybody, but I'm in love,
I truly am!" Verenitsyn, of course, has a fit right there and
then, and the suitors don't know what's coming next, she's
still sticking to her guns. So there you have it – that's the
kind of strange goings-on in our neck of the woods!

NATALYA PETROVNA: I don't find anything strange
about it. It's surely possible to love two people at the
same time.

RAKITIN: You think so?

NATALYA PETROVNA: I think... well, actually, I don't
know. Maybe all it proves is that you don't love
either one.

SHPIGELSKY: Mm, yes. I see. I see...

NATALYA PETROVNA: Your story was very good, but
you haven't made me laugh, just the same.

SHPIGELSKY: My dear lady, who's going to make you
laugh now, for goodness' sake? That's not what you need.

NATALYA PETROVNA: Oh, and what do I need?

SHPIGELSKY: The Lord alone knows!

NATALYA PETROVNA: You're such a bore – you're as
bad as Rakitin.

SHPIGELSKY: You do me too much honour, ma'am.

ANNA S: Well, that's that over. Ooohh... my feet have
absolutely gone to sleep.

NATALYA PETROVNA: That's what you get for sitting
so long.

(*SHPIGELSKY and RAKITIN begin a whispered conversation.*)

ANNA S: That's seventy kopecks you owe me, my dear sir.
(*SCHAAF makes an ironic bow.*) You can't have it all your
own way. You're looking quite pale today, Natasha. Are
you all right? Doctor, is she well?

SHPIGELSKY: Oh yes, absolutely!

ANNA S: Well, I'll have a lie-down before dinner. I'm dead on my feet. Liza, come. Ooohh, these legs of mine... (*Exits to the ballroom with LIZAVETA BOGDANOVNA. NATALYA PETROVNA accompanies her. SHPIGELSKY, RAKITIN and SCHAAF remain downstage.*)

SHPIGELSKY: (*Offering his snuffbox.*) Well, Herr Schaaf, *wie befinden Sie sich?*

SCHAAF: Good. *Sehr gut.* And how are you?

SHPIGELSKY: Oh, not too bad, thank you. (*To RAKITIN.*) You really don't know what's up with Natalya Petrovna today?

RAKITIN: No, I honestly don't.

SHPIGELSKY: Well, if you don't know... (*Meets NATALYA PETROVNA, re-entering from the ballroom.*) Natalya Petrovna, I have a little business with you.

NATALYA PETROVNA: Really? What sort of business?

SHPIGELSKY: I need a word with you in private.

NATALYA PETROVNA: Oh dear, you alarm me.
(*RAKITIN meanwhile walks back and forth with SCHAAF, whispering in German. SCHAAF is amused: "Ja, ja, ja, jawohl, jawohl sehr gut.".*)

SHPIGELSKY: Actually, this matter doesn't only concern you...

NATALYA PETROVNA: What do you mean?

SHPIGELSKY: Well, the fact is – a good friend of mine has asked me to find out... to inquire what your intentions are with respect to your ward – Vera Aleksandrovna.

NATALYA PETROVNA: My intentions?

SHPIGELSKY: To come straight to the point, this friend of mine...

NATALYA PETROVNA: Surely he doesn't want to marry her?

SHPIGELSKY: Well, yes, precisely.

NATALYA PETROVNA: You're joking.

SHPIGELSKY: Indeed I'm not.

NATALYA PETROVNA: Good heavens, she's still a child. What a strange commission you've been given!

SHPIGELSKY: What's so strange about it, Natalya Petrovna? My friend...

NATALYA PETROVNA: You're being terribly diplomatic, Shpigelsky. Who exactly is this friend of yours?

SHPIGELSKY: Well, if you'll forgive me – you haven't said anything definite yet, about my...

NATALYA PETROVNA: Oh please, Doctor, no more. Vera's still a child. You know that perfectly well, Mister Ambassador. Anyway, here she comes.

(*VERA and KOLYA run in from the ballroom.*)

KOLYA: Rakitin, tell them to give us some glue, we need glue...

NATALYA PETROVNA: Where've you been? (*Strokes VERA's cheek.*) You're quite flushed.

VERA: We've been in the garden.

(*SHPIGELSKY bows to her.*)

Good afternoon, Doctor.

RAKITIN: What do you want glue for?

KOLYA: We need it. Aleksei Nikolaich is making us a kite. Tell them...

RAKITIN: Wait, in a minute...

SCHAAF: *Erlauben Sie....* Master Kolya has not finished his reading lesson today. (*Takes KOLYA's hand.*) *Kommen Sie...*

KOLYA: *Morgen, Herr Schaaf, morgen...*

SCHAAF: (*Testily.*) *Morgen, morgen, nur nicht heute, sagen alle faule Leute... Kommen Sie...*

NATALYA PETROVNA: Who were you out walking with all this time? I haven't seen you since morning.

VERA: With Aleksei Nikolaich... and Kolya.

NATALYA PETROVNA: Aha! Kolya, what's the meaning of this?

KOLYA: Herr Schaaf... Mama...

RAKITIN: They've been off making a kite, and now he's got to have his lesson.

SCHAAF: *Gnädige Frau...*

NATALYA PETROVNA: Do as you're told, Kolya, you've run around quite enough today. Go on, go with Herr Schaaf.

SCHAAF: (*Leads KOLYA out to the ballroom.*) *Es ist unerhört!*

KOLYA: (*Whispers to RAKITIN.*) You will get us some glue? (*RAKITIN nods.*)

SCHAAF: (*Tugging at KOLYA.*) *Kommen Sie, mein Herr...*
(*They exit to the ballroom, and RAKITIN follows.*)

NATALYA PETROVNA: (*To VERA.*) Sit down. You must
be tired...

VERA: No, not in the least.

NATALYA PETROVNA: Doctor, look at her – isn't she
tired?

SHPIGELSKY: Yes, but it's good for her, surely.

NATALYA PETROVNA: I'm not saying it isn't. So, what
were you doing in the garden?

VERA: Just playing, running around. First we watched them
digging down at the weir, then Aleksei Nikolaich
climbed up a tree after a squirrel, really high, and began
shaking the top branches. Actually, we were quite scared.
Then the squirrel dropped down, at last, and Trésor
almost caught it, only it got away.

NATALYA PETROVNA: And after that?

VERA: After that Aleksei Nikolaich made Kolya a bow,
and so quickly, too. Then he crept up behind our cow in
the meadow, and suddenly jumped on her back. The cow
took fright, and started running and kicking, and he just
laughed. Aleksei Nikolaich said he'd make us a kite then,
so we came back here.

NATALYA PETROVNA: You're a child, you really are just
a child, aren't you? Don't you think so, Doctor?

SHPIGELSKY: Yes, I agree.

NATALYA PETROVNA: Well, there we are.

SHPIGELSKY: But that's no obstacle, is it. On the contrary...

NATALYA PETROVNA: You think not? (*To VERA.*) So,
you had a jolly time?

VERA: Oh yes, ma'am – Aleksei Nikolaich is so funny.

NATALYA PETROVNA: Is he indeed? Vera darling, how
old are you? Yes, a child. Just a child...
(*RAKITIN enters from the ballroom.*)

SHPIGELSKY: Oh dear, I quite forgot. Your coachman's
ill, and I haven't been to see him yet.

NATALYA PETROVNA: What's wrong with him?

SHPIGELSKY: A fever – actually, he's not in any sort of danger.

NATALYA PETROVNA: You'll have dinner with us, Doctor?

SHPIGELSKY: Yes, if I may. (*Exits to the ballroom.*)

NATALYA PETROVNA: *Mon enfant, vous feriez bien de mettre une autre robe pour le diner...* Come here. (*Kisses her on the forehead.*) You're such a child!

RAKITIN: (*To VERA, giving her a wink.*) I've sent your young man everything he needs.

VERA: Thank you so much, Mikhail Aleksandrych. (*Exits.*)

RAKITIN: Alone at last. Natasha, tell me, what's the matter?

NATALYA PETROVNA: Nothing, *Michel.* Nothing. And if there was... well, it's past now. Sit down. It happens to us all, surely. A few passing clouds. Why are you looking at me like that?

RAKITIN: I'm just looking at you. I'm happy.

NATALYA PETROVNA: *Michel,* open the window. The garden's so lovely! (*RAKITIN opens the window.*) Hello, wind! It's as if it's been waiting for a chance to rush in. Look, it's taken over the whole room – we shan't get rid of it now...

RAKITIN: And you're so soft and gentle now, like the evening after a storm.

NATALYA PETROVNA: After a storm... Was there really a storm?

RAKITIN: Gathering.

NATALYA PETROVNA: Honestly? You know, *Michel,* I can't imagine a kinder person than you. It's the truth. No, don't – I want to say this. You're so understanding, so gentle, and constant. You never change. I owe you so much.

RAKITIN: Natasha, why are you saying all this to me now?

NATALYA PETROVNA: I don't know. I'm happy, I feel relaxed. Just let me talk, please don't stop me.

RAKITIN: You're so kind, like an angel.

NATALYA PETROVNA: You wouldn't have said that this morning... But do listen, *Michel,* you know what I'm like, you must forgive me. Our relationship is so pure, and open, yet there's something not quite right about it. We can look Arkady in the eye, we've nothing to hide from anyone, and that's the truth. But... well, that's why it's hard for me at times, I feel awkward, I get into a foul mood, and I tend to take it out on other people, like a child, and especially on you. You don't resent being honoured in this way?

RAKITIN: No, on the contrary...

NATALYA PETROVNA: It's even fun, sometimes, to torment the person you love... love, yes, I can say that too, like Pushkin's Tatyana: *"Why should I dissemble?*

RAKITIN: Natasha, you...

NATALYA PETROVNA: (*Interrupting him.*) Yes, I love you. But shall I tell you something, Rakitin? Do you know what I find strange? I love you, and it's such a clear feeling, and so peaceful. I'm not disturbed by it, it's such a warm feeling, but... You've never once made me cry, and maybe you should have. What does it mean?

RAKITIN: A question like that doesn't need an answer.

NATALYA PETROVNA: After all, we've known each other a long time.

RAKITIN: Four years. Yes, we're old friends.

NATALYA PETROVNA: Friends... No, you're more than a friend to me.

RAKITIN: Natasha, please don't bring that up. I'm afraid for my happiness, as if it might slip away through your fingers.

NATALYA PETROVNA: No, no, no. That's the whole point, you're too kind. You give in to me too easily. You've spoiled me. You really are too kind, do you hear?

RAKITIN: Yes, ma'am.

NATALYA PETROVNA: I don't know about you, but I don't wish for any other happiness. A lot of women would envy me. Isn't that so?

RAKITIN: I'm in your power. Do with me as you wish...
(*ISLAEV is heard in the ballroom: "So, have you sent for him?".*)

NATALYA PETROVNA: It's him! I can't bear to see him now... Goodbye! (*Exits to the study.*)

RAKITIN: What is this? The beginning of the end, or just the end? Or is it the beginning?

(*ISLAEV enters.*)

ISLAEV: Hello, *Michel.*

RAKITIN: We've already said hello today.

ISLAEV: Oh, sorry – I'm absolutely run ragged. You know, it's a strange thing! The Russian peasant is very shrewd, quick-witted, I honestly do respect our peasants. But all the same there are times... well, you can talk till you're blue in the face, explaining something, and you think, right, that's clear, and it's a complete waste of time. The Russian peasant just has no... no what d'you call it...

RAKITIN: So you're still pottering around down there at the weir?

ISLAEV: He has no... how shall I put it... no love for work. No, he's got no liking for work at all. He won't let you make your point, not properly. "Yes, sir! Right away, sir!" he says, but to what? He hears all right, but he doesn't take anything in. Now, you look at the Germans – there's a thing! No, our Russians have no patience. Still, I do respect them. Where's Natasha, do you know?

RAKITIN: She was here a minute ago.

ISLAEV: And what time is it? It must be time for dinner. I've been on my feet since morning. It's been non-stop. And I still haven't been at the building site. I don't know where the time goes. It's terrible, you just can't keep up! Oh yes, I can see you're laughing at me, but what on earth can I do? We've all got our cross to bear. I'm a forceful person, I was born to run things, to take charge, and nothing else. There was a time when I had other ideas – oh yes, and made a mess of them! Got my fingers burnt, and no mistake! So, isn't Belyaev here yet?

RAKITIN: Who's Belyaev?

ISLAEV: He's our new tutor, a Russian. He's a regular shrinking violet, but well, he'll get used to us. He's no fool. I asked him to check on the building work today, see how...

(*BELYAEV enters.*)

Ah, here he is! Well, how is it? How are they getting on? They'll be doing nothing, I suppose, eh?

BELYAEV: No, sir. They're busy.

ISLAEV: Have they put up the second stage yet?

BELYAEV: Yes, they've started on the third.

ISLAEV: What about the cross-beams, did you tell them?

BELYAEV: Yes, I did.

ISLAEV: Well? What did they say?

BELYAEV: They say they've never done it any other way.

ISLAEV: Hm. Is the carpenter there? Yermil?

BELYAEV: He's there.

ISLAEV: Ah!... Well, thanks anyway.

(*NATALYA PETROVNA enters.*)

Ah, Natasha! Hello!

RAKITIN: Why do you keep saying hello to people? That's twenty times already!

ISLAEV: It's because I'm run off my feet, I told you. By the way, I haven't shown you my new winnowing-machine, have I? Come and have a look, it's most interesting. You wouldn't believe it, it blows up a positive hurricane.

We've still time before dinner – would you like to see it?

RAKITIN: I don't mind.

ISLAEV: What about you, Natasha – won't you come with us?

NATALYA PETROVNA: Honestly, what do I know about winnowing-machines! No, you go – just don't stay too long.

ISLAEV: (*Exits with RAKITIN.*) We'll be back in a minute...

(*BELYAEV is about to follow them.*)

NATALYA PETROVNA: (*To BELYAEV.*) Aleksei Nikolaich, where are you going?

BELYAEV: I'm... I'm...

NATALYA PETROVNA: Oh well, if you want to go for a walk...

BELYAEV: No, ma'am, I've been out all morning!

NATALYA PETROVNA: Well, in that case, sit down. Sit here. We haven't had a proper talk yet. We've hardly been introduced. And I do want to get to know you.

BELYAEV: Ma'am, I... I'm deeply flattered.

NATALYA PETROVNA: You're afraid of me now, I can see that, but once you get to know me, you'll stop being afraid. Tell me... tell me, how old are you?

BELYAEV: I'm twenty-one, ma'am.

NATALYA PETROVNA: Are your parents still living?

BELYAEV: My mother's dead. Father's still alive.

NATALYA PETROVNA: And your dear mother – did she pass away a long time ago?

BELYAEV: Yes, ma'am.

NATALYA PETROVNA: But you still remember her?

BELYAEV: Of course. Yes.

NATALYA PETROVNA: And your Papa lives in Moscow?

BELYAEV: No, no – in the country.

NATALYA PETROVNA: Ah! So – have you any brothers or sisters?

BELYAEV: One sister.

NATALYA PETROVNA: And you're very fond of her?

BELYAEV: Yes, ma'am. She's much younger than me.

NATALYA PETROVNA: And what's her name?

BELYAEV: Natalya.

NATALYA PETROVNA: Natalya? Now isn't that odd – I'm called Natalya too... And you love her very much?

BELYAEV: Yes, ma'am.

NATALYA PETROVNA: So – tell me, what do you think of my Kolya?

BELYAEV: He's a fine boy.

NATALYA PETROVNA: Isn't he? And he's so affectionate! He's already managed to attach himself to you.

BELYAEV: Well, I'll do my best... I'm just pleased to...

NATALYA PETROVNA: You see, the thing is, Aleksei, I'd like to make a really sensible person out of him. I don't know if I'll succeed, but in any event I want him to look back on his childhood with pleasure, always. Let him grow up freely, that's the main thing. I was brought up quite differently myself – my father wasn't a bad man, but he was stern and irritable. Everyone in the house, not least my dear Mama, was afraid of him. My brother and I used

to cross ourselves, in secret, whenever he called us to him.
Now and again my father would decide to give me a hug,
but even with his arms around me, I remember being
scared stiff. My brother walked out on him when he grew
up – possibly you've heard about it. It was terrible, I'll
never forget that day. But right to the end of his life, I was
his obedient daughter. He used to call me his consolation,
his Antigone – Father went blind in his last years – but no
amount of tender embraces could wipe away those first
impressions of my childhood. I was afraid of him, an old
blind man, and I never felt free in his presence. I suppose
the traces of that shyness, of being so long constrained,
have never entirely left me. At first sight, I know, I must
seem... how shall I put it... cold, perhaps? Anyway,
I realise I'm telling you about myself, instead of talking to
you about Kolya, but I just want to say that I know from
personal experience, how good it is for a child to grow up
freely. I daresay you weren't repressed as a child?

BELYAEV: I don't know what to say. Certainly, I wasn't
repressed. Nobody took any notice of me.

NATALYA PETROVNA: Surely your dear father...

BELYAEV: He didn't really care. He spent all his time
going round the neighbours' houses, on business. Well,
not exactly business, but that's how he earned his bread,
you might say, through them. Offering his services.

NATALYA PETROVNA: I see. So nobody took any
interest in your education?

BELYAEV: To tell you the truth, ma'am – no. And I suppose
it's pretty obvious. I'm well aware of my deficiencies.

NATALYA PETROVNA: Perhaps. But all the same... By the
way, Aleksei, was that you singing in the garden yesterday?

BELYAEV: When, ma'am?

NATALYA PETROVNA: Last night, near the pond. Was
it you?

BELYAEV: Yes, ma'am. I'm sorry, I didn't think... it's so
far from here to the pond... I didn't think anyone could
hear me...

NATALYA PETROVNA: Good heavens, why are you
apologising? You have a fine, clear voice, and you sing
very well. Have you studied music?

BELYAEV: No, not at all. I sing by ear, and only very
simple songs.

NATALYA PETROVNA: Well, you sing them beautifully.
Sometime I'll ask you... not just now, but when we're
better acquainted, when we've become friends. I mean,
we shall be good friends, shan't we, Aleksei? I feel I can
trust you, my chattering to you like this proves it.
(*She holds out her hand. BELYAEV takes it uncertainly, and
kisses it. NATALYA PETROVNA hastily withdraws her hand,
just as SHPIGELSKY enters.*)

NATALYA PETROVNA: Oh, it's you, Doctor... Mr Belyaev
and I were just...

SHPIGELSKY: You wouldn't believe what's going on here,
dear lady. I go into the servants' quarters, ask for your
sick coachman, and lo and behold! – there's my patient
sitting at the table, stuffing his face with onion pancakes!
So much for medicine, eh, if you're relying on illness for
an honest profit!

NATALYA PETROVNA: Yes, indeed...
(*BELYAEV is about to exit.*)
Aleksei Nikolaich, I forgot to tell you...

VERA: (*Running in from the ballroom.*) Aleksei! Aleksei!

NATALYA PETROVNA: What is it? What is it you want?

VERA: Someone wants him.

NATALYA PETROVNA: Who wants him?

VERA: Kolya... I mean, Kolya asked me about the kite...

NATALYA PETROVNA: Oh. *On n'entre pas comme cela dans
une chambre... Cela ne convient pas.* (*To SHPIGELSKY.*)
What time is it, Doctor? Your watch is always right – it
must be time for dinner.

SHPIGELSKY: Let me see. It's now – I can tell you it's
now – it's twenty minutes past four.

NATALYA PETROVNA: Ah, you see? Dinner-time.
(*She crosses to the mirror to fix her hair. VERA meanwhile whispers
to BELYAEV. They laugh. NATALYA PETROVNA, watched by
SHPIGELSKY, observes them in the mirror.*)

BELYAEV: Not really?

VERA: Yes, yes, she fell off.

NATALYA PETROVNA: What's that? Did someone fall?

VERA: No, ma'am – Aleksei Nikolaich had put up a swing, and Nanny took it into her head to...

NATALYA PETROVNA: (*To SHPIGELSKY.*) By the way, Doctor, I'd like a word with you. (*To VERA.*) She wasn't hurt, was she?

VERA: Oh no, ma'am!

NATALYA PETROVNA: Yes. Even so, Aleksei Nikolaich, you ought not to...

MATVEI: (*Enters from the ballroom.*) Dinner is served, ma'am.

NATALYA PETROVNA: Ah! Now where's Arkady? He's with Rakitin, and they're late again.

MATVEI: They're already at table, ma'am.

NATALYA PETROVNA: And what about Mama?

MATVEI: She's at table too, ma'am.

NATALYA PETROVNA: Well, let's go in then. Vera, *allez en avant avec monsieur.*

(*MATVEI exits, followed by BELYAEV and VERA.*)

SHPIGELSKY: (*To NATALYA PETROVNA.*) You were going to say something?

NATALYA PETROVNA: Oh yes! Yes, of course... I was thinking – we must talk again about... about your proposal.

SHPIGELSKY: You mean about Vera Aleksandrovna?

NATALYA PETROVNA: Yes. I'll think it over. I'll give it some thought.

(*They exit to the ballroom.*)

(*End of Act One.*)

ACT TWO

The scene is the garden. To right and left, under the trees, stand benches, and there are raspberry-bushes upstage centre. KATYA and MATVEI enter from the right. KATYA is carrying a basket.

MATVEI: So what's it to be, Katerina? Speak up, please, I've got to know.

KATYA: Matvei, I really...

MATVEI: Katerina, you know perfectly well the way I feel about you. All right, I'm a little older in years, maybe, it's not as if I can dispute it. But I've looked after myself, I'm still in my prime. And I'm good-natured, you know that too, so what more d'you want?

KATYA: Matvei, I do have feelings for you, believe me, and I'm grateful, I truly am. I just think we should wait, that's all.

MATVEI: Heavens above, Katerina, what are we waiting for? If I can just remind you, you didn't use to talk like that. And when it comes to respect, well, I think I can vouch for myself there. You'll have all the respect you want, none better, and you won't have to ask for more. Besides which, I'm not a drinking man, no, and you won't hear a bad word about me from any of my masters.

KATYA: Honestly, Matvei, I don't know what to say...

MATVEI: Oh come on, Katerina, it's just lately you've started talking like this.

KATYA: What do you mean? Just lately what?

MATVEI: I don't know... it's just that before, well, you used to behave differently with me.

KATYA: Watch out – it's that German.

MATVEI: Oh, damn him. He's like a stork, that long nose of his! But you and I'll need to have a talk. (*Exits right.*)
(*SCHAAF enters left, a fishing-rod over his shoulder.*)

SCHAAF: Katerin! Where are you going?

KATYA: I've been told to pick the raspberries, Herr Schaaf.

SCHAAF: Raspberries? Raspberries are very fine fruit. You like raspberries?

41

KATYA: Yes, I do.

SCHAAF: Ha-ha! And I too... I also. Whatever you like, I like also. Katerin, wait, stay a little...

KATYA: I can't, I've no time. The housekeeper'll shout at me.

SCHAAF: Oh, that doesn't matter. Look, I'm going to... How do you say... to fish? Fish, you understand, yes? To take fish. You like that? Fish?

KATYA: Yes, sir.

SCHAAF: Ha-ha! Yes, and I too, I also. And you know what I will tell you, Katerin? In German, there is a little song... (*Sings.*) *'Kathrinchen, Kathrinchen, wie lieb' ich dich so sehr!'*... That is in Russian: *'Oh, little Katerin, pretty little Katerin, how I love you so!'* (*Makes to put his arm around her.*)

KATYA: No, don't, please! You should be ashamed of yourself – look, there are people coming. (*Flees into the raspberry bushes.*)

SCHAAF: *Das ist dumm.*

(*Enter right NATALYA PETROVNA, on RAKITIN's arm.*)

NATALYA PETROVNA: Ah, Herr Schaaf! You're going fishing?

SCHAAF: That is so, ma'am.

NATALYA PETROVNA: And where's Kolya?

SCHAAF: With Lizaveta Bogdanovna – piano lesson...

NATALYA PETROVNA: I see. And you're all alone?

SCHAAF: Quite alone, yes.

NATALYA PETROVNA: You haven't seen Mr Belyaev?

SCHAAF: No, I have not.

NATALYA PETROVNA: We'll come with you, Herr Schaaf, if you don't mind. We'll watch you catching fish, all right?

SCHAAF: I'm very pleased.

RAKITIN: (*Sotto voce.*) What on earth for?

NATALYA PETROVNA: Come on, let's go, *mon beau ténébreux...*

(*All three exit right.*)

KATYA: (*Emerging from the bushes.*) They've gone... Huh! That German!... (*Resumes picking raspberries, sings.*)

Fire won't burn, and pitch won't boil,
But my heart melts and burns like fire...
Yes, Matvei is absolutely right!
But my heart melts and burns like fire,
Dear father, mother, not for you...
Oh, what huge raspberries!...
Dear father, mother, not for you...
Phew! The heat! And it's so stuffy...
Dear father, mother, not for you...
No, my heart melts...
(*BELYAEV and VERA enter left. BELYAEV is carrying a kite.*)
BELYAEV: Why have you stopped singing, Katya? (*Sings.*)
No, my heart melts for a fine young maid...
KATYA: Those aren't the words we sing.
BELYAEV: Really? What, then? (*KATYA laughs.*) What's that
you're doing, picking raspberries? Let's have a taste.
KATYA: Take them all...
BELYAEV: Now why would I do that? Vera Aleksandrovna,
will you have some? That's plenty.
KATYA: No, take the lot.
BELYAEV: No no, Katya. Thanks all the same. (*To VERA.*)
Look, let's sit down on the bench. We've got to attach its
tail. You can help me.
(*They sit down. BELYAEV hands her the kite.*)
There you are. Now watch, hold it up straight. What's the
matter?
VERA: I can't see you properly.
BELYAEV: What on earth do you want to see me for?
VERA: I mean, I can't see how you're tying on the tail.
BELYAEV: Oh! Well, look, hold on. Katya, why aren't you
singing? Go on, please.
(*KATYA begins singing again.*)
VERA: Tell me, Aleksei Nikolaich – did you sometimes fly
kites in Moscow too?
BELYAEV: No, I've no time for kites in Moscow! Now, hold
on to the string... that's fine. What, you think we've
nothing else to do in Moscow?
VERA: What do you do in Moscow?

BELYAEV: What do you mean? We study, listen to the professors.

VERA: Study what?

BELYAEV: Oh, everything.

VERA: You must be a very good student. Better than all the rest.

BELYAEV: No, I'm not. Better than the rest? No, I'm too lazy.

VERA: Why? Why are you lazy?

BELYAEV: God knows! I must've been born lazy.

VERA: Do you have any friends in Moscow?

BELYAEV: Yes, of course. Oh dear, this isn't strong enough.

VERA: Are you fond of them?

BELYAEV: Of course I am! I mean, aren't you fond of your friends?

VERA: Friends... I haven't any.

BELYAEV: I mean girlfriends.

VERA: Yes.

BELYAEV: You do have girlfriends?

VERA: Yes. Only I don't know why, but... well, I haven't really thought about them lately. I haven't even answered Liza Moshnina, and she did ask me to in her letter.

BELYAEV: Anyway, why are you saying you've no friends? What am I?

VERA: Oh, well, you're different. (*After a pause.*) Aleksei Nikolaich!

BELYAEV: What?

VERA: Do you write poetry?

BELYAEV: No. Why?

VERA: Oh, nothing. One of the girls at boarding-school used to write poetry.

BELYAEV: (*Tugs at the knot with his teeth.*) There we are! Was it any good?

VERA: I don't know. She used to read it to us, and we'd cry.

BELYAEV: What on earth for?

VERA: From pity. We felt so sorry for her!

BELYAEV: You went to school in Moscow?

VERA: Yes, at Madame Beaulieu's. Natalya Petrovna took me away from there last year.

BELYAEV: Do you like Natalya Petrovna?

VERA: Yes, I do. She's so kind. I'm very fond of her.

BELYAEV: And a little frightened of her, perhaps?

VERA: Just a little.

BELYAEV: So who sent you to school?

VERA: That was Natalya Petrovna's mother. I grew up in her house. I'm an orphan.

BELYAEV: You're an orphan? You don't remember your mother or father?

VERA: No.

BELYAEV: My mother's dead too. We're both orphans. Still, it can't be helped, there's no point in moping about it.

VERA: They say orphans make friends easily with each other.

BELYAEV: Really? And what do you think?

VERA: I think it's true.

BELYAEV: I wonder how long I've been here now?

VERA: Today's the twenty-eighth day.

BELYAEV: What a memory! There now, that's the kite finished. Have a look at that tail! We must go and fetch Kolya.

KATYA: Would you like some more raspberries?

BELYAEV: No, thanks, Katya.

(*KATYA withdraws.*)

VERA: Kolya's with Lizaveta Bogdanovna.

BELYAEV: It's a shame keeping a boy indoors on a day like this!

VERA: Lizaveta Bogdanovna would only hold us back...

BELYAEV: Oh no, I wasn't talking about her...

VERA: Kolya couldn't come without her. Incidentally, she spoke very highly of you yesterday.

BELYAEV: Really?

VERA: Don't you like her?

BELYAEV: She doesn't bother me. Let her stick to her snuff! Why are you sighing?

VERA: Oh, no reason. How clear the sky is!

BELYAEV: Is that why you're sighing? Are you bored, perhaps?

VERA: Bored? No! Sometimes I don't even know myself why I sigh... I'm definitely not bored. On the contrary...

I don't know, I suppose I must be a bit low. I went upstairs yesterday for a book, and I suddenly sat down on the stairs and started to cry, can you imagine? Goodness knows why, but for ages afterwards, the tears just kept welling up. What does it mean? I feel fine...

BELYAEV: It's growing pains. You're growing up. These things happen. Actually, your eyes were a bit puffy last night.

VERA: And you noticed?

BELYAEV: Of course.

VERA: You notice everything.

BELYAEV: Not really. Not everything.

VERA: Aleksei Nikolaich...

BELYAEV: Yes?

VERA: What on earth was I going to ask you? Honestly, I've forgotten what I wanted to ask.

BELYAEV: What, are you so absent-minded?

VERA: No, but... oh, yes! I know what I was going to say. You told me you had a sister, I think?

BELYAEV: Yes, I have.

VERA: Tell me, does she look like me?

BELYAEV: Heavens, no. You're much nicer-looking.

VERA: That's not possible! Your sister... oh, I'd love to be in her place.

BELYAEV: What do you mean? You'd like to live in our simple little house?

VERA: No, I didn't mean that... Is your home really so small?

BELYAEV: Very small. Not at all like this.

VERA: What do they want with so many rooms, anyway?

BELYAEV: Well, why not? Some day you'll realise why they need all those rooms.

VERA: Some day? When?

BELYAEV: When you're the mistress of your own house.

VERA: Do you think so?

BELYAEV: You'll see. Well, Vera Aleksandrovna, we'll go and fetch Kolya, shall we?

VERA: Why don't you call me Vera?

BELYAEV: And why don't you call me Aleksei?

VERA: Yes, why not? Oh!

BELYAEV: What is it?

VERA: Natalya Petrovna's coming.

BELYAEV: Where?

VERA: Over there – coming along the path with Rakitin.

BELYAEV: Let's go and fetch Kolya. He must've finished his lesson by now.

VERA: Yes, let's. Otherwise I'm afraid she'll give me a row. (*They exit left. KATYA hides. NATALYA PETROVNA and RAKITIN enter right.*)

NATALYA PETROVNA: Isn't that Mr Belyaev going off with Vera?

RAKITIN: Yes, that's them.

NATALYA PETROVNA: It's as if they're running away from us.

RAKITIN: Possibly.

NATALYA PETROVNA: Well, I must say, I don't think it's proper for Vera, alone like that with a young man in the garden. She's only a child, of course, but it's not very discreet. I'll speak to her.

RAKITIN: How old is she?

NATALYA PETROVNA: Seventeen! Yes, she's seventeen already. It's so hot today. I'm tired, let's sit down. Has the Doctor left?

RAKITIN: Yes, he has.

NATALYA PETROVNA: It's too bad you couldn't get him to stay. I don't know what possessed that man to become a country doctor. He's very amusing. He makes me laugh.

RAKITIN: Indeed, and I thought you weren't in a laughing mood today.

NATALYA PETROVNA: What made you think that?

RAKITIN: Oh, nothing.

NATALYA PETROVNA: Because I've no time for senti-ment today? No, I give you fair warning – absolutely nothing is likely to move me. But that's not going to stop me laughing, quite the contrary. Anyway, I wanted to have a little chat with the Doctor.

RAKITIN: May one know what about?

NATALYA PETROVNA: No, one may not. You know
  enough about me without that – what I think, what I do.
  It's so boring.

RAKITIN: I'm sorry... I wasn't suggesting...

NATALYA PETROVNA: I'd like to keep at least something
  back from you.

RAKITIN: Honestly! Anyone listening to you would think
  I knew everything...

NATALYA PETROVNA: And don't you?

RAKITIN: Now you're poking fun at me.

NATALYA PETROVNA: You mean you really don't know
  everything that goes on my mind? Well, in that case
  I don't think much of you. What, a man who watches me
  from morning till night?

RAKITIN: Is that a reproach?

NATALYA PETROVNA: A reproach? No, I can see now –
  you're not very perceptive.

RAKITIN: Perhaps not. But since I watch you from morning
  till night, you'll permit me to offer an observation...

NATALYA PETROVNA: On my account? Please do.

RAKITIN: You won't be angry with me?

NATALYA PETROVNA: Heavens, no! I'd like to be, but no.

RAKITIN: These past weeks, Natasha, you've been in some
  sort of constant state of irritation, it's something inside
  you, as if you can't help yourself – as if you're inwardly
  struggling, confused about something. I wasn't aware of
  it before my visit to the Krinitsyns'. It's quite recent.
  Now and again you let out such a deep sigh – the way
  someone extremely tired sighs, someone who can't find
  any ease.

NATALYA PETROVNA: So – what conclusion do you
  draw from that, Mr Observer?

RAKITIN: None. But it does worry me.

NATALYA PETROVNA: Well, I thank you most humbly
  for your concern.

RAKITIN: Besides which...

NATALYA PETROVNA: Please change the subject.
  (*A silence.*)

RAKITIN: You weren't planning to go out today?

NATALYA PETROVNA: No.

RAKITIN: Why ever not? It's a beautiful day.

NATALYA PETROVNA: Inertia. Tell me... you know
Bolshintsov, don't you?

RAKITIN: What, our neighbour?

NATALYA PETROVNA: Yes.

RAKITIN: What sort of question's that? We were playing
cards with him at your house, just a few days ago.

NATALYA PETROVNA: I meant, what kind of man is he?

RAKITIN: Bolshintsov?

NATALYA PETROVNA: Yes, yes, Bolshintsov.

RAKITIN: Well, quite frankly, I wasn't expecting that!

NATALYA PETROVNA: Weren't expecting what?

RAKITIN: That you'd start quizzing me about Bolshintsov!
He's a fat, stupid, rather dull person – apart from that,
I've nothing against him.

NATALYA PETROVNA: He's not quite as stupid, nor as
dull as you imagine.

RAKITIN: Perhaps not. To be honest, I haven't scrutinised
the gentleman that closely.

NATALYA PETROVNA: What, you haven't observed him?

RAKITIN: Why did he suddenly come into your mind?

NATALYA PETROVNA: No reason.

(*A silence.*)

RAKITIN: Look, Natasha, how beautiful that dark-green
oak tree is against the deep blue of the sky. It's
absolutely drenched in sunlight, and what strong
colours... How much indestructible life and power there
is in that tree, especially when you compare it with that
little birch sapling. It seems about to dissolve entirely
into the sun, its tiny leaves shine with a kind of liquid
glow, as if they're melting, yet it's lovely too...

NATALYA PETROVNA: Shall I tell you something,
Rakitin? I noticed a long time ago... You're so intensely
aware of the so-called beauties of Nature, and you talk
about them very elegantly and cleverly – so elegantly
and cleverly, that I imagine nature must be grateful

beyond words for your exquisitely-turned phrases. You pay court to Nature, like some perfumed marquis on red high-heels, in pursuit of a pretty peasant wench. There's only one snag: I sometimes think Nature simply wouldn't know how to appreciate your subtle observations, just as the peasant girl wouldn't understand the courtly *politesse* of the marquis. Nature is much simpler, cruder even, than you suggest, because Nature's healthy, thank God. Birches don't melt, and they don't swoon, either, like neurotic women.

RAKITIN: *Quelle tirade!* Nature's healthy – so, in other words, I'm a sickly creature.

NATALYA PETROVNA: You're not the only sickly creature – we're neither of us too healthy.

RAKITIN: Oh yes, I'm well aware of this technique for saying the most unpleasant things to a person, in the most inoffensive manner. Instead of telling him straight to his face, thus: you're a fool, sir – all you need do is smile sweetly and make the same point: you know, we're fools, you and I.

NATALYA PETROVNA: You're offended? Oh, don't be silly, what nonsense! All I meant was that we're both... well, you don't like the word 'sickly'... that we're both old, very old.

RAKITIN: What do you mean old? I don't consider myself old.

NATALYA PETROVNA: No, seriously, listen to me... just look at us sitting here now, and a quarter of an hour ago, two truly young creatures may well have been sitting on this very same bench.

RAKITIN: Belyaev and Vera, you mean? Well, naturally, they're younger than us. There's a few years' difference between us, that's all, but that doesn't make us old.

NATALYA PETROVNA: The difference between us isn't simply age.

RAKITIN: Ah, I see! You envy them their *naiveté*, their freshness, their innocence – in other words, their silliness.

NATALYA PETROVNA: You think so? You honestly think they're silly? Well, I can see everyone's silly today, as far as you're concerned. No, you don't understand me. And silly, besides! Who cares? What's so wonderful about cleverness, if it isn't amusing? There's nothing more tiresome than gloomy thoughts.

RAKITIN: Hm. Why don't you come right out with it, instead of beating about the bush? I don't amuse you – that's what you mean. So why make cleverness in general the scapegoat for my sins?

NATALYA PETROVNA: No, you've got it all wrong.
(*KATYA emerges from the bushes.*)
So, have you picked all the raspberries, Katya?

KATYA: Yes, ma'am.

NATALYA PETROVNA: Let me see... Oh, what lovely berries! They're so red – and your cheeks are even more red. Now, off you go.
(*KATYA exits.*)

RAKITIN: That's another young creature to your taste.

NATALYA PETROVNA: Of course.

RAKITIN: Where are you going?

NATALYA PETROVNA: Well, firstly, I'm going to see what Vera's up to. It's time she was home. Secondly, I must confess our conversation has upset me a little. We'd better call a halt to our discussions on Nature and youth for the time being.

RAKITIN: Perhaps you'd rather walk alone?

NATALYA PETROVNA: Frankly, yes. We'll meet again soon. After all, we're still friends, aren't we? (*Offers him her hand.*)

RAKITIN: Good heavens, yes!

NATALYA PETROVNA: Goodbye. (*Puts up her parasol and exits.*)

RAKITIN: What's the matter with her? Oh, it's nothing. Just a mood. Moody? I haven't noticed that in her before. On the contrary, I can't think of a more even-tempered woman. What's causing it? Hm, they're so funny, these people with one single idea in their minds, one aim, one *raison d'être* – like myself, for example. She was quite right – you observe trivial details from morning till night, and you become trivial yourself. That's the way it is, but I can't live without her. In her presence I'm more than just happy, you can't call that feeling happiness. I belong to her completely, parting from her would be, without exaggeration, exactly like parting with my life. What's wrong with her? What's the meaning of that inner turmoil, and those bitter remarks, as if she can't help herself? Is she getting bored with me? Hm. I've never been under any illusions – I know very well what kind of love she feels for me, but I did hope that in time, that placid emotion... I had some hope! But can I be right? Do I dare hope? I'll admit my situation's really rather comical – almost contemptible. Well, why even talk about it? She's an honest woman, and I'm no Don Juan. Unfortunately. Enough! Let's put all that nonsense right out of our heads! What a beautiful day it is! Yes, she scored a palpable hit. My 'exquisitely-turned' phrases... She's very clever, especially when she's in a bad mood. And why this sudden inclination towards simplicity and innocence? This Russian tutor – she talks a lot about him. Frankly, I can't see anything special about him. He's just a student, like any other. She surely isn't... no, it's not possible. She's out of sorts, she doesn't know what she wants, so she sinks her claws into me. Yes, a child always slaps its nurse. What a flattering comparison! Still, I mustn't interfere. Once this fit of nostalgia's over, she'll be the first to laugh at this lanky young stripling, this fresh-faced youth. Well, that's not a bad interpretation, Rakitin old chap, but is it accurate? God only knows! We shall see. It won't be the first time, my dear fellow, that after a great deal of soul-searching, you've given up any sort of conjecture or speculation, to sit with your arms folded and calmly await developments. Meanwhile, you must admit you feel thoroughly ill at ease, and bitter... but that's your *métier,* after all. Ah! Here he is in person, our spontaneous young man. Yes, here he comes, and I haven't had a proper chat with him yet. Let's see what he's made of.

(*BELYAEV enters.*)

Aleksei Nikolaich! You've been taking the air too?

BELYAEV: Yes, sir.

RAKITIN: Though I must say, the air's not all that fresh today. It's frightfully hot, but it's just about bearable under these lime trees, in the shade. Have you seen Natalya Petrovna?

BELYAEV: I've just met her... She's gone back to the house with Vera Aleksandrovna.

RAKITIN: But wasn't it you I saw here with Vera, about a half-hour ago?

BELYAEV: Yes, it was. I was out walking with her.

RAKITIN: I see. So, how do you like life in the country?

BELYAEV: I love the country. The only trouble is the hunting round here's very poor.

RAKITIN: You like hunting, then?

BELYAEV: Yes. What about you?

RAKITIN: Me? No, I'm a poor shot, I must confess. I'm too lazy.

BELYAEV: Well, I'm lazy too – but not when it comes to walking.

RAKITIN: I see. So, in what way lazy? Reading?

BELYAEV: No, I love reading. I just can't be bothered working. I can't keep my mind on anything for long, especially not the same subject.

RAKITIN: Like chatting with the ladies, for instance?

BELYAEV: Now you're laughing at me. Actually, I'm rather afraid of them.

RAKITIN: What gave you the idea... what made you think I was laughing at you?

BELYAEV: Oh, nothing. It doesn't matter, anyway. Tell me, where can you get hold of gunpowder around here?

RAKITIN: In town, I think. It's sold there under the name of poppy-seed. Is it fine quality you need?

BELYAEV: No, just rifle grade. I don't want it for shooting, it's to make fireworks.

RAKITIN: Oh? You know how to...

BELYAEV: Yes, I do. I've already picked out a spot, at the

back of the pond. I gather it's Natalya Petrovna's name-day next week, so that would be ideal.

RAKITIN: Natalya Petrovna will be very pleased at that attention on your part. She likes you, I can tell you that.

BELYAEV: I'm very flattered. Oh, incidentally, sir, I believe you have a magazine delivered. Would you let me have a look at it?

RAKITIN: Yes, of course, it'll be my pleasure. There's some very good poetry in it.

BELYAEV: I'm afraid I'm not keen on poetry.

RAKITIN: Why not?

BELYAEV: Well, comic verse strikes me as a bit contrived, and there's not much of it anyway. As for romantic poetry – I don't know, there's something false about it.

RAKITIN: You prefer novels?

BELYAEV: Yes, I like a good novel. But what I most enjoy are critical articles.

RAKITIN: Really, why?

BELYAEV: Because they're written from the heart.

RAKITIN: And what about yourself? Are you involved in literature?

BELYAEV: No, sir! What's the point of writing, if God hasn't given you any talent – I mean, people would laugh. Actually, what I find curious – perhaps you'd oblige me by explaining – is why an otherwise intelligent person, the moment he picks up a pen, starts foaming at the mouth? No, writing's not for me – pray God I can just understand what's written!

RAKITIN: Well, I'll tell you this, Aleksei Nikolaich – there aren't many young men with as much commonsense as you have.

BELYAEV: I'm most humbly grateful to you for the compliment. (*A pause.*) Yes, I've picked out a spot behind the pond for the fireworks, so I can have Roman candles burning on the water.

RAKITIN: That'll be very beautiful, I'm sure. Excuse me, Aleksei Nikolaich, but I wonder if I might ask – do you know French?

BELYAEV: No. I once translated a novel by Paul de Kock, "The Dairymaid of Montfermeil" – you've possibly heard of it – for fifty roubles in notes, but I don't know a word of French. Believe it or not, I translated *'quatre-vingt-dix'* as 'four-twenty-ten'! A case of needs must, I'm afraid. It's a shame, though. I would like to know French. Just that damnable laziness of mine. I'd like to read Georges Sand in French. But the pronunciation... I mean, how are you supposed to cope with that? *En, on, un, une...* awful!

RAKITIN: Well, you can always get help...

BELYAEV: I'm sorry, what time is it, please?

RAKITIN: It's half past one.

BELYAEV: Why does Lizaveta Bogdanovna keep Kolya so long at the piano? He'll be dying to get away by now.

RAKITIN: Well, he does need to study.

BELYAEV: Yes, of course. You shouldn't have to say that, sir – and I shouldn't have to be told. You're right, we don't want everybody turning out an idle layabout like me.

RAKITIN: Oh, come, come...

BELYAEV: No, I know what I'm talking about.

RAKITIN: Yes, but on the other hand, I also know, and quite possibly the thing you regard as a flaw, that is, your casualness, your easy manner – is exactly what people like about you.

BELYAEV: What people?

RAKITIN: Natalya Petrovna, for one.

BELYAEV: Natalya Petrovna? I certainly don't feel easy, as you call it, when I'm with her.

RAKITIN: You don't?

BELYAEV: Well, for goodness' sake, sir, surely it's a man's education that counts? It's all right for you... I honestly don't understand you... What's that? That sounded like a corncrake in the garden... (*Makes to exit.*)

RAKITIN: It might have been... where are you going?

BELYAEV: To get my gun.

(*He makes to exit, and meets NATALYA PETROVNA, entering.*)

NATALYA PETROVNA: Mr Belyaev, where are you going?

BELYAEV: I... I...

RAKITIN: He's going to fetch his gun. He heard a corncrake just now in the garden.

NATALYA PETROVNA: No, please don't shoot in the garden. Let the poor bird live. Besides, you'll frighten Grandmama.

BELYAEV: Yes, ma'am.

NATALYA PETROVNA: Oh, come, sir, you should be ashamed of yourself. 'Yes, ma'am' – what sort of answer's that? How can you talk like that? Now stay here. Rakitin and I are taking charge of your education. Yes, yes, we are. We've spoken about you more than once – there's a conspiracy afoot, I give you fair warning. You'll surely allow me a hand in your education?

BELYAEV: Goodness, ma'am, I...

NATALYA PETROVNA: And firstly – don't be so shy, it doesn't suit you at all. Yes, we'll take you in hand. After all, we're such old fogeys, and you're a young man – isn't that the truth? Now look how nicely everything's turning out. You'll be looking after Kolya, and I... and we'll look after you.

BELYAEV: I should be most grateful.

NATALYA PETROVNA: Good! Now, what were you talking about just now with Rakitin?

RAKITIN: He was just telling me how he had translated a French novel, without knowing a word of French.

NATALYA PETROVNA: There you are, you see? We shall teach you French. Incidentally, what have you done with your kite?

BELYAEV: I carried it back home. I thought you weren't... you didn't seem very pleased...

NATALYA PETROVNA: Whatever gave you that idea? Because I took Vera... was it because I took Vera home? No, it was... No, you're mistaken. Anyway, I'll tell you what – Kolya will have finished his lesson by now, so let's go and fetch him, and Vera, and the kite – would

you like that? And we'll all go together down to the
meadow, shall we?

BELYAEV: With pleasure, Natalya Petrovna.

NATALYA PETROVNA: Splendid. Now, come on, let's go.
Come on, take my hand, don't be so awkward. Let's go,
quickly.

(*They exit.*)

RAKITIN: So full of life... so happy. I've never seen that
look on her face before. And what a sudden change!
Souvent femme varie.... As for me, well... I'm definitely
not to her liking today, that's clear. So! We'll see what
develops. Can she really be...? No, it's not possible.
But that smile, that gentle, radiant, welcoming look...
God forbid I should discover the pangs of jealousy,
especially senseless jealousy! Well, well, what brings
them here?

(*SHPIGELSKY and BOLSHINTSOV enter.*)

Good afternoon, gentlemen. I must admit I wasn't
expecting to see you again, Doctor...

SHPIGELSKY: Well, actually, I was, er... I didn't think I'd
be back either. But there I was, on my way to look in on
Bolshintsov, and he's already sitting in his carriage, to
come here. So, I turned the shafts round there and then,
and came back with him.

RAKITIN: Well, anyway, you're most welcome.

BOLSHINTSOV: Yes, I was just getting ready to...

SHPIGELSKY: The servants told us everyone was in the
garden. At least, there was nobody in the drawingroom.

RAKITIN: What, you didn't bump into Natalya Petrovna?

SHPIGELSKY: When?

RAKITIN: Just now.

SHPIGELSKY: No. We didn't come here directly from the
house. Bolshintsov wanted to see if there were any
mushrooms in the spinney.

BOLSHINTSOV: I... I...

SHPIGELSKY: Oh come on, we all know you're an
absolute hound for brown-caps. So, Natalya Petrovna's
gone home? Really? Well, we'd better go back too.

BOLSHINTSOV: Yes, of course.

RAKITIN: Actually, she's gone home to call everybody out. I think they're going to fly the kite.

SHPIGELSKY: Splendid! They ought to be outdoors in weather like this.

RAKITIN: You can stay here. I'll tell her you've arrived.

SHPIGELSKY: Goodness, dear sir, why put yourself to so much bother?

RAKITIN: No, no, I've got to go in anyway...

SHPIGELSKY: Oh well, in that case, we won't hold you back. No fuss, mind...

RAKITIN: Goodbye, gentlemen. (*Exits.*)

SHPIGELSKY: Goodbye. (*To BOLSHINTSOV.*) Well then, sir...

BOLSHINTSOV: What was all that stuff about mushrooms, Doctor? I don't understand – what mushrooms?

SHPIGELSKY: Oh, I see – and perhaps you'd rather I'd told him that poor old Bolshintsov here took fright, and wouldn't come direct, insisted on taking a detour?

BOLSHINTSOV: Well, I suppose so... but really, mushrooms? I don't know, maybe I'm making a mistake.

SHPIGELSKY: No doubt you are, my friend. And you'd better give it some thought. Anyway, we're here now, as you wished. Just take care you don't fall flat on your face.

BOLSHINTSOV: Well, all right, Doctor, but it was you – I mean, you told me – I'd like to know definitely, what her answer...

SHPIGELSKY: My dear good sir! From your village to here it's over ten miles, and you've asked me the same question at least three times every mile. What more do you want? Now, do listen, I'm telling you this, just to please you, one more time. All Natalya Petrovna said to me was, "I don't..."

BOLSHINTSOV: Yes.

SHPIGELSKY: Yes? What do you mean 'yes'? I haven't told you anything yet. What she said was, "I don't know Mr Bolshintsov very well, but he seems a good man. On

the other hand, I haven't the slightest intention of forcing
Vera, but if he wishes to call on us, and proves worthy..."

BOLSHINTSOV: Worthy? She said, "Worthy"?

SHPIGELSKY: "If he proves worthy of her favour, then
Anna Semyonovna and I won't stand in the way..."

BOLSHINTSOV: "Won't stand in the way"? Did she
actually say that? "Won't stand in the way"?

SHPIGELSKY: Yes, yes, yes. What a peculiar fellow you
are! "We won't stand in the way of their happiness."

BOLSHINTSOV: Hm.

SHPIGELSKY: "Their happiness", yes. But take note, sir,
of the task that's ahead of you – you've now got to
convince Vera Aleksandrovna herself that marriage with
you will be precisely that, her happiness – you have to
win her favour.

BOLSHINTSOV: Yes, yes, to win her – that's it, you're
quite right.

SHPIGELSKY: And you absolutely insisted I bring
you here today, so let's see, what action do you
intend to take?

BOLSHINTSOV: Action? Yes, of course   action. I have to
win her, that's right. The only thing is, Doctor – if you
don't mind, as my dearest friend – I must confess to a
certain weakness. I mean, you said I asked you to bring
me here today.

SHPIGELSKY: You didn't ask, you demanded, most
insistently.

BOLSHINTSOV: Well, yes, I suppose I did. But you see –
well, when I'm at home – I mean, when I'm at home
I feel ready for anything, but now I'm a bundle of
nerves, I really am.

SHPIGELSKY: What on earth are you nervous about?

BOLSHINTSOV: It's the risk.

SHPIGELSKY: Wha-a-at?

BOLSHINTSOV: It's risky. I'm taking a big risk. I must
confess to you, Doctor, as my...

SHPIGELSKY: As your dearest friend, we know, we know.
Go on...

59

BOLSHINTSOV: You're absolutely right, of course.
Anyway, I must confess to you that I've had very few
relationships, so to speak, with ladies, with the female
sex in general. And I'll be quite open with you, Doctor,
I simply haven't a clue what to talk about with a person
of the opposite sex – on one's own, besides, and
especially with young ladies.

SHPIGELSKY: You astonish me. I mean, what can't you
talk about to a person of the opposite sex, especially a
young lady, and especially on your own?

BOLSHINTSOV: Yes, that's all very well for you, but what
about me? That's the very reason I had to come running
to you. It's the first step that counts in these affairs, they
say, so couldn't you give me something to start the
conversation, some sort of casual remark, a few words, just
to get me going? Then I'll manage somehow by myself.

SHPIGELSKY: I'm not going to give you any sort of
phrase, my dear sir, because there's nothing that'll do you
any good – but I will give you some advice, if you like.

BOLSHINTSOV: Please do, dear friend. And if there's any
way I can show my gratitude... well, you know...

SHPIGELSKY: Oh, stop it. What am I doing, making a
deal with you?

BOLSHINTSOV: I mean, about the little troika, you can
rest assured...

SHPIGELSKY: For heaven's sake, will you stop! Now look,
Bolshintsov – you're a splendid person in every respect,
there's no doubt about it, a person of exceptional qualities...

BOLSHINTSOV: Oh, please...

SHPIGELSKY: Besides which, you possess three hundred
serfs, am I right?

BOLSHINTSOV: Three hundred and twenty, yes.

SHPIGELSKY: Not mortgaged?

BOLSHINTSOV: I don't owe a single kopeck.

SHPIGELSKY: Well, there you are, then. As I've been
trying to tell you, you're an absolutely splendid person,
and a fine catch for anyone. And you're telling me
you've had very little to do with ladies...

BOLSHINTSOV: Well, it's true. You might say I've been
avoiding the opposite sex since childhood.

SHPIGELSKY: So what? That's not a vice in a husband,
quite the contrary. All the same in certain circumstances
– for example, when you make your first declaration of
love – you ought to have at least something to say, isn't
that so?

BOLSHINTSOV: Oh, absolutely, I agree.

SHPIGELSKY: Otherwise Vera Aleksandrovna might
think you're feeling unwell, and it'll be all over. Besides
which, although you're quite presentable, by and large,
you're not exactly striking, you don't hit someone
between the eyes, if you know what I mean, and that's
what's needed nowadays.

BOLSHINTSOV: (*Sighs.*) That's what's needed nowadays.

SHPIGELSKY: Well, it pleases the young ladies. Yes,
and then there's your age, of course. In short, you
won't get anywhere on charm alone. Maybe you
shouldn't bother with pretty speeches. You can't rely
on them, anyway. And you can rely on something
much firmer and more solid, yes, your personal
qualities, my dear sir, and your three hundred and
twenty serfs. If I were you, I'd simply tell Vera
Aleksandrovna...

BOLSHINTSOV: What, on my own?

SHPIGELSKY: Yes, absolutely on your own! "Vera
Aleksandrovna!" I'd say...
(*BOLSHINTSOV mouths every word after SHPIGELSKY.*)
"I love you, and I'm asking for your hand in marriage.
I'm a kindhearted chap, straightforward, quiet, and I'm
not exactly poor. You'll have complete freedom with me,
and I shall try to please you in all things. Please make
enquiries about me, and pay me, if you will, just a little
more notice than you have done hitherto, then give me
your answer, whatever it may be, at your convenience.
I'm prepared to wait, and even consider it a pleasure".

BOLSHINTSOV: Consider it a pleasure... Yes, yes,
you're absolutely right. There's only one thing, Doctor

– I think you used the word 'quiet' – as if to say I'm a quiet person.

SHPIGELSKY: Well, why not? You are quiet, aren't you?

BOLSHINTSOV: Well, yes, but I mean, I'm wondering – will that be acceptable? Wouldn't I be better to say something like, for instance....

SHPIGELSKY: For instance?

BOLSHINTSOV: Well, for instance... for instance... All right, I'll just say 'quiet'.

SHPIGELSKY: Now, sir, listen carefully – hear me out. The more simply you express yourself, the less flowery you make your speech, the better the whole business will go, believe me. The main thing is not to keep harping on, don't force the issue. Vera Aleksandrovna's still very young, you might scare her off. Give her time to think over your proposal properly. Oh yes, and another thing – after all, you did ask me for my advice. Anyway, now and again you have a tendency, my dear sir, to say things like 'sparrowgrass' and 'taters'. Well, of course, that's fine, but actually, 'asparagus' and 'potatoes' are a bit more usual. They're more in common use, as you might say. And I remember on one occasion you called some hospitable local gent a *bon voyeur*... Yes – "He's a real *bon voyeur!*", you said. That's a good phrase too, of course, but unfortunately it doesn't mean anything. All right, I'm no great shakes at French myself, but I know that much. No, give the flowery stuff a miss, and I'll guarantee your success. Ah, they're all coming now.

(*BOLSHINTSOV makes to withdraw.*)

Where on earth are you going? Mushrooms again? The main thing is not to be shy!

BOLSHINTSOV: You're sure Vera Aleksandrovna doesn't know anything yet?

SHPIGELSKY: Oh, for heaven's sake!

BOLSHINTSOV: Well, I'm depending on you...

(*He blows his nose. Enter NATALYA PETROVNA, VERA, BELYAEV with his kite, KOLYA, and behind them RAKITIN and LIZAVETA BOGDANOVNA.*)

NATALYA PETROVNA: Ah, good afternoon, gentlemen, good afternoon, Doctor – I wasn't expecting you today, but I'm always pleased to see you. Good afternoon, sir.

SHPIGELSKY: It was this gentleman – he absolutely insisted on bringing me here.

NATALYA PETROVNA: I'm much obliged to him, but do you really have to be forced to visit us?

SHPIGELSKY: Good heavens, no! But I was here just this morning, and left... no, of course not.

NATALYA PETROVNA: Ah, you see, you're contradicting yourself, Mr Ambassador!

SHPIGELSKY: Anyway, I must say, dear lady, it gives me great pleasure to see you in such high spirits, at least as far as I can tell.

NATALYA PETROVNA: Oh, come – do you really need to remark on that – it's surely not that rare an occurrence?

SHPIGELSKY: No, not at all, but...

NATALYA PETROVNA: *Monsieur le diplomate,* you're getting more mixed up by the minute.

KOLYA: *Maman,* please, when are we going to fly the kite?

NATALYA PETROVNA: Whenever you like. Aleksei Nikolaich, and you, Vera, let's all go down to the meadow. I don't think you'll find it very interesting, gentlemen. Lizaveta Bogdanovna, and you, Rakitin, I'm leaving our good friend Bolshintsov here in your care.

RAKITIN: And just what makes you think we won't be interested?

NATALYA PETROVNA: Well, you're such clever people – it'll seem silly to you, I'm sure. However, as you wish, we're not stopping you... Let's go.
(*NATALYA PETROVNA, VERA, BELYAEV and KOLYA all exit.*)

SHPIGELSKY: (*To BOLSHINTSOV.*) So, my good friend – give your arm to Lizaveta Bogdanovna.

BOLSHINTSOV: With the greatest of pleasure...

SHPIGELSKY: (*To RAKITIN.*) And we'll come with you, if you don't mind, sir. Just look at them racing down the path. Let's go and watch them flying this kite, even though we're such clever people. Bolshintsov, you don't mind walking on ahead?

BOLSHINTSOV: Well, I must say, the weather's very nice today.

LIZAVETA B: Yes, very.

SHPIGELSKY: (*To RAKITIN.*) And you and I ought to have a chat, sir... (*RAKITIN laughs.*) What is it?

RAKITIN: Nothing – nothing at all. I just think it's funny, us bringing up the rear – the *arrière-garde*.

SHPIGELSKY: Ah well, the *avant-garde,* as you know, can very easily become the *arrière-garde*... it depends which direction you're facing.

(*They exit.*)

(*End of Act Two.*)

ACT THREE

The setting as Act One. RAKITIN and SHPIGELSKY enter from the ballroom doors.

SHPIGELSKY: So anyway, Rakitin, I'm asking you to assist me, please.

RAKITIN: But how can I assist you, Doctor?

SHPIGELSKY: How? Look, put yourself in my place. Of course, I'm not involved in this affair personally. I've acted, one might say, out of a desire to please... and that kind heart of mine'll be the death of me yet!

RAKITIN: Oh come, there's no danger of that.

SHPIGELSKY: Well, it's still not out in the open, but I'm in fact in a really awkward position. I've brought Bolshintsov here at Natalya Petrovna's bidding, and conveyed her answer to him, with her permission, but now I get the distinct feeling, for one thing, that I've made a stupid blunder, and for another, Bolshintsov won't give me any peace. They're avoiding him, and they won't speak to me...

RAKITIN: What on earth possessed you to get mixed up in this anyway? I mean, between ourselves, Bolshintsov's an absolute idiot.

SHPIGELSKY: Between ourselves? That's a joke. It's not exactly news, is it? Anyway, since when did only clever people get married? Whatever else we do, we can't stop fools marrying. You say I got mixed up in this business... that's not so. What actually happened was that a friend asked me to put in a good word for him – what else could I do? I could hardly refuse, could I? I'm a kind person, I can't say no. So, I carry out my friend's wishes, and I'm told: "We thank you most humbly, but please don't go to any more trouble..." I understand, and drop the matter. Then suddenly I'm being invited, even encouraged, you might say. So, I do as I'm told, and then they're indignant. I mean, what have I done wrong?

RAKITIN: Who said you'd done anything wrong? I'm only surprised you're making such a fuss.

SHPIGELSKY: Because the man keeps pestering me, that's why.

RAKITIN: Oh, come...

SHPIGELSKY: Besides which, he's an old friend.

RAKITIN: Really? Well, that's a different matter.

SHPIGELSKY: Oh, all right, I'll be frank with you. You're not easily fooled. The fact is, well... he's promised me... well, my trace-horse is on its last legs, so he's promised me...

RAKITIN: A new trace-horse?

SHPIGELSKY: No, actually three, a whole team.

RAKITIN: You should have said that earlier!

SHPIGELSKY: Now, please don't think... I wouldn't have agreed to act as go-between in this business for anything, it's absolutely contrary to my nature, if I hadn't known Bolshintsov to be the most honourable man. Well, anyway, there's only one thing I want now, and that's a definite answer – yes or no.

RAKITIN: So the affair's gone as far as that, has it?

SHPIGELSKY: What do you mean? We're not talking about marriage, simply permission to call on her.

RAKITIN: And who on earth's going to forbid you?

SHPIGELSKY: Oh, honestly – forbid! Of course, if it were anyone else... but Bolshintsov's a timid soul, an innocent, like something out of the Golden Age, still wet behind the ears. He's got no self-confidence, he needs a bit of encouragement. Besides which, his intentions are entirely honourable.

RAKITIN: And his horses are good.

SHPIGELSKY: His horses are good. (*Offers RAKITIN his snuff-box.*) Would you care for some snuff?

RAKITIN: No, thank you.

SHPIGELSKY: So, as you see, Rakitin, I'm not trying to deceive you. Why should I? It's all perfectly above board. A man of principle, well-to-do, mild-mannered... If he's acceptable, fine. If he isn't, then let them say.

RAKITIN: This is all splendid, I dare say, but what's it to do with me? I don't see how I can help.

SHPIGELSKY: Oh come, sir! We all know much Natalya Petrovna respects you. She'll even do as you tell her now and again. Seriously, Rakitin, be a friend, put in a good word for us.

RAKITIN: And you think he'll make a good husband for Vera?

SHPIGELSKY: I'm convinced of it. If you don't believe me, just wait and see. After all, the main thing in a marriage, as you know yourself, is a good, solid character. And what could be more solid than Bolshintsov! Ah, I think that's Natalya Petrovna now... Oh, dear friend and benefactor, just think! Two chestnut trace-horses, a bay mare in the shafts! Now, go to work!

RAKITIN: Well, all right.

SHPIGELSKY: Believe me, I'm depending on you... (*Exits to the ballroom.*)

RAKITIN: What a crafty devil that Doctor is! Vera... with Bolshintsov! Well, why not? There's many a worse match than that. I'll do his bidding, what happens after that's no concern of mine!

(*NATALYA PETROVNA enters from the study.*)

NATALYA PETROVNA: Oh, it's you... I thought you were in the garden.

RAKITIN: You sound displeased...

NATALYA PETROVNA: Now, don't start! You're by yourself?

RAKITIN: The Doctor's just left.

NATALYA PETROVNA: Huh, the local Talleyrand... What was he saying to you? Is he still hovering around?

RAKITIN: I can see our local Talleyrand, as you call him, isn't exactly in your good books. On the other hand, yesterday...

NATALYA PETROVNA: He makes me laugh; he's quite funny, but... well, he pokes his nose into other people's affairs. It isn't nice. Besides which, despite all his fawning, he's actually quite rude, a bit of a nuisance. He's a terrible cynic.

RAKITIN: That wasn't your opinion of him yesterday.

NATALYA PETROVNA: Perhaps not. So what was he saying?

RAKITIN: He was telling me about... Bolshintsov.

NATALYA PETROVNA: That stupid creature?

RAKITIN: And you had a different opinion of him yesterday too.

NATALYA PETROVNA: Yesterday isn't today.

RAKITIN: For everyone else, yes – obviously not for me.

NATALYA PETROVNA: What do you mean by that?

RAKITIN: For me, today's the same as yesterday.

NATALYA PETROVNA: I understand your reproach, but you're mistaken. Yesterday I wouldn't have admitted I had anything to reproach myself with... No, don't contradict me. I know, and you know too, what I'm referring to. And today I can admit it. I've been thinking things over. Believe me, *Michel,* no matter what silly ideas I've had, no matter what I've said or done, there's no one I depend on, as I do you. There's no-one I love, as I love you. Don't you believe me?

(*A brief silence.*)

RAKITIN: I believe you. But you look so sad today... what's wrong?

NATALYA PETROVNA: This much I'm convinced of, Rakitin – you can't be responsible for yourself in any given circumstance, you can't guarantee anything. I mean, often we don't understand our own past, so how can we be answerable for our future? You can't bind the future in chains.

RAKITIN: That's true.

NATALYA PETROVNA: Listen to me – I want to be frank with you, and perhaps I'll hurt you a little, but I know my keeping quiet will only hurt you more. I'll confess to you, *Michel...* this young student... this Belyaev has made a considerable impression on me.

RAKITIN: I know.

NATALYA PETROVNA: You've noticed? Since when?

RAKITIN: Since yesterday afternoon.

NATALYA PETROVNA: I see.

RAKITIN: A few days ago, if you remember, I spoke about the change that was taking place in you. At that time I had no idea what to attribute it to. But yesterday, after our conversation, and at the meadow... oh, if you had been able to see yourself! I didn't recognise you, you'd become a different person. You were laughing, skipping, jumping for joy like a schoolgirl, your eyes shining, your cheeks flushed, and you were looking at him with such trusting curiosity, so delightedly, and so attentively, you were smiling so... Even now your face is lit up, just remembering.

NATALYA PETROVNA: No, please, Rakitin – for God's sake don't turn away. Listen to me – why are you exaggerating? I've been smitten by his youth, that's all. I've never been young, *Michel,* from my childhood on, right up until now. I mean, you know what my life's been like. I'm not used to it, so all this has rushed to my head, like wine, but it'll pass, I know it will, as quickly as it came. It's not worth discussing. Only please don't turn your back on me, don't pull your hands away. Help me...

RAKITIN: Help you... what cruel words. Natasha, you don't know yourself what's happening to you. You're certain it's not worth discussing, and yet you ask for help. Obviously, you feel you need it!

NATALYA PETROVNA: Well, yes... that is... I'm turning to you as a friend.

RAKITIN: Yes, ma'am. And I'm willing to justify your confidence in me once I've summoned up a little courage, if you don't mind...

NATALYA PETROVNA: Courage? There isn't going to be any... any unpleasantness, surely? Nothing's changed, has it?

RAKITIN: No, of course not! Everything's just as it was.

NATALYA PETROVNA: But what are you thinking, *Michel?* You can't seriously be suggesting...

RAKITIN: I'm not suggesting anything.

NATALYA PETROVNA: Can you, of all people, really have such a low opinion of me?

RAKITIN: Oh, stop it, for God's sake. We'd better have a talk about Bolshintsov. The Doctor's expecting an answer in the matter with Vera, you know that.

NATALYA PETROVNA: You're angry with me.

RAKITIN: Me? Of course I'm not. But I feel sorry for you.

NATALYA PETROVNA: What? Now that does annoy me! You should be ashamed of yourself, *Michel.* You say the Doctor's expecting an answer? And just who asked him to interfere?

RAKITIN: He assured me, that you yourself...

NATALYA PETROVNA: Possibly, possibly... Although I don't think I said anything definite. Besides which, I am allowed to change my mind. Oh, who gives a damn anyway! Shpigelsky's got a finger in every pie – he can't expect to succeed all the time – not in his line of work.

RAKITIN: He simply wants to know what response...

NATALYA PETROVNA: What response? *Michel,* please don't... Give me your hand. Why are you looking at me so coldly, why all that chilly politeness? What've I done wrong? I mean, is this really my fault? I came to you in the hopes of hearing some good advice, I didn't hesitate for a second, I didn't dream of holding anything back, and here you... I can see I shouldn't have been so open with you. It would never have entered your mind. You suspected nothing, and you've been deceiving me. Now God only knows what you're thinking.

RAKITIN: Me? Oh, for Heaven's sake!

NATALYA PETROVNA: Give me your hand, please... You've decided to turn your back on me? Well, so much the worse for you. Although I suppose I can't really blame you. You're jealous!

RAKITIN: I don't have the right to be jealous, Natasha. How can you say that?

NATALYA PETROVNA: (*After a pause.*) Very well. But as far as Bolshintsov is concerned, I haven't yet had a talk with Vera.

RAKITIN: I can send her to you now.

NATALYA PETROVNA: What on earth for? Oh, all right, do as you wish.

RAKITIN: So, you want me to send her?

NATALYA PETROVNA: *Michel,* one last thing... You said just now you were sorry for me – is this your way of showing it? Do you really...

RAKITIN: Shall I send her?

NATALYA PETROVNA: (*Exasperated.*) Yes.

(*RAKITIN exits to the study.*)

This one, too! What's the matter with me! Him... and now him! And I was so relying on him. And what about Arkady? Oh, God! I haven't given him a thought! It's time to put a stop to all this, I can see...

(*VERA enters.*)

Yes, it's time I did.

VERA: You wanted to see me, Natalya Petrovna?

NATALYA PETROVNA: Ah! Vera, my dear, it's you – yes, I did ask to see you.

VERA: Are you feeling all right?

NATALYA PETROVNA: Me? Yes, why?

VERA: I just thought...

NATALYA PETROVNA: No, I'm fine. I'm feeling a little warm, that's all. Now, sit down.

(*VERA sits.*)

Tell me, Vera – you're not busy with anything at the moment, are you?

VERA: No, ma'am.

NATALYA PETROVNA: The reason I ask is because we need to have a talk... a serious talk. You see, my dear, up until now you've been a child, really, but you're seventeen now. You're a bright girl – it's time you gave a little thought to your future. You know I love you like a daughter – my house will be your home, always – but, well, in other people's eyes you're an orphan. You haven't any means, and in time you may well tire of constantly living off other people. Tell me this – would you like to be your own mistress, in complete charge of your own home?

71

VERA: I don't know what you mean, ma'am.

NATALYA PETROVNA: I've been asked for your hand in marriage. You weren't expecting that, I can see. I must confess I thought it a little strange myself. You're still so young. I needn't tell you I haven't the slightest intention of forcing you. In my opinion, it's too early yet for marriage. I simply thought it my duty to inform you... Vera, what is it? Are you crying? Why, you're trembling all over – you're surely not afraid of me, Vera?

VERA: I'm in your power, Natalya Petrovna.

NATALYA PETROVNA: Vera, why should you be crying? How can you say you're in my power? What do you take me for? I'm speaking to you as a daughter, and you're... Oh, really – you're in my power? Well, kindly burst out laughing this minute – that's an order!

(*VERA smiles through her tears.*)

That's better.

(*NATALYA PETROVNA puts her arm round her.*)

Vera, my child, treat me as you would your own mother – or no, better still, think of me as your older sister, and let's you and I put our heads together on all these marvellous things. Would you like that?

VERA: I would, ma'am.

NATALYA PETROVNA: Well, then, listen... Move up a little closer. That's better. Firstly, since you're my sister, let's assume I don't have to tell you that you're at home here – such a pretty face is at home anywhere. So it shouldn't even enter your head that you could be a burden to anyone, that anyone might want rid of you – do you follow me? But one fine day, along comes your sister and says, "Just think, Vera, someone wants to marry you..." You see? What are you going to say to her? That you're still too young, that you haven't given any thought to marriage?

VERA: Yes, ma'am.

NATALYA PETROVNA: No, no, don't say 'Yes, ma'am'. Is that how sisters talk? 'Yes, ma'am'?

VERA: Well... no.

NATALYA PETROVNA: Anyway, your sister agrees with you, the proposal's turned down, and that's the end of the matter. But supposing he's a fine man, well-to-do, and let's say he's prepared to wait, and all he wants is permission to see you now and again, in the hope that you'll eventually grow to like him.

VERA: But who is this suitor?

NATALYA PETROVNA: Aha! You're curious. You can't guess?

VERA: No.

NATALYA PETROVNA: You saw him only today... True, he's not particularly handsome, and he's not all that young... Bolshintsov.

VERA: Bolshintsov?

NATALYA PETROVNA: Yes... Bolshintsov.

VERA: (*Suddenly begins to laugh, then stops.*) You aren't joking?

NATALYA PETROVNA: No, but I can see Bolshintsov's wasting his time here. If you'd burst out crying at the mention of his name – well, he might have had some hope, but you burst out laughing. The only thing he can do now is take himself off home.

VERA: I'm sorry, but I honestly wasn't expecting... I mean, do people still get married at his age?

NATALYA PETROVNA: Good heavens, how old do you think he is? He isn't fifty yet. He's still in his prime.

VERA: Well, maybe so, but he's so funny-looking...

NATALYA PETROVNA: All right, let's not discuss him any further. He's dead and buried. God rest his soul! Besides, one thing's certain – a man like Bolshintsov couldn't please a young girl like you. You all want to marry for love, without a second thought, isn't that the truth?

VERA: Well, yes, Natalya Petrovna, but... I mean, surely you married Arkady Sergeyich for love?

NATALYA PETROVNA: Yes, of course. For love. Yes, Vera. I called you a young girl just now, but the young girls are right. Anyway, that's the end of the matter.

Bolshintsov's out of the running. To tell you the truth, I wouldn't really like to see his bloated old features alongside your lovely little fresh face, although he's a nice enough person. So you see now why you'd no need to fear me? How quickly it's all been settled! Honestly, you've been treating me as if I were your benefactress. And you know how much I hate that word.

VERA: Please forgive me, Natalya Petrovna.

NATALYA PETROVNA: Oh, nonsense. You're sure you're not afraid of me?

VERA: No. I love you, I'm not afraid of you.

NATALYA PETROVNA: Well, thank you. Perhaps we can be better friends now, and not hide anything from each other. I mean, supposing I were to say to you, "Vera, now tell me, just between ourselves: you don't want to marry Bolshintsov – is it purely because he's much older than you, and isn't exactly handsome?"

VERA: Isn't that enough?

NATALYA PETROVNA: I'm not disputing the fact... but there isn't any other reason, is there?

VERA: I hardly know him.

NATALYA PETROVNA: That's true. But you're not answering my question.

VERA: No, there's no other reason.

NATALYA PETROVNA: Honestly? Well, in that case I would advise you to think it over. I know it won't be easy to fall in love with Bolshintsov, but I must say again, he's a fine man. If you were in love with someone else, well, that would be a different matter. But you're sure your heart's still intact?

VERA: I'm sorry?

NATALYA PETROVNA: You don't love anyone else?

VERA: I love you... and Kolya. And I love Anna Semyonovna...

NATALYA PETROVNA: No, I don't mean that kind of love, you don't understand me. For instance, among all the young men, whom you might have seen either here, or on visits – isn't there any of them you like?

74

VERA: Oh yes, ma'am – I like some of them, but...

NATALYA PETROVNA: At the Krinitsyns' party, for example, I noticed you danced three times with that tall officer – what's his name?

VERA: An officer?

NATALYA PETROVNA: Yes, the one with the big moustache.

VERA: Oh, that one? No, I don't like him.

NATALYA PETROVNA: Well, what about Shalansky?

VERA: Shalansky's quite nice, but... no, I don't think he's interested in me.

NATALYA PETROVNA: Why not?

VERA: Well... I think he's more interested in Liza Velsky.

NATALYA PETROVNA: Really? You noticed that? What about Rakitin?

VERA: Well, I do love him...

NATALYA PETROVNA: I know, like a brother. How about Belyaev, then?

VERA: Aleksei Nikolaich? Yes, I like him.

NATALYA PETROVNA: Yes, he's a fine young man. Only he's so shy with everybody.

VERA: Oh no, ma'am. He's not shy with me.

NATALYA PETROVNA: Really?

VERA: Yes, he talks all the time with me. Perhaps he seems that way with you because... well, he's afraid of you. He hasn't got to know you yet.

NATALYA PETROVNA: And how do you know he's afraid of me?

VERA: He told me so.

NATALYA PETROVNA: He told you that? Obviously he's more open with you than with other people.

VERA: I don't know how he is with other people. Maybe it's because we're both orphans. Besides which... well, I'm just a child in his eyes.

NATALYA PETROVNA: You think so? Actually, I like him too. He must have a kind heart.

VERA: Oh, the kindest! If you only knew, ma'am – all the servants love him. He's so gentle. And the way he speaks to everyone, he'll help anybody. Why, a few days ago he carried an old beggar-woman in his arms, from the main road, right up to the hospital. He picked a flower for me once, off such a steep cliff that I had to shut my eyes, I was so frightened... I was sure he'd fall and injure himself, but he's so agile! You saw yourself how quick he was down at the meadow yesterday.

NATALYA PETROVNA: Yes, that's true.

VERA: You remember, when he was chasing the kite, how he leapt over that huge ditch? Oh yes, that's just child's play to him.

NATALYA PETROVNA: And he really did pick a flower for you in such a dangerous place? Obviously he's in love with you.

VERA: And he's always so jolly... high-spirited...

NATALYA PETROVNA: Yes, all the same it is strange. When he's with me he's so...

VERA: But as I said, that's because he doesn't know you. Look, I'll tell him... I'll tell him he's got nothing to fear from you – that's so, isn't it? That you're really very kind...

NATALYA PETROVNA: Thank you.

VERA: I mean, you'll see... and he does listen to me, even though I'm younger than him.

NATALYA PETROVNA: I'd no idea you and he were such good friends. Anyway, Vera, do be careful. He's a splendid young man, of course, but you know – at your age, well, it's not exactly right. People might think... I remarked on it yesterday in the garden, you remember? On the other hand, I've no wish to stand in the way of your affections, I've too much confidence in you both for that. Still, you won't be angry with me, my dear, for being so pedantic. We old fuss-pots just have to annoy young people with our dire warnings. Anyway, I'm wasting my time saying these things – after all, you like him, and nothing more, isn't that so?

VERA: Ma'am, I...

NATALYA PETROVNA: Now why are you looking at me like that again? Is that really how you look at a sister?

Vera, listen to me, come closer. Let's suppose your sister, your real sister, were to whisper to you now: "Vera, do you honestly love nobody?" Eh? What would you say to her? Mm? Those lovely eyes are trying to tell me something...

(*VERA suddenly presses her face to NATALYA PETROVNA's bosom.*)

You love him? Tell me, do you love him?

VERA: Oh, God! I don't know what I feel...

NATALYA PETROVNA: Oh, you poor thing – you're in love... You're in love... but what about him? Vera, is he?

VERA: Why are you asking me? I don't know. Maybe. I don't know, I don't know...

(*VERA looks up.*)

Natalya Petrovna, what's the matter?

NATALYA PETROVNA: With me? Nothing. Why? No, nothing.

VERA: You're quite pale, Natalya Petrovna. What's wrong? Let me call someone...

NATALYA PETROVNA: No, no, there's no need. It's nothing. It'll pass. Look, it's passed already.

VERA: Let me at least call someone.

NATALYA PETROVNA: Indeed, no. I... I want to be alone. Leave me. Will you, please? We'll talk another time. Now go, please.

VERA: You're not angry with me, Natalya Petrovna?

NATALYA PETROVNA: Why should I be? No, not at all. On the contrary, I'm most grateful to you for your trust. Just leave me, please, for the moment.

VERA: (*Tearfully.*) Natalya Petrovna...

NATALYA PETROVNA: Leave me alone, please.

(*VERA exits to the study. NATALYA PETROVNA remains motionless a few moments.*)

Everything's clear now. These children love each other... Well? So much the better... God grant them happiness! (*Laughs.*) And I... That I could think... She gave herself away so quickly. I must admit, I didn't suspect a thing. Certainly, this news has come as a shock. Still, never

mind, it's not over yet. My God, what am I saying?
What's the matter with me? I hardly recognise myself –
what've I become? What am I doing? I'm trying to
marry this poor girl off to... to an old man! And getting
the Doctor involved – he can guess what's going on, he's
dropping hints... Arkady, and Rakitin... And me...
I mean, what in God's name... am I jealous of Vera? Am
I in love with him, is that it? Are you still in any doubt?
Yes, you're in love, you wretched woman! How it
happened – I've no idea. It's as if I've been poisoned.
Suddenly my whole world's been smashed, scattered,
swept away... He's afraid of me. They're all afraid of me.
What does he see in me? What am I to him, someone
like me? He's young, and she's young. And as for me...
What value would he place on me? They're both stupid,
as Rakitin says. Oh, how I hate him, he's so damned
clever! And Arkady, dear, kind, trusting Arkady – God
in Heaven, I wish I were dead! Honestly, I think I'm
going out of my mind. Why am I exaggerating like this?
All right, I've had a shock – it's such a bizarre feeling,
this is the first time I've... I've... yes! The first time – I'm
in love now for the very first time! He'll have to leave.
Yes. And Rakitin too. It's time I came to my senses. I've
allowed myself one false step, and now see what's
happened. This is what I've come to. What was it about
him that attracted me? One thing's sure, it's a terrible
feeling... Arkady! Yes, I'll rush into his arms, I'll beg him
to forgive me, to protect me, to save me. Arkady, and
no-one else! All other men are strangers to me, and must
remain strangers. But... is there really no other way?
That girl... she's just a child. She could be mistaken. It's
all just children's games with them. So why should
I think... no, I'll have it out with him myself, I'll ask
him... Really? You're still hoping? You still live in hope?
Hope of what! Oh God, don't make me despise myself!
(*RAKITIN enters from the study, agitated.*)
RAKITIN: Natasha... (*She does not stir.*) What can have
happened between her and Vera? Natalya Petrovna...

NATALYA PETROVNA: Who is it? Oh, it's you.

RAKITIN: Vera told me you were unwell... I...

NATALYA PETROVNA: I'm fine. What gave her that idea?

RAKITIN: No, Natasha, you're not well – just look at you.

NATALYA PETROVNA: All right, maybe I'm not, but what's it to do with you? What is it you want? Why've you come?

RAKITIN: I'll tell you why I've come. I've come to beg your forgiveness. Half an hour ago I was unspeakably stupid and rude to you. Please forgive me. The truth is, Natasha, that no matter how modest his desires and... and his hopes, it's hard for a man not to lose his head, even if only for an instant, when they're suddenly snatched from him. However, I've come to my senses now, I understand my situation, and my fault in all this, and I wish only one thing – your forgiveness. Look at me, please – don't you turn your back on me too. Natasha, it's your old friend Rakitin here, the man who wishes nothing but to be allowed to serve you, your mainstay, as you used to call me. Don't deprive me of your trust, make use of me, and forget that I ever... Forget anything that might have offended you...

NATALYA PETROVNA: Yes, yes... Oh, I'm sorry, Rakitin, I didn't take in a word you were saying.

RAKITIN: I was saying... I was asking your forgiveness, Natasha. I was asking if you would let me be your friend still.

NATALYA PETROVNA: Oh, Rakitin, tell me – what's the matter with me?

RAKITIN: You're in love.

NATALYA PETROVNA: I'm in love... But that's crazy, Rakitin. It's not possible. Can it really be so sudden? You're saying I'm in love?

RAKITIN: Yes, you're in love, you poor woman. Don't try and deceive yourself.

NATALYA PETROVNA: So what can I do now?

RAKITIN: I'll tell you, Natasha, if you promise me...

NATALYA PETROVNA: You know, that young girl, Vera, she loves him... They're in love with each other.

RAKITIN: In which case that's another good reason for...

NATALYA PETROVNA: I've had my suspicions for a long time, but she confessed everything just now... just a moment ago...

RAKITIN: (*Sotto voce.*) Poor woman!

NATALYA PETROVNA: Well, it's time I came to my senses. You were about to say something, I think... For God's sake, Rakitin, advise me, please, tell me what to do...

RAKITIN: I'm willing to advise you, Natasha, but on one condition.

NATALYA PETROVNA: What is it, tell me?

RAKITIN: Promise me you won't suspect my motives. Tell me you believe in my unselfish desire to help you. And you must help me, too. Your trust in me will give me strength – otherwise you'd better let me remain silent.

NATALYA PETROVNA: No, go on, go on.

RAKITIN: You don't doubt me?

NATALYA PETROVNA: Tell me.

RAKITIN: All right. Listen to me... He's got to leave. Yes, he must. I'm not going to talk about... about your husband... your duty. Coming from my lips, words like that are out of place. But these children love one another. You've just told me that. Imagine yourself now coming between them – it would destroy you!

NATALYA PETROVNA: He must go away. What about you? Will you stay?

RAKITIN: Me? I... No, I have to leave too. For your peace of mind, your happiness, for Vera's happiness – he and I both... we must go away forever.

NATALYA PETROVNA: You know, Rakitin, I'd got to such a state... That poor girl, that orphan, entrusted to my care by her mother – I was virtually on the point of marrying her off to that stupid, ridiculous old man! And I just couldn't do it, Rakitin – the words froze on my lips, when she burst out laughing

at the idea. Yet I made all the arrangements with
that Doctor, I let him smile meaningfully at me.
I put up with those smiles, his compliments, his
innuendoes... Oh God, I feel as if I'm on the brink
of an abyss, save me!

RAKITIN: You see I was right, Natasha. He has to leave –
we both must. There's no other way.

NATALYA PETROVNA: And afterwards, what is there to
live for?

RAKITIN: Good God, has it come to that? Natasha, you'll
get over this, believe me – it'll pass. How can you ask
what there is to live for?

NATALYA PETROVNA: Yes, yes, what've I got to live for,
when everyone is abandoning me?

RAKITIN: But your family... Look, if you want, I can stay
on a few days after his departure, so that...

NATALYA PETROVNA: Oh yes, I see now. You're
counting on old habits, on our former friendship.
You're hoping I'll come to my senses, and return to
you, isn't that so? Yes, I know you well enough.

RAKITIN: Natalya Petrovna! Why are you insulting me?

NATALYA PETROVNA: I can see what you're up to, but
you're deluding yourself.

RAKITIN: What? After all your promises? After all I've
done for you, and only for you, for your happiness, for
your position in society – that you should finally...

NATALYA PETROVNA: Oh yes, and how long has that
been a concern of yours? Why didn't you say anything
about it before?

RAKITIN: Natalya Petrovna, I'm leaving here today, I'm
going right this minute, and you'll never see me again...
(*Makes to exit.*)

NATALYA PETROVNA: (*Embraces him.*) *Michel,* forgive me,
please – I don't know what I'm saying. You see what a
state I'm in. Please forgive me.

RAKITIN: Natasha...

NATALYA PETROVNA: Oh, *Michel,* I can't tell you hard it
is for me... Help me, please, I'm dead without you...

(*The ballroom door opens. ISLAEV and ANNA SEMYONOVNA enter.*)

ISLAEV: Well, I've always been of the opinion that...
(*He catches sight of RAKITIN and NATALYA PETROVNA, astonished. NATALYA PETROVNA hurriedly exits.*)
What's the meaning of this? What's going on?

RAKITIN: Er... nothing. It's just...

ISLAEV: Is Natalya Petrovna unwell?

RAKITIN: No, but...

ISLAEV: Why did she run out like that? What were you two talking about? It looked as if she'd been crying. And you were consoling her. What's going on?

RAKITIN: Nothing, honestly.

ANNA S: What do you mean by nothing, Mikhail Aleksandrych? I'll go and see... (*Makes to enter the study.*)

RAKITIN: No, please – you'd better leave her in peace for the moment.

ISLAEV: What is the meaning of all this? For God's sake, tell me!

RAKITIN: It's nothing, I swear to you. Look, I promise I'll explain everything to you both today, I give you my word. But for the moment, please, just trust me, don't ask me anything – and don't disturb her.

ISLAEV: Well, all right, but this is surprising. This has never happened before with Natasha. It's rather unusual.

ANNA S: The point is, what could've made Natasha cry? And why did she go out? I mean, are we strangers?

RAKITIN: No, of course not – how can you say that? Please listen to me – the fact is... well, to be honest, we haven't finished our conversation. And I'm obliged to ask you – both of you – to leave us alone for a few moments.

ISLAEV: What on earth...? D'you mean there's some secret between you?

RAKITIN: Yes, a secret... but you'll know soon enough.

ISLAEV: Let's go, Mama. We'll leave them alone. Let them finish their mysterious discussion.

ANNA S: But...

ISLAEV: Come on, let's go. You heard him promise to explain everything.

RAKITIN: You can rest assured...

ISLAEV: Oh, I'm perfectly assured! (*To ANNA SEMYONOVNA.*) Come on. (*They exit.*)

RAKITIN: Natasha... Natasha, come out, please.

NATALYA PETROVNA: (*Emerges from the study.*) What did they say?

RAKITIN: Nothing, you can relax. They were a little surprised, certainly. Arkady thought you were unwell. He noticed you were upset. Sit down, Natasha, please, you're hardly able to stand. I told him... I asked him not to disturb you... to leave us alone.

NATALYA PETROVNA: He agreed?

RAKITIN: Yes. Actually, I had to promise him I'd explain everything tomorrow. Why did you run out?

NATALYA PETROVNA: Why? What on earth are you going to say?

RAKITIN: I... I'll think of something. That doesn't matter. We've got to make the most of this breathing-space now. We can't go on like this, you know that. You're in no state to endure any more emotional upheaval. And it's unworthy of you. I myself... Anyway, that's not the point. You've got to be firm, that's all – I'll get by. Natasha, you do agree?

NATALYA PETROVNA: About what?

RAKITIN: About the necessity of... of our leaving. You agree? In which case there's nothing to hinder us, and if you'll let me, I'll have a word with Belyaev right now. He's a decent chap, he'll understand.

NATALYA PETROVNA: You're going to have a word with him? You? What can you say to him?

RAKITIN: I... I...

NATALYA PETROVNA: Rakitin, listen to me – don't you feel as if we're both going crazy? I've taken fright, I've frightened you, and most likely it's all for no reason.

RAKITIN: What do you mean?

NATALYA PETROVNA: It's true. I mean, what are we doing? It seems so long ago now, doesn't it, that everything was quiet and peaceful in this house, then suddenly... How did all this happen? We've all gone mad. No, it's finished – we've made big enough fools of ourselves. We'll carry on living just as before. And there'll be nothing for you to explain to Arkady. I'll tell him myself about our little escapades, and we'll both have a good laugh. No, I don't need any go-between with my husband!

RAKITIN: Natasha, you really do frighten me now. You're smiling, and yet you're as pale as death. Don't you recall anything of what you said a quarter of an hour ago?

NATALYA PETROVNA: Huh, what didn't I say! Anyway, I can see now what's going on. It was you yourself raised this storm, to make sure you wouldn't go down alone.

RAKITIN: You see? Again suspicion, again reproach. Natasha, God forgive me, but are you doing this to torment me, or do you simply regret your frankness?

NATALYA PETROVNA: I regret nothing.

RAKITIN: Then what am I supposed to think?

NATALYA PETROVNA: Rakitin, if you so much as breathe one word from me, or about me to Belyaev, I'll never forgive you.

RAKITIN: Ah, so that's it! Well, rest assured, Natalya Petrovna – not only will I say nothing to Mr Belyaev, I won't even bid him goodbye, as I quit this place. I've no intention of intruding where I'm not wanted.

NATALYA PETROVNA: I see – you think perhaps I've changed my mind about... about his leaving?

RAKITIN: I don't think anything.

NATALYA PETROVNA: Well, on the contrary, I'm so convinced of the necessity, as you put it, of his departure, that I intend to dismiss him myself. Yes, I'll tell him myself.

RAKITIN: You will?

NATALYA PETROVNA: Yes. And right now. Please send him to me.

RAKITIN: What? Now?

NATALYA PETROVNA: Yes. Please do this for me, Rakitin. And you see, I'm perfectly calm. Besides which,

I won't be disturbed now, so it's the ideal moment. I'd be most grateful to you. I want to ask him a few questions.

RAKITIN: Good heavens, he'll tell you nothing. He's admitted to me himself that he feels uneasy in your presence.

NATALYA PETROVNA: Oh? You've been discussing me with him?

(*RAKITIN shrugs.*)

NATALYA PETROVNA: I'm sorry, *Michel,* forgive me – and please send him to me. I'll dismiss him, you'll see, and that'll be the end of it. It'll all pass and be forgotten, like a bad dream. Send him in, do. I really must have a talk with him, once and for all. You'll be pleased with me. Go on.

RAKITIN: As you please. Your wish is my command.

(*Makes to exit.*)

NATALYA PETROVNA: *Michel...* Thank you.

RAKITIN: Please – spare me your gratitude. (*Exits to the ballroom.*)

NATALYA PETROVNA: He's a decent man. But did I ever really love him, ever? He's right. Belyaev must go. But how can I dismiss him? I just wish I knew exactly how fond he was of that girl. Maybe it's all nonsense. How did I ever get into such a state? What was the point of all that carry-on? Anyway, it's over and done with now. I'd just like to know what he has to say. Of course, he's got to leave, he must... he must go. Maybe he won't answer me. After all, he is afraid of me. Well, what of it? So much the better. There won't be so much to talk about... And I have a headache. Shouldn't I leave it until tomorrow? Maybe I should. I feel as if they've been watching me the whole time today. That's the state I've reached. No, better to get it over with now. One last effort, and I'm free! Oh, yes! I need peace and freedom so desperately!

(*BELYAEV enters.*)

It's him...

BELYAEV: Natalya Petrovna, Mr Rakitin says you want to see me.

NATALYA PETROVNA: That's right. I need to... to clarify a few things.

BELYAEV: Clarify?

NATALYA PETROVNA: Yes... clarify. I have to tell you, Aleksei Nikolaich, I'm... I'm not satisfied with you.

BELYAEV: May I know the reason?

NATALYA PETROVNA: Please, hear me out. I... I... To be honest, I'm not sure where to begin. Anyway, I must tell you that my dissatisfaction isn't on account of any sort of negligence on your part. On the contrary, I'm very pleased with the way you've been looking after Kolya.

BELYAEV: So tell me, what can it be?

NATALYA PETROVNA: You needn't be alarmed. It's not a particularly serious fault. You're young – I daresay you've never lived in a strange house. You couldn't have foreseen...

BELYAEV: Natalya Petrovna...

NATALYA PETROVNA: Yes, of course, you want to know what this is all about, and I can well understand your impatience. So – I have to tell you that Vera... Vera has confessed everything to me.

BELYAEV: Vera Aleksandrovna? What on earth could she confess? And what's it got to do with me?

NATALYA PETROVNA: You really don't know what she could confess? You can't guess?

BELYAEV: Me? No, not at all.

NATALYA PETROVNA: Well, in that case, forgive me. If you honestly can't guess, then I must ask your forgiveness. I thought... well, I was mistaken. But let me tell you, I don't believe you. And I can understand what's making you say that. I have every respect for your discretion.

BELYAEV: Natalya Petrovna, I haven't the faintest idea what you're talking about.

NATALYA PETROVNA: Honestly? D'you really think you can convince me you haven't noticed that child's feelings for you, Vera's feelings?

BELYAEV: Vera Aleksandrovna's feelings? I scarcely know what to say. Good heavens, as far as I know I've always treated Vera Aleksandrovna the same as...

NATALYA PETROVNA: The same as everyone else, isn't that so? Well, whatever the situation, whether you genuinely don't know, or whether you're pretending, the fact of the matter is this – that young girl's in love with you. She herself admitted it to me. So now I must ask you, as an honourable man, what you intend to do.

BELYAEV: What I intend to do?

NATALYA PETROVNA: Yes.

BELYAEV: This is all so unexpected, Natalya Petrovna.

NATALYA PETROVNA: Aleksei Nikolaich, I can see I've handled this matter rather awkwardly. You don't understand me. You think I'm angry with you, but... well, I'm just a little uneasy. And that's only natural. You needn't worry. Let's sit down. I'll be frank with you, Aleksei Nikolaich, and you can be at least a little more trusting with me. You really mustn't be so distant with me. Vera's in love with you... that's not your fault, of course. I'm willing to concede that it isn't your fault. But you do see, Aleksei Nikolaich, she's an orphan, and my ward. I'm responsible for her, for her future happiness. She's still very young, and I'm quite certain this feeling you've inspired in her will soon pass. At her age, love isn't lasting. Nevertheless, you understand it was my duty to warn you. Playing with fire is a dangerous business. Anyway, now that you're aware of her feelings, I've no doubt you'll change your behaviour towards her, you'll steer clear of meetings, and walks in the garden... Won't you? I feel I can depend on you. With anyone else I'd have been afraid to speak so openly.

BELYAEV: Natalya Petrovna, believe me, I do appreciate...

NATALYA PETROVNA: No, what I'm saying is that I have no doubts about you... and besides, all this is to remain a secret, just between us two.

BELYAEV: I must admit – everything you've told me seems so strange. Of course, I wouldn't presume to doubt you, but...

NATALYA PETROVNA: Listen to me, Aleksei Nikolaich. Everything I've said just now, I've said on the assumption that as far as you're concerned, there's nothing... Because if there were... Of course, I still hardly know you, but I already know you well enough to see no reason to oppose your intentions. You're not wealthy, but you're young, you have a good future, and when two people love each other... Let me say again, I simply thought it my duty to warn you, as an honourable man, about the consequences of your friendship with Vera, but of course if you...

BELYAEV: Natalya Petrovna, I honestly don't know what you mean.

NATALYA PETROVNA: I'm not asking for a confession, believe me – I don't need to, I can see by your manner what the situation is. However, I must tell you that Vera has a notion that you're not exactly indifferent to her.

BELYAEV: Natalya Petrovna, I can see it's impossible for me to remain under your roof.

NATALYA PETROVNA: I think you might at least wait until I dismiss you...

BELYAEV: You've been very frank with me. Allow me to be equally frank with you. I don't love Vera Aleksandrovna – at least not in the way you're suggesting.

NATALYA PETROVNA: Is that really what I...

BELYAEV: And if Vera is attracted to me, if she's got the idea that I'm not indifferent to her, as you put it, then I've no wish to deceive her. I'll tell her everything myself, the whole truth. But after this sort of discussion, you can understand it would be very difficult for me to stay on. My situation would be extremely awkward. I needn't tell you how hard it'll be for me to leave this place, but there's nothing else for it. I'll always think of you with gratitude. Now if you'll allow me to leave... I'll have the honour of bidding you farewell later.

NATALYA PETROVNA: As you wish. Though I must
confess I didn't expect this. That's certainly not why
I wanted to have this talk. I simply wanted to warn you...
Vera's still a child. Maybe I placed too much significance
on all this. I really can't see the necessity for your
leaving. Still, if that's what you want.

BELYAEV: Natalya Petrovna, it's honestly impossible for
me to stay here any longer.

NATALYA PETROVNA: Obviously you find parting with
us very easy!

BELYAEV: No, Natalya Petrovna – not easy.

NATALYA PETROVNA: Well – I'm not in the habit of
detaining people against their will, but I must confess,
this is all very unpleasant.

BELYAEV: Natalya Petrovna... I don't want to cause you the
slightest unpleasantness... I'll stay.

NATALYA PETROVNA: I see... I wasn't expecting you to
change your mind so quickly. I'm grateful to you, but...
Let me think it over. Perhaps you're right. Perhaps you
really should leave. I'll think it over, and I'll let you
know. You don't mind if I leave you in the dark until
this evening?

BELYAEV: I'm willing to wait, as long as you please.
(*Makes to exit.*)

NATALYA PETROVNA: Promise me one thing...

BELYAEV: Yes, ma'am?

NATALYA PETROVNA: I think you were going to discuss
this with Vera... I'm not sure that's a good idea. Anyway,
I'll let you know my decision. I'm beginning to think
you really should go. Good day.
(*BELYAEV exits to the ballroom.*)
Oh, I'm so relieved! He doesn't love her... So instead
of dismissing him, I'm actually holding onto him?
He will stay. But what am I going to tell Rakitin?
What've I done? And what right did I have to
broadcast that poor girl's love? Why? First to worm a
confession out of her, a half-confession, and then to
be so ruthless, so crude... He might even have been

falling in love with her. What right had I to crush that tender bud? Did I really crush it? Maybe he's been deceiving me. After all, I was trying to deceive him! No, no, he's too decent for that... he's not like me! And why was I in such a hurry? Why give the whole show away at once? What've I done? If only I could've foreseen... Oh, how I tried to trick him, how I lied to him, while he...! How freely and boldly he spoke out. I bow down before him, this is a man indeed! I had no idea. No, he must leave. If he stays, I'll lose every last remnant of my self-respect, I'm certain of it. He must go, or I'm ruined! I'll write to him, before he's had a chance to see Vera again. He must leave! (*Exits quickly to the study.*)
(*End of Act Three.*)

ACT FOUR

The scene is a large empty hallway, with bare walls and a rough stone floor. Six peeling whitewashed brick pillars support the ceiling, three at either side. On the left are two open windows and a door leading into the garden; on the right, a door out to a corridor, leading to the house proper; upstage centre is an iron door to a storeroom. There is a green painted garden bench beside the first pillar on the right, and a few spades, watering-cans and pots in the corner. It is evening, and the rays of the setting sun fall through the window onto the floor. KATYA enters, crosses briskly to the window and looks out at the garden.

KATYA: No, he's nowhere to be seen. And they told me he was going to the conservatory. That means he still hasn't come out. Oh well, I'll just wait till he passes. He's got to come this way. They say he's leaving. What'll we be like without him? And my poor lady! How she kept asking me... Well, why not do her a good turn? He can have a talk with her for the last time. Phew, it's so hot today! I think that's a spot of rain... They're surely not coming here? Indeed they are – Heavens above!
(Makes to run out, but hides behind a pillar. SHPIGELSKY and LIZAVETA BOGDANOVNA enter from the garden.)

SHPIGELSKY: We can wait out the shower here. It'll soon pass.

LIZAVETA B: Yes, all right.

SHPIGELSKY: What is this building? A storehouse, is it?

LIZAVETA B: No, that's the storehouse there. They say Islaev's old father built this place when he returned from foreign parts.

SHPIGELSKY: Ah, I see what it is – Venice, if I'm any judge. Let's sit down a moment. Well, my dear, you must admit that shower came on rather inconveniently. It interrupted our discussion at a most delicate moment.

LIZAVETA B: Doctor...

SHPIGELSKY: Still, there's no-one here to stop us picking up where we left off. You were saying, incidentally, that Anna Semyonovna's out of sorts today?

LIZAVETA B: Yes, she is. She even dined in her room.

SHPIGELSKY: Really? Heavens, that's terrible.

LIZAVETA B: She found Natalya Petrovna in tears this morning. With Rakitin. He's like one of the family, of course, but all the same... Anyway, Rakitin's promised to explain.

SHPIGELSKY: I see! Well, she needn't be alarmed. If you want my opinion, Rakitin's never been a danger, and even less now, than before.

LIZAVETA B: What do you mean?

SHPIGELSKY: Just this. He's a terribly clever chap. And you know, some people break out in a rash, but these clever types break out in talk, hot air all over. No, my dear, you needn't worry about chatterers, they're not dangerous, but the silent ones, a little bit crazy, prone to moods, very broad head at the back – well, they're the dangerous ones.

LIZAVETA B: Tell me, is Natalya Petrovna really unwell?

SHPIGELSKY: She's as unwell as you or I.

LIZAVETA B: She wouldn't eat anything at dinner.

SHPIGELSKY: It isn't only illness that kills the appetite.

LIZAVETA B: So you dined with Bolshintsov?

SHPIGELSKY: That's right. I drove out to his place. I came back just for you, I swear to God.

LIZAVETA B: Oh, really! Anyway, I'll tell you something, Doctor – Natalya Petrovna's angry with you for some reason. She mentioned you at table in terms that weren't exactly complimentary.

SHPIGELSKY: Is that so? Well, obviously their ladyships aren't too pleased, when people have sharp eyes. You do what they ask, assist them – yes, and you even have to pretend you don't know what they're up to. That's what they're like. Well, anyway, we'll see. I suppose Rakitin's down in the dumps?

LIZAVETA B: Yes, he seems to be out of sorts too.

SHPIGELSKY: Hm. And how about Vera Aleksandrovna? And Belyaev?

LIZAVETA B: No, they're decidedly out of sorts, all of them. I really can't imagine what's got into them today.

SHPIGELSKY: Well, what you don't know won't put years on you, my dear. Good luck to them, I say. Let's you and I talk about our own little matter. Look, the shower still hasn't stopped... Shall we?

LIZAVETA B: What are you asking me, Doctor?

SHPIGELSKY: Oh, come, Lizaveta Bogdanovna – why so coy? Why are you fluttering your eyelids all of a sudden? After all, it's not as if we're young things! All that palaver, all that drooping and sighing, it doesn't suit the likes of us. We should discuss things in a calm, businesslike manner, as befits people of our age. Anyway, here's the question – we like each other – at least, I'm assuming you do like me.

LIZAVETA B: Doctor, really...

SHPIGELSKY: Oh well, all right then – I suppose as a woman you've got to put on these airs. Let's assume we like each other. And we're also well matched in other respects. I feel bound to say, of course, on my own part, that I'm not exactly high-born, but there again, you're not of noble extraction either. I'm not well off – actually, if I were, I wouldn't need to... (*Laughs.*) Still, I have a decent practice, my patients don't all die. You, by your own admission, have fifteen thousand in cash – if you'll allow me to observe, that's not at all bad. Besides which, I imagine you're pretty fed up with the life of a governess, then being at the old woman's beck and call, partnering her at whist, yes ma'am, no ma'am – that can't be much fun either. As for me, it's not that I'm bored by the bachelor life, but I'm getting old, and well, my cooks are robbing me blind. Anyway, all this seems to be going along nicely. But here's the snag, my dear – the fact is, we don't know each other at all. Or to be more precise, you don't know me. I do know you, your character's well known to me. And I won't say you don't have your failings. Being a spinster's made you a little crabby, but well, that's no real problem. A wife's like putty in the hands of a good husband. But I'd like you to get to know me before the wedding, otherwise you might start complaining afterwards, and I don't want to deceive you.

LIZAVETA B: Well, Doctor, I think I've had a chance to observe your character too...

SHPIGELSKY: You have? That's hardly a woman's forte. I mean, for instance, you no doubt think I'm quite a jolly chap – a joker, right?

LIZAVETA B: You've always struck me as a very amiable person.

SHPIGELSKY: Well, there you are. That just shows how easily you can be mistaken. Just because I play the fool in front of strangers, tell funny stories, defer to people, you've got the idea that I'm a jolly person. But if I didn't need them, these people, I wouldn't give them a second glance. Yes, and wherever I can, if it's not too risky, you understand, I'll hold them up to ridicule too. And I'm under no illusions, incidentally. There are certain people, I know, to whom I'm absolutely indispensable, who can't do without me, yet they consider they have the right to despise me. But I don't owe them a thing. Natalya Petrovna, for one – d'you think I can't see through her? "Oh, my dear Doctor, I truly do love you, you've such a wicked tongue..." Oh yes, keep on cooing, my little dove. No, I can't abide these fine ladies – all the while smiling at you, and screwing up their little eyes, like so, and sheer nastiness written all over their faces. They despise us, and that's the truth of it. I know well why she spoke so disparagingly about me today. They're an amazing lot. Just because they wash in eau-de-cologne every day, and speak so nonchalantly, dropping their words all over the place – oh, do pick them up – yes, they think they can't be caught out. But that's not so at all – no, they're mortal beings, just like us poor sinners!

LIZAVETA B: Doctor... you surprise me.

SHPIGELSKY: I knew I would. And perhaps you'll see
now that I'm not at all a jolly chap, possibly none too
kind, even. But I don't want to pass myself off to you
as something I've never been. However much of an
act I put on for the gentry, no-one's ever made a fool
of me, no-one's yet led me by the nose. Yes, I'd say
they're even a bit afraid of me. They know I can bite.
Once about three years ago, a certain gentleman,
some son of the soil or other, grabbed me at table
and stuck a radish in my hair, just for fun. And what
d'you think I did? Well, right there and then, without
losing my temper, you understand, and in the most
courteous manner, I challenged him to a duel. The
poor worm was practically paralysed with fright, and
our host made him apologise – I tell you, the effect
was extraordinary! Of course, I knew in advance that
he wouldn't fight. So, you see, my dear, I do have
some pride. Anyway, this is how my life's turned out.
My talents are pretty limited, too. I was no great
shakes as a student. I'm a rotten doctor, there's no
point in trying to conceal it, and any time you fall
ill, it won't be me that'll treat you. If I'd had the
talent and education, I'd have headed for St.
Petersburg. Of course, there's no call for a decent
doctor round here – I'll do for the locals. As for my
personal disposition, I ought to warn you, my dear,
that at home I'm gloomy and taciturn, very
demanding. I'm rather partial to being humoured and
well looked after. I like people to observe my little
habits, and feed me well. On the other hand, I'm not
jealous or miserly, and when I'm not there you can
do whatever you like. As far as so-called romantic
love between us is concerned, well, there's no point
in even talking about it, as I suppose you know.
Nevertheless, I fancy you could manage to live under
one roof with me – as long as you tried to keep me
sweet, and didn't cry in front of me, that I really

can't abide! And I'm not given to finding faults. There, that's my confession. Well, ma'am, what have you to say to that?

LIZAVETA B: What can I say, Doctor? If you haven't blackened your own character deliberately...

SHPIGELSKY: What do you mean, blackened my character? Don't forget that anyone else would've kept quiet about their shortcomings, since you hadn't noticed them, and then after the wedding, well, the game's up then, it's too late. But I'm too proud for that. Yes, too proud, and you needn't look at me like that. I've no intention of pretending, and lying to my future wife, not for fifteen, not for a hundred thousand, even though I'd stoop as low as you like to a stranger for a sack of flour. That's the way I am. I'll grin all the time at people, but inwardly I'm thinking, 'What a blockhead you are, my friend, and you're walking right into my trap', whereas with you I say what I think. Well, I'm not saying everything I think, even to you, but at least I'm not trying to hoodwink you. No doubt I seem a complete eccentric to you, but just wait, one of these days I'll tell you my life story. You'll marvel I've managed to stay in one piece at all. Possibly your own childhood wasn't exactly blessed either, but I'll tell you this, my dear lady, you just can't imagine genuine, grinding poverty... Anyway, I'll tell you all about that some other time. As for now, you'd better think over what I've just had the honour of proposing. Consider it most carefully, this little matter, when you're alone, and communicate your decision to me. You're an intelligent woman, as far as I've been able to observe. You're... Incidentally, how old are you?

LIZAVETA B: I'm... I'm thirty.

SHPIGELSKY: Now, that's not true – you're at least forty.

LIZAVETA B: Forty nothing, I'm thirty-six!

SHPIGELSKY: Well, certainly not thirty. That's a habit you'll need to get rid of. I mean, a married woman of thirty-six isn't at all old. And you shouldn't take snuff, either. I think the rain's stopped.

LIZAVETA B: Yes, it has.

SHPIGELSKY: So, you'll give me your answer in a day or two?

LIZAVETA B: I'll tell you my decision tomorrow.

SHPIGELSKY: That's what I like! Now that is sensible! Good for you, my dear lady! Right – give me your hand and we'll set off home.

LIZAVETA B: Let's go.

SHPIGELSKY: Oh, by the way – I haven't kissed your hand, and I believe that is called for... Well, just this once, here goes! There you are. (*Makes to exit.*)

LIZAVETA B: So, Doctor, you honestly think Rakitin isn't a dangerous person?

SHPIGELSKY: Yes, I do.

LIZAVETA B: You know something, Doctor? I think Natalya Petrovna has recently... I mean, I think Mr Belyaev... She's been paying him a good deal of attention, wouldn't you say? Yes, and Vera – what about her? That couldn't be the reason they were...

SHPIGELSKY: There's something else I forgot to tell you, my dear. I myself am terribly inquisitive, but I can't abide nosy women. Let me explain. As I see it, a wife ought to be both inquisitive and observant – it can be extremely useful for her husband – but only with other people. You take my meaning? With other people. As it happens, if you really do want my opinion of Natalya Petrovna, Vera, Belyaev, and the generality of people around these parts, then listen, if you will, and I'll sing you a little song. I have an execrable voice, so don't expect much.

LIZAVETA B: A song!

SHPIGELSKY: Listen! First verse:

> Oh, there was an old woman who had a grey goat,
> There was an old woman who had a grey goat,
> Yes, sir! Indeed, sir! A little grey goat!
> Yes, sir! Indeed, sir! A little grey goat!

Second verse:
>   And the little goat went for a walk in the woods,
>   The little goat went for a walk in the woods,
>   Yes, sir! Indeed, sir! A walk in the woods!
>   Yes, sir! Indeed, sir! A walk in the woods!

LIZAVETA B: I really don't understand...

SHPIGELSKY: Listen, please! Third verse:
>   And the grey wolves ate the little goat up,
>   The grey wolves ate the little goat up...

(*SHPIGELSKY jumps up and down.*)
>   Yes, sir! Indeed, sir! They ate the goat up!
>   Yes, sir! Indeed, sir, they ate the goat up!

Anyway, let's go now. I've got to have a word with Natalya Petrovna, by the way. Perhaps she won't bite me. If I'm not mistaken, she still needs me. Come on.

(*They exit to the garden. KATYA emerges from behind the pillar.*)

KATYA: I thought they'd never leave! Well, that Doctor's spiteful right enough – the things he was saying! And he calls that singing? I'm only afraid Mr Belyaev'll have gone back to the house by now. They *would* have to come here! And what about Lizaveta Bogdanovna? She'll be the Doctor's wife... Now, there's a turn-up! Anyway, I don't envy her. (*Looks out of the window.*) Well, that's the grass had a good soaking... it smells nice. Mmm – that's the scent off the bird-cherry... Oh, here he comes now. Mr Belyaev!... Mr Belyaev!...

BELYAEV: Is someone calling me? Oh, it's you, Katya. What is it?

KATYA: Come inside, I've something to tell you.

BELYAEV: Oh? All right, then. (*Enters by the door.*) Here I am.

KATYA: You didn't get soaked in the rain?

BELYAEV: No, I stayed in the greenhouse with Potap... he's your uncle, I understand?

KATYA: That's right, sir. He's my uncle.

BELYAEV: You're looking very pretty today.

(*He takes a peach out of his pocket.*)

Would you like it?

KATYA: No, thanks very much, sir, but you eat it yourself.

BELYAEV: Oh, come on, did I refuse when you offered me raspberries yesterday? Take it... I picked it for you, honestly.

KATYA: Well, thank you very much

BELYAEV: That's better. So, what was it you wanted to tell me?

KATYA: The young lady... Vera Aleksandrovna asked me... She'd like to see you.

BELYAEV: Really? Well, I'll go and find her at once.

KATYA: No, sir, she'll come here. She wants to have a talk with you.

BELYAEV: She's coming here?

KATYA: Yes, sir. You see, here... well, nobody ever comes to this place. You won't be disturbed. She loves you very much, sir – and she's such a kind person. I'll fetch her now, shall I? And you'll wait?

BELYAEV: Yes, of course.

KATYA: I won't be a minute. (*Makes to exit.*) Sir, is it true what they're saying – that you're leaving us?

BELYAEV: Leaving? No... who told you that?

KATYA: You're not leaving? Oh, thank heavens! We'll be back in a minute. (*Exits to the house.*)

BELYAEV: This is extraordinary! What's happening to me is simply amazing! I honestly didn't expect any of this. Vera loves me... Natalya Petrovna knows... Vera confessed everything to her... it's astonishing! Vera's such a kind, sweet child, but what's the meaning of this note, for instance? From Natalya Petrovna, in pencil. "Please don't leave, don't make any decisions, until I speak to you." What does she want to speak to me about? Such stupid thoughts going through my mind! Frankly, this is all very embarrassing. If someone had told me a month ago, that I... that I'd be... I just can't think straight since that conversation with Natalya Petrovna. Why is my heart pounding like this? And now it's Vera who wants to see me. What can I say to her? At least I'll find out what's going on. Maybe Natalya Petrovna's angry with me... but what on earth for? This is all so strange, so very strange.

(*VERA and KATYA appear at the door, and he hastily conceals the note.*)

KATYA: Don't be afraid, miss, you go on up to him. I'll keep a look out. Don't be frightened. Oh, sir! (*She closes the window and exits to the garden.*)

BELYAEV: Vera... you wanted to see me. Come over here, please, and sit down. Now then. You've been crying?

VERA: It's nothing... I came to ask your forgiveness, Aleksei Nikolaich.

BELYAEV: What for?

VERA: I heard... I heard you had an unpleasant conversation with Natalya Petrovna. And you're leaving. You've been dismissed.

BELYAEV: Who told you that?

VERA: Natalya Petrovna herself. I met her after your talk with her. She told me that you yourself didn't want to stay here any longer. But I think you've been dismissed.

BELYAEV: Tell me, does everyone know about this?

VERA: No, only Katya. I had to tell her. I wanted to speak with you, to ask your forgiveness. You can imagine how difficult this is for me now. I mean, I'm the cause of it all, it's all my fault.

BELYAEV: You, Vera?

VERA: I couldn't have expected... Natalya Petrovna... Anyway, I've forgiven her. Please forgive me too. I was a very foolish child this morning, but now...

BELYAEV: Vera, nothing's been decided yet. Perhaps I'll stay on.

VERA: You say nothing's been decided. No, it's all settled, it's finished. I mean, look how you are with me now, then remember just yesterday in the garden... I can see Natalya Petrovna's told you everything.

BELYAEV: Vera...

VERA: She's told you everything, I can see it. She wanted to catch me out, and like a fool I walked straight into her trap. But she gave herself away too. I'm not that much of a child. Oh, no!

BELYAEV: What do you mean?

VERA: Aleksei Nikolaich, did you really want to leave us?

BELYAEV: Yes.

VERA: Why? Aren't you going to answer me?

BELYAEV: Vera Aleksandrovna, you're not mistaken.
Natalya Petrovna did tell me.

VERA: What, for example?

BELYAEV: Vera... This is honestly impossible for me, you
must understand.

VERA: Perhaps she told you I was in love with you?

BELYAEV: Yes.

VERA: Well, that's a lie...

BELYAEV: What?

VERA: At least, I didn't say that to her, and I don't
remember... Oh, how cruelly she's treated me! And
you... is that why you want to leave?

BELYAEV: Vera, surely you can see...

VERA: He doesn't love me!(*Covers her face.*)

BELYAEV: Vera, give me your hand. Listen to me, please –
there must be no misunderstanding between us. I love
you as a sister. I love you because it's impossible not to.
Please forgive me, if I've... I've never been in a situation
like this... I don't want to hurt you, but I'm not going to
pretend. I know you like me, that you've grown fond of
me. But just ask yourself, what good could come of this?
I'm still only twenty, I haven't a penny to my name.
Please, don't be angry with me. I honestly don't know
what to say.

VERA: Good God, as if I'd asked you for anything! Why
are people so cruel, so heartless...

BELYAEV: Vera, I didn't want to hurt you.

VERA: I'm not blaming you, Aleksei Nikolaich. You've
done nothing wrong. It's all my own fault, and I've been
punished for it! I don't even blame her. She's a good
woman, I know that, she just couldn't help herself. She
lost her head, that's all.

BELYAEV: Lost her head?

VERA: Natalya Petrovna is in love with you, Belyaev.

BELYAEV: What?

VERA: She's in love with you.

BELYAEV: What are you saying?

VERA: I know what I'm saying. This afternoon has aged
me. I'm no longer a child, believe me. She's taken it
into her head to be jealous... of me! What do you think
of that?

BELYAEV: No, it's not possible!

VERA: Not possible? Then why did she suddenly decide to
marry me off to that old man, what's his name –
Bolshintsov? Why did she send the Doctor to me, why
did she herself try to talk me round? Oh yes, I know
what I'm saying! If you could've seen how her
expression changed, when I told her... Oh, you just can't
imagine how cunningly, how craftily she wormed that
confession out of me. Yes, she's in love with you,
Belyaev, it's all too clear.

BELYAEV: Vera Aleksandrovna, you're mistaken,
I assure you.

VERA: I'm not mistaken. Believe me, I'm not. If she doesn't
love you, then why did she torture me like that? What
had I done to her? Jealousy excuses everything. Oh,
what's the point of talking! And now look – why is she
dismissing you? She thinks that you... that you and I...
Well, she needn't worry! You can stay!

BELYAEV: She hasn't dismissed me yet, Vera. I've already
told you nothing's been decided.

VERA: Really?

BELYAEV: Yes. Why are you looking at me like that?

VERA: Ah! I see... Yes, yes, she's still hoping...
(*NATALYA PETROVNA appears in the doorway, catches sight of
VERA and BELYAEV.*)

BELYAEV: What are you saying?

VERA: Yes, I see it all now. She's had second thoughts, now
she realises I'm no threat to her. And what am I,
anyway? A silly little girl, whereas she...

BELYAEV: Vera, how can you imagine...

VERA: Yes, and after all, who knows? Maybe she's right –
maybe you do love her.

BELYAEV: Me?

VERA: Yes, you – why are you blushing?

BELYAEV: Vera, I...

VERA: You love her, or you might grow to love her? You're
not answering my question.

BELYAEV: Good God, what do you want me to say? Vera,
you're upset – calm down, for heaven's sake...

VERA: Oh, you're treating me as if I were a child. You
don't think I even merit a straight answer. You just want
rid of me, you're trying to humour me! (*Makes to exit,
suddenly sees NATALYA PETROVNA.*) Natalya Petrovna...

NATALYA PETROVNA: Yes, it's me. I came to fetch
you, Vera.

VERA: And exactly what gave you the idea of coming
here? You've been searching for me, perhaps?

NATALYA PETROVNA: Yes, I have been looking for you.
You're being a little indiscreet, Vera. It isn't the first time
I've told you. And you, Aleksei Nikolaich – you've
forgotten your promise. You've let me down.

VERA: Oh, stop it, for God's sake, Natalya Petrovna, that's
enough! I've had enough of your speaking to me like a
child. From today onwards I'm a woman – a woman,
just like you.

NATALYA PETROVNA: Vera...

VERA: He hasn't betrayed you. It wasn't he who wanted
this meeting. Anyway, he doesn't love me, you know
that, there's no need to be jealous.

NATALYA PETROVNA: Vera!

VERA: Just believe me, and don't try any more tricks. They
won't serve any purpose now. I can see right through
you, I assure you I can. I'm not your ward, Natalya
Petrovna, for you to look after 'like an elder sister'. I'm
your rival.

NATALYA PETROVNA: Vera, you forget yourself.

VERA: Maybe I do, but who's driven me to this? I don't
understand myself, how I've found the courage to speak
to you like this. Maybe I can speak like this because
I've no longer anything to hope for, because it suited

you to crush me. And you've managed that quite
successfully. But listen to me – I've no intention of
deceiving you, as you did me – so you'd better know,
I've told him everything.

NATALYA PETROVNA: What could you tell him?

VERA: What? Only everything I managed to observe, that's
all. You were hoping to worm everything out of me,
without giving yourself away. But that was where you
made your mistake, Natalya Petrovna – you over-
estimated your powers.

NATALYA PETROVNA: Vera, Vera, think what you're
saying...

VERA: So tell me I'm mistaken... Tell me you don't love
him. After all, he's told me he doesn't love me!
(*NATALYA PETROVNA is dumbstruck. VERA remains
motionless a few moments.*)
Natalya Petrovna, forgive me... I... I don't know what
came over me, forgive me, please – please don't be too
hard on me... (*She bursts into tears and runs out.*)
(*A silence.*)

BELYAEV: Natalya Petrovna, I can assure you...

NATALYA PETROVNA: No, please... It's true. Vera's right.
It's time I... it's time I stopped play-acting. I've wronged
her, and you. You have every right to despise me. I've
debased myself in my own eyes. There's only one course
open to me, if I'm to win back your respect – honesty,
complete honesty, whatever the consequences. In any
case, I'm seeing you for the last time, this is the last time
I'll speak with you. I love you.

BELYAEV: Natalya Petrovna, you?

NATALYA PETROVNA: Yes, me. I love you. Vera wasn't
deceived, and she hasn't deceived you. I fell in love
with you the very first day you arrived, but I didn't
realise it myself until yesterday. I've no intention of
justifying my behaviour... it was unworthy of me. But
at least you can understand now, perhaps forgive me.
Yes, I was jealous of Vera. In my mind's eye I'd
married her off to Bolshintsov, to get her out of my

way, and away from you. I took advantage of my age,
my position, to pry her secret out of her, and –
naturally, I didn't expect it – gave myself away in the
process. I love you, Belyaev, but you should know –
it's only pride that has forced this confession from me.
The little comedy I've been playing up till now has
finally turned sour on me. You can't remain here.
Anyway, after what I've just said, you'll no doubt feel
very uncomfortable in my presence, and you yourself
will want away from here as quickly as possible. I'm
certain of that. It's that certainty that's given me the
courage to speak. Of course, I don't want you to take
away unpleasant memories of me. You know
everything now. Possibly, I've spoiled things for you.
Maybe if all this hadn't happened, you'd have fallen in
love with Vera. I've only one excuse, Aleksei
Nikolaich... I couldn't help any of this. You're not
answering me? Well, I can understand that. You've
nothing to say to me. It's extremely distressing for a
man who's not in love, to hear a declaration of love.
I'm grateful for your silence. Believe me, when I told
you I loved you, I had no ulterior motive... not like
before. I wasn't counting on anything. On the
contrary, I wanted to throw off my mask once and for
all – I can assure you it's not something I'm used to.
In any case, what's the point of scheming and
dissembling, when it's all out in the open? Why go on
pretending, when there's no-one to deceive? It's all
over between us. I won't try and detain you any
longer. You can leave here without a word to me,
without so much as a goodbye. I'll consider that not
only not impolite, I'll even be grateful to you. There
are occasions when good manners are out of place –
worse than rudeness. Obviously, we haven't been fated
to know each other. Goodbye. No, it wasn't our
destiny... but at least I hope you've stopped seeing me
as that domineering, secretive, scheming creature...
Goodbye, forever. You're not leaving?

BELYAEV: No, I can't leave... I can't leave like this! Listen
to me, please. Natalya Petrovna, you've just said you
don't want me to take away an unpleasant memory of
you, but neither do I want you to remember me as a
man who... oh, God! – I don't know how to say this...
please forgive me. I've no idea how to speak to ladies...
Till now, the few women I've known weren't like this at
all. You say it wasn't our destiny to know one another,
but honestly, how could I – a simple, barely educated
boy – how could I even dream of friendship with you?
Bear in mind who you are, and who I am! I mean,
could I have even dared to think... With your
upbringing... And what am I saying about upbringing?
Just look at me, in this old coat, and you with your
scented dresses... Heavens above! Yes, of course I was
afraid of you, and I'm afraid of you even now. I'm not
exaggerating when I say I looked on you as a superior
being, and all the while you're saying... you're telling
me that you love me... you, Natalya Petrovna! Me! I can
feel my heart pounding as never before – and it's not
just from shock, it's not because my vanity's been
flattered, no, it's nothing to do with vanity... But
I can't... I can't leave like this, whatever you say.

NATALYA PETROVNA: What have I done!

BELYAEV: Natalya Petrovna, for God's sake, believe me...

NATALYA PETROVNA: Aleksei Nikolaich, if I didn't
know you for an honourable man, a man to whom a lie
is inconceivable, God only knows what I might be
thinking. I might indeed be regretting my frankness. But
I believe you. I don't want to hide my feelings from you.
I'm grateful to you, for what you've just said. I know
now why we didn't become friends – that it wasn't
anything about me personally that held you back, only
my position. It's all for the best, of course, but I feel
easier now parting with you... Goodbye. (*Makes to leave.*)

BELYAEV: Natalya Petrovna, I know it's impossible for
me to remain here, but I can't begin to tell you
everything that's going on inside me. You love me... it

terrifies me even to utter those words. This is all so new to me. I think I'm seeing you, hearing you, for the very first time, but I'm aware of only one thing – I must leave. I feel I can't be responsible for what might...

NATALYA PETROVNA: Yes, yes, Belyaev, you must go. Now that you've made yourself clear, you can leave. And is it really possible, that after all I've done – oh, believe me, if I'd had even the slightest hint of what you've just told me – that confession, Belyaev, would've died on my lips. I simply wanted to end all the confusion, I wanted to do penance, to punish myself, I wanted to make a clean break. If I'd imagined...

BELYAEV: I believe you, Natalya Petrovna, I believe you. I myself, just a quarter of an hour ago... how could I have thought... Only today, at our last meeting just before dinner, for the first time I felt something strange, something extraordinary, as if a hand was squeezing my heart, and such a burning feeling in my breast. It's true I was very distant with you before, as if I didn't even like you, but when you told me today that Vera Alcksandrovna thought...

NATALYA PETROVNA: No, please, Belyaev – we mustn't even think of that. We mustn't forget that we're speaking to one another now for the last time – that you're leaving tomorrow...

BELYAEV: Oh, yes! Yes, I'm leaving tomorrow! Now that I still can... And this will all pass. You see, I don't want to exaggerate. I'll leave, and after that, it's in God's hands. I'll take with me only one memory, I'll remember forever, that you loved me. But how was it possible that I didn't know you until now? I mean, you're looking at me now. How could I ever have tried to avoid your eyes? How could I ever have been so timid in your presence?

NATALYA PETROVNA: You told me just now you were afraid of me.

BELYAEV: Was I? That's true... I'm surprising even myself. Can this really be me, speaking so boldly? I don't recognise myself.

NATALYA PETROVNA: And you're not deceiving yourself?

BELYAEV: About what?

NATALYA PETROVNA: About the way you feel. Oh, God, what am I doing? Listen to me, Belyaev, please. You must help me. No woman's ever been in a situation like this. I haven't the strength to go on, truly. Maybe it's for the best, to make a clean break, but at least we've come to know each other. Give me your hand, and wish me goodbye forever.

BELYAEV: Natalya Petrovna, I don't know how to say goodbye to you... my heart's so full. May God give you... (*Presses her hand to his lips.*) Goodbye. (*Makes to exit.*)

NATALYA PETROVNA: Belyaev...

BELYAEV: Natalya Petrovna...

NATALYA PETROVNA: Stay...

BELYAEV: What?

NATALYA PETROVNA: Stay, and let God be our judge!

BELYAEV: (*Goes to embrace her.*) Natalya Petrovna...
(*At that moment RAKITIN appears in the doorway, stands looking at the pair a few moments.*)

RAKITIN: They're looking for you everywhere, Natasha.

NATALYA PETROVNA: Oh, it's you... Who's looking for me?
(*BELYAEV bows to NATALYA PETROVNA and makes to exit.*)
So, you are leaving, Aleksei Nikolaich? Please, don't forget... you know...
(*BELYAEV exits to the garden.*)

RAKITIN: Arkady's looking for you. I must confess, I didn't expect to find you here. However, on my way past...

NATALYA PETROVNA: You heard our voices. I bumped into Belyaev here, and we explained a few things. This is obviously a day for explanations, but we can go home now...

RAKITIN: May I know... what decision...

NATALYA PETROVNA: Decision? I don't know what you mean?

RAKITIN: In that case, I understand everything.

NATALYA PETROVNA: There you go again – all these mysterious hints! Anyway, I explained myself to him, and everything's in order again. It was all nonsense, blown up out of all proportion. Everything you and I discussed, that was simply childishness. It's best forgotten now.

RAKITIN: Natalya Petrovna, I'm not interrogating you.

NATALYA PETROVNA: Now, what was it I wanted to tell you? Oh, I don't remember. It doesn't matter. Let's go now. It's all over... it's all in the past.

RAKITIN: Yes, it's all over. You must be angry with yourself now... for your frankness earlier today.

NATALYA PETROVNA: Rakitin... You've still not spoken with Arkady?

RAKITIN: No, ma'am, I have not. I haven't yet managed to prepare myself. You understand, I'll have to invent something.

NATALYA PETROVNA: Oh, this is intolerable! What do they want from me? They watch me every step of the way. Rakitin, I feel terribly guilty...

RAKITIN: Natasha, don't trouble yourself – what's the point? I mean, that's life, isn't it. But it's obvious Mr Belyaev is still something of a tyro! Why on earth was he so embarrassed, why did he run off like that? Well, I suppose in time... you'll both learn to act. Now, let's go.

(*ISLAEV is heard behind the garden door: "He came here, you say?", then ISLAEV and SHPIGELSKY enter.*)

ISLAEV: Yes, indeed, he's here. Ho ho! And Natasha's here too! What's going on? The sequel to this afternoon's little discussion? It's obviously a very important topic.

RAKITIN: I've just met Natasha here...

ISLAEV: Just met her? Well, this is some meeting place, wouldn't you say?

NATALYA PETROVNA: You've just dropped by here yourself...

ISLAEV: I dropped by here because...

NATALYA PETROVNA: Because you were looking for me?

ISLAEV: Yes – I was looking for you. Won't you come back to the house? There's tea ready. It'll soon be dark.

NATALYA PETROVNA: Let's go.

ISLAEV: Hm, it might be possible to make two good rooms for the gardeners out of this place, or else another servants' hall – what d'you think, Doctor?

SHPIGELSKY: Yes, indeed.

ISLAEV: Let's go by the garden, Natasha. (*He makes to exit, still hasn't looked at RAKITIN.*) Well, gentlemen, what're you waiting for? Let's go and have some tea. (*Exits.*)

SHPIGELSKY: Well then, Rakitin, let's go. Give me your arm. You and I are obviously fated to bring up the rear.

RAKITIN: Really, Doctor – if you'll allow me to say so, you make me sick!

SHPIGELSKY: Actually, if you did but know it, my dear chap, I make myself sick! Come on, let's go...
(*They exit.*)
(*End of Act Four.*)

ACT FIVE

The setting as Acts I and III. It is morning. ISLAEV is looking through some papers.

ISLAEV: No! I definitely can't do any work today. It's as if a nail's been driven into my head. I must confess I didn't expect it. I didn't expect to be as upset as this. What am I going to do? That's the problem. Matvei!

MATVEI: *(Entering.)* Yes, sir, what is it?

ISLAEV: Call the bailiff. Yes, and tell the workmen at the weir to wait for me. Off you go.

MATVEI: Yes, sir.

ISLAEV: Yes, it's a real problem.

ANNA S: *(Entering.)* Arkady, dear...

ISLAEV: Ah! It's you, Mama. How are you?

ANNA S: I'm well, thank God. *(Sighs.)* I'm quite well. Thank God.

ISLAEV: You're sighing – what's the matter?

ANNA S: Oh, Arkady, as if you didn't know what I'm sighing about!

ISLAEV: What do you mean?

ANNA S: Arkady dear, I'm your mother. You're a grown man, of course, a sensible adult, but I am your mother, just the same. And that's a great word – mother!

ISLAEV: Please come to the point.

ANNA S: You know what I'm hinting at, my dear. Your wife, Natasha – she's a splendid woman, of course, and her behaviour up until now has been exemplary – but she's still so young, Arkady! And youth...

ISLAEV: I know what you're trying to say – you think her relationship with Rakitin...

ANNA S: God preserve us! I wasn't thinking anything of the...

ISLAEV: You didn't let me finish. You think her relationship with Rakitin isn't entirely... well, clear. These clandestine conversations, these tears – all that seems strange to you.

ANNA S: So what did he eventually say to you, Arkady – what was their conversation about? He's said nothing to me.

ISLAEV: Mama dear, I haven't interrogated him. And he's obviously in no hurry to satisfy my curiosity.

ANNA S: So what do you intend to do now?

ISLAEV: What do I intend? Why, nothing.

ANNA S: What do you mean, nothing?

ISLAEV: Just that – nothing.

ANNA S: Well, I must confess I'm surprised. You're the master in your own home, of course, you know what's right and wrong better than I. However, do think of the consequences...

ISLAEV: Mama, you've no need to be alarmed, honestly.

ANNA S: But, my dear, I'm a mother... well, anyway, you know best. To tell you the truth, I'd come to you with the intention of offering to act as a go-between.

ISLAEV: No, Mama, please – I must ask you not to concern yourself on that score. Please do as I ask!

ANNA S: As you wish, Arkady, as you wish. I won't say another word. I tried to warn you, I've done my duty, and now – well, I'll just hold my tongue.

ISLAEV: You're not going out for a drive today?

ANNA S: I felt I just had to warn you, that's all. You're too trusting, my dear. You judge everybody by yourself! Believe me, true friends are all too rare these days!

ISLAEV: Mama...

ANNA S: I'm saying nothing, not another word! Besides, what's the point of me talking, an old woman. No doubt I've gone senile! But I was brought up by standards – and I've tried to instil them in you. Well, anyway, get on with your work, I won't hold you back. I'll leave you... (*Makes to exit.*) Well? Oh, all right, you know best! (*Exits.*)

ISLAEV: Why on earth is it that people, who actually do love you, have to poke their fingers into your wound? And all the while they're convinced they're easing your pain – that's the funny part! Anyway, I can't really blame mother. She means well – besides, how can I stop her giving advice? But that isn't the point. What am I going

to do? Oh well, the simpler the better. Diplomatic
subtleties aren't my line. I'm the first to get tangled up in
them. (*Rings the bell.*)
(*MATVEI enters.*)
Mr Rakitin – is he at home, do you know?

MATVEI: He is, sir. I've just seen the gentleman in the
billiard room.

ISLAEV: I see. Well, ask him to come to me.

MATVEI: Yes, sir. (*Exits.*)

ISLAEV: I'm not used to altercations of this sort. I hope
they won't often be repeated. I've a strong constitution,
God knows, but I can't bear this. Phew!
(*RAKITIN enters from the ballroom.*)

RAKITIN: You sent for me?

ISLAEV: Yes. *Michel,* I think you owe me something.

RAKITIN: I do?

ISLAEV: What do you mean? You surely haven't forgotten
your promise? About... about Natasha crying, and all
that. When Mama and I broke in on you, you remember,
you told me there was some kind of secret between you,
which you were going to explain.

RAKITIN: Did I say a secret?

ISLAEV: You did.

RAKITIN: What possible secret can there be between us?
We were having a conversation.

ISLAEV: About what? And why was she crying?

RAKITIN: You know, Arkady, there are times like that in a
woman's life – even the happiest of women...

ISLAEV: Oh, stop, Rakitin, this is impossible. I can't stand
seeing you in this situation. Your embarrassment's
causing *me* more distress than you. I mean, we're old
friends – you've known me since childhood. I wouldn't
know how to pretend – yes, and you've always been open
with me. Let me put just one question to you. I give you
my word of honour, I won't doubt the sincerity of your
reply. You love my wife, don't you? You know what
I mean – you love her in the way... Well, in a word, you

love my wife with the sort of love that's difficult to
admit to a husband – yes?

RAKITIN: Yes, I love your wife... in that way.

ISLAEV: Thank you for your honesty, *Michel*. You're an
honourable man. Anyway – what are we going to do
now? Sit down, please – let's discuss this business
together. I know Natasha, I know her worth. But
I also know my own worth. I can't compare with you,
Michel... no, don't interrupt me, please – I can't stand
against you. You're more intelligent, finer, more
attractive all round. I'm a simple man. Natasha does
love me, I think, but she's got eyes... well, obviously,
she must find you attractive. And there's something
else I want to say – I noticed your mutual attraction
a long time ago. But I'd always trusted you both, and
nothing had come out in the open... Oh God, I don't
know how to say these things! But after yesterday's
little scene, after your second rendezvous last night –
I mean, what are we to do? If I'd even caught you on
my own, but there were witnesses – Mama, and that
villain Shpigelsky. Well, what have you to say,
Michel, eh?

RAKITIN: Arkady, you're perfectly within your rights...

ISLAEV: That's not the issue – what are we going to do?
I must tell you, *Michel* – I might be a simple man, but
I know this much – it does no good to wreck other
people's lives, and there are times when insisting on your
rights is sinful. And I didn't get that out of any book, my
friend – that's conscience speaking. To give a person
their freedom... well, let them go! Only it'll need
thinking over. It's too important.

RAKITIN: And I've already thought it over.

ISLAEV: What?

RAKITIN: I must go away. I'm leaving.

ISLAEV: You mean that? What, right away from here?

RAKITIN: Yes.

ISLAEV: That's... those are strong words! But maybe you're
right. It'll be difficult for us with you gone. God knows,

it may not even do any good. But you see things more clearly, you know best. I think you've made the right decision. You are a threat to me, my friend. Yes, you're a danger to me. I mean, what I said just now, about freedom and all that... Maybe I wouldn't survive! For me, life without Natasha... And there's something else, my friend – this while back, especially the last few days, I've seen a great change in her. She seems to be in some sort of constant state of agitation, and that frightens me. That's true, isn't it – I'm not mistaken?

RAKITIN: No, you're not mistaken.

ISLAEV: There you are, you see? So, you're leaving?

RAKITIN: Yes.

ISLAEV: Hm. Well, this is all very sudden. And of course you had to look so obviously embarrassed, when Mama and I found you...

MATVEI: (*Entering.*) That's the bailiff now, sir.

ISLAEV: Let him wait.

(*MATVEI exits.*)

Michel, you won't be away too long, will you? I mean, this is such a trifling matter.

RAKITIN: I don't know, to be honest. I think... yes, a long time.

ISLAEV: You surely don't take me for some sort of Othello? I honestly don't think there's ever been a conversation like this between two friends – not since the dawn of time! I can't part with you like this, I just can't...

RAKITIN: (*Pressing his hand.*) You can let me know when it's possible for me to return.

ISLAEV: And there's no-one here to take your place. Certainly not Bolshintsov!

RAKITIN: There are others...

ISLAEV: Who? Krinitsyn? That silly creature? Of course, Belyaev's a fine chap, but really, compared with you, there's a world of difference!

RAKITIN: You think so? You don't know him, Arkady. Keep an eye on him, I advise you. Are you listening? He's a very... a very remarkable man.

ISLAEV: Oh, stuff! That's why you and Natasha kept going on about taking him in hand, educating him. Ah! This is him now, I think. Anyway, my dear friend, it's all settled – you're going away, for a short while... well, one of these days. There's no hurry, we'll have to prepare Natasha. I'll reassure Mama. And God grant you happiness! You've taken a great weight off my mind. Embrace me, my dear good friend!
(*BELYAEV enters.*)
Oh, it's you! Well, well... and how are things?

BELYAEV: Fine, thank you, sir.

ISLAEV: And where's Kolya?

BELYAEV: He's with Herr Schaaf.

ISLAEV: Ah, splendid! Well, gentlemen, goodbye for the moment. I still haven't been anywhere today – neither the weir, nor the building site. I haven't even looked through these papers. Well, *au revoir!* Matvei! Matvei! Come along with me! (*Exits.*)

BELYAEV: How are you feeling today, sir?

RAKITIN: About the same as usual, thank you. And yourself?

BELYAEV: I'm well.

RAKITIN: That's obvious.

BELYAEV: What do you mean?

RAKITIN: Just that... from the look on your face. Ah! You've put on a new coat today. And what's this I see? A flower in your buttonhole?
(*BELYAEV tears it out.*)
What are you doing that for? For heaven's sake, why? It's very becoming... Oh, by the way, if there's anything you need, I'm going into town tomorrow.

BELYAEV: Tomorrow?

RAKITIN: Yes. And from there on to Moscow, most likely.

BELYAEV: To Moscow? But I thought you told me just yesterday, you were intending to stay here a month or so.

RAKITIN: Yes. However, business... the way things have worked out...

BELYAEV: And you'll be away for some time?

RAKITIN: I don't know... yes, probably.

BELYAEV: May I ask... is Natalya Petrovna aware of your
   intention?
RAKITIN: No. Why do you ask about her specifically?
BELYAEV: Did I? I don't know...
RAKITIN: Aleksei Nikolaich, it seems there's no-one else
   in the room, apart from ourselves. It's a bit odd,
   continuing to play out this charade, don't you think?
BELYAEV: I don't know what you mean, sir.
RAKITIN: Really? You honestly don't know why I'm
   leaving?
BELYAEV: No.
RAKITIN: That's strange. Still, I'm willing to believe you.
   Perhaps you genuinely don't know the reason. Would
   you like me to tell you why I'm leaving?
BELYAEV: If you wish.
RAKITIN: Well, as you see – and I'm relying on your
   discretion, by the way – you found me with Arkady
   Sergeyich just now. We'd been having a rather serious
   talk. Indeed, it's as a consequence of that talk I've
   decided to leave. And do you know why? I'm telling
   you all this because I consider you an honourable
   man. Well, he somehow imagined that I... well, that
   I was in love with Natalya Petrovna. Now, what do you
   think of that? A strange idea, wouldn't you say?
   Anyway, I'm grateful to him for not play-acting with
   me, putting me under observation and all that, but
   simply coming right out with it to my face. So – tell
   me now, what you would do in my place? Of course,
   there are no grounds whatsoever for his suspicions,
   but they are troubling him. For a friend's peace of
   mind, a decent man sometimes has to sacrifice his
   own... pleasure. So you see, that's why I'm leaving. I'm
   sure you'll approve of my decision, yes? I mean, you'd
   do exactly the same thing in my place, wouldn't you?
   You'd leave too?
BELYAEV: Perhaps.
RAKITIN: I'm very pleased to hear that. Of course, I'm
   not disputing the fact that my intended departure has its

funny side – as if I consider myself to be a threat. However, you do understand, a woman's honour is a very serious matter. Speaking of which – of course I'm not referring to Natalya Petrovna – but I've known women, pure and innocent at heart, veritable children, in spite of their intelligence, who as a direct consequence of that purity and innocence, are all the more prone to sudden infatuation. So, for that reason, who knows? Excessive caution in such cases is perhaps no bad thing – the more so since... Anyway, my dear Belyaev, no doubt you still think of love as the greatest bliss imaginable, yes?

BELYAEV: I've not yet experienced it, but yes, I think being loved by the woman one loves must be a great happiness.

RAKITIN: May God grant that you hold on to such pleasant convictions! In my opinion, Belyaev, any kind of love, happy or unhappy, it doesn't matter which, is an absolute disaster if you surrender to it completely. You wait and see! You've perhaps still to discover how those gentle hands can torture a man, with what tender solicitude they can tear your heart to pieces. Yes, you wait! You'll find out how much burning hatred lies hidden beneath that ardent love! And you'll remember me, when you long for peace, as a sick man longs for health – the most mindless, common-or-garden peace, when you'll envy any free, untroubled soul. You wait and see! You'll find out what it means to hang on a woman's skirts, what it means to be enslaved, intoxicated – and how humiliating and tiresome that slavery can be! You'll discover, eventually, what a high price we pay for these wretched trifles. But why am I telling you all this? You won't believe me. In fact, I'm very pleased that you approve – yes, yes, one can't be too careful in situations like this.

BELYAEV: Thank you for the lesson, sir, although I didn't need it.

RAKITIN: You must forgive me, please, I'd no intention of... I've no right to give anyone a lesson. I was just rambling...

BELYAEV: For no reason?

RAKITIN: Exactly – for no particular reason. I simply wanted to... I mean, up until now, you've had no opportunity to study women. Women are... well, they're very headstrong creatures.

BELYAEV: To whom are you referring?

RAKITIN: Nobody. No-one in particular.

BELYAEV: Women in general, is that it?

RAKITIN: Yes, perhaps. I really don't know how I've fallen into this didactic manner, but if you'll allow me to offer you a piece of sound parting advice... Good God, what sort of adviser am I! Please, you must excuse my silly chatter...

BELYAEV: No, not at all.

RAKITIN: So, anyway – you don't need anything from town?

BELYAEV: Nothing, thanks. But I'm sorry you're leaving.

RAKITIN: I thank you most humbly. Believe me, I am too...
(*NATALYA PETROVNA and VERA enter from the study.*)
I've been most pleased to make your acquaintance....
(*Shakes his hand.*)

NATALYA PETROVNA: Good afternoon, gentlemen.

RAKITIN: Good afternoon, Natalya Petrovna... Vera...
(*BELYAEV bows in silence to NATALYA PETROVNA and VERA.*)

NATALYA PETROVNA: And what've you been up to?

RAKITIN: Oh, nothing.

NATALYA PETROVNA: Vera and I've been strolling in the garden. It's so lovely today. The lime-trees smell so sweet, we've been walking under them the whole time. It's so nice in the shade, listening to the bees buzzing overhead... (*To BELYAEV, shyly.*) We'd hoped we might meet you there.
(*BELYAEV is silent.*)

RAITKIN: (*To NATALYA PETROVNA.*) Ah! So even you're taking note of the beauties of nature? Aleksei

Nikolaich couldn't walk in the garden. He's wearing a new coat today.

BELYAEV: Oh, of course, I only have the one, and I might tear it in the garden – isn't that what you mean?

RAKITIN: Not at all – I hadn't the slightest...

(*VERA crosses to the settee, and busies herself with her sewing. A brief, distinctly painful silence.*)

Oh yes, by the way, I forgot to tell you, Natalya Petrovna – I'm leaving today.

NATALYA PETROVNA: You're going away? Where to?

RAKITIN: Into town. On business.

NATALYA PETROVNA: Not for too long, I hope?

RAKITIN: That depends.

NATALYA PETROVNA: Well, do make sure you come back soon. Aleksei Nikolaich, are these your drawings Kolya's been showing me? Did you do these?

BELYAEV: Yes, ma'am. I... they're just trifles...

NATALYA PETROVNA: On the contrary, they're quite charming. You have a real gift.

RAKITIN: It seems you're discovering fresh talents in Mr Belyaev by the day.

NATALYA PETROVNA: Perhaps... All the better for him. (*To BELYAEV.*) No doubt you have other drawings – would you show them to me?

(*BELYAEV bows.*)

RAKITIN: Anyway, I've just remembered, I've still to pack my things. *Au revoir.* (*Makes to exit.*)

NATALYA PETROVNA: You'll come and say goodbye to us?

RAKITIN: Of course.

BELYAEV: Rakitin, wait – I'll come with you. I'd like a word with you...

RAKITIN: Oh?

(*They exit to the ballroom.*)

NATALYA PETROVNA: (*After a pause.*) Vera!

VERA: What do you want?

NATALYA PETROVNA: Vera, for God's sake, don't be like that with me. Vera, please... Vera...

(*VERA says nothing. NATALYA PETROVNA kneels down quietly before her. VERA tries to raise her up, then turns away.*)
Vera, please forgive me. Vera, don't cry. I've hurt you, I know, it's all my fault. Can you really not forgive me?

VERA: (*Tearfully.*) Get up, please get up...

NATALYA PETROVNA: Vera, I'm not getting up until you forgive me. It's hard for you, I know, but think – is it really any easier for me? Think, Vera. I mean, you know everything. The only difference between us is that you've done me no harm, you're not to blame, whereas I...

VERA: And that's the only difference! No, no, there's another difference between us. You're so gentle today, so kind, so loving...

NATALYA PETROVNA: That's because I feel guilty.

VERA: Really? Is that the only reason?

NATALYA PETROVNA: What other reason could there be?

VERA: Natalya Petrovna, please don't torment me any more, don't keep asking me.

NATALYA PETROVNA: Oh, Vera – I see you can't forgive me.

VERA: You're so kind and gentle today, because you feel loved.

NATALYA PETROVNA: Vera!

VERA: Well – isn't that the truth?

NATALYA PETROVNA: Believe me – you and I are equally unhappy.

VERA: He loves you!

NATALYA PETROVNA: Vera, why do we have to torture one another? It's time we both came to our senses. Think of my position, the position we're both in. It's my fault, of course, but our secret's already known to two people here... Vera, instead of tormenting each other with suspicions and reproaches, wouldn't it be better if we tried to find some way out of this terrible situation together? Some way to save ourselves? D'you think I can cope with all this agitation, all these crises? Or have you forgotten who I am? Vera, you're not even listening to me.

VERA: He loves you...

NATALYA PETROVNA: Vera, he's going away.

VERA: Oh, leave me alone!

ISLAEV: (*Off-stage.*) Natasha? Natasha, where are you?

NATALYA PETROVNA: I'm in here. What is it?

ISLAEV: (*Off-stage.*) Do come in, please – I've something to say to you.

NATALYA PETROVNA: In a moment.

(*She holds out her hand to VERA, who does not stir. NATALYA PETROVNA exits to the study.*)

VERA: He loves her! And I've got to stay in her house! Oh! This is too much...

(*SHPIGELSKY pokes his head round the ballroom door, looks round circumspectly, then tiptoes up to VERA.*)

SHPIGELSKY: Vera... Vera Aleksandrovna...

VERA: Who is it? Oh, it's you, Doctor...

SHPIGELSKY: What's the matter, my dear young lady – are you unwell, perhaps?

VERA: No, I'm fine.

SHPIGELSKY: I'll feel your pulse, shall I? Hm... why is it so fast? Oh, my dear, dear young lady, you won't listen to me, but it's for your own good, that's all I want.

VERA: Doctor Shpigelsky...

SHPIGELSKY: Yes, Vera Aleksandrovna... Heavens, what a look! Yes, I'm listening.

VERA: This gentleman... Bolshintsov, this acquaintance of yours, is he really a good man?

SHPIGELSKY: My friend Bolshintsov? An absolutely excellent, honourable man – a model of virtue, an example to us all.

VERA: He's not ill-natured?

SHPIGELSKY: Good heavens, no – the soul of kindness. He's not a man, he's a lump of dough, honestly – you can take him and mould him. You wouldn't find a better-natured fellow anywhere, not if you were to search high and low. No, he's not a man, he's a angel.

VERA: You'll vouch for him?

SHPIGELSKY: As I would for myself!

VERA: In that case you can tell him... tell him I'm willing to marry him.

SHPIGELSKY: Really?

VERA: Only as soon as possible – do you hear? As soon as possible.

SHPIGELSKY: Well, tomorrow, if you like... yes, why not! Well done, Vera! Yes, bravo, my dear young lady! I'll dash over and tell him right this minute. I'll make him happy with this, yes! Goodness, what an unexpected turn of events! You know, he absolutely dotes on you, Vera.

VERA: I didn't ask you that, Doctor.

SHPIGELSKY: Whatever you say, Vera, whatever you say. But you'll be happy with him, you'll be grateful to me, you'll see... Well, I'll say no more. So, I can tell him?

VERA: Yes, yes, you can.

SHPIGELSKY: Very well – I'll set off right now, then. *Au revoir.* That's someone coming, incidentally. (*At the doorway, pulls an astonished face.*) *Au revoir!* (*Exits*)

VERA: Anything, anything, rather than stay here. Yes. I've made up my mind. I can't stay in this house, not for anything. I can't stand that look of hers, so meek and mild, the way she smiles, I just can't bear to see her so smug, basking in her good fortune. And she's happy all right, no matter how she pretends to be sad and miserable. I can't bear her to touch me.

(*BELYAEV enters from the ballroom.*)

BELYAEV: Vera, are you alone?

VERA: Yes.

BELYAEV: I'm glad you're alone. I wouldn't have come in otherwise. Vera, I've come to say goodbye to you.

VERA: To say goodbye?

BELYAEV: Yes, I'm going away.

VERA: You're leaving? You're going away too?

BELYAEV: Yes. Vera, you must see I can't possibly remain here. My being here has already done too much damage. Apart from the fact that I've somehow or other upset both you and Natalya Petrovna, I've also managed to wreck long-standing friendships. It's thanks to me that Rakitin's leaving, and that you've quarrelled with your guardian. It's time to put a stop to all this. After I've gone, I hope, it'll all calm down again, and go back to normal. Turning the heads of wealthy ladies and young girls really isn't my style. You'll forget about me, and in time you'll probably wonder how all this could've happened. I'm puzzled by it even now. I've no wish to deceive you, Vera – I'm afraid to stay here, I'm frankly terrified. I can't be responsible for what might... You know, I'm not used to all this. I feel so awkward. It's as if everyone's looking at me. Well, anyway, it's quite impossible. I mean, here... with both of you...

VERA: Well, you needn't concern yourself on my account. I won't be here much longer.

BELYAEV: What do you mean?

VERA: That's my secret. But I shan't be in your way, believe me.

BELYAEV: There you are, you see? Why shouldn't I leave? I mean, look at me – it's as if I've carried a plague into this house – everyone's fleeing from me. Isn't it better if I simply vanish from the scene, while there's still time? I've just come from a long conversation with Rakitin. You can't imagine how hurt and embittered he was. He even poured scorn on my new coat, and quite right, too. He's absolutely right. Yes, I've got to leave. Believe me, Vera Aleksandrovna, I can't wait until I'm bowling along in the cart, on the main road out of this place. I'm suffocating here, I need the open air. I can't tell you how miserable I am, yet at the same time relieved, like a man setting off on a long voyage, across the sea – he feels wretched at parting with his friends, he's scared, even, but all the while the sea's making such a cheerful sound, the wind feels so fresh on his face, that the blood starts racing in his veins, no matter how heavy his heart is. Yes, I'm definitely leaving. I'm going back to Moscow, to see my friends, and start work again...

VERA: I think you love her. You love her, and yet you're going away.

BELYAEV: Vera, please – what's the point? Can't you see it's all over? Finished. It flared up, and then died again, like a spark. Let's part as friends, please. It's time I was going. I've come to my senses. Look after yourself, be happy, we'll meet again some day. I'll never forget you, Vera Aleksandrovna. I've grown very fond of you, believe me. Give her this note for me, please.

VERA: A note?

BELYAEV: Yes, I can't say goodbye to her.

VERA: You're surely not leaving right now?

BELYAEV: Yes. I've said nothing to anyone about this... that is, apart from Rakitin. He approves. I'm setting off now, and I'll walk as far as Petrovskoye. I'll wait for Rakitin there, and we'll drive into town together. I'll write from town, and they can send on my things. So you see, it's all arranged. Anyway, you can read that note. It's just a couple of words.

VERA: You really are leaving?

BELYAEV: Yes, I am. Give her the note and tell her... No, don't tell her anything. What's the use? Someone's coming. Goodbye. (*He exits hurriedly.*)

(*NATALYA PETROVNA emerges from the drawingroom.*)

NATALYA PETROVNA: Vera... What's the matter?

(*VERA silently holds out the note to her.*)

A note? From whom?

VERA: Read it.

NATALYA PETROVNA: You alarm me. (*Reads the note, suddenly collapses into the armchair.*)

VERA: Natalya Petrovna...

NATALYA PETROVNA: He's leaving! He didn't even want to say goodbye to me... Oh! At least he said goodbye to you!

VERA: He didn't love me.

NATALYA PETROVNA: Anyway, he's no right to leave like this. I want... He can't do this. Who told him he could just break off so stupidly? This is contempt, that's what it is. I... What makes him think I wouldn't have decided to... Oh, my God, my God!

VERA: Natalya Petrovna, you told me yourself that he would have to leave. You remember?

NATALYA PETROVNA: It's all right for you now – he's leaving. We're equals now, you and I...

VERA: Natalya Petrovna, you said a moment ago – these were your very own words – instead of torturing one another, it'd be better if we tried to find some way out of this situation together, some way to save ourselves. Well, we're saved now.

NATALYA PETROVNA: Oh...

VERA: I understand you, Natalya Petrovna. Don't worry – I won't upset you with my presence for much longer. We can't go on living here together.

NATALYA PETROVNA: Why are you saying this, Vera? Surely you're not abandoning me too? Yes, you're right, we're saved now. It's all over – everything's back to normal.

VERA: Don't worry, Natalya Petrovna.

(*ISLAEV enters from the study.*)

ISLAEV: (*To VERA.*) Does she know he's leaving?

VERA: (*Puzzled.*) Yes... she knows.

ISLAEV: Why is he going so soon? Natasha... Natasha, it's me. Aren't you well, my love? I'd advise you to lie down for a bit, honestly.

NATALYA PETROVNA: I'm fine, Arkady. It's nothing.

ISLAEV: But you're so pale. Please, listen to me – have a little rest.

NATALYA PETROVNA: Well, all right.

ISLAEV: There – you see? Do you want me to accompany you?

NATALYA PETROVNA: Oh! I'm not that weak! Vera, come with me.

(*RAKITIN enters from the ballroom.*)

RAKITIN: Natalya Petrovna, I've come to...

ISLAEV: Ah, *Michel!* Come over here, please! (*Sotto voce.*)
Look, why on earth did you have to tell her everything
now? I mean, I asked you not to, didn't I? What was all
the hurry for? I found her here in a terrible state.

RAKITIN: I don't know what you mean.

ISLAEV: You told Natasha you were leaving.

RAKITIN: And you think that's the reason for the state
she's in?

ISLAEV: Ssshh! She can see us. Aren't you going to your
room, Natasha?

NATALYA PETROVNA: Yes... I'm going.

RAKITIN: Natalya Petrovna... goodbye!
(*NATALYA PETROVNA makes no response.*)

ISLAEV: You know, Natasha, this is one of the finest
people...

NATALYA PETROVNA: Yes, yes, I know – he's a splendid
person – you're all splendid people, all of you, yes. The
only thing is...
(*Suddenly rushes out, followed by VERA. ISLAEV sits down at
the table in silence.*)

RAKITIN: So, and what's my position? Wonderful – she's
nothing to say. Really, it's quite invigorating. That's
my farewell, after four years of love? Fine, excellent –
serve the old windbag right. Well, it's all for the best,
thank God. It's time to put an end to these unhealthy,
consumptive relationships. (*To ISLAEV.*) Well, Arkady
– goodbye.

ISLAEV: (*Tearfully.*) Goodbye, old friend. It's not... oh dear,
this isn't exactly easy. I didn't expect this, old chap. Like
a bolt from the blue. Well, anyway – it'll all come right
in the end. Thanks all the same, I do thank you. You're...
you're a true friend.

RAKITIN: Oh, this is too much! Goodbye.
(*He makes to exit to the ballroom. SHPIGELSKY rushes in.*)

SHPIGELSKY: What's going on? They tell me Natalya
Petrovna's ill.

ISLAEV: Who told you that?

SHPIGELSKY: Some young girl... her maid...

ISLAEV: No, it's nothing, Doctor. I think it's best not to disturb Natasha for the moment.

SHPIGELSKY: Oh well, that's fine! And you're heading for town, they tell me?

RAKITIN: Yes. On business.

SHPIGELSKY: I see. On business...

(*ANNA SEMYONOVNA, LIZAVETA BOGDANOVNA, KOLYA and SCHAAF rush in from the ballroom.*)

ANNA S: What's going on? What's the matter? What's up with Natasha?

KOLYA: What's wrong with Mama? What's the matter with her?

ISLAEV: There's nothing the matter with her – I've just seen her. What's the matter with you all?

ANNA S: For heaven's sake, Arkady, they told us Natasha was ill.

ISLAEV: Well, you shouldn't have believed them.

ANNA S: What are you so annoyed about, Arkady dear? We're understandably concerned.

ISLAEV: Yes, of course.

RAKITIN: Anyway, it's time I was going.

ANNA S: You're leaving?

RAKITIN: Yes, I'm leaving.

ANNA S: I see. Well, now I understand.

KOLYA: Papa...

ISLAEV: What is it?

KOLYA: Why has Aleksei Nikolaich gone away?

ISLAEV: Gone where?

KOLYA: I don't know. He just kissed me, put on his cap, and left. And it's time for my Russian lesson now.

ISLAEV: He'll be back soon, most likely. Anyway, we can always send after him.

RAKITIN: (*Sotto voce to ISLAEV.*) Don't bother sending for him, Arkady. He won't be coming back.

(*ANNA SEMYONOVNA strains to hear. SHPIGELSKY is whispering to LIZAVETA BOGDANOVNA.*)

ISLAEV: Meaning what?

RAKITIN: He's leaving too.

ISLAEV: Going away? Where to?

RAKITIN: To Moscow.

ISLAEV: What d'you mean Moscow? What's happening, is everybody going mad today or something?

RAKITIN: Just between ourselves – Vera's fallen in love with him. Anyway, as an honourable man, he's made up his mind to leave. Now you can see why...

ISLAEV: Me? I can't see anything. My head's spinning. What is there to understand in all this? Everyone's flying off in different directions, like partridges, and all because they're honourable men! And it's all happened so suddenly, all on the same day...

ANNA S: What's all this? You're saying that Mr Belyaev...

ISLAEV: It's nothing, Mama, nothing! Herr Schaaf, would you please give Kolya his lesson now in place of Mr Belyaev? Please take him away.

SCHAAF: Yes, sir.

KOLYA: But, Papa...

ISLAEV: Go on, go on!

(*SCHAAF leads KOLYA out.*)

Now, Rakitin, I'll see you off. I'll tell them to saddle up a mare, and I'll wait for you at the weir. And Mama, please, for God's sake, don't disturb Natasha – nor you either, Doctor... Matvei! Matvei! (*Hurriedly exits.*)

(*ANNA SEMYONOVNA raises her eyes to the heavens, as if wishing to remain aloof from all that is going on around her.*)

SHPIGELSKY: (*To RAKITIN.*) Now then, Rakitin, how would you like a lift to the main road in my new troika?

RAKITIN: I see. So you've got your horses already?

SHPIGELSKY: Well, I had a little talk with Vera Aleksandrovna. So – may I?

RAKITIN: Please! Anna Semyonovna, I have the honour...

ANNA S: Goodbye, Mikhail Aleksandrych – I wish you *bon voyage*...

RAKITIN: I thank you most humbly. Lizaveta Bogdanovna...

(*He bows to her, then exits to the ballroom.*)

SHPIGELSKY: (*Kisses ANNA SEMYONOVNA's hand.*)
Goodbye, dear lady...

ANNA S: Ah! Are you leaving too, Doctor?

SHPIGELSKY: Yes, ma'am. Some of my patients, they're a
bit... you know. Besides which, as you can see, my
presence isn't needed here.
(*Bows to the company, winks slyly at LIZAVETA
BOGDANOVNA.*)
Au revoir... (*Exits.*)

ANNA S: (*To LIZAVETA BOGDANOVNA.*) Well, then – what
do you make of all this, my dear, eh?

LIZAVETA B: I don't know what to say, ma'am.

ANNA S: You've heard Belyaev's leaving too...

LIZAVETA B: Oh dear, ma'am – perhaps I won't be here
much longer either. I'm leaving too.
(*ANNA SEMYONOVNA stares at her, speechless with
astonishment.*)
(*The End.*)

STONY BROKE

Characters

ZHAZIKOV (TIMOFEI PETROVICH)
a young man

MATVEI
His valet, an old man

BLINOV (VASILY VASILIEVICH)
his neighbour, a country landowner

A RUSSIAN MERCHANT

A GERMAN SHOEMAKER

A FRENCH ARTIST

A GIRL

A COACHMAN

A STRANGER

A DOG-FANCIER

A LITHOGRAPHER'S CLERK

Scenes from the life of a young nobleman in St. Petersburg.

The scene is a decently furnished room. ZHAZIKOV is sleeping on the bed behind the screen. MATVEI enters and goes up to the bed.

MATVEI: Sir! Your honour! Please, sir – you've got to get up!
(*A silence:*)
Sir! Your honour!

ZHAZIKOV: Mm?

MATVEI: Please, sir – it's time you were up.

ZHAZIKOV: What time is it?

MATVEI: It's a quarter past ten, sir.

ZHAZIKOV: (*Suddenly springing to life.*) What! Why didn't you waken me before this? Didn't I tell you yesterday?

MATVEI: Sir, I tried to waken you, but you wouldn't get up.

ZHAZIKOV: Well, you should've pulled the blanket off me. Let me get dressed, quickly. (*Flings on a dressing gown and emerges from behind the screen.*) Oh God... (*Crosses to the window.*) It must be freezing outside. It's cold enough in this room. Matvei, be a good chap and light the stove.

MATVEI: Sir, there's no wood.

ZHAZIKOV: What d'you mean, no wood? It's not all gone, surely?

MATVEI: There's been none for a week now, sir.

ZHAZIKOV: What nonsense is this? What've you been heating the place with?

MATVEI: I haven't been heating it, sir.

ZHAZIKOV: (*After a brief silence.*) Hm... That's obviously why I've been cold. Well, we must get our hands on some wood. Anyway, we'll discuss that later. Meanwhile, have you put on the samovar?

MATVEI: I have, sir.

ZHAZIKOV: Good. Let's have some tea, quick.

MATVEI: In a minute, sir. We've run out of sugar too.

ZHAZIKOV: Out of sugar? What, all of it?

MATVEI: Yes, sir.

ZHAZIKOV: (*Indignantly.*) Well, I really can't be doing without tea! Go and chase up some sugar somewhere, go on!

MATVEI: But, your honour, where am I going to get it?

ZHAZIKOV: In the grocer's, for heaven's sake – ask for it on tick. Tell him I'll pay him tomorrow.

MATVEI: Sir, they don't trust us in the grocer's any more – he shouts abuse at me.

ZHAZIKOV: How much do we owe him?

MATVEI: Seven roubles and sixty kopecks.

ZHAZIKOV: What? Miserable wretch! Well, anyway, have another try – maybe he'll let you have it.

MATVEI: He won't, sir.

ZHAZIKOV: Look, tell him your master's expecting money from home any day now – two days at the most – tell him we'll pay him in full immediately. Well, go on!

MATVEI: Sir, there's no point – he won't give us it, I know he won't.

ZHAZIKOV: He won't?! That's because you're stupid! You're grovelling to this shopkeeper, as if you're begging a favour. You don't have any... oh, I don't know what you call it in Russian, you wouldn't understand me anyway.
(*The doorbell rings. ZHAZIKOV rushes to hide behind the screen, and speaks in a whisper from there.*)
Don't let anybody in! Nobody! Do you hear? Tell them I left town this morning...
(*MATVEI exits. ZHAZIKOV stops his ears with his fingers. The SHOEMAKER speaks with a thick German accent.*)

SHOEMAKER: (*Off-stage.*) Is the master home?

MATVEI: (*Off-stage.*) No, he's not.

SHOEMAKER: *Gotts Donnerwetter!* He's not there?

MATVEI: No, he isn't at home, I'm telling you.

SHOEMAKER: Will he be back soon?

MATVEI: I don't know. No, he won't.

SHOEMAKER: What's going on? This isn't right. I need my money.

MATVEI: He's gone away, I told you – he's had to go away on business.

SHOEMAKER: Hm... I'll just wait.

MATVEI: You can't do that.

SHOEMAKER: I'll wait.

MATVEI: You can't. Look, clear off – I've got to go out myself soon.

SHOEMAKER: I'll wait.

MATVEI: No, you can't wait.

SHOEMAKER: I want my money, I need it – I'm not leaving.

MATVEI: Go away, please!

SHOEMAKER: This is a disgrace! A gentleman, and this is how he behaves! It's shameful...

MATVEI: Dammit, will you clear off? I can't stand here for the next hour chatting to you!

SHOEMAKER: So when will I get my money? My money – when?

MATVEI: Come back the day after tomorrow.

SHOEMAKER: What time?

MATVEI: The same time.

SHOEMAKER: Right then, goodbye.

MATVEI: Goodbye.

(*The sound of the outer door closing. MATVEI enters.*)

ZHAZIKOV: (*Timidly looking out from behind the screen.*) Has he gone?

MATVEI: Yes, sir.

ZHAZIKOV: Good, good. Damn German! It's money money all the time with him... I can't stand Germans! Right, you can go for sugar now.

MATVEI: But, sir...

ZHAZIKOV: I don't want to hear it! What, d'you want me to do without tea today? Steal some if you have to, but go! Do you hear?

(*MATVEI exits.*)

That old fool's no use for anything. I'll have to send for another man, a bit younger. (*A brief silence.*) Still, I must get hold of some cash from somewhere... Who'll give me a loan? Yes, that's the question....

(*The doorbell rings.*)

Damn it to hell, another creditor! And I've sent Matvei out for sugar!

(*Rings again.*)

I can't open the door to that fiend...

(*And again.*)

It's a creditor, it must be – the swine!

(*And again.*)

Listen to that – damned insolence! (*Makes to answer it.*)
No, I can't – it's not proper!

(*A long despairing ring.*)

Go on, ring all you like! (*Shudders.*) He's pulled the bell
out of its socket, surely! How dare he! Hold on,
supposing it isn't a creditor? What if it's the postman
with a money-order? No, the postman wouldn't ring like
that – he'd come back another time.

(*MATVEI enters.*)

Where on earth did you get to? Someone's torn out the
bell while you were away. It's absolutely unbelievable.
Well, have you brought the sugar?

MATVEI: (*Takes a grey paper package out of his pocket.*) Here
you are, sir.

ZHAZIKOV: That's it? (*Opens the package.*) There's only
four lumps here, and they're covered in dust.

MATVEI: Sir, it took me all my time even to get those.

ZHAZIKOV: Oh well, they'll have to do. Let's have the tea,
then. (*Begins humming an Italian aria.*) Matvei!

MATVEI: Yes, sir?

ZHAZIKOV: Matvei, I think I'll order a new livery for you.

MATVEI: As you please, sir.

ZHAZIKOV: What do you reckon? A new livery in the
latest fashion, sort of greyish lilac, with light blue
shoulder-knots...

(*The doorbell rings.*)

Damn!

(*Again vanishes behind the screen. MATVEI exits.*)

MERCHANT: (*Off-stage.*) Good day, my dear sir – is your
master still abed?

MATVEI: (*Off-stage.*) No, he's gone out.

MERCHANT: Gone out, you say?

MATVEI: That's right.

MERCHANT: I see. Must've got up early. There isn't any money lying around, is there?

MATVEI: No, sir, not at the moment, I must confess. There soon will be, though.

MERCHANT: Meaning when, exactly? I don't mind waiting, if it's not going to be too long.

MATVEI: No, you'd be better to call back in two or three days, sir.

MERCHANT: I see. So – there definitely isn't any money.

MATVEI: Not at this time, sir, no.

MERCHANT: You know, it's not as if he owes that much. But I've practically worn my boots out, trying to collect it.

MATVEI: Another couple of days, sir.

MERCHANT: So, that'll be Thursday? Or should I look in on Friday, d' you think? Or else Saturday?

MATVEI: Make it Saturday, sir, that's fine.

MERCHANT: Right, I'll come back on Saturday. (*After a brief silence.*) You're sure there's no money lying around?

MATVEI: (*With a sigh.*) None, sir.

MERCHANT: So. When should I come back?

MATVEI: Saturday, sir – that's what we said.

MERCHANT: Saturday? Well, all right, I'll come back on Saturday. And you definitely haven't any money?

MATVEI: God in heaven! No, sir, no!

MERCHANT: Not even twenty-five roubles?

MATVEI: No, no – not even a half-kopeck.

MERCHANT: Twenty? Two tenners?

MATVEI: Now, where would I get hold of that?

MERCHANT: So you've no money, none at all?

MATVEI: No! No! No!

MERCHANT: So when should I call back?

MATVEI: Saturday, Saturday.

MERCHANT: You couldn't make it sooner?

MATVEI: Sooner if you like, it's up to you.

MERCHANT: I'll come on Friday.

MATVEI: Right, that's fine.

MERCHANT: And I'll get the money then?

MATVEI: Yes, sir.

MERCHANT: And you haven't any now?

MATVEI: No, none.

MERCHANT: So – Friday, you said?

MATVEI: Yes!

MERCHANT: Round about this time?

MATVEI: Yes, yes.

MERCHANT: Or else Saturday, right?

MATVEI: It's up to you.

MERCHANT: So I'll come back on either Friday or Saturday, whichever's more convenient. Whichever I find easier, you understand.

MATVEI: It's up to you, sir.

MERCHANT: Possibly Friday... But there's definitely no chance of getting the money now?

MATVEI: Good God almighty!

MERCHANT: Right, it's Saturday, then. I bid you good-day, sir.

MATVEI: Goodbye.

MERCHANT: It's been a pleasure, sir. I'll call back on Friday or Saturday, about this time. Goodbye, sir.
(*The sound of the outer door closing. MATVEI enters, pale and sweating.*)

ZHAZIKOV: (*Emerging from behind the screen.*) What are you playing at, Matvei? You've been talking to that fool for a whole hour. Who was it?

MATVEI: (*Glumly.*) The furniture-maker.

ZHAZIKOV: I don't owe him anything, do I?

MATVEI: Fifty-two roubles.

ZHAZIKOV: Really? What for? That desk's all cracked, look at it. It's quite incredible. In future I'll get all my furniture from Hambs, those English people. I can't abide Russian workmen. All those long beards, they're like goats! They may be cheap, but they're rotten.
(*The doorbell rings.*)
Damn it to hell! Not again! They don't give you a minute to yourself! I can't even get a drink of tea in peace, it's frightful!

(*Disappears behind the screen. MATVEI goes out into the hall.*)

GIRL: (*Off-stage.*) Hello? Is the master at home?

(*ZHAZIKOV peeps out quickly from behind the screen.*)

MATVEI: (*Off-stage.*) No, he's been gone since this morning.

ZHAZIKOV: (*Loudly.*) Who is it?

GIRL: I thought you said he wasn't at home?

MATVEI: Well, you'd better come in... If he himself says...

(*A GIRL of about seventeen enters, carrying a parcel, and wearing a hat and coat.*)

ZHAZIKOV: (*With an ingratiating smile.*) Well, what can I do for you?

MATVEI: It's the girl from the laundry.

ZHAZIKOV: (*A little taken aback.*) Ah. What do you want?

GIRL: (*Hands him a bill.*) I've come to collect this, sir.

ZHAZIKOV: (*Coolly.*) I see. (*Glances over the bill.*) Well, this is fine. Eleven roubles, forty kopecks. Fine. Come back tomorrow, if you will.

GIRL: Sir, my mistress told me to get it today.

ZHAZIKOV: Yes, and I'd give it to you today with pleasure... (*Smiles.*) but I've no small change, would you believe it? Absolutely none.

GIRL: I'll get change for you, sir, I can go to the shop.

ZHAZIKOV: No, you'd be better to come back another time... (*Toying with the tassels of his dressing-gown.*) Anyway, tomorrow, all right? Or later today even, after dinner...

GIRL: No no – it's got to be now, please. My mistress'll shout at me.

ZHAZIKOV: Oh, what a cruel woman! To shout at you – why, that's the very height of injustice! Honestly, I just can't understand... What's your name, my dear?

GIRL: Matryona, sir.

ZHAZIKOV: Well, Matryona my sweet, I like you very much...

GIRL: No, sir, please – give me the money. The amount's there on the bill.

ZHAZIKOV: And believe me, I shall pay you, I'll pay in full. It's just that I'm absolutely stuck...

(*The doorbell rings.*)

Oh, damn and blast! Goodbye, my darling, I'll see you tomorrow. Come back tomorrow, you shall have it in full. Goodbye, my sweet little angel!

GIRL: No, no, I can't...

(*ZHAZIKOV vanishes behind the screen.*)

MATVEI: Now, off you go, my dear – go on...

GIRL: But my mistress'll shout at me.

MATVEI: Go, please – go now... (*Propels her out.*)

ZHAZIKOV: (*Calls after MATVEI.*) Take her out the back way! D'you hear? (*To himself.*) In case she bumps into somebody... God, what a mess! An absolute disgrace! She's a real peach, too, dammit! I'll just have to...

(*The doorbell rings. ZHAZIKOV again hides behind the screen.*)

STRANGER: (*A coarse, gruff voice, off-stage.*) Is he in?

MATVEI: (*Off-stage, nervously.*) No, sir, no – he isn't.

STRANGER: You're lying!

MATVEI: Honest to God, sir...

STRANGER: So what's your master up to, eh? Having a laugh at me somewhere, is he? Does he think I'm his skivvy? I give him money, and I've got to come running up here for it every day? Right, let's have a pen and paper, I'll leave a note for him.

MATVEI: Of course, sir.

STRANGER: Here, take my coat, you miserable old dog.

(*A large, stout man with black side-whiskers enters. MATVEI hands him a piece of paper and a pen. The STRANGER sits down at the table, muttering, and begins to write. A dead silence reigns behind the screen. After a few moments, the STRANGER rises.*)

Here, give him this. Your master, d'you understand?

MATVEI: Yes, sir.

STRANGER: And you can tell this master of yours I've no time for jokes. I'll have your master put in jail, that's what I'll do. Yes, I'll fix his wagon!

(*Exits. Puts on his galoshes noisily in the hallway. The outer door closes. After a few minutes, ZHAZIKOV emerges from behind the screen.*)

ZHAZIKOV: (*Indignantly.*) What a swine! Who does he think he is, trying to frighten me, eh? No, my friend, you won't get away with that. You just don't know me, sir! (*Reads the letter.*) Oh, the swine! Vile, ill-bred wretch! (*Tears the letter in shreds.*) Uncouth, ignorant peasant! And I'm as bad, for dealing with scum like that in the first place! Good God, he has the nerve to threaten me! (*Paces up and down the room, in agitation.*) Right, I'll have to take steps...

(*The doorbell rings.*)

Oh, my God! (*Vanishes behind the screen again.*)

MATVEI: (*Off-stage.*) What do you want?

COACHMAN: (*Off-stage.*) His honour hired me to drive him yesterday, and...

MATVEI: Drive him where?

COACHMAN: To Podyachesky, and then from there to the Sands...

MATVEI: Well, what do you want?

COACHMAN: He told me to come today for my money.

MATVEI: How much?

COACHMAN: Thirty kopecks.

MATVEI: Fine, come back tomorrow.

COACHMAN: (*After a pause.*) Yes, sir.

ZHAZIKOV: (*Emerging from behind the screen.*) Oh yes, I need money, no question of it – it's an absolute necessity... Matvei!

(*MATVEI enters.*)

Do you know where General Schöntzl lives?

MATVEI: Yes, sir.

ZHAZIKOV: Then you can take him a letter from me. Off you go, I'll call you when it's ready. (*Sits down at the table and begins to write.*) Oh, these pens are disgusting! I'll have to get some in the English shop... (*Reads aloud.*) "Your Excellency, permit me to approach you with this humble... (*Corrects it.*) with this most humble request: could you let me have a loan of three hundred roubles in cash for a few days? I am extremely embarrassed at having to trouble you, but I place my trust in your indulgence, and I shall be most exceedingly grateful. I shall of course repay the money in full by the due date. I remain, your most sincere and devoted..." Does that seem all right? It's a little familiar, but that's no bad thing. Shows a certain independence, a casual outlook on life... I mean, it's not as if I'm some nobody, dammit. No, I'm a nobleman! Hm... might do the trick?... Matvei!

(*MATVEI enters.*)

Here, deliver this. And don't hang about, please – come straight back. He lives practically round the corner.

MATVEI: (*Exits.*) What would I hang about for?

ZHAZIKOV: Anyway, worth a try? I think he'll do it.
He's a decent chap, and he likes me. Meanwhile,
I haven't touched my tea yet. It'll be cold. (*Drinks.*) Hm,
it's frozen. Well, it can't be helped. (*After a brief silence.*)
I need to keep myself busy, somehow... No, I can't – I'll
wait for Matvei. I wonder if he'll bring me something?
Supposing he doesn't find him at home? What's the
time? (*Goes over to the clock.*) Half-past eleven. (*Thinks for
a moment.*) I should try and write something. What shall
I write? (*Stretches out on the sofa.*) This is rotten! (*Starts
up.*) Matvei!... No, it can't be him yet. (*Begins to recite.*)
    'Tis sad to think that all in vain
    To us was given youth...
Yes, 'tis sad indeed. Pushkin's a great poet. What's
keeping Matvei? (*Thinks again.*) You know, to tell the
truth, I did wrong in not going into the military. In the
first place, it would've been better than this; and in the
second – well, I think I have a natural aptitude for
strategy. I'm sure I do. Still, you can't turn the clock
back. No, I'm sorry, my dear sir, but that's something
you can't do.

(*MATVEI enters. ZHAZIKOV buries his head in his pillows,
covers his eyes with his hands and shouts.*)

All right, I know, I know! He wasn't at home, was he.
Come on, he was out, right? Tell me, quickly!

MATVEI: No, sir. He was at home.

ZHAZIKOV: (*Lifts his head.*) What? He was at home? And did you get an answer?

MATVEI: I did indeed, sir.

ZHAZIKOV: (*Turns his head away, not daring to look, and stretches out a hand.*) Let's have it, let's have it... (*Feels the envelope.*) Ugh! It's not exactly bulky! (*Takes the letter, and peers at it, screwing up his eyes.*) What! (*Opens his eyes.*) This is my own letter!

MATVEI: Yes, sir – His Excellency wrote something on the back of it.

ZHAZIKOV: Oh, I see, I see – it's a refusal! Damn long-nosed scoundrel! I can't even read his answer... (*Flings the letter aside.*) I know what he's written anyway... (*Picks up the letter.*) Well, I suppose I'd better read the thing – maybe he hasn't turned me down flat... maybe he's promising... (*To MATVEI.*) Listen, did he hand you the letter in person?

MATVEI: No, sir, he sent one of the servants out with it.

ZHAZIKOV: Hm. Well, let's see what it says. (*Begins reading, with an ironic smile.*) Oh, he's a fine fellow... "My dear sir, I cannot comply with your request. However, I beg to remain..." However, he begs to remain! Huh! So much for good will! So much for amicable relations! (*Flings the letter aside.*) Damn him to hell, absolutely!

MATVEI: (*With a sigh.*) It's not our lucky day!

ZHAZIKOV: Who said you could stick your oar in? Look, clear off, I've got work to do, d'you understand?
(*MATVEI exits. ZHAZIKOV paces up and down the room.*) This is dreadful... what am I going to do? (*Sits down at the table.*) I must get down to work.
(*He stretches, picks up a French novel, opens it at random and begins to read. MATVEI enters.*)

MATVEI: (*Barely audible.*) Sir... Your honour...

ZHAZIKOV: What is it now?

MATVEI: Sir, there's somebody outside – Mr Naumov's valet...

ZHAZIKOV: (*In a whisper.*) Sidor?

MATVEI: Yes, sir.

ZHAZIKOV: What's he want?

MATVEI: He says he needs money, sir – his master's going back to his village, he says, and he's taking him with him, so he's come to ask for his money.

ZHAZIKOV: How much do I owe him?

MATVEI: It'll come to about five hundred roubles now, with interest, sir.

ZHAZIKOV: Did you tell him I was at home?

MATVEI: Indeed I didn't, sir.

ZHAZIKOV: Good, that's fine. But why didn't I hear the doorbell?

MATVEI: He came up the back stairs, sir.

ZHAZIKOV: (*Whispering, heatedly.*) What are you playing at, letting people come up the back stairs? How come they know there's a back way, eh? Dear God, they could come in and rob us blind! This is a disgrace, I won't put up with it, d'you hear? They can use the front stairs!

MATVEI: Yes, sir. I'll send him away now, sir. Only he keeps asking me when he can come back to collect his money.

ZHAZIKOV: When... when... when... Well, tell him in a week's time, all right?

MATVEI: Yes, sir. But you will try to give him some money, sir, won't you?

ZHAZIKOV: Why? Is he a relation of yours? One of your in-laws or something?

MATVEI: He is, sir, yes.

ZHAZIKOV: So that's why you're making such a fuss about him? Oh, all right, on you go... I'll pay him, I'll pay him...

(*MATVEI exits.*)

They're all the same, these people... I know the sort... (*Settles down to his French novel again, then suddenly lifts up his head.*) But what about His Excellency, eh? So much for him! Oh yes, my father's old friend, served in the army alongside him, and all that!... (*Rises, crosses to the mirror and begins to sing.*)

> Be still, my raging passions,
>
> Sleep thou, my hopeless heart...

Still, I've got to work. (*Sits down at the table.*) Yes, must work, I must...

(*Enter MATVEI.*)

Is that you, Matvei?

MATVEI: Yes, sir.

ZHAZIKOV: What's going on?

MATVEI: Sir, there's a dog-fancier at the door. He's asking for you, says you told him to come to the house a couple of days ago.

ZHAZIKOV: Oh yes, so I did, so I did... Has he brought a dog with him?

MATVEI: (*Gloomily.*) Yes, sir, he has.

ZHAZIKOV: Well, let's see him, bring him in... Is it a retriever? Come in, come in, my dear chap!

(*A man enters in a coarse flannelette greatcoat, with a scarf tied round his cheeks. He is leading an old, filthy dog on a string. ZHAZIKOV peers at the dog through a lorgnette.*)

What's her name?

DOG-FANCIER: (*In a dull, wheezy voice.*) Minder.

(*The dog looks up timidly at its master, and gives a fitful wag of its stumpy tail.*)

ZHAZIKOV: And is she a good dog?

DOG-FANCIER: Excellent, sir. Minder, *ici!*

ZHAZIKOV: Can she fetch things?

DOG-FANCIER: She certainly can, sir. (*Pulls out his cap from underneath his arm and flings it on the floor.*) *Pile, apporte!* (*The dog retrieves his cap.*)

ZHAZIKOV: Good, good – but what's she like in the field?

DOG-FANCIER: Absolutely first-class, sir... *Couche! Debout!* Come on, move!

ZHAZIKOV: How old is she?

DOG-FANCIER: This is her third winter, sir... Hey, where are you going? (*Jerks the dog to heel.*)

ZHAZIKOV: Well, what sort of price are you looking for?

DOG-FANCIER: Fifty roubles, sir – I can't take less.

ZHAZIKOV: What? That's ridiculous – I'll give you thirty.

DOG-FANCIER: Can't do it, sir – I'm letting her go cheap as it is.

ZHAZIKOV: All right, I'll give you ten roubles.

(*MATVEI's expression is a picture of anguish.*)

DOG-FANCIER: No, sir, absolutely not.

ZHAZIKOV: Oh, to hell with it... what's her pedigree?

DOG-FANCIER: It's a good one, sir.

ZHAZIKOV: Good?

DOG-FANCIER: We don't keep bad dogs, sir. God forbid!

ZHAZIKOV: Really? You never keep them?

DOG-FANCIER: No, what would we do that for?

ZHAZIKOV: (*To MATVEI.*) She looks not a bad dog – what do you think?

MATVEI: (*Through gritted teeth.*) Not bad, sir.

ZHAZIKOV: Would you take thirty-five roubles for her?

DOG-FANCIER: Forty roubles, sir, that's my bottom price – I'm giving her away at forty.

ZHAZIKOV: No, no, not a chance!

DOG-FANCIER: Well, all right, you can take her, what the hell.

ZHAZIKOV: Not before time. And she's a good dog?

DOG-FANCIER: Oh, sir, she's a fantastic dog – you won't find one like her in the whole town.

ZHAZIKOV: (*Slightly embarrassed.*) Well, the thing is, my dear chap – I do have some money just now, but I've another purchase to make with it, you understand... but if you'd care to drop in tomorrow, about the same time, hm? Or the day after tomorrow, say, only a bit earlier.

DOG-FANCIER: Fair enough. You give me a small deposit, and I'll leave the dog here.

ZHAZIKOV: No, sorry, I can't do that.

DOG-FANCIER: A rouble'll do.

ZHAZIKOV: No, I'd rather pay the whole thing in one lump.

DOG-FANCIER: (*Heading for the door.*) Look, sir... if you give me the money now you can have her for thirty roubles.

ZHAZIKOV: I can't give it you now.

DOG-FANCIER: Well, twenty, then.

ZHAZIKOV: I'm sorry, my dear chap, it's absolutely impossible.

DOG-FANCIER: Twenty roubles – d'you want her?

ZHAZIKOV: Are you being funny? I've said I can't.

DOG-FANCIER: (*Making to exit.*) Right then, Minder – *ici!* (*With a bitter smile.*) Huh, it's obvious your honour hasn't got any money, and never had! Minder – *ici! Ici,* you rascal!

ZHAZIKOV: How dare you, sir!

DOG-FANCIER: And he has the cheek to ask me up here!... *Ici!*

ZHAZIKOV: Clear off, you vulgar lout! Matvei, show him the door! Fling him out!

DOG-FANCIER: Take it easy, I'll see myself out...

ZHAZIKOV: Matvei, I'm ordering you...

DOG-FANCIER: (*From the hallway.*) You lay a hand on me, you old bugger!

(*MATVEI follows him out.*)

ZHAZIKOV: (*Shouting after him.*) Fling him out! Knock his block off! Go on, get out! (*Begins pacing up and down the room.*) What a impertinent creature! And that dog of his isn't up to much, frankly. I'm glad I didn't buy it. But he'd no right to be rude – how dare he! (*Sits down on the sofa.*) God, what a day it's turned out! I haven't done a stroke since morning, and I haven't got hold of any money either. And I need some cash right now, I really do... Matvei!

MATVEI: (*Entering.*) Yes, sir?

ZHAZIKOV: I want you to take a letter to Krinitsyn.

MATVEI: Yes, sir.

ZHAZIKOV: Matvei!

MATVEI: Yes, sir, what is it?

ZHAZIKOV: What d'you think, will he give me some money?

MATVEI: No, sir, he won't.

ZHAZIKOV: Yes, he will! (*Clicks his tongue.*) You wait and see.

MATVEI: He won't, sir.

ZHAZIKOV: Why on earth not?

MATVEI: (*After a brief silence.*) Sir, if you'll allow me, an
old fool, to say a word...

ZHAZIKOV: Go on.

MATVEI: (*Clears his throat.*) Sir, if I may say... it's not right,
sir, the way you live here. You're our master, sir, by
birth, you're a landowner by inheritance – why should
you want to live here in the city, sir, in dire need, and in
trouble all the time? You have a family estate, sir, you
know right well. Your mother, by the grace of God, is in
good health – you ought to go and live with her, on your
own property, your own land, sir.

ZHAZIKOV: What, have you had a letter from my mother?
It's her tune you're singing, that's obvious.

MATVEI: Sir, I have indeed received a letter from my
mistress. She has esteemed me worthy, so to speak,
and I've written to her about your health, sir, as she
commanded me, all the details. If I may say so, sir,
she is very concerned for you: she asked me to write
and tell her all about you, what you're doing, who
your friends are, where you go – tell me everything,
she says. And she's threatened me, sir, she says I'll be
in her bad books, she'll give me a hard time if I don't.
You tell your master, she says, that his mother's very
concerned for him – it's all there written down, sir –
and you tell him it's not right, him living in
Petersburg with no job, and wasting money, who ever
heard the like? That's what she says, sir.

ZHAZIKOV: (*With a forced smile.*) So, what did you write
back to her?

MATVEI: I told the mistress, I said, thanks be to God
everything's going nicely, and what she told me to do,
I've done exactly as she said, and I'd pass her message
on to your honour, and then report back to her. Oh, let's
go back home, master, to the country, you could live
like a lord there, in your own little house, with a wife to
look after you... Why d'you stay here, sir? Every time the
bell rings you jump like a startled rabbit, and you've no
money – you don't even eat properly.

ZHAZIKOV: No, it's too boring in the country – the
neighbours are all so ignorant, and the girls just stare at
you and sweat with fright, if you try to talk to them.

MATVEI: Oh, sir! And what are they like here, eh? And the
gentlemen that call on your honour? God almighty, sir,
they're not much to look at, are they – shabby, mean little
creatures, sick-faced and coughing all the time – God
forgive me, they're more like sheep than people. But back
home, well! True enough, it's not like it used to be, no
indeed, sir. Your grandfather Timofei, God bless him, was
so tall and broad-shouldered – when he got mad, sir, and
started shouting at you in that piercing voice of his, well,
you'd wish you were dead! He was the master, and no
mistake! But if he took a liking to you, or if he happened
to be in a good mood, he'd reward you, sir, yes, he'd give
you so much you'd be sick for days! And his wife, our old
mistress, what a good soul she was. Never touched a drop
before dinner, she didn't – no, not a drop

ZHAZIKOV: Well, I'm not going back to the country, I'd
go crazy there.

MATVEI: And you'll have money there too! I mean, the
state of us here, sir – all right, I'm only your serf, but
look at me! It's a disgrace – look... (*Holds open the skirts of
his kaftan.*) These are trousers in name only, sir. But in
the country there's plenty of everything! Snug little
houses, you can sleep all day if you like, eat whatever
you want... Whereas here, if I may say so, I've not once
had a decent meal. And what about the hunting, sir,
chasing after hares and martens, ch? Besides which, it'd
be a comfort to your dear mother, in her old age.

ZHAZIKOV: Well, maybe I could go back to the country.
Trouble is, they wouldn't let me out again. I'd never be
able to get clear of the place. Ye gods, I might even wind
up married!

MATVEI: And what's wrong with that, sir? It's the
Christian thing to do.

ZHAZIKOV: No, don't say another word, don't even
mention it!

MATVEI: Well, it's up to you, of course. Anyway, sir, I'll
say again, I just don't feel right in this place. I mean,
God preserve us, sir, what if somebody was to steal
something from us, eh? I'd just die, and it'd serve me
right, because I hadn't looked after the master's things.
But how can I do that, sir? Of course, that's my job, as a
serf – I never go anywhere, just sit from morning till
night out in the hall... but it's not like in the country, my
mind's not at ease, sir. At times a shiver goes right
through me, I'm sitting there shaking like a leaf, sir, and
praying to God. I can't even have a proper nap in the
afternoon. And what are the servants like here, eh?
They've no respect, sir, they're frightened of nobody.
Between us serfs and them, well, there's just no
comparison. And they go around looking as if butter
wouldn't melt! Thieves and robbers, sir, scum of the
earth, that's what they are. Some of them, God forgive
me, look as if they've never had a lesson in their lives!
I mean, what sort of existence have we here, sir?
Compared with the country, eh? You've got respect
there, and honour, and a bit of peace. You're my lord and
master, sir, my benefactor, but listen to an old fool,
please. I served your grandfather, and your father and
mother, sir, and I've seen plenty in my life: I've seen
Italians, and Germans, and Frenchmen from Odessa, I've
seen the lot, sir, I've been all over the place. But I've
never seen anywhere to beat our own village. So take my
advice, sir, listen to an old man...
(*The doorbell rings.*)
See, there you go again – just about jumped out of your
skin!

ZHAZIKOV: Go, go – open the door!
(*MATVEI exits, ZHAZIKOV remains motionless, does not go
behind the screen this time.*)

ARTIST: (*Off-stage.*) Monsieur Jazikoff?

MATVEI: (*Off-stage.*) Who do you want?

ARTIST: *Monsieur Jazikoff?*

MATVEI: He's not in.

ARTIST: (*Astonished.*) Not in? *Comment* 'not in'? *Sacré Dieu!*

MATVEI: And who are you?

ARTIST: *Voilà ma carte, voilà ma carte.*

MATVEI: Well, you've squawked enough, you damn raven!
(*The door closes. MATVEI enters and hands ZHAZIKOV the card.*)

ZHAZIKOV: (*Without looking at it.*) Oh, I know who it
was... it's the artist, the Frenchman – I told him to come
today and paint my portrait... Oh well, it can't be helped.
Anyway, I must write to Krinitsyn, things are getting
really bad.
(*He sits down at the table and begins to write. Then he stands
up, goes across to the window and reads aloud.*)
"My dear Fedya, please help to get a friend out of
trouble, and don't let him perish in the flower of his
youth. Send me two hundred and fifty roubles in cash, or
even two hundred. You can give the money to the bearer,
and I shall be grateful to you until my dying day. Please,
Fedya, don't refuse me. Be my father and benefactor.
Yours, etc."
That'll do, I think. Right, Matvei, here's the letter, you'd
better take a cab. (*Seeing that MATVEI is about to object.*)
Use the same coachman I already owe money to. He
knows us, he'll accept credit. Now, hand over the letter
and wait for an answer – d'you hear? You absolutely
must get an answer!

MATVEI: Yes, sir.

ZHAZIKOV: Off you go, Matvei – God speed and good
luck! Well, go on!
(*MATVEI exits.*)
Dammit, when you come to think of it, Matvei's not far
wrong. I like his simple, straightforward ideas. It
certainly is better back home. Especially in summer. And
I do like the Russian countryside. Anyway, I can always
come back to St. Petersburg in the winter. True enough,
our neighbours are mostly pretty uneducated, but there
are a few kind and quite clever people among them. You
can even have a decent conversation with some of them.
You can develop them, show them the way, so to speak,

without them being aware – yes, you can even do them a bit of good. As for the girls, well, it's a known fact, they're like putty in your hands, you can do what you like with them. (*Begins pacing around the room.*) Frankly, the only bad thing about the country is the poverty and oppression you see there... that's rather disagreeable for somebody with my ideals, not at all nice. But then again, there's the riding, and hunting – a great many pleasures, one must admit.(*Thinks.*) Hm... I'll have to order up some new clothes... buy some ties... got to be properly turned out. I'll have a new hunting-coat made. Pity I didn't buy that dog today. She'd have come in handy. Oh, well, I can always find another. Better pick up a few more books, too. I should write one myself, on some new theme, something that nobody's ever thought of... Yes, that'll be rather nice. I wouldn't want to stay in the country in winter, but who's going to make me do that, eh? Matvei's right, absolutely... you shouldn't ignore old people. Sometimes they... yes, they do indeed! And besides, I really ought to see my mother again. She might even give me some money. She'll kick up a fuss, but she'll give me it. Yes, I'll go to the country. (*Crosses to the window.*) But how am I ever going to part with St. Petersburg? Goodbye, St. Petersburg! Farewell, beloved capital! And farewell to thee also, Vera my sweet! I did not expect such a hasty departure! (*Sighs.*) God, I'm leaving so much behind here... (*Sighs again.*) And I'll pay all my debts. Yes, I'll go! Without fail, I'll go!
(*The doorbell rings.*)
Damn! And Matvei's not here – where the hell has he got to?
(*The bell rings again.*)
It can't be a creditor – they don't ring like that, and besides it's not their time!
(*And again.*)
I'd better go and open it... *Courage!* What the hell, I'm going back to the country anyway!
(*Exits to the hall – sounds of delighted greetings.*)

Vasily, dear friend! Is it you? What brings you here?
(*A gruff voice answers, "It's me... It's me".*) Take off your
coat, and come inside.

(*ZHAZIKOV re-enters, along with VASILY VASILIEVICH
BLINOV, a country landowner, with enormous curled moustaches
and a puffy face.*)

Have you been in town long, my dear sir? I'm so pleased
to see you, I'm absolutely delighted! Sit down, sit down...
Here, take this armchair, you'll be more comfortable.

I really am so pleased – I can't believe my eyes!

BLINOV: (*Sits down.*) Let me catch my breath. (*Wipes
the perspiration from his face.*) Well, you live high up
here – whew!

ZHAZIKOV: Have a rest, my dear Vasily, do... Heavens,
am I glad to see you! I'm so grateful to you – where are
you staying?

BLINOV: At the London Hotel.

ZHAZIKOV: And have you been there long?

BLINOV: Since last night. I tell you, that road! So full of
pot-holes you had to hang onto your seat!

ZHAZIKOV: You shouldn't have troubled yourself, Vasily –
you shouldn't have come out today. You should've rested
after the road, and you could've sent for me.

BLINOV: Oh, stuff and nonsense, I'm not some old woman.
(*Looks round the room.*) You're pretty cramped here. Your
old lady sends her regards – says she thinks you've
forgotten her. Still, she's a woman, she's probably lying.

ZHAZIKOV: Anyway, my mother's well?

BLINOV: Fine... she gets by.

ZHAZIKOV: And how are your own folk?

BLINOV: They're fine too.

ZHAZIKOV: So, are you staying here long?

BLINOV: God knows. I'm here on business.

ZHAZIKOV: (*Sympathetically.*) On business, eh?

BLINOV: Yes, otherwise the devil himself wouldn't have
dragged me away. I'm too fond of home. I've a
damned neighbour to thank – the swine's got me
involved in a lawsuit.

ZHAZIKOV: Really?

BLINOV: Yes, damn the man! But I'll show him, the scoundrel! Anyway, you're in the civil service here, right?

ZHAZIKOV: Well, I'm not working at the moment, but...

BLINOV: So much the better. You can help me copy out the documents, hand in the petitions, drive round the city...

ZHAZIKOV: I'd consider that a pleasure, my dear Vasily...

BLINOV: Yes, of course, of course... (*Stops and looks ZHAZIKOV straight in the eye.*) Now, let's have a drop of vodka – I'm frozen stiff.

ZHAZIKOV: (*Fussing around.*) Vodka... Oh, what a shame! I don't have any vodka, and I've just sent my servant out... oh, dear!

BLINOV: What, you've no vodka? Well, you don't take after your father. (*Seeing that ZHAZIKOV continues to search.*) It doesn't matter, I'll do without.

ZHAZIKOV: My man'll be back any minute.

BLINOV: You know, that damned neighbour of mine – he's a retired major – he's going on about some boundary line. And there's no sign of any boundary line! Show me where it is, I say, show me where it's indicated.
(*ZHAZIKOV is listening intently.*)
I mean, the property's mine, isn't it? But that scoundrel, damn him, keeps trespassing on my land. And my steward, naturally, sticks up for his rights – that's the master's land, he says, keep off. So they beat him up, yes, give him a terrible beating! Draws his own boundary line, he does – to suit himself, dammit! Anyway, he starts ploughing, ready for another scrap – oh no, you don't, says my man. Then I suddenly appear, and at first, you know, he backs off. Then I see his clerk riding up, with his cap on – don't you insult us, he says, so I punched him in the teeth. Things got out of hand then, and that neighbour of mine, the swine, he's taking me to court. Claims I started the fight, and robbed him of his land. Damn villain! I robbed him? I stole his land? Since when? Anyway, some nice gentlemen arrived, they tried all sorts,

but he made even more of a mess, damn him! He lodged
an official complaint, and so did I. A decision was
reached, and it came out in my favour, I think, but that
swine Pafnutyev had it overturned. So I fired off an appeal
to the district court, and that scoundrel jumps into a
carriage and gallops up here to do the same. No, my
friend, I says, you're not taking me for a fool – I promptly
did likewise, and here I am. Now, that's what my swine of
a neighbour's been up to!

ZHAZIKOV: You don't say! Why, that's frightful!

BLINOV: Well, that's how it goes. Anyway, what about
you? Are you well?

ZHAZIKOV: I am, Vasily, thank God. Can't complain.

BLINOV: And do you go to the theatre?

ZHAZIKOV: I do, indeed. Quite often.

BLINOV: Listen – why don't you take me to the theatre?

ZHAZIKOV: With the greatest of pleasure, my dear friend
– yes, surely.

BLINOV: Take me to see a tragedy. Yes, something Russian
– something really morbid, you know?

ZHAZIKOV: It'll be my pleasure.

BLINOV: And where are you dining today?

ZHAZIKOV: Me? Well, wherever you fancy, dear sir.

BLINOV: Take me to a café, then – somewhere decent, of
course. I like a bit of... you know... (*Laughs.*) You haven't
a bite to eat here, have you? Eh?

ZHAZIKOV: To tell you the truth, I'm absolutely...

BLINOV: (*Stares hard at him.*) Listen, Timofei, my dear chap...

ZHAZIKOV: Yes?

BLINOV: Do you have any money?

ZHAZIKOV: Yes, yes... of course I have.

BLINOV: Hm, I thought you... well, you know. So how
come you've nothing to eat in the house?

ZHAZIKOV: Well, it's just one of those things, and my
servant's not in... I've no idea where he's got to!

BLINOV: He'll be back. Anyway, you'll want to eat
soon, right?

ZHAZIKOV: Why's that?

BLINOV: I like to keep regular hours. And you're taking me to see a tragedy – Karatygin, if you don't mind?

ZHAZIKOV: Oh, absolutely.

BLINOV: Well, then – get dressed, and we'll go for dinner.

ZHAZIKOV: In a little while, Vasily.

BLINOV: Timofei, listen, listen...

ZHAZIKOV: What is it?

BLINOV: Listen, they say you have girls here – mam'selles, eh? – who can ride standing up, is that true?

ZHAZIKOV: Oh, in the circus? Yes, that's true.

BLINOV: Can they really do that? Are they pretty?

ZHAZIKOV: Yes, they are.

BLINOV: They'll be fat, I suppose.

ZHAZIKOV: No, not very.

BLINOV: Really? You'll show me them, right?

ZHAZIKOV: Yes, if you wish.

> (*The doorbell rings. ZHAZIKOV is thrown into confusion.*)
> Er... that'll be for me.
> (*Exits to the hall and opens the door. We hear his voice: "Oh, come in." A lithographer's CLERK enters, carrying a rolled-up print.*)
> You're from the lithographer's, I believe.

CLERK: That's right, sir. I've brought your pictures.

ZHAZIKOV: What pictures?

CLERK: The ones you chose yesterday, sir.

ZHAZIKOV: Oh yes, of course. Have you brought the invoice?

CLERK: Yes, sir.

ZHAZIKOV: (*Takes the bill and goes over to the window.*) Right... give me a minute...

BLINOV: (*To the clerk.*) So, you're a local man, my friend?

CLERK: (*A little surprised.*) Yes, sir.

BLINOV: And who's your master?

CLERK: Mr Kuroplekhin, sir.

BLINOV: And you pay quit-rent, I suppose?

CLERK: That's right, sir.

BLINOV: How much a year?

CLERK: A hundred roubles.

BLINOV: Really? And you've got a passport to stay in town?

CLERK: Yes, sir.

BLINOV: A yearly passport?

CLERK: Yes, sir.

BLINOV: So, how are you getting along?

CLERK: Not bad, sir. Getting along slowly.

BLINOV: Slowly but surely, eh?

CLERK: (*Through gritted teeth.*) Too true, sir.

BLINOV: And what's your name?

CLERK: Kuzma.

BLINOV: Hm...

ZHAZIKOV: (*Going up to BLINOV.*) My dear Vasily, I'm terribly sorry... I hate to bother you, believe me, but you couldn't by any chance let me have a loan of twenty roubles – just for a day or two, no longer?

BLINOV: I thought you said you had money?

ZHAZIKOV: Yes, yes, I do have – I have some money, if that's what you mean, but I've got to pay for the apartment, so, well, you know...

BLINOV: Right, I'll give it to you. (*Takes out a soiled roll of banknotes.*) How much? A hundred? Two hundred?

ZHAZIKOV: Well, I only need twenty right now, but if you'd be so kind, then yes, please – a hundred and ten, say, or a hundred and fifteen.

BLINOV: Here's two hundred.

ZHAZIKOV: Thank you, I'm most grateful... and I'll return this in full tomorrow, or the day after tomorrow, at the latest... (*Turns to the clerk.*) This is for you, my dear sir. I'll call in at the shop again today, choose a few more things.

CLERK: Thank you very much, sir. (*Exits.*)

BLINOV: Now, let's go and have dinner.

ZHAZIKOV: Indeed, let's go, my friend. I'll take you to the Saint-Georges and treat you to champagne, the like of which...

BLINOV: Has this Saint-Georges place got an organ?

ZHAZIKOV: No, it hasn't.

BLINOV: To hell with it, then! Take me to a café with an organ.

ZHAZIKOV: With pleasure, sir.
(*MATVEI enters.*)
Ah, you've come back! Well, was he in?

MATVEI: He was, sir, and I got an answer.

ZHAZIKOV: (*Takes the note and casually glances over it.*) Well, so be it!

MATVEI: (*To BLINOV.*) Mr Blinov, sir! How are you? Give me your hand, sir!

BLINOV: (*Gives him his hand.*) Good morning, my friend.

MATVEI: (*Bows.*) How are you keeping, sir?

BLINOV: Fine, fine.

MATVEI: Thanks be to God, sir, eh?

ZHAZIKOV: (*Flings the note on the floor.*) Scum of the earth! Matvei! Help me get dressed!

MATVEI: Yes, sir – will you be wearing your patent-leather boots?

ZHAZIKOV: I suppose so...

BLINOV: What, aren't you dressed? Just fling on a coat.

ZHAZIKOV: Yes, why not! Now, let's go, my dear sir.

BLINOV: Right, let's be off. And you'll take me to a tragedy, and show me the mam'selles...

MATVEI: (*Quietly, to ZHAZIKOV.*) But, sir... what about the country?

ZHAZIKOV: (*Going out with BLINOV.*) What on earth are you on about? To hell with the country!
(*They exit.*)

MATVEI: (*With a sigh.*) It's too bad! (*Watches BLINOV as he goes out, sighs.*) The good old days are gone! And the gentry, well, they're a changed folk! (*Exits to the hall.*)
(*Curtain.*)
(*End of the Play.*)

ONE OF THE FAMILY

Characters

YELETSKY (PAVEL NIKOLAEVICH)

a St Petersburg civil servant, collegiate counsellor rank, 32; cold, dry, very far from foolish, and rather prim. He is dressed simply and tastefully. An average sort, not malicious, but unfeeling

YELETSKAYA (OLGA PETROVNA, NÉE KORINA)

his wife, 21. She is a kindhearted, gentle creature; now and again dreams of high society, but is afraid of it; loves her husband, behaves with absolute decorum. Very well dressed

KUZOVKIN (VASILY SEMYONICH)

an impoverished gentleman, living on charity in the Yeletsky household, 50; wears a coat with a stand-up collar and brass buttons

TROPACHEV (FLEGONT ALEKSANDRYCH)

a neighbour of the Yeletskys, 36, unmarried; a landowner, possessing 400 serfs; tall, quite presentable, but loud voiced and pompous; served in the cavalry, and retired with the rank of lieutenant; regularly travels to St Petersburg, and is getting ready to go abroad; coarse-grained by nature, and even rather mean; dressed in a green frock-coat, tan trousers, a tartan waistcoat, and a silk cravat with an enormous pin; wears patent-leather boots, and carries a gold-topped cane; close-cropped hair, *à la malcontent*

IVANOV (IVAN KUZMYCH)

another neighbour, 45; a placid and rather silent being, not without his own sort of pride, a friend of Kuzovkin's; prone to melancholy; wears an ancient brown frock-coat, a faded yellowish waistcoat, and grey trousers; extremely poor

KARPACHOV

Another neighbour, 40; a very stupid person, moustachioed, looking for all the world like Tropachev's adjutant; not particularly well off; wears a dolman jacket and baggy trousers; speaks in a deep bass voice

TREMBINSKY (NARTSYS KONSTANTINYCH)
The Yeletskys' general factotum and major-domo, 40; an aggressive, rather shrill fusspot; in truth, a beastly individual; well turned out, as befits a major-domo of a wealthy household; speaks correctly, but with a provincial accent

KARTASHOV (YEGOR)
The bailiff, 60; a rather bloated, somnolent man; steals whenever the opportunity arises; wears a long blue coat

PRASKOVYA (IVANOVNA)
The housekeeper, 50; a dry, spiteful, and irritable creature; wears a headscarf and a dark coloured dress; constantly muttering

MASHA
A chambermaid, 20; a fresh, lively girl

ANPADIST
A tailor, 70, a decrepit, half-crazy old man, worn out from his long years of service

PYOTR
A servant, 25; a sturdy young lad; given to scoffing and tomfoolery

VASKA
A Cossack boy, 14

ACT ONE

The scene is a large public room in the house of a wealthy land-owner; to the right are two windows, and a door leading into the garden; to the left, a door to the drawingroom, and facing, to the hall. Between the windows stands a pull-out table, and on the table is a chessboard. Downstage left is another table, and two armchairs, and there is access to a corridor between the drawingroom and the hall.

TREMBINSKY: (*Off-stage.*) This is a mess! The whole place is a shambles, everywhere I turn! There's absolutely no excuse!... (*Entering, accompanied by the servant PYOTR and the Cossack boy VASKA.*) I have precise written instructions from the mistress, I'm in charge here, and you'd better all do as I say! (*To PYOTR.*) Do you understand me?

PYOTR: Yes, sir.

TREMBINSKY: The mistress and her husband will be arriving today... they've sent me on ahead, and what are we doing here? Absolutely nothing! (*Turns to the Cossack boy.*) And what are you doing? You like lounging around too, eh? Have you got nothing to do? (*Catches hold of his ear and tugs it.*) D'you think you get free meals here? You people live off the rest of us, we know your sort! Clear off! Get to work!

(*The COSSACK BOY exits. TREMBINSKY sits down in an armchair.*)

Ye gods, I'm absolutely worn out! (*Leaps up again.*) Why haven't I seen the tailor? Where on earth's the tailor?

PYOTR: (*Looks out into the hall.*) He's here, sir.

TREMBINSKY: Well, why doesn't he come in? What's he waiting for? Come in, my dear fellow, what's your name? (*ANPADIST enters and stands by the door, his hands behind his back.*)

(*To PYOTR.*) Is this the tailor?

PYOTR: It is indeed, sir.

TREMBINSKY: (*To ANPADIST.*) How old are you, my dear fellow?

ANPADIST: I'm in my seventieth year, sir.

TREMBINSKY: (*To PYOTR.*) Is he the only tailor you have?

PYOTR: 'Fraid so, sir. There was another, but he turned out a wrong 'un. On account of he had a foul mouth on him.

TREMBINSKY: (*Raising his hands in the air.*) What a mess! (*To ANPADIST.*) Well then, old man, have you made up the order?

ANPADIST: I have, sir.

TREMBINSKY: And you've sewn the new collars onto the livery coats?

ANPADIST: I have, sir. Only, you see, sir, there wasn't enough yellow cloth, sir...

TREMBINSKY: So what on earth did you use?

ANPADIST: Well, sir, they fished an old petticoat out of the store-room for me, and it was sort of yellow.

TREMBINSKY: (*Waving his arms.*) Don't say any more! Oh well, there's nothing we can do about it. We can't drive into town for cloth now. Right, off you go.
(*ANPADIST makes to exit.*)
And watch your step, sir! Look lively, otherwise... Oh, go on, go on!
(*ANPADIST exits. TREMBINSKY sits down, and instantly leaps to his feet again.*)
Oh yes! Are they clearing the paths in the garden?

PYOTR: Indeed they are, sir, yes. They've roped in the young fellows from the village, all the bachelors.

TREMBINSKY: (*Goes up to PYOTR.*) And who exactly are you?

PYOTR: (*Puzzled.*) What d'you mean, sir?

TREMBINSKY: (*Goes up even closer.*) Who are you? I'm asking you, just who do you think you are?

PYOTR: (*Increasingly bewildered.*) Me, sir?

TREMBINSKY: (*Right into PYOTR's face.*) Yes, you! You, sir! You! Who are you?

PYOTR: I'm Pyotr.

TREMBINSKY: No, sir, you're a servant, that's what you
are! Your business is the house. And cleaning the lamps,
that's your business too. But the garden's none of your
concern. Whether they sent in single men, or any other
sort, is nothing to do with you. That's up to the bailiff.
I didn't ask you that, and I didn't want an answer. Your
business is to go and fetch the bailiff. That's your
business.

PYOTR: Well, he's coming here himself, sir.

(*YEGOR enters from the hall.*)

TREMBINSKY: Ah, Mr Kartashov! You've arrived just in
time, sir. Tell me, please, have you given orders for the
garden, concerning the...

YEGOR: I have, sir. There's no need to worry... Would you
care for a pinch of snuff, sir?

TREMBINSKY: (*Takes a pinch of YEGOR's snuff.*) You
wouldn't believe the trouble I've had this morning, Mr
Kartashov. I'll tell you freely, sir, I didn't expect to find
a big estate like this in such a mess! Not in your area, of
course – not the farming side of things, but the house...

YEGOR: Ah yes, sir.

TREMBINSKY: I mean, you can imagine, for example:
I ask: 'Do we have any musicians?' The master and
mistress have to be properly welcomed, you understand.
So they tell me we have. All right, I say, bring them in.
And would you believe it? All the musicians are out
doing various other jobs. One's a gardener, one's a
shoemaker, the bass is looking after the cattle. Now what
do you think of that? And the instruments are a mess
too. I had endless trouble sorting them out. (*Has another
pinch of snuff.*)

YEGOR: You're in a troublesome line of work, sir.

TREMBINSKY: Yes, I daresay I don't get paid for nothing.
Anyway, are the musicians on the porch now?

YEGOR: They are indeed, sir. There was a spot of rain, so
they took themselves off to the servants' hall: they say
their instruments'll get wet. But I chased them out, sir.
We don't want them missing the signal, when the folks

have to be welcomed. And they can keep their
instruments under their coats.

TREMBINSKY: That's quite right. Well, I think that's
everything in order now.

YEGOR: Don't you worry, Mr Trembinsky. (*Looks over at
PYOTR.*) What are you hanging around for? Clear off,
back where you belong, d'you hear?
(*PYOTR exits to the hall. MASHA runs on from the corridor.*)
Hey, hey, hey – where are you running to, young lady?

MASHA: Oh, leave me alone, Yegor. Praskovya's got me
absolutely worn out already. (*Dashes out into the hall.*)
(*YEGOR watches her go, then turns to TREMBINSKY and
winks. TREMBINSKY smiles.*)

YEGOR: Now, sir, would you happen to know the time,
please?

TREMBINSKY: (*Looks at his watch.*) A quarter to eleven.
The master and mistress'll be here any minute.
(*KUZOVKIN appears in the hall, pauses, makes a sign to someone
behind the door, enters cautiously and goes towards the table
near the windows.*)

YEGOR: I'll just dash into the office. The elder won't have
combed his beard, and he'll want to kiss the folks too...
(*Exits, colliding with KUZOVKIN.*)

KUZOVKIN: Good morning, Yegor Alekseyich.

YEGOR: (*Irritably.*) Oh, Kuzovkin, I haven't time for you
now! (*Exits to the hall.*)
(*KUZOVKIN goes over to the window.*)

TREMBINSKY: (*Looks round and catches sight of KUZOVKIN.
Aside.*) Now, then – who's this?
(*KUZOVKIN bows to TREMBINSKY. TREMBINSKY nods
coldly, and speaks to him offhandedly.*)
So, you've come too? I suppose you want to meet the
young master and mistress as well, eh?

KUZOVKIN: Yes, sir, of course.

TREMBINSKY: Well, all right. Are you pleased? (*Without
waiting for an answer.*) Are those your best clothes?

KUZOVKIN: Yes... I mean...

TREMBINSKY: Fine, that's all right. You can sit here in
the corner.

(*KUZOVKIN bows.*)

Heavens, I almost forgot – Pyotr!... Pyotr!... Pyotr, are you there? What's going on? Is there nobody in the hall?

IVANOV: (*Pokes his nose round the hall door.*) Yes, sir, what do you want?

TREMBINSKY: (*A little taken aback.*) Oh, excuse me... How did you happen to be...

IVANOV: (*Coming no further.*) I'm Ivanov – Ivan Kuzmych... I'm a friend of his... (*Points to KUZOVKIN.*)

KUZOVKIN: (*To TREMBINSKY.*) A neighbour, sir – a local man.... He's come to see me.

TREMBINSKY: (*Drawling, and shaking his head.*) Oh, sirs – this isn't the time, or the place.

(*PYOTR emerges from the hall, pushing right past IVANOV. IVANOV withdraws.*)

(*To PYOTR.*) Where did you disappear to? Now, follow me... I want to see what you've done in that office. Most likely it won't be at all what I ordered. You people just can't be trusted.

(*They exit to the drawingroom. KUZOVKIN remains alone.*)

KUZOVKIN: (*After a silence.*) Vanya? Hello, Vanya?

IVANOV: (*From the hall, without showing himself.*) What?

KUZOVKIN: It's all right, Vanya, you can come in.

IVANOV: (*Slowly enters.*) I'd better leave.

KUZOVKIN: No, stay. What are you worried about? You've come to see me, so come in. Sit down, do. This is my corner here.

IVANOV: We'd be better going into your room.

KUZOVKIN: We can't go into my room now. They're sorting out the laundry in it... they've put a lot of featherbeds in there too. Anyway, what's wrong with here?

IVANOV: No, I'd better go home.

KUZOVKIN: No, Vanya, you're staying here. Sit down, have a seat. And I'll sit down too.

(*KUZOVKIN does so.*)

The master and mistress'll be here any minute. You can have a look at them.

IVANOV: What's to look at?

KUZOVKIN: What do you mean, what's to look at? Olga
Petrovna got married in St Petersburg. Don't you want to
see what her husband's like? Anyway, we haven't seen
her for ages. Over six years. So sit down.

IVANOV: Honestly, Vasily...

KUZOVKIN: Sit down, for goodness' sake. Don't take any
notice of that new major-domo. Never mind him, he's
just doing his job.

IVANOV: So, has Olga Petrovna married a rich husband?
(*Sits down.*)

KUZOVKIN: I don't know about that, Vanya, but he's a
government official, they say, quite high up. Well, that's
only right for Olga Petrovna. She couldn't go on living
with her aunt forever.

IVANOV: Yes, but suppose the new master flings us out,
Vasily?

KUZOVKIN: Now why would he do that?

IVANOV: It's you I'm talking about, really.

KUZOVKIN: (*With a sigh.*) I know, Vanya, I know. You've
got some property, at least, but I don't even own the
clothes I stand up in. They're all off somebody else's
back. Still, perhaps the new master won't fling me out.
The old master, God bless him, he didn't fling me out,
not even when he was angry.

IVANOV: Yes, but you don't know these young Petersburg
types, Vasily.

KUZOVKIN: What? Surely they're not so...

IVANOV: They're absolutely dreadful, it seems. I don't
know them either, but that's what I've heard.

KUZOVKIN: (*After a moment's silence.*) Well, we'll see. I'll
put my trust in Olga Petrovna. She won't let me down.

IVANOV: Won't let you down? She's probably forgotten all
about you. I mean, she left here with her aunt, after her
mother died – she was just a child when she went away,
How old was she? She wasn't even fourteen. You used to
play with her dolls along with her – so what? She won't
even look at you.

KUZOVKIN: No, Vanya, no.

IVANOV: Well, you'll see.

KUZOVKIN: Anyway, that's enough of that, Vanya, please.

IVANOV: You wait and see.

KUZOVKIN: Stop it, Vanya, please... Listen, let's have a game of chess, eh? What d'you say?
(*IVANOV is silent.*)
What are you sitting like that for? Come on, my friend, let's have a game. (*Picks up the chess set, and begins laying out the pieces.*)

IVANOV: (*Helps him.*) You've picked a fine time, I must say. The major-domo won't let you, for sure.

KUZOVKIN: We're not bothering anybody, are we?

IVANOV: The young couple'll be here any minute.

KUZOVKIN: So, we'll stop when they arrive. Now, which hand – right or left?

IVANOV: They'll fling us both out, Vasily, you'll see. Left hand. It's your move.

KUZOVKIN: Mine... right, this is how I'm starting today.

IVANOV: Hm... what sort of move's that? Anyway, I'm doing this.

KUZOVKIN: And I'll go here.

IVANOV: And I'll go here.
(*There is a sudden noise from the hall. The COSSACK BOY Vaska dashes in at full tilt, shouting: "They're coming! They're coming! Mr Trembinsky! They're coming!" KUZOVKIN and IVANOV leap to their feet.*)

KUZOVKIN: (*Greatly agitated.*) They're coming? Are they here?

VASKA: (*Shouts.*) Yes, somebody waved, to give the signal – they're coming!
(*TREMBINSKY's voice is heard off-stage: "What's going on? Have the master and mistress arrived?" He and PYOTR rush in from the drawingroom.*)

TREMBINSKY: (*Shouts.*) The musicians! Get the musicians into place!
(*Runs out into the hall, followed by PYOTR and the COSSACK BOY. MASHA hurries in from the corridor.*)

MASHA: Are the folks coming?

KUZOVKIN: Yes, yes.

(*IVANOV gloomily withdraws into the corner. MASHA rushes into the corridor, shouting: "They're coming!". After a moment, PRASKOVYA bursts in from the corridor, and TREMBINSKY from the hall.*)

PRASKOVYA: Are they coming?

TREMBINSKY: Call the girls in here – the girls, quickly!

PRASKOVYA: (*Shouts into the corridor.*) Girls! Girls! Hurry!

YEGOR: (*Rushes in from the hall.*) Mr Trembinsky, the bread and salt!

TREMBINSKY: (*At the pitch of his voice.*) Pyotr! Pyotr! The bread and salt! Where's the bread and salt!

(*Six girls enter from the corridor, in festive dress.*)

Get into the hall, girls, the hall!

(*The girls run into the hall, colliding with PYOTR in the doorway. He is bearing a platter with an enormous round loaf and a salt-dish.*)

PYOTR: Watch what you're doing, you mad things!

TREMBINSKY: (*Snatches the platter from PYOTR and hands it over to YEGOR.*) Right, take this, and go out onto the porch, go on.

(*He thrusts him out along with PYOTR and PRASKOVYA, and hurries out after them, shouting into the hall: "Where are all the servants? Get everybody out here!".*)

PYOTR: (*Off-stage.*) Somebody call Anpadist!

A VOICE: (*Off-stage.*) The constable's taken away his boots...

TREMBINSKY: (*Off-stage.*) Get the footmen out here!

GIRLS: (*Off-stage.*) They're coming! They're coming!

TREMBINSKY: (*Off-stage.*) Now, quiet, everybody! Quiet!

(*A profound silence reigns. KUZOVKIN, who has been in a state of high excitement all this time, but has scarcely moved from the spot, eagerly strains to listen. Suddenly the band strikes up, a very shaky rendering of: "Let the Victory Roll Resound!" A carriage drives up to the porch, and after some conversation, the music stops. The sounds of greeting are heard, and a few moments later, OLGA PETROVNA and her husband enter; he is carrying the round loaf. Behind them come TREMBINSKY, YEGOR, with*) *the platter, PRASKOVYA, and the rest of the household, who remain, however, in the doorway.*)

OLGA: (*To her husband, with a smile.*) Well, Paul, we're home at last.

(*YELETSKY squeezes her hand.*)

I'm so happy! (*Turning to the servants.*) Thank you! Thank you! (*Then pointing to YELETSKY.*) This is your new master... I ask you to love and respect him... (*To her husband.*) *Rendez cela, mon ami.*

(*YELETSKY hands the loaf to YEGOR.*)

TREMBINSKY: (*Bowing deeply from the waist.*) If it would please you to order something to eat... or some tea, perhaps...

OLGA: No, thank you – not yet. (*To her husband.*) I want to show you the whole house, and your study. I haven't been home for seven years... seven years!

YELETSKY: Show me, please do.

PRASKOVYA: (*Taking OLGA's hat and coat.*) Our dear, darling mistress...

OLGA: (*Smiles in response, and looks round the room.*) Our house has grown old, though... and the rooms seem smaller.

YELETSKY: (*In the manner of a kindly preceptor.*) It always seems that way... You were a child when you left here.

KUZOVKIN: (*Who hasn't once taken his eyes off OLGA, goes up to her.*) Olga Petrovna, if you please... (*His voice breaks.*)

OLGA: (*Doesn't recognise him at first.*) Oh... oh, it's Mr Kuzovkin... Mr Kuzovkin... how are you? I didn't recognise you.

KUZOVKIN: (*Kisses her hand.*) Please... allow me to... congratulate...

OLGA: (*To her husband.*) This is an old family friend, Mr Kuzovkin...

YELETSKY: (*Bows.*) Pleased to meet you.

(*IVANOV in the background also bows, although no-one has noticed him yet.*)

KUZOVKIN: (*Bows to YELETSKY.*) Welcome, welcome, sir... we're all so happy...

YELETSKY: (*Bows to him again, then speaks to his wife in an aside.*) Who is he?

OLGA: (*Aside.*) He's a poor gentleman, he lives here free with us. (*Aloud.*) Anyway, let's go – I want to show you the whole house... this is where I was born, Paul, this is where I grew up...

YELETSKY: Let's go, it'll be a pleasure... (*Turning to TREMBINSKY.*) And kindly order my valet... my luggage is outside...

TREMBINSKY: (*Hurriedly.*) Yes, sir, of course!

OLGA: Come on, Paul.

(*They exit to the drawingroom.*)

TREMBINSKY: (*To all the servants, sotto voce.*) Well, my friends, you can now go about your business. Yegor, you stay here in the hall, in case the master wants anything. (*YEGOR and the other servants exit to the hall; PRASKOVYA and the maids go out into the corridor.*)

PRASKOVYA: (*In the doorway.*) Go on, go on... and what are you laughing at, Masha? (*Exits.*)

TREMBINSKY: (*To KUZOVKIN and IVANOV.*) And what about you gentlemen – are you staying here?

KUZOVKIN: We'll stay here.

TREMBINSKY: All right... Only, please don't... you know... (*Gestures vaguely.*) For heaven's sake, otherwise it'll all come back on me... (*Exits on tiptoe to the hall.*)

KUZOVKIN: (*Watches him go out, then quickly turns to IVANOV.*) Well, Vanya, what do you think of her? How she's grown, eh? And hasn't she turned out a real beauty! And she hasn't forgotten me! You see, Vanya, you see? I was right after all.

IVANOV: She hasn't forgotten you? Then why did she call you Mr Kuzovkin, instead of Vasily?

KUZOVKIN: Oh, you're impossible, Vanya! What difference does it make, first name, second name? You surely know that, a clever person like you. And she introduced me to her husband. What a fine-looking man! And so handsome! Oh yes, he must be a government official – what do you think, Vanya?

IVANOV: I've no idea, Vasily. Anyway, I'd better go.

KUZOVKIN: Honestly, Vanya – what's got into you? You're not your old self at all – 'I'd better go, I'd better go...' You'd do better to tell me what you thought of our young mistress.

IVANOV: She's very nice, I'm not saying she isn't.

KUZOVKIN: Her smile alone is worth... And what about her voice, eh? So sweet, like a little bird. And she loves her husband, that's quite obvious. What d'you think, Vanya? I mean, it's obvious, isn't it.

IVANOV: God only knows, Vasily.

KUZOVKIN: Shame on you, Vanya! It's a sin to talk like that. Everyone's happy, and you... Oh, they're coming back again!

(*OLGA and YELETSKY enter from the drawingroom.*)

OLGA: It's not a very grand house, as you can see, but we're content with what we have.

YELETSKY: Really, it's a splendid house – beautifully arranged.

OLGA: Anyway, let's go into the garden now.

YELETSKY: With pleasure. However, I'd like a few words with your bailiff first

OLGA: (*Reproachfully.*) With my bailiff?

YELETSKY: (*Smiles.*) With our bailiff. (*Kisses her hand.*)

OLGA: Well, if you like. I'll take Mr Kuzovkin with me. Mr Kuzovkin, shall we go into the garden?

KUZOVKIN: (*Beaming with pleasure.*) Please... I... I...

YELETSKY: Put on your hat, Olya.

OLGA: I don't need it. (*Flings a scarf over her head.*) Come on, Mr Kuzovkin...

KUZOVKIN: Olga Petrovna... if you'll permit me... please, this is one of... this is one of our neighbours, Ivanov... (*IVANOV is embarrassed, bows.*)

OLGA: I'm pleased to meet you. Would you like to come with us into the garden? (*IVANOV bows.*) Give me your arm, Mr Kuzovkin.

KUZOVKIN: (*Unable to believe his ears.*) I'm sorry?

OLGA: (*Laughing.*) Look, like this... (*Takes his arm, and puts hers through it.*) Now, you see what I mean, Mr Kuzovkin? (*They exit through the french windows, followed by IVANOV. YELETSKY walks over to the french windows, watches them go, then returns to the table at left and sits down.*)

YELETSKY: Hello! Who's there? Is anyone there?

PYOTR: (*Entering from the hall.*) Yes, sir?

YELETSKY: What's your name, my good man?

PYOTR: Pyotr, sir.

YELETSKY: Ah. Well, go and fetch me the bailiff... what's-his-name – Yegor, isn't it?

PYOTR: That's right, sir.

YELETSKY: Well, go and get him.
(*PYOTR exits. A moment later YEGOR enters, pauses in the doorway, and puts his hands behind his back.*)
(*Officiously.*) Ah, Yegor, tomorrow I intend to inspect Madame Yeletskys estate.

YEGOR: Yes, sir.

YELETSKY: Do we have many serfs here?

YEGOR: Three hundred and eighty-four, of the male sex, sir, in Timofeyevo, according to the last census, but there's more than that.

YELETSKY: How many more?

YEGOR: (*Coughs behind his hand.*) There'll be about a dozen or so.

YELETSKY: Hm... Right, I want you to find out precisely, and report back to me. Are there any allotments?

YEGOR: There's a patch round the cottage, sir.

YELETSKY: (*Looks at YEGOR with a puzzled expression.*) Hm... And is there much decent land?

YEGOR: A fair bit, sir. Over five hundred acres planted.

YELETSKY: (*Again looks doubtfully at YEGOR.*) And how much unproductive land?

YEGOR: (*After some hesitation.*) Well, sir, I'm not sure how to say... There's the bushes... and there's gullies, too. And then there's the manor land, and the pasture. (*Gathering his thoughts.*) It's being cut for hay, sir.

YELETSKY: (*Knitting his brows.*) Yes, but how much, exactly?

YEGOR: Nobody knows, sir. The land's never been surveyed. It might be marked on the plan. Anyway, there must be about a thousand acres.

YELETSKY: (*Sotto voce.*) The whole thing's a mess! (*Aloud.*) Are there any woods?

YEGOR: About seventy acres, sir, and a bit more.

YELETSKY: (*After a pause, thinking aloud.*) So, that means there'll be about twelve hundred acres all told?

YEGOR: Twelve hundred? No, getting on for two thousand, more like.

YELETSKY: But you've just said... (*Stops short.*) Yes... yes... that's what I was going to say. So, is everything clear?

YEGOR: Yes, sir.

YELETSKY: (*In all seriousness.*) Now, tell me – do the peasants round here behave themselves? Are they quiet?

YEGOR: They're good people, sir. They need a good talking-to, at times.

YELETSKY: Hm... They're not ruined, are they?

YEGOR: Heavens, sir, how could they be? Absolutely not. No, mostly they're quite content.

YELETSKY: Well, I'll look into all that for myself tomorrow. You can go now. Oh, by the way – tell me, who's that gentleman who's living here?

YEGOR: That's Kuzovkin, sir – Vasily Petrovich. He's a nobleman, but he gets free board here, sir. He's been here since the old master's time. You might say he kept him here for amusement.

YELETSKY: And has he been staying here long?

YEGOR: Oh yes, sir. It's been twenty years no since the old master died, and Mr Kuzovkin moved in here while he was still alive.

YELETSKY: Right, that's fine... And do you have an office here?

YEGOR: Couldn't do without one, sir.

YELETSKY: Well, I'll inspect all these things tomorrow. You can go now.

(*YEGOR exits.*)

Hm... I think this bailiff's a fool. Anyway, we'll see. (*Stands up and walks round the room.*) So... here I am in the country, in my own village. It's rather strange. But nice. (*The voice of TROPACHEV is heard outside in the hall: "Have they arrived? Today?"*)
Now, who's this?

PYOTR: (*Entering from the hall.*) Sir, that's Mr Tropachev – he'd like to see you. What shall I tell him?

YELETSKY: (*Aside.*) Who is this, I wonder? The name sounds familiar... (*Aloud.*) Send him in.

TROPACHEV: (*Enters.*) Good morning, Pavel Nikolaich, *bonjour!*
(*YELETSKY bows, clearly a little puzzled.*)
You don't recognise me, I think... You remember, in St Petersburg, at Count Kuntsov's house...

YELETSKY: Oh yes, I do beg your pardon... I'm pleased to meet you, sir. (*Shakes his hand.*)

TROPACHEV: I'm your nearest neighbour. I live about a mile from here. I drive past your house on my way into town. I knew they were expecting you, so I thought I'd just pop in to check, but if I've come at a bad time, then please say so. *Entre gens comme il faut,* as they say... well, why stand on ceremony, eh?

YELETSKY: No, not at all, sir – indeed, I hope you'll stay to dinner... although I've no idea what our country chef has in store for us.

TROPACHEV: (*Strikes a pose, toying with his cane.*) Oh, good heavens, sir, I know you live like kings here. And I trust you'll do me the honour of dining at my house one of these days. You wouldn't believe how pleased I am that you've come. There are so few decent types around here, *des gens comme il faut. Et madame?* How is she? I knew her as a child. Oh yes, I know your wife, sir, I know her well. And I congratulate you, Pavel Nikolaich, most heartily. Hee-hee! But she probably won't remember me at all. (*Again strikes a pose, stroking his side-whiskers.*)

YELETSKY: She'll be delighted to see you. She's just gone for a stroll in the garden with this... with this gentleman who boards here.

TROPACHEV: (*Contemptuously.*) Oh, him! You know, he acts as a sort of court jester here... Still, he's peaceable enough. Incidentally, I brought another gentleman with me... he's out in the hall. May I...?

YELETSKY: Why, certainly. What on earth is he doing in the hall?

TROPACHEV: *Oh, ne faîtes pas attention.* That's his way, it doesn't matter. He boards with me too, on account of his poverty. He travels around with me – it's a bit of a bore, you know, driving on one's own. But please, don't worry about him... *je vous en prie.* (*Goes over to the hall door.*) Karpachov! Come on in, dear chap!
(*KARPACHOV enters and bows.*)
Pavel Nikolaich, may I have the honour...

YELETSKY: I'm pleased to meet you, sir.

TROPACHEV: (*Takes YELETSKY's arm and quietly turns him away from KARPACHOV, who discreetly withdraws.*)
C'est bien, c'est bien. So, are you staying with us long, sir?

YELETSKY: I'm taking three months' leave.
(*They begin pacing around the room.*)

TROPACHEV: Hm, that's not very much. Still, I suppose you couldn't take any more. And I daresay they weren't keen to release you. Hee-hee! But you've got to have a break, eh? So, do you hunt, sir?

YELETSKY: You know, I've never once had a gun in my hand? However, I bought myself a dog, just before this trip. Is there much game around here?

TROPACHEV: There is indeed. And if you'll allow me, sir, I'll take you in hand, make a real sportsman out of you.
(*To KARPACHOV.*) Have we got a hunt in Malinniko?

KARPACHOV: (*From the corner, in a deep voice.*) Two. And there's three in Kamenny Ridge.

TROPACHEV: Oh, good!

KARPACHOV: Fedul the woodcutter was saying just the other day, that in Gorelo...
(*OLGA enters from the garden, along with KUZOVKIN and IVANOV. KARPACHOV breaks off, and bows.*)

OLGA: Oh, Paul, our garden's so lovely... (*Stops, on catching sight of TROPACHEV.*)

YELETSKY: (*To OLGA.*) My dear, allow me to introduce...

TROPACHEV: (*Interrupting YELETSKY.*) Oh, please, please – we're old friends... Olga Petrovna probably doesn't recognise me, and that's not surprising. I knew her *comme ça*... (*Indicating about a yard from the floor. He strikes a pose, and continues with a smile.*) Tropachev... you remember your old neighbour Tropachev, surely? The one who used to bring you toys from town? You were such a sweet little thing then – but now... (*Gives the last word a significant emphasis, bows, takes a step backwards and then straightens up, extremely pleased with himself.*)

OLGA: Oh, m'sieu Tropachev, of course! Yes, now I recognise you... (*Gives him her hand.*) You wouldn't believe how happy I am, now that we're here.

TROPACHEV: (*Sweetly.*) What, only now that you're here?

OLGA: (*Smiles in response.*) My childhood all came back to me, so vividly... Paul, you really must come into the garden with me. I'll show you an acacia tree I planted myself. It's much taller than me now.

YELETSKY: (*To OLGA, indicating KARPACHOV.*) This is m'sieu Karpachov – also a neighbour.
(*KARPACHOV bows, and withdraws into the corner, in which KUZOVKIN and IVANOV have already managed to position themselves.*)

OLGA: I'm pleased to meet you...

TROPACHEV: (*To OLGA.*) Ne faîtes pas attention. (*Aloud, rubbing his hands.*) So, you're here in your own village at last – mistress of the house, eh? Time flies, *n'est-ce pas?*

OLGA: I trust you'll be dining with us?

YELETSKY: I've already invited... *pardon*... what's your name again, sir?

TROPACHEV: Tropachev.

YELETSKY: I've already invited Mr Tropachev. Only I'm afraid dinner might not be...

TROPACHEV: Oh, nonsense!

OLGA: (*Leads YELETSKY a little way apart.*) He's come at a rather awkward time.

YELETSKY: Yes... Still, he seems a decent enough chap.

TROPACHEV: (*Also withdraws, and rather absently swaying from side to side, and gnawing the top of his cane, goes up to KUZOVKIN and speaks to him in an undertone.*) So, you're here, eh? And how are you?

KUZOVKIN: Praise be, I'm well, sir – thank you very much.

TROPACHEV: (*Pointing with his elbow at KARPACHOV.*) I take it you know him?

KUZOVKIN: Oh yes, of course, sir. We know each other.

TROPACHEV: So... so... (*To IVANOV.*) And what's your name again? You're here too?

IVANOV: Yes, sir.

OLGA: (*To TROPACHEV.*) M'sieu... m'sieu Tropachev...

TROPACHEV: (*Quickly turns round.*) *Madame?*

OLGA: We're old friends, you and I – so we needn't stand on ceremony, right?

TROPACHEV: Of course not.

OLGA: Then if you'll allow me to go to my room... We've only just arrived, and I must look out some things.

TROPACHEV: Please do, Olga Petrovna. And you, Mr Yeletsky, don't mind me, make yourself at home, hee-hee! I'll have a little chat with these gentlemen here...

OLGA: You're an old friend, of course, but I don't feel at ease in these travelling clothes...

TROPACHEV: (*Smirking.*) Well, I wouldn't accept that as a... as an excuse, if I didn't know how much... I mean, you ladies and your toilette... how much pleasure, so to speak, you always take... (*Gets mixed up, bows and strikes a pose.*)

OLGA: (*Laughs.*) You're a wicked man, sir. Anyway, I shall leave you gentlemen – goodbye for the moment. (*Exits to the drawingroom.*)

TROPACHEV: Pavel Nikolaich, allow me to congratulate once again... You're a lucky man, I may say.

YELETSKY: (*Smiles and shakes his hand.*) You're quite right, Mr... er... Mr Tropachev.

TROPACHEV: But listen, perhaps I'm detaining you?

YELETSKY: No no, on the contrary, sir. And in fact, if you'd like to come with me... as a landowner, you might find it interesting.

TROPACHEV: (*Goes up to YELETSKY and presses his hand to his belly.*) Pavel Nikolaich, I am at your disposal.

YELETSKY: If you like, we could walk over to the granary before lunch. It's only a few steps away, just beyond the garden.

TROPACHEV: *Enchanté!* Lead the way.

YELETSKY: You'd better take your hat. (*Shouts.*) Hello? Is there anyone there?

(*PYOTR enters.*)

Tell them to prepare lunch.

PYOTR: Yes, sir. (*Exits.*)

TROPACHEV: Karpachov'll come with us, if you don't mind.

YELETSKY: No, not at all.

(*They exit, KARPACHOV following.*)

KUZOVKIN: (*Quickly turns to IVANOV.*) Now, Vanya, tell me – what do you think of our Olya?

IVANOV: Well, what can I say? She's quite pretty.

KUZOVKIN: And so affectionate, isn't she?

IVANOV: Oh yes – she's not like him.

KUZOVKIN: What on earth's wrong with him? I mean, think, Vanya – he's an important man, he's got into the habit of acting like that. He'd obviously like to... well, you know, he just can't. That's what's demanded of him, in those places. But did you notice her eyes, Vanya?

IVANOV: No, Vasily, I didn't.

KUZOVKIN: Honest to God, I'm surprised at you, my friend. That's not nice, Vanya, it really isn't.

IVANOV: Maybe not. Anyway, I'm not saying she... Look out, here comes the major-domo.

KUZOVKIN: (*Lowering his voice.*) Well, let him come. We're not doing anything.

(*TREMBINSKY and PYOTR enter. PYOTR is carrying a tray with lunch things.*)

179

TREMBINSKY: (*Moving a table into the middle of the room.*) Put it down here, and watch you don't break anything. (*PYOTR sets down the tray and begins spreading the tablecloth. TREMBINSKY takes it from him.*) Here, I'll do that. You go and fetch the wine. (*PYOTR exits. TREMBINSKY sets the table, and looks askance at KUZOVKIN.*) Huh, it's all right for some, born with a silver spoon in their mouths. People like us have to slave for every scrap of bread, and they get it all for nothing. Where's the justice in this world, I ask you, eh? It's a strange business, right enough.

KUZOVKIN: (*Gingerly touches TREMBINSKY's shoulder. TREMBINSKY looks at him in surprise.*) You've brushed against the wall... you've got your coat dirty...

TREMBINSKY: Is that all? Who cares? Leave it alone! (*PYOTR enters with some bottles of wine, and champagne in a bucket, which he puts on a little table by the door.*) Now, come on, look lively. (*Takes the bottles and puts them on the table.*) Oh, and you can take this chess set away. The gentlemen'll have no time for that. Anyway, what sort of game is it? The gentry never play it, do they. (*PYOTR removes the chess set.*)

IVANOV: (*To KUZOVKIN, quietly.*) Goodbye, my friend.

KUZOVKIN: Where are you going?

IVANOV: Home.

KUZOVKIN: No, don't – stay.

YEGOR: (*Looks in from the hall.*) Mr Trembinsky! Mr Trembinsky!

TREMBINSKY: What is it?

YEGOR: Where has the master gone?

TREMBINSKY: To the granary. What do you want with him?

YEGOR: To the granary... Oh, God! (*He is about to run off, but suddenly straightens up, puts his hands behind his back, and presses himself against the door. YELETSKY, TROPACHEV and KARPACHOV enter.*)

YELETSKY: (*To TROPACHEV.*) So... *vous êtes content?*

TROPACHEV: *Très bien, très bien, tout est très bien...* Ah,
Yegor, good morning!
(*YEGOR bows. TROPACHEV claps him on the shoulder.*)
This is an excellent man, Pavel Nikolaich. You can rely
on him absolutely.
(*YEGOR bows again and exits.*)
Ah, and here's lunch. (*Goes up to the table.*) Good heavens,
this is an entire dinner! *Comme c'est bien servi! (Lifts the
silver cover off one of the dishes.*) Snipe? I say! This
might've been dished up by Saint-George himself! He's a
damnable rogue, Saint-George, but he does a glorious
dinner. Last time I ate there I was out a couple of
hundred...

YELETSKY: Shall we sit down? (*Calls.*) Let's have some
chairs here!
(*PYOTR sets out the chairs, TREMBINSKY fusses around the
gentlemen. YELETSKY and TROPACHEV sit down.*)

TROPACHEV: (*To KARPACHOV.*) You too, Karpach... (*To
YELETSKY.*) C'est comme cela que je l'appelle... Vous
permettez?*

YELETSKY: Yes, help yourself. (*To KUZOVKIN and IVANOV,
who still haven't budged from their corner.*) Gentlemen, why
on earth aren't you sitting? Please, sit down...

KUZOVKIN: (*Bows.*) Thank you very much, sir. We'll just
stay here...

YELETSKY: Sit down, please.
(*KUZOVKIN and IVANOV meekly sit down at the table. From
the audience's viewpoint, TROPACHEV is sitting on
YELETSKY's left; KARPACHOV, a little apart on the right,
with KUZOVKIN and IVANOV beside him. TREMBINSKY,
with a napkin over his arm, stands behind YELETSKY; PYOTR
is by the door.*)
(*Lifting the cover from one of the dishes.*) Now, gentlemen,
for what the good Lord has provided...

TROPACHEV: (*With his mouth full.*) Parfait, parfait!* You
have a wonderful chef, Pavel Nikolaich...

YELETSKY: You're too kind. Now, tell me – do you think
there'll be a good harvest this year?

TROPACHEV: (*Still chewing.*) I think so. (*Takes a drink of wine.*) Your good health, sir! Karpach, why aren't you drinking to Pavel Nikolaich's health?

KARPACHOV: (*Leaping to his feet.*) Long life to our most worthy master... (*Downs the glass in one gulp.*) ... and every kind of blessing! (*Sits down.*)

YELETSKY: Thank you.

TROPACHEV: (*To KARPACHOV, nudging YELETSKY with his elbow.*) We should appoint you marshal of the nobility, eh? What do you think?

KARPACHOV: Heavens, no. What earthly use would I be to them?

TROPACHEV: In point of fact, Pavel Nikolaich, if it weren't for your duties... this is a splendid cheese... if it weren't for your duties, you know, you really ought to be our marshal!

YELETSKY: Oh, please...

TROPACHEV: No, I'm not joking. (*To KUZOVKIN.*) And why aren't you drinking to Pavel Nikolaich's health, eh? (*To IVANOV.*) And you too, eh?

KUZOVKIN: (*A little embarrassed.*) I am very pleased to...

TROPACHEV: Karpach, pour him a drink... fill him up. Go on, don't stand on ceremony.

KUZOVKIN: (*Stands up.*) To the health of our most esteemed master and mistress... (*Bows, drinks, and sits down.*) (*IVANOV also bows, and drinks in silence.*)

TROPACHEV: Ah, bravo! (*To YELETSKY.*) Now just wait... *Nous allons rire.* He's quite entertaining, but you need to get him drunk first. (*To KUZOVKIN, toying with a knife.*) So, how are things these days, Mr what's-your-name? I haven't seen you in ages. You're getting by, I trust?

KUZOVKIN: Yes, sir. Getting by, sir, as you say.

TROPACHEV: Good, good. That's fine. So, will you get Vetrovo back eventually, or not?

KUZOVKIN: (*Lowering his eyes.*) You're making fun of me, sir.

TROPACHEV: Eh? Good heavens, what gives you that idea? I'm interested in you, that's all. I'm not joking.

KUZOVKIN: (*With a sigh.*) There's been no decision yet, sir.

TROPACHEV: Really?

KUZOVKIN: No, sir.

TROPACHEV: Well, you'll just have to be patient. (*To YELETSKY, with a wink.*) Pavel Nikolaich, you perhaps don't know that you have landed gentry here, in the person of Mr Kuzovkin – a genuine landowner, with his own property, no less – or to be more accurate, an heir – the legal heir to the village of Vetrovo, and Ugarovo besides... How many serfs, would you say?

KUZOVKIN: According to the eighth census, there are forty-two in Vetrovo, but I don't get all of it.

TROPACHEV: (*To YELETSKY, sotto voce.*) He's completely crazy about this Vetrovo. (*Aloud.*) And how many acres have you got?

KUZOVKIN: (*Beginning to lose his shyness.*) Well, after deducting a seventh share, and various other legal requirements – about two hundred acres or so.

TROPACHEV: So how many serfs will you get?

KUZOVKIN: I don't know how many. A lot of them have run away, sir.

YELETSKY: Tell me, why don't you take possession of your estate?

KUZOVKIN: It's the lawsuit, sir.

YELETSKY: Lawsuit? With whom?

KUZOVKIN: Well, it turns out there are other heirs, sir. There are also debts – to the government, and some private ones besides.

YELETSKY: So how long has this case been going on?

KUZOVKIN: (*Gradually becoming more animated.*) Oh, a long time, sir. Since while the old master was still alive, God rest him! I should've been done with it, but I'd no money. And no time, either. I should've gone into town, of course, and asked somebody to look after it for me, but I didn't have the time. The stamped paper alone costs a fortune. And I'm a poor man, sir.

TROPACHEV: Karpach, pour him another glass.

KUZOVKIN: Oh, no thank you, sir...

TROPACHEV: Nonsense. (*Has a drink himself.*) Your good
health!
(*KUZOVKIN stands up, bows, and drinks.*)
Come on, what's the matter with you? This isn't fair,
you're going to spoil our fun!

KUZOVKIN: So what can I do, sir? This past year,
I haven't even bothered to collect the information...
(*TROPACHEV shakes his head reproachfully.*)
Certainly, I have a man there... I'm relying on him, but
the Lord only knows what he's up to.

TROPACHEV: (*Glances at YELETSKY.*) And just who is
this man, might one ask?

KUZOVKIN: Well, by rights I shouldn't say, but... oh,
what's the odds?... His name's Lychkov, Ivan Lychkov –
do you happen to know him?

TROPACHEV: No, I don't. What does he do?

KUZOVKIN: Oh, now... he's a district solicitor... or at
least, he used to be. Not around here, though – in
Venyovo. He makes a fair living nowadays, but he's
more involved in business.

TROPACHEV: (*Still looking at YELETSKY, who is beginning
to smile at KUZOVKIN.*) And this gentleman, Lychkov,
promised to help you?

KUZOVKIN: (*After a pause.*) He did, sir. I was godfather to
his second boy, sir, and that's why he promised. I'll sort
out this case for you, he said, just wait. And he's a real
expert, is Mr Lychkov.

TROPACHEV: Really?

KUZOVKIN: Oh yes, sir, he's well known in these parts.

TROPACHEV: Yes, but you say he's retired from the law
these days, he's gone into business.

KUZOVKIN: That's true, sir. That's just the way things
turned out for him, but he's a real gem of a man! Only
I haven't seen him for ages.

TROPACHEV: How long?

KUZOVKIN: Oh, it'll be over a year now, sir.

TROPACHEV: Good heavens, man, you shouldn't do that!
That's not good, you know.

KUZOVKIN: You're absolutely right, sir. B⌐
   you advise me to do?

YELETSKY: Perhaps you can tell us what

KUZOVKIN: (*Clearing his throat, and becom*
   heated.) The trouble is, Pavel Nikolaich⌐
   being so bold, but... well, you did ask. The trouble is
   this, sir: the village of Vetrovo... To tell you the truth,
   I've never once spoken in the presence of a dignitary...
   you'll forgive me if I'm a bit...

YELETSKY: Speak out, go on.

TROPACHEV: (*Gesturing to KARPACHOV to fill*
   KUZOVKIN's glass.) Another little glass, eh?

KUZOVKIN: Oh, no thank you, sir.

TROPACHEV: Some Dutch courage?

KUZOVKIN: Well... perhaps a little... (*Drinks, then wipes
his mouth with his handkerchief.*) Anyway, sir, as I was
saying, this village of Vetrovo I just referred to... this
same village came to me in direct line of descent from
my grandfather Maxim Kuzovkin – he was a major in
the army, sir, you may have heard of him. It was left
to two brothers, Maxim's sons, my father Semyon, and
my uncle Niktopolion. My father Semyon, and his
brother, my uncle, never divided the property while
they were alive, and my uncle died without leaving
any children – which I'd like you to note, sir – but he
only died after the death of my own father, Semyon.
However, they had a sister, Katerina, and she married
a certain Yagushkin, Porfiry, his name was, and this
Porfiry Yagushkin had a son, Ilya, by his first wife, a
Polish woman, and this Ilya was a fierce drunkard, a
proper rogue, and my uncle Niktopolion gave this
Ilya – at least, according to his sister Katerina – a
note for seventeen hundred roubles, and Katerina
herself gave her husband another note for seventeen
hundred, plus one from my father, only this time for
two thousand roubles, endorsed by the district
magistrate Galushkin, and his wife had a piece of it
too... Well, anyway, just then my father, God rest him,

up and died, and the notes were handed over for redemption. Niktopolion doesn't know where to turn, so he says he hasn't divided the property with his nephew. Katerina demands a fourteenth share, and the government taxes also come up for collection. A dreadful business, sir! Galushkin's wife suddenly starts clamouring for her money... Niktopolion says that's the nephew's responsibility, but how can I be responsible, sir, if I've not even come of age yet? Anyway, Galushkin decides to sue him. And the Polish woman's son went to court too, he wouldn't even spare his own stepmother. I'm not letting her off, he says, she got my maid Akulina into the habit of drinking, he says... So the porridge was fairly boiling, the petitions started rolling through the courts. First the district court, then the regional court, then from the regional court back to the district court, with all sorts of inscriptions on them. And after the death of Niktopolion, things just got worse. I tried to get possession of my estate, and I'm handed an order – on account of unpaid taxes, the village of Vetrovo has to be sold at auction. The German Hanginmeister proclaims his rights, and suddenly the peasants come running, like partridges. The district marshal reads me a lecture at my own door, trustees, trustees, he keeps shouting, but trustees of what? The rightful heir isn't given possession, and his own stepmother Katerina brings a complaint against the Polish woman's son Ilya to the Senate, the highest court in the land...
(*Stopped in his tracks by the general hilarity, KUZOVKIN falls silent, acutely embarrassed. TREMBINSKY, who has been observing the gentlemen intently, and a little uncertainly all this time, joining in discreetly in their merriment, shrieks with laughter behind his hand. PYOTR, standing by the door, has a stupid grin on his face. KARPACHOV is laughing heartily, though a little circumspectly. TROPACHEV is in fits. YELETSKY is laughing somewhat contemptuously, screwing up his eyes. Only IVANOV, who has several times*

tugged KUZOVKIN's sleeve, during the narration, sits with his head bowed.)

YELETSKY: (*Laughing, to KUZOVKIN.*) Go on, sir, please – why have you stopped?

TROPACHEV: Yes, go on, what's-your-name, do.

YELETSKY: I... I'm sorry... it seems I've disturbed...

TROPACHEV: I know what the matter is... you're too shy – isn't that it, you're shy?

KUZOVKIN: (*In a subdued voice.*) Yes, sir.

TROPACHEV: Well, we'll need to fix that, won't we. (*Lifts up an empty bottle.*) Waiter! Let's have some more wine! (*To YELETSKY.*) *Vous permettez?*

YELETSKY: By all means. (*To TREMBINSKY.*) Isn't there any champagne?

TREMBINSKY: Yes, sir, of course.

(*Hurries over to the ice-bucket and brings it to the table. KUZOVKIN smiles, and toys with the buttons of his own coat.*)

TROPACHEV: (*To Kuzovkin.*) Now, that's not very nice, my esteemed sir. Mustn't be shy in respectable company, you know, it's not done. (*To YELETSKY, pointing to the champagne bucket.*) What – chilled already? *Mais c'est magnifique.* (*Pours out a glass.*) This is an excellent vintage, obviously. (*To KUZOVKIN.*) Here you are. And you mustn't refuse... Anyway, you were telling us a few things, and you got carried away – where's the harm in that? Pavel Nikolaich, tell him to drink up...

YELETSKY: Here's to the future owner of Vetrovo! Your good health, sir! Drink up, Mr... er, drink up, Mr Kuzovkin!

(*KUZOVKIN drinks.*)

TROPACHEV: That's what I like to see!

(*He stands up along with YELETSKY; they all stand up and move downstage.*)

What a superb lunch! (*To KUZOVKIN.*) So, what's the outcome? Who's your case with now, eh?

KUZOVKIN: (*Beginning to get excited from the champagne.*) Well, with Hanginmeister's heirs, of course.

TROPACHEV: And who might he be?

KUZOVKIN: He's a German, obviously. He bought up all the notes, you see, though some people say he just took them. That's my opinion too. He just frightened the womenfolk and took them.

TROPACHEV: And what was Katerina doing? And the Polish woman's son, Ilya?

KUZOVKIN: Oh! They're all dead and gone now. The Polish woman's son burned to death, in a tavern on the highway – he was drunk, and there was a fire. (*To IVANOV.*) Stop tugging at my sleeve! I'm trying to explain something to the gentlemen, it's perfectly all right. They've asked me to, I'm not doing anything wrong.

YELETSKY: Let him be, Mr Ivanov, we're enjoying listening to him.

KUZOVKIN: (*To IVANOV.*) You see? (*To YELETSKY and TROPACHEV.*) I mean, what am I asking for, gentlemen? I'm asking for justice, a proper ordering of things by law. I'm not ambitious. What do I want with ambition? Judge between us, I say, and if I'm in the wrong, well, so be it. But if I'm in the right... if I'm in the right...

TROPACHEV: (*Interrupting him.*) Now, what about another little glass?

KUZOVKIN: Oh no, sir, thank you very much. I mean, that's all I'm asking, sir...

TROPACHEV: Well, let me give you a hug, my friend, in any event.

KUZOVKIN: (*A little taken aback.*) Sir, I'm greatly honoured... I'm extremely...

TROPACHEV: No no, I like you a lot... (*Puts his arm round KUZOVKIN and keeps it there a few moments.*) I'd give you a kiss, my dear chap, but no, I think I'll save that for later!

KUZOVKIN: As you please, sir.

TROPACHEV: (*Winking at KARPACHOV.*) Go on, Karpach, it's your turn...

KARPACHOV: (*With a throaty chuckle.*) Now then, Mr Kuzovkin, let me press you to my heart...

(*Hugs KUZOVKIN and spins round with him. They all laugh,
each in his own way.*)

KUZOVKIN: (*Tearing himself free from KARPACHOV's
embrace.*) That's enough, sir!

KARPACHOV: Oh, don't be so stubborn. (*To
TROPACHEV.*) You'd be better telling him to sing a song,
Mr Tropachev. He's a first-rate singer.

TROPACHEV: Do you sing, my friend? Oh, please, show
us your talent.

KUZOVKIN: (*To KARPACHOV.*) What are you making up
stories about me for? I'm no singer.

KARPACHOV: Well, you used to sing after dinner in the
old master's time, didn't you?

KUZOVKIN: (*Lowering his voice.*) In the master's time, yes,
but I've grown old since then...

TROPACHEV: Good heavens, sir, you're not old!

KARPACHOV: (*Pointing at KUZOVKIN.*) He used to sing,
and dance, too!

TROPACHEV: Really? Well, I can see you're a brave chap,
sir. Now, be a good friend, what do you say?... (*To
YELETSKY, aside.*) C'est un peu vulgaire – but, well, this
is the country. (*Aloud to KUZOVKIN.*) Come on, sir, what
are you waiting for? What about "Down Our Street"?
(*Begins to sing "Down Our Street".*) Well, go on.

KUZOVKIN: Please, sir, I'd rather not...

TROPACHEV: The man's downright obstinate... Yeletsky,
you tell him.

YELETSKY: (*A little diffidently.*) Now, Mr Kuzovkin, you
don't want to sing for us?

KUZOVKIN: Oh, not at my age, sir, please. I'm too old.

TREMBINSKY: (*Smiling ingratiatingly at the company.*) If
I remember rightly, sirs, he was quite outstanding at Mr
Ivanov's brother's wedding, not so long ago.

TROPACHEV: You see?

TREMBINSKY: He danced right across the room,
squatting on his heels.

TROPACHEV: Oh well, in that case, you can't refuse us.
You surely don't want to offend Mr Yeletsky and me?

KUZOVKIN: Sir, that was of my own free will.

TROPACHEV: Well, now we're asking you. Really, you should bear in mind that your refusal might be construed as ingratitude. And ingratitude... ugh, that's an extremely nasty vice!

KUZOVKIN: But I've no sort of voice, sir, truly. And as far as gratitude is concerned, I'm very well aware of my obligations, sir, and willing to make any sacrifice...

TROPACHEV: But we're not asking you to make a sacrifice... Just sing us a song, that's all. Go on... (*KUZOVKIN is silent.*)
Well?

KUZOVKIN: (*After a moment's silence, begins to sing "Down Our Street", but his voice gives out at the second word.*) No, I can't, sir... Honest to God, sir, I just can't...

TROPACHEV: Oh, come on, don't be shy.

KUZOVKIN: No, sir, I'm not going to sing.

TROPACHEV: You won't?

KUZOVKIN: I can't, sir.

TROPACHEV: Well, in that case, do you know what I'm going to do? You see this glass of champagne? I'm going to pour it down your collar!

KUZOVKIN: (*Agitated.*) Please, sir, don't do that! I don't deserve that. No-one's ever... please, sir, don't, this is embarrassing...

YELETSKY: (*To TROPACHEV.*) *Finissez...* You can see he's upset.

TROPACHEV: (*To KUZOVKIN.*) So you don't want to sing?

KUZOVKIN: Sir, I can't.

TROPACHEV: You don't want to sing? (*Advancing towards him.*) Right, then... one!

KUZOVKIN: (*Pleadingly.*) Mr Yeletsky...

TROPACHEV: Two! (*Getting ever closer to KUZOVKIN.*)

KUZOVKIN: (*Retreating, pathetically.*) Please, sir... why are you treating me like this? I don't even have the honour of knowing you, sir... And I'm a gentleman myself, sir, let me inform you... I can't sing, honestly... you saw that for yourself, sir...

TROPACHEV: For the last time...

KUZOVKIN: Stop it, for goodness' sake! I'm not your clown.

TROPACHEV: Why not? It wouldn't be the first time, would it?

KUZOVKIN: (*Losing his temper.*) Find somebody else to make a fool of!

YELETSKY: Leave him alone, please.

TROPACHEV: Oh, very well. But you do know he used to play the clown here in your father-in-law's time?

KUZOVKIN: That's all in the past now. (*Wipes his face.*) And there's something wrong with my head today, sir, there is, honestly.

YELETSKY: That's all right. Do as you please, sir.

KUZOVKIN: (*Dejectedly.*) You won't be angry with me, sir, will you.

YELETSKY: Oh, nonsense! Why on earth should I be?

KUZOVKIN: Another time, I'd be happy to do it. (*Trying to appear cheerful.*) But please be so good as to forgive me, sir, if I've offended in any way. I got a little heated, gentlemen, I'm afraid. I'm too old, that's what it is, and I'm not used to drinking.

TROPACHEV: Well, at least have another glass.

KUZOVKIN: (*Delightedly.*) With pleasure! Yes, sir, with the greatest of pleasure! (*Takes the glass and drinks.*) To our dear, esteemed host!

TROPACHEV: And you still won't sing for us?

KUZOVKIN: (*The wine has been having its effect on him for quite some time, but with this glass, and now that the danger is past, he suddenly seems very drunk.*) I can't, sir, honest to God. (*Laughs.*) True enough, I used to be a fair singer in my day. But times have changed, and these days what am I? A nonentity, that's all. Same as him. (*Points at IVANOV and laughs.*) No use to anybody. Still, if you'll forgive me... I'm too old, that's all. I mean, look at what I've drunk today. Two or three glasses, that's all, and it's gone to my head.

TROPACHEV: (*Who has meanwhile been whispering to KARPACHOV.*) Oh, nonsense – that's what you think! (*KARPACHOV exits, laughing, and takes PYOTR with him.*) Anyway, why didn't you finish telling us your story?

KUZOVKIN: That's right. Of course. I didn't finish it. Well, I'm ready, if you want me to. (*Laughs.*) Only you'll have to indulge me a little... If I can just sit down... It's my legs... they won't hold me up...

TROPACHEV: (*Offering him a chair.*) Please do, what's-your-name – have a seat.

KUZOVKIN: (*Sits down facing the audience and speaks in a rather slurred voice, getting drunker by the minute.*) Now, where did I stop? Oh yes – Hanginmeister. Well, this Hanginmeister, he's German, of course. What did he care? He worked in the... he worked in the commissary department, he'd steal whatever he could lay his hands on... so anyway, he says now the note's his. But I'm a gentleman. Yes, what was I going to say? Well, anyway, he says, either pay up, or hand over the estate... either pay up, or hand over the estate... either pay up... or hand over the... hand over the... either...

TROPACHEV: You're falling asleep, my friend, wake up.

KUZOVKIN: (*Gives a start, and carries on, half-asleep, speaking with some difficulty.*) Who? Me? Not at all – what makes you think... well, anyway.... I'm not asleep. People sleep at night, and this is daytime. It's surely not night, is it? Anyway, about this Hanginmeister... This Hanginmeister... Han... gin... meister... He's my real enemy. People say one thing and another, but I say no, I say Hanginmeister... Han-gin-meister – he's the one who's ruined me...
(*KARPACHOV enters with a huge dunce's cap made out of blue sugar paper, and with a wink to TROPACHEV, steals up behind KUZOVKIN. TREMBINSKY bursts out laughing. IVANOV, pale and dejected, looks down at his feet.*)
And I know why he doesn't like me... I know he's ruined my whole life, this Hanginmeister... Right from when I was a child...

(*KARPACHOV carefully places the cap on KUZOVKIN's head.*)
But I forgive him... God help him... Yes, God help him...
(*Everyone is giggling. KUZOVKIN stops, and looks round, bewildered. IVANOV goes up to him, takes him by the arm, and hisses in his ear: "Look what they've put on your head... they're making a fool of you!" Kuzovkin lifts his hands to his head, feels the dunce's cap, slowly lowers his hands to his face, closes his eyes and begins to weep, murmuring through his tears: "Why? Why? Why?", without removing the cap. TROPACHEV, TREMBINSKY and KARPACHOV are still giggling. PYOTR is also laughing, looking round from behind the door.*)

YELETSKY: That's enough. You should be ashamed of
yourself, Mr Kuzovkin, crying over such a trivial thing.

KUZOVKIN: (*Taking his hands away from his face.*) Trivial?
No, it's not trivial, Mr Yeletsky... (*Stands up and flings
the dunce's cap to the floor.*) On the very day of your
arrival... the very first day... (*His voice is breaking.*) This
is how you treat an old man, sir... an old man! Like
this! Why? Why should you trample me in the mud?
What harm have I ever done you? Tell me, please!
And I was so happy, looking forward to your
coming... Why, Mr Yeletsky?

TROPACHEV: Oh, for heaven's sake, what's the matter
with you?

KUZOVKIN: (*Turning pale, beginning to lose control of
himself.*) I'm not speaking to you. You were pleased to
make a fool of me, sir, and you're happy. I'm speaking to
you, Pavel Nikolaich. Just because your late father-in-law
used to have a little fun with me, for the bread he gave
me, and the old shoes – does that mean you must also?
Oh, yes, I paid for those little gifts he made me, with
bitter tears! What, are you envious of me too? Oh, Pavel
Nikolaich! Shame on you, sir, shame on you! An
educated man, from St Petersburg!

YELETSKY: (*Haughtily.*) Now, look here – you seem to
have forgotten yourself. Go to your room, sir, and sleep
it off. You're drunk, you can barely stand.

KUZOVKIN: (*Even more recklessly.*) I'll sleep it off all right, Pavel Nikolaich... Maybe I am drunk, but who got me that way, eh? That's not the point, sir. And note this – you've held me up to ridicule in front of everybody, you've flung mud at me, the very first day of your homecoming... and if I wanted, if I were to say one word...

IVANOV: (*Sotto voce.*) Vasily, remember where you are!

KUZOVKIN: Leave me alone! Oh yes, my dear sir, if I were to tell...

YELETSKY: Oh! The man's blind drunk, he doesn't know what he's saying!

KUZOVKIN: Excuse me, sir. I'm drunk, yes, but I know what I'm saying. I mean, look at you now: a great man, a government official, well educated – and look at me: a clown, a fool, without so much as a kopeck to my name, a beggar, living on charity... but do you know who I am, sir? You're married, yes... But who did you marry, eh?

YELETSKY: (*Tries to usher TROPACHEV out.*) I do beg your pardon, I really didn't expect this kind of nonsense...

TROPACHEV: Well, it's my fault, I suppose...

YELETSKY: (*To TREMBINSKY.*) Take him away, please...
(*Makes to go into the drawingroom.*)

KUZOVKIN: No, wait a minute, dear sir... You haven't yet told me who you've married...
(*OLGA appears in the doorway of the drawingroom, and stands there looking bewildered. Her husband signals to her to go away, but she doesn't understand him.*)

YELETSKY: (*To KUZOVKIN.*) Get out of here!

TREMBINSKY: (*Goes up to KUZOVKIN and takes him by the arm.*) Come on...

KUZOVKIN: (*Pushes him away.*) Stop pulling me, you!
(*Pursuing YELETSKY.*) Yes, you're the master, a great man, isn't that so? And you're married to Olga Petrovna... Olga Korina... And the Korins are an old family, an old established family... but do you know who she really is? Olga Petrovna? Eh? She's... She's my daughter!

(*OLGA vanishes.*)

YELETSKY: (*Stopped in his tracks, as though thunderstruck.*)
What! Have you gone mad?!

KUZOVKIN: (*After a moment's silence, clutches his head.*) Yes,
I've gone mad...

(*He rushes out, staggering, from the room, followed by IVANOV.*)

YELETSKY: (*Turning to TROPACHEV.*) The man's crazy...

TROPACHEV: Oh, for sure!

(*They exit quietly to the drawingroom. TREMBINSKY and
KARPACHOV look at each other in astonishment.*)

(*Curtain.*)

ACT TWO

The scene is a drawingroom, richly furnished in the old-fashioned manner. To the right is a door leading into the sitting-room, to the left another leading to OLGA PETROVNA's room. OLGA is sitting on a settee, with her housekeeper PRASKOVYA standing nearby.

PRASKOVYA: (*After a silence.*) Well then, ma'am, which of the girls do you wish me to appoint as your personal maids?

OLGA: (*A little impatiently.*) Whichever you like.

PRASKOVYA: Akulina, the lame girl, is very good. So is Marfa, Marchukov's daughter. Will you have them?

OLGA: What do you call that girl... she's quite good-looking... the one in the blue dress?

PRASKOVYA: (*Doubtfully.*) The blue dress? Oh, yes, that must be Mashka you mean. Well, it's up to you, ma'am, but she's a rather pert creature, really quite cheeky. She's extremely disobedient, and her behaviour in general leaves something to be desired. However, if that's your wish, ma'am...

OLGA: I like the look of her, but if she's so badly behaved...

PRASKOVYA: Dreadful, ma'am. She's quite impossible, not worth even... (*Falls silent.*) Oh, ma'am, you look so lovely – you're so like your dear mother! Like a perfect angel, it makes me so happy just to look at you... Let me kiss your hand, ma'am...

OLGA: All right... now off you go, Praskovya.

PRASKOVYA: Yes, ma'am. You're sure you don't want anything?

OLGA: No, nothing, thank you.

PRASKOVYA: Very well, ma'am. I'll go and tell Akulina and Marfa then, shall I?

OLGA: Yes, that'll be fine.

(*PRASKOVYA makes to exit.*)

Oh, and tell someone I'd like a word with Pavel Nikolaich.

PRASKOVYA: Yes, ma'am. (*Exits.*)

OLGA: (*Alone.*) What does it mean? What was it
I overheard yesterday? I haven't been able to sleep the
whole night. That old man must be mad... (*Rises, begins
pacing around the room.*) "She's my daughter..." Yes, yes,
those were his exact words. But that's madness...
(*Stops.*) My husband still doesn't suspect anything...
Here he comes now.
(*YELETSKY enters, looking very worried.*)

YELETSKY: You wanted to see me, Olya?

OLGA: Yes, I wanted to ask you... The paths round the pond
in the garden are quite overgrown with grass. They've
cleaned them up in front of the house, but they seem to
have forgotten those... Perhaps you could tell them...

YELETSKY: I've already given orders.

OLGA: Ah. Thank you... Oh, and you might ask them to
buy some little bells in town – they're for my cows, to
hang round their necks.

YELETSKY: I'll see that's done. (*Makes to exit.*) Is there
anything else you'd like?

OLGA: Well... are you busy at the moment?

YELETSKY: I've had the accounts brought in from the office.

OLGA: Oh, well, in that case I won't detain you... we can
ride out to the woods before dinner.

YELETSKY: Yes, of course. (*Again makes to exit.*)

OLGA: Darling...

YELETSKY: Yes?

OLGA: Listen... tell me, please... I didn't have time to ask
you last night, but what exactly was the trouble at
lunch yesterday?

YELETSKY: Oh, that? Nothing, really. A little unpleasantness,
that's all – I'm just annoyed it happened on the very day of
our homecoming. Actually, it was partly my fault. We took
it into our heads to get that old man, Kuzovkin, drunk – or
rather, it was really our neighbour's idea, Monsieur
Tropachev. Anyway, he was quite amusing to start with,
chattering on with all sorts of tales – then he got a bit out
of hand, said some pretty stupid things... well, it doesn't
matter. It's not worth mentioning.

OLGA: I see. Well, it seemed to me as if...

YELETSKY: Oh, no, no... we'll just have to be more careful in future, that's all. (*After a pause.*) Anyway, I've taken the necessary steps.

OLGA: What steps?

YELETSKY: Well... it was nothing, really, but I mean, there were other people present, they saw and heard it all, and it's not right in a respectable house. So, as I say, I've made certain arrangements.

OLGA: What arrangements?

YELETSKY: Well... actually, I... well, I explained to the old man how awkward it would be for him to continue living here, after that sort of carry-on, as you yourself said. And he immediately agreed with me – he was quite sober by then. Of course, he's got no money, nothing to live on, but we can send him to one of your other villages, find him a room there, fix him up with a regular income, bed and board, and so on. He'll be very happy with that... I won't deny him anything, that goes without saying.

OLGA: Really, darling, don't you think you're being a little hard on him, for such a trifle? He's been living in this house for so long now... he's got used to it, he's known me since I was a child. I think he should stay.

YELETSKY: Olya, no – I have my reasons. Of course we can't be too hard on the old man, especially since he wasn't quite himself. Nevertheless, you must let me manage this affair in my own way. I say again, I have good reason – it's really quite important.

OLGA: As you wish.

YELETSKY: Anyway, I think he's already packed his things.

OLGA: He surely won't leave without saying goodbye?

YELETSKY: No, I think he'll come to say goodbye. However, if that's going to be... well, a bit awkward for you, you needn't see him.

OLGA: On the contrary, I should very much like a word with him.

YELETSKY: As you wish, Olya my dear, but I wouldn't advise it. You're likely to be upset – he's an old man, after all, he's known you since childhood. And to be honest, I frankly shouldn't like to change my decision.

OLGA: No, no, you needn't worry. I'm just afraid he might leave without saying goodbye. Darling, please send someone to see if he's still here.

YELETSKY: Yes, of course. (*Rings.*) *Vous êtes jolie, comme un ange, aujourd'hui.*

PYOTR: (*Entering.*) You rang, sir?

YELETSKY: Yes, be a good chap, go and find out if Mr Kuzovkin's still here. (*Looks at OLGA.*) So you want him to come and say goodbye?

PYOTR: Very well, sir. (*Exits.*)

OLGA: Darling... I have another request to make.

YELETSKY: (*Tenderly.*) Yes, of course. What is it?

OLGA: Well... when he comes... Kuzovkin... please leave me alone with him.

YELETSKY: (*After a pause, with a cold smile.*) Mm... I think... not. No, it'll be very awkward for you.

OLGA: Not at all. Please – I have something I want to discuss with him. Something I need to ask him... I really would like a word with him in private.

YELETSKY: (*Looking at her fixedly.*) Is it about yesterday? Is it possible you...

OLGA: (*With the most innocent expression.*) What, darling?

YELETSKY: (*Hurriedly.*) Nothing, nothing – do as you please.

(*KUZOVKIN enters, looking very pale.*)

OLGA: Good morning, Vasily Petrovich...

(*KUZOVKIN bows silently.*)

How are you? (*To YELETSKY.*) *Eh bien, mon ami? Je vous en prie...*

YELETSKY: *Oui, oui.* (*To KUZOVKIN.*) You've got everything packed?

KUZOVKIN: (*Dully.*) Everything's packed.

YELETSKY: Olga Petrovna would like a word with you... to say goodbye to you. And please, if there's anything you need, do tell her... (*To OLGA.*) *Au revoir...* You won't be long with him, will you?

OLGA: I don't know. I don't think so.

YELETSKY: Very well... (*Exits to the sitting-room.*)

(*OLGA sits down on the settee and motions KUZOVKIN towards an armchair.*)

OLGA: Please be seated, Vasily Petrovich.

(*KUZOVKIN bows, and remains standing.*)

Please... Sit down...

(*KUZOVKIN does so. For a few moments, OLGA doesn't know where to begin.*)

Well... I hear you're leaving us.

KUZOVKIN: (*Without looking up.*) That's right, ma'am.

OLGA: My husband told me about it. You must believe me, I'm very unhappy that...

KUZOVKIN: Please – don't concern yourself, ma'am. I'm most grateful to you, truly...

OLGA: Well... you'll be just as comfortable in your new home – even more so. You needn't worry, I'll see to everything.

KUZOVKIN: I'm much obliged to you, ma'am, but I honestly don't deserve all this. A bite to eat, and a corner somewhere – I don't need anything more, ma'am. (*After a silence, he rises to go.*) If I might say goodbye now... I've been very foolish... please forgive an old man.

OLGA: Why are you in such a hurry? Stay, please...

KUZOVKIN: As you wish, ma'am. (*Sits down again.*)

OLGA: (*After a pause.*) Vasily Petrovich, listen... tell me honestly what happened yesterday morning.

KUZOVKIN: It was my fault, ma'am, no-one else's.

OLGA: Yes, but how did you come to...

KUZOVKIN: Please, ma'am, don't ask me... it doesn't matter. I was to blame, and that's all there is to it. Pavel Nikolaich is quite right. He should have punished me even more severely. I shall pray for him as long as I live.

OLGA: Quite frankly, I can't see any great fault. I mean, you're no longer a young man – most likely you're not used to drinking, and well, you got a little noisy, that's all.

KUZOVKIN: No, ma'am, please – don't make excuses for me. I thank you most humbly, but only I know my own guilt.

OLGA: Or perhaps you said something to offend my husband, or Mr Tropachev?

KUZOVKIN: (*Hanging his head.*) It was my own fault.

OLGA: (*A note of agitation.*) Vasily Petrovich, listen... do you remember everything you said?

KUZOVKIN: (*Shudders, then looks up at OLGA, slowly.*) Ma'am, I don't know what I said.

OLGA: Apparently you said something...

KUZOVKIN: (*Hurriedly.*) It was a lie, ma'am – a barefaced lie. I just said the first thing that came into my mind. I'm so sorry, ma'am – I wasn't in my right mind.

OLGA: Yes, yes... but for something like that suddenly to come into your mind...

KUZOVKIN: God knows why, ma'am, it just did. Sheer madness, that's all. I've got quite out of the way of drinking, that's true. And I got drunk, and that's what happened. God only knows what I said! These things happen. But I'm to blame, ma'am, and rightly punished for it. (*Makes to rise.*) I'll say goodbye now, ma'am... Please don't think too badly of me.

OLGA: I can see you don't want to be open with me. You needn't be afraid of me. I'm not Pavel Nikolaich. I dare say you're afraid of him, because you don't know him, and he does look quite forbidding. But why should you be afraid of me? I mean, you've known me since I was a child.

KUZOVKIN: Ma'am, you have the heart of an angel. Have mercy on a poor old man.

OLGA: Heavens! On the contrary, I would like...

KUZOVKIN: Please, ma'am, don't remind me of your childhood, I feel bad enough as it is... I'm bitterly unhappy. To have to leave your house in my old age – and through my own fault...

OLGA: Vasily Petrovich, listen to me – there's still a way out of your troubles. Only you must be frank with me. Listen... I... (*Suddenly rises, and walks a little way apart.*)

KUZOVKIN: Ma'am, please – don't concern yourself, it's not worth it, honestly. I'll pray for you even there. And you'll think of me now and again, and say, "Well, old man Kuzovkin was devoted to me..."

OLGA: Vasily Petrovich... are you truly devoted to me? Do you truly love me?

KUZOVKIN: Oh, my dear lady – just say the word, and I would die for you.

OLGA: No, no, I'm not asking for your life, I just want the truth... the truth, that's all.

KUZOVKIN: Yes.

OLGA: What you shouted... your last words... I heard them.

KUZOVKIN: (*Scarcely able to speak.*) What... last words?

OLGA: I heard... what you said about me.

(*KUZOVKIN rises from the armchair and falls to his knees.*) Is it true?

KUZOVKIN: (*Stammering.*) Oh, God, oh no... oh, forgive me, ma'am... have mercy... it was madness, I've already told you... (*His voice breaks.*)

OLGA: No, you don't want to tell me the truth.

KUZOVKIN: A moment of madness – oh, please forgive me, ma'am...

OLGA: (*Seizing him by the hand.*) No, no! For the love of God, I'm begging you – please, tell me – is it true? Is it? (*A silence.*)

For God's sake, why are you torturing me like this?

KUZOVKIN: You want to know the truth?

OLGA: Yes, yes – tell me. Is it true?

(*KUZOVKIN looks up at OLGA. His expression reveals a fierce inner struggle. Suddenly he hangs his head and whispers, "It's true." OLGA hurriedly steps back from him and stands motionless. KUZOVKIN covers his face with his hands. The sitting-room door opens, and YELETSKY enters. At first he does not notice KUZOVKIN, who is still kneeling, and goes up to his wife.*)

YELETSKY: Well, then – have you finished? (*Stops short in amazement.*) Et voilà, je vous ai dit... He's begging your forgiveness...

OLGA: Darling, leave us alone...

YELETSKY: (*Puzzled.*) Mais, ma chère...

OLGA: Please, darling – leave us...

YELETSKY: (*After a pause.*) Well, all right, but I hope you'll
    explain this riddle to me...
    (*OLGA nods her head, and YELETSKY slowly exits. She then
    goes up to the sitting-room door, locks it, and turns to KUZOVKIN,
    who is still kneeling.*)

OLGA: Please, get up – do as I say.

KUZOVKIN: (*Slowly rises.*) Olga Petrovna... (*He is obviously
    at a loss for words.*)

OLGA: (*Motioning him to the settee.*) Please sit down.
    (*KUZOVKIN does so. OLGA remains standing, a little way off
    and to one side.*)
    Vasily Petrovich... you understand my position...

KUZOVKIN: (*Weakly.*) Yes, yes, my dear lady, I can see...
    I simply lost my mind... Please let me leave, before I do
    any more harm. I don't know what I'm saying.

OLGA: (*Breathing heavily.*) No, stop... The deed's done now.
    You can't take back your words. You must tell me
    everything... the whole truth... now.

KUZOVKIN: But I...

OLGA: (*Quickly.*) Listen, I want you to understand my
    position, and yours, once and for all... And you have
    either slandered my mother, in which case you are to
    leave this house immediately, and never come into my
    presence again...
    (*She points towards the door. KUZOVKIN attempts to stand up,
    but slumps back down again.*)
    Ah, so you're staying? You see, you're not leaving...

KUZOVKIN: (*Mournfully.*) Oh, God in heaven...

OLGA: I want to know everything... You must tell me
    everything, do you hear?

KUZOVKIN: (*In despair.*) Yes... yes... You shall know
    everything, since that's the unhappy fate that has befallen
    me... Only please don't look at me like that, Olga
    Petrovna... otherwise I... I just can't...

OLGA: (*Trying to smile.*) Vasily Petrovich, I...

KUZOVKIN: (*Meekly.*) I'm sorry... my name is Vasily
    Semyonych...

(*OLGA is embarrassed, shrugs her shoulders. She remains at some distance from KUZOVKIN.*)

Yes... well, anyway... where shall I begin?

OLGA: (*Confused.*) Vasily Semyonych, please... wherever you wish, just as long as I...

KUZOVKIN: (*On the verge of tears.*) But I can't... I can't speak when you...

OLGA: (*Reaches out her hand to him.*) Calm yourself, please... just tell me. You can see what a state I'm in. Pull yourself together.

KUZOVKIN: Yes. Yes, dear lady. Well... where shall I begin? Oh, God... Yes, yes. That's it. If you'll permit me, I'll tell you a little bit first. Well... Here goes... I was just over twenty at the time... I have to say, I had been born to poverty, and eventually I was left without even a bite to eat, because of an injustice, I may tell you... Anyway, I had no proper upbringing, needless to say, and your late father...

(*OLGA shudders.*)

Your late father, God bless him, took pity on me, otherwise I would've gone under. You can stay in my house, he said, until I find you a position. That's how I came to move into your father's house. Well, of course, it wasn't an easy matter, finding me a place, so I stayed on here. Your father was still a bachelor at that time, but he started seeing your mother a couple of years later, and eventually married her. So, anyway, he was living with your mother, and she gave him two sons... both boys died soon afterwards. Olga Petrovna, I have to tell you that your late father was a very hard man... very strict, God forgive him, and a little too ready with his fists. And when people like that get angry, well, they just forget themselves. He used to drink a lot, too. Still, he was a good man at heart, and he was my benefactor. Well, anyway, your father and mother lived together quite happily at first. But that didn't last. Your dear mother, God bless her, was a perfect angel, I may say, a very beautiful woman... Oh, yes... But then Fate... There

was a neighbour of ours at that time, a young woman...
And your father got very attached to her... Olga
Petrovna, please forgive me, if I'm...

OLGA: Go on.

KUZOVKIN: Well, you asked me to tell you... Oh, God
help me, wretched sinner that I am! Your father got
involved with this woman, may God punish her – and
he would visit her every single day, and often not even
come home at night. Things went from bad to worse.
Your mother used to sit all alone, whole days on end,
saying nothing. Either that or just weep. And of course,
I'm sitting there, my heart's breaking, but I daren't
open my mouth. Anyway, what could I say, a stupid
creature like me? And the other neighbours, I have to
say, the local landowners, never came near your father,
he'd driven everybody away from the house with his
arrogance. So your mother had no-one to exchange so
much as a word with. She used to sit there, the poor
woman, by the window, not even reading a book, just
gazing out at the road, and the fields. Meanwhile while
father – God only knows why, because no-one dared
contradict him – but your father's temper got even
worse. He became so violent, it was dreadful. And
what's really astonishing is that he took into his head to
be suspicious of your mother, and God knows there was
no-one to be jealous of. He would drive off somewhere,
and leave her locked up, for heaven's sake! He would
fly into a rage at the most trifling thing. And the harder
your mother tried to placate him, the angrier he got.
Finally, he stopped talking to her altogether, and just
cast her aside. Oh, Olga Petrovna, Olga Petrovna – you
have no idea what your poor mother suffered then! You
don't remember her, my dearest child, you were too
young when she died. She was such a kind soul, there's
no-one like her left on this earth. And she loved your
father so much! He wouldn't even look at her, and yet
when he was away she did nothing but talk about him
the whole time – how could she make things right, what

could she do to please him? And then suddenly one day your father packed his things and left – yes, for Moscow, he says, I'm going away by myself, on business. But that woman was waiting for him at the very next station, and they went away together – for six months... yes, for six long months, Olga Petrovna! And not so much as a letter home, all that time. Then he suddenly appeared again, in a foul mood, raging... We discovered later that she'd thrown him over. So he locked himself into his room, wouldn't even show his face. Even the servants were astonished at his behaviour. Your dear mother finally couldn't stand it any longer... she crossed herself – yes, the poor creature was so frightened of him – and went into his room. At first she tried to talk him round, but he suddenly started shouting at her, and lifted a stick to her... (*KUZOVKIN looks at OLGA.*) I'm so sorry, Olga Petrovna.

OLGA: You're telling me the truth, Vasily Semyonych?

KUZOVKIN: May God strike me down dead on this spot.

OLGA: Go on.

KUZOVKIN: So... then he... Oh, Olga Petrovna, he abused your mother most dreadfully, in word and in... in other ways... The poor woman was almost out of her mind, and she ran back into her own room. He shouted for the servants, even the ones in the distant fields. And then... then... something happened... (*His voice falters.*) Olga Petrovna, I can't go on... God help me, I just can't...

OLGA: (*Without looking at him.*) Tell me. (*After a pause, impatiently.*) Tell me!

KUZOVKIN: Very well. Ma'am, it's my guess that this terrible insult somehow turned your dear mother's mind... a sickness took hold of her... I can see her even now... she went into the icon-room, and stood for a while in front of the icons. Then she lifted her hand as if to cross herself, suddenly turned round and walked out... she even started laughing, very quietly... It was as if the Evil One had got the better of her. I was almost frightened to look at her. She wouldn't eat anything,

didn't speak, just kept staring at me. And in the
evening... Ma'am, in the evenings I used to sit with her
in this very room. Sometimes we'd play cards, to pass
the time, and sometimes we'd talk a little... Well, ma'am
– that evening... (*He is almost choking with emotion.*)
Ma'am, your dear mother... she sat saying nothing for
ages, then she suddenly rushed towards me... Olga
Petrovna, I almost worshipped your mother, I loved her
dearly, and she suddenly said to me: "Vasily Semyonych,
I know you love me, and he despises me – he's cast me
aside, he's insulted me... Well, then, I'm going to..."
Ma'am, she must have lost her reason, because of the
injury she'd suffered – she didn't know what she was
doing... And I... I... I don't understand it, ma'am, my
head was spinning – it frightens me even now to think of
it, but that evening, she suddenly... Oh, God – Olga
Petrovna, have mercy on a poor old man... I can't go
on... I'd sooner have my tongue cut out!
(*OLGA silently turns away. KUZOVKIN looks at her, and
continues in agitation.*)
Ma'am, I left the house the very next day, as you can
imagine. I remember running off into the forest at dawn.
And the day after that, a messenger comes galloping into
the yard... He told them the master had fallen from his
horse, he'd fatally injured himself, and he was lying
unconscious somewhere... the very next day, Olga
Petrovna, the very next day! Your mother immediately
ordered a carriage and went to see him. He was lying in
a little village on the steppe, in a priest's house, about
thirty miles away. She drove as fast as she could, but he
was dead by the time she got there... Oh, dear God! We
thought she'd go out of her mind completely. She was
sick right up until the time of your birth, and she didn't
get any better afterwards... You know yourself, she wasn't
long for this world...
(*Hangs his head.*)

OLGA: (*After a long silence.*) Then perhaps... perhaps I am
your daughter. What proof do you have?

KUZOVKIN: (*Agitated.*) Proof? What proof could I have, Olga Petrovna? I don't have any proof! How would I dare? And if it hadn't been for yesterday's misfortune, I'd never have uttered a word, not even on my death-bed – I'd have torn my tongue out sooner! If only I'd died yesterday! Until yesterday, not a single soul knew about it – please, ma'am, you must believe me. Living here on my own, I didn't even dare think of it. After the death of your... your father, I wanted to run away, as far as my legs would carry me, but I hadn't the strength, I'm sorry to say – I was afraid of poverty, of being in dire need. So I stayed, it's my own fault. But while I was with your dear mother, ma'am, while she was still alive, I never mentioned it, I didn't breathe a word about it. Proof! For the first few months I didn't even see your mother – she shut herself up in her room, and apart from her maid Praskovya, she wouldn't let anyone else near her. Later... Later on, I did see her, but I swear before God, I was afraid to look her in the eye... Proof! Olga Petrovna, please, I'm not a criminal, and I'm not a fool – I know my place. If you hadn't commanded me... please, ma'am, don't get upset. What is there to worry about? What proof do I have? You don't even need to believe me, an old fool like me. I've told a lie, and that's that. I mean, sometimes I don't know what I'm saying myself... My mind's going... Don't believe me, Olga Petrovna, that's all. What proof have I!

OLGA: No, Vasily Semyonych, I won't try to dissemble with you... You couldn't have made up a story like that. Slandering the dead, it's too awful... (*She turns away from him.*) No, I believe you.

KUZOVKIN: (*Feebly.*) You believe me?

OLGA: Yes... (*Looks at him and shudders.*) But this is frightful, terrible! (*Quickly moves away.*)

KUZOVKIN: (*Reaches out to her.*) Olga Petrovna, please, don't worry. I understand you. With your upbringing... If it wasn't for that, I would tell you what I'm really like – I know myself well enough. Do you think I don't feel all

this? Believe me, I love you as if you were my own. And
after all, you are my... (*Hastily rises.*) Have no fear, that
word shall never pass my lips. Forget everything we've
said, and I shall leave here today, this very moment.
I can't stay here any longer, it's impossible. And I can
pray for you just as well... (*Tears well up in his eyes.*) For
you, and your dear husband, wherever I am. It's my own
fault – yes, I can say I've deprived myself of my last
chance of happiness. (*Weeps.*)

OLGA: (*Intensely agitated.*) What can this mean? He is my
father, after all... (*Turns round and catches sight of him
weeping.*) He's crying... No, please don't cry... (*She goes up
to him.*)

KUZOVKIN: (*Holds out his hand to her.*) Goodbye, Olga
Petrovna...
(*OLGA also holds out her hand to him, a little indecisively – she
tries to force herself to embrace him, but turns on her heel with a
shudder and flees into the study. KUZOVKIN remains rooted to
the spot. He clutches his heart.*)
Oh God, oh God, what's happening to me?

YELETSKY. (*Off-stage.*) Olya, you've locked the door!
Olya!

KUZOVKIN: (*Coming to his senses.*) Who's that?... It's him...
Yes... What now?

YELETSKY: (*Off-stage.*) Olya, Mr Tropachev's come to see
us. *Je vous l'annonce...* Olya, answer me, please... Vasily
Semyonych, are you there?

KUZOVKIN: Yes, sir.

YELETSKY: And where is Olga Petrovna?

KUZOVKIN: She's gone out, sir.

YELETSKY: Oh! Open the door, please.
(*KUZOVKIN opens the door. YELETSKY enters, looks round
the room.*)
This is all very peculiar. (*To KUZOVKIN, coldly, unsmiling.*)
You're leaving?

KUZOVKIN: Yes, sir.

YELETSKY: I see. So, exactly what was the outcome of
your conversation?

KUZOVKIN: Conversation... There wasn't any conversation, sir, to be honest. I simply asked Olga Petrovna's forgiveness.

YELETSKY: And what did she say?

KUZOVKIN: She said she was no longer angry with me... and now I'm getting ready to leave.

YELETSKY: So, the upshot was, Olga Petrovna did not change my decision?

KUZOVKIN: Not at all, sir.

YELETSKY: Hm... I'm very sorry... but you do understand, Vasily Semyonych, that I can't...

KUZOVKIN: Oh, absolutely not, sir – I couldn't agree more. You've treated me most graciously, sir. I thank you from the bottom of my heart.

YELETSKY: Well, I'm pleased to see you at least acknowledge your fault. Anyway... goodbye. And please – if you should need anything, don't hesitate to ask. I've given orders to the steward, of course, but you can approach me directly in any event.

KUZOVKIN: Thank you very much, sir. (*Bows.*)

YELETSKY: Goodbye, Mr Kuzovkin. Oh, wait a moment – one more thing... Er... Mr Tropachev has just called on us – he's coming in here now... I'd like you to repeat what you told me this morning, in his presence.

KUZOVKIN: Very well, sir.

YELETSKY: Good. (*To TROPACHEV, as he enters.*) Mais venez donc! Venez donc!
(*TROPACHEV goes up to him, striking a pose as usual.*)
Well, then – who won?

TROPACHEV: I did, of course. But that's an exceptionally fine billiard table you have. Would you believe it? Monsieur Ivanov declined to play with me! I've got a headache, he says. Monsieur Ivanov has a headache, eh? *Et madame?* I trust she's well?

YELETSKY: She is, thank goodness. She'll be in presently.

TROPACHEV: (*With easy familiarity.*) You know, your coming here is a real stroke of luck for us country types

– hee-hee, *une bonne fortune...* (*Looks round and spots KUZOVKIN.*) Goodness me, are you here too? (*KUZOVKIN silently bows.*)

YELETSKY: (*To TROPACHEV, nodding in KUZOVKIN's direction.*) Yes, he's terribly embarrassed today, after yesterday's nonsense – he's been begging everybody's pardon since this morning.

TROPACHEV: Really? Obviously can't hold his liquor, eh? Well, what do you say?

KUZOVKIN: (*Without looking up.*) It's my own fault, sir. I lost my head completely.

TROPACHEV: Aha! You see? Well, then, my lord Vetrovo... (*To YELETSKY.*) You know, people do have some funny ideas. After that, it's no surprise there's some madman... oh, I don't know... he thinks he's the Emperor of China, for instance, or another one who imagines he's got the sun and moon, and God knows what else, inside his stomach! Hee-hee! Yes, that's the way of it, my lord Vetrovo.

YELETSKY: (*Anxious to change the subject.*) Hm... yes. Now, there was something I was meaning to ask you, sir... oh yes, when shall we go hunting?

TROPACHEV: Whenever you like. I mean, you can see I don't stand on ceremony with you. I was here yesterday, and I'm back again today. So, you should be the same with me. Hold on a second, I'll ask Karpachov. He knows more about these things. He'll tell us where to go. (*Goes over to the drawingroom doors.*) Karpachov! Come here, my friend! (*To YELETSKY.*) He's a first-rate shot, though I always murder him at billiards. (*KARPACHOV enters.*) Karpachov – Mr Yeletsky here wants to go hunting tomorrow – where should we go, eh?

KARPACHOV: We should go to Koloberdovo, and head for Vokhryak. There'll be plenty of blackcock there now.

YELETSKY: Is it far from here?

KARPACHOV: It's about twenty miles by road, but it'll be a bit less cross-country.

YELETSKY: Well, that's fine.

(*PRASKOVYA enters from the study.*)

Yes, what is it?

PRASKOVYA: (*Curtseys to YELETSKY.*) Sir, the mistress would like to see you.

YELETSKY: What for?

PRASKOVYA: I don't know, sir.

YELETSKY: Tell her I'm coming in a moment. (*To TROPACHEV.*) Will you excuse me, sir?

(*PRASKOVYA exits.*)

TROPACHEV: (*Shaking his head.*) Oh, my dear sir, how can you ask such a question? Go on, please do...

YELETSKY: I shan't keep you waiting.

(*Exits. KUZOVKIN, who has been standing near the door all this time, tries to take advantage of this moment to leave.*)

TROPACHEV: (*To KUZOVKIN.*) Now where d'you think you're going, my dear fellow? Stay there, we'll have a chat.

KUZOVKIN: Sir, I must go.

TROPACHEV: Oh, nonsense, there's no need. All right, you're a little embarrassed, perhaps, but that's silly – after all, that happens to everybody, surely? (*Takes him by the arm and leads him downstage.*) What I mean is, we all get drunk once in a while, but I must confess, you really surprised us yesterday! That's some family connection you've dug up, eh? You've some imagination, I must say!

KUZOVKIN: It was sheer foolishness, sir.

TROPACHEV: Well, of course, but it was amazing just the same. I mean, why precisely a daughter? Fantastic! Though you must admit you wouldn't turn down a daughter like that, eh? (*Pokes him in the ribs.*) Come on, admit it – you wouldn't, would you? (*To KARPACHOV.*) He's no fool, is he. What do you think?

(*KARPACHOV laughs.*)

KUZOVKIN: (*Tries to free his arm from TROPACHEV's grasp.*) Sir, please...

TROPACHEV: Why did you get so angry with us yesterday, eh? Come on, tell me.

KUZOVKIN: (*Turns away, barely audible.*) I'm sorry, sir...

TROPACHEV: Yes, you are. Well, God will forgive you.
She's your daughter, right?
(*KUZOVKIN is silent.*)
Listen, my dear chap, why don't you ever come to my
place? I'd give you a good dinner.

KUZOVKIN: Thank you very much, sir.

TROPACHEV: It's not bad, you can ask this fellow if you
like. (*Indicating KARPACHOV.*) You could tell me about
this Vetrovo business again.

KUZOVKIN: (*Dully.*) Yes, sir.

TROPACHEV: I don't think you've said hello to
Karpachov today yet, have you. (*To KARPACHOV.*)
Karpach, haven't you said hello to Mr Kuzovkin this
morning?

KARPACHOV: No, sir, I haven't.

TROPACHEV: Mm, that's not very nice, is it.

KARPACHOV: I'll do it right now...
(*He goes up to KUZOVKIN with arms outstretched. KUZOVKIN
retreats. The study door is suddenly flung open and YELETSKY
enters, pale and agitated.*)

YELETSKY: (*Annoyed.*) Mr Tropachev, I thought I asked
you to leave Mr Kuzovkin in peace...
(*TROPACHEV turns round in surprise and looks at YELETSKY.
KARPACHOV remains motionless.*)

TROPACHEV: (*Slightly embarrassed.*) Well, you might
have... I don't remember...

YELETSKY: (*Rather dry and snappish.*) Yes, indeed, sir –
I must confess I'm surprised you're so keen... a man of
your upbringing... your education... that you indulge in
such... well, such frankly silly games. And two days in
succession, moreover.

TROPACHEV: (*Signs to KARPACHOV, who immediately
springs back, out of the way.*) Well, yes, my dear sir, but
surely... I mean, of course, I... Actually, I'm in complete
agreement with you... Although, then again... By the way,
sir, is your good lady well?

YELETSKY: Yes... she'll be in presently. (*Smiles, and grips TROPACHEV's hand.*) You must excuse me, I'm a little out of sorts today.

TROPACHEV: Oh, think nothing of it, my dear sir. Anyway, you're quite right. It doesn't do to be too familiar with these people.
(*YELETSKY winces.*)
What glorious weather we're having!
(*A moment's silence.*)
Yes, you're absolutely right. It's a bad business, staying too long in the country. *On se rouille à la campagne...* It's frightful. Such a bore, you know? There's nothing else to do...

YELETSKY: Mr Tropachev, please, don't give it another thought.

TROPACHEV: No no, it's fine – I'm just speaking generally – just making a general observation.
(*Again, a brief silence.*)
Mm, I don't think I mentioned – I'm going abroad this winter.

YELETSKY: Really? (*To KUZOVKIN, who is again on the point of leaving.*) Mr Kuzovkin, please – wait there... I want to have a talk with you.

TROPACHEV: Yes, I'm thinking of spending a couple of years there. Now, what about *madame?* Shall we have the pleasure of her company today?

YELETSKY: Yes, of course. Meanwhile, perhaps you'd like to take a stroll in the garden? It's a good time for it, don't you think? *Un petit tour?* Only you won't mind if I don't accompany you. I need to have a word with Mr Kuzovkin... I'll be a few minutes, that's all.

TROPACHEV: Feel free, my dear Yeletsky – ha-ha, don't mind me. And don't hurry over your business – this mortal creature and I will meanwhile enjoy the beauties of nature! Yes, I could die for nature! *Venez ici,* Karpach!
(*Exits with KARPACHOV.*)
(*YELETSKY follows them to the door, and locks it. He then returns to KUZOVKIN, and stands with his arms folded.*)

YELETSKY: My dear sir, yesterday I looked upon you as a foolish and intemperate man. Today, I am bound to consider you a slanderer and intriguer! No no, don't interrupt me... A slanderer and intriguer! Olga Petrovna has told me everything. No doubt, my dear sir, you were not expecting that. What explanation can you offer me for your conduct? You confessed to me in person this morning, that everything you said yesterday was a fiction, pure and simple, and now, in conversation with my wife...

KUZOVKIN: Sir, I'm truly sorry... My heart...

YELETSKY: I couldn't care less about your heart. I'm asking you again – you were lying, weren't you? (*KUZOVKIN is silent.*)
You were lying?

KUZOVKIN: I've already told you, sir – I didn't know what I was saying yesterday.

YELETSKY: But you do know what you said today. And after that, you have the nerve to look a decent man in the eye? You're still not destroyed by shame?

KUZOVKIN. Mr Yeletsky, I swear to God, you're too hard on me. Think, please – what benefit could I expect to gain from my talk with Olga Petrovna?

YELETSKY: I'll tell you what benefit. You hoped by this ridiculous story to arouse her compassion. You were counting on her generous spirit... it was money you were after. Oh yes, sir – money. And I'm bound to tell you you've achieved your goal. Now listen here – my wife and I have resolved to give you whatever sum you need to live on, with the proviso, however...

KUZOVKIN: I don't want anything!

YELETSKY: Please, don't interrupt me, sir! With the proviso, that you take up residence somewhere very far away from here. And on my part, I would like to add the following: that in accepting this sum of money from us, you admit to having lied... I can see that word grates on your ears, sir... you admit to having fabricated this whole story, and consequently you forfeit any right to...

KUZOVKIN: I won't take a kopeck from you!

YELETSKY: What? You're holding out? Am I supposed to think you told the truth? Explain yourself, sir!

KUZOVKIN: I have nothing to say. Think whatever you like about me, but I'm not taking any money.

YELETSKY: Well, I've never heard anything like it! Does that mean you're staying on here?

KUZOVKIN: No, I'm leaving this very day!

YELETSKY: You're leaving? But what state are you leaving Olga Petrovna in? You should have thought of that, if you had a drop of feeling left in you.

KUZOVKIN: Please, sir, let me go. God help me, my head's spinning. What is it you want from me?

YELETSKY: I want to know if you'll accept this money. Perhaps you think the sum isn't significant – we'll give you ten thousand roubles.

KUZOVKIN: I can't accept anything.

YELETSKY: You can't? Then perhaps my wife is your... God, I can't get my tongue round the word!

KUZOVKIN: I don't know anything. Please let me go. (*Makes to exit.*)

YELETSKY: This is too much! I can force you to obey me, you do realise that?

KUZOVKIN: And how will you do that, sir, may I ask?

YELETSKY: Look, don't make me lose my patience! Don't force me to remind you what you are!

KUZOVKIN: I'm a member of the nobility, sir – that's what I am!

YELETSKY: Hah! Some nobleman, I must say!

KUZOVKIN: Be that as it may, sir – I can't be bought.

YELETSKY: Now, listen here...

KUZOVKIN: Maybe you can treat your underlings in St. Petersburg that way, but...

YELETSKY: Listen to me, you stubborn old man – you surely don't want to offend your benefactress, do you? You've already admitted the injustice of your words – why not put Olga Petrovna's mind at ease, finally, and

take the money we're offering you? Or are you so rich
that ten thousand roubles doesn't matter to you?

KUZOVKIN: I'm not rich, Mr Yeletsky, but this gift of
yours is a bitter pill to take, and I've swallowed
enough shame already. Indeed I have, sir. You say
I need money – well, I don't. I won't accept a single
rouble from you, sir.

YELETSKY: Oh, I know what you're up to! You're
pretending to be unselfish, because you hope you'll gain
more that way. Well, I'm telling you for the last time:
either you accept this money under the conditions I've set
out to you, or I'll be forced to resort to... to resort to...

KUZOVKIN: For God's sake, what do you want from me!
I'm leaving, but that isn't enough for you. You want me
to disgrace myself, you want to buy me... No, absolutely
not, sir, never!

YELETSKY: Oh, to hell with it! I'll...

(*Just at that moment, TROPACHEV's voice is heard outside in
the garden; he is singing, "I am here, Inezilla, I am here at your
window...".*)

This is intolerable! (*Goes over to the window.*) I'm coming,
I'm coming! (*To KUZOVKIN.*) I'm giving you a quarter
of an hour to think it over... After that, on your own head
be it! (*Exits.*)

KUZOVKIN: Oh, Lord, what are they trying to do to me!
I might as well be buried alive. I've ruined myself. My
tongue's my own worst enemy. This gentleman... God in
heaven, he spoke to me as if I were a dog! As if I had no
soul! If he'd even just killed me!

(*OLGA emerges from the study, holding a paper. KUZOVKIN
looks round.*)

Oh, Lord...

OLGA: (*Goes up to KUZOVKIN, hesitantly.*) I wanted to see
you one more time...

KUZOVKIN: (*Without looking at her.*) Olga Petrovna... why
did you... your husband... why did you tell him...

OLGA: Mr Kuzovkin, I have no secrets from him.

KUZOVKIN: Yes, but...

OLGA: (*Hurriedly.*) He believed me... (*Lowering her voice.*) And he agrees to everything.

KUZOVKIN: Agrees? Agrees to what?

OLGA: Mr Kuzovkin, you're a good man... an honourable man... You'll understand me. Tell me frankly – can you stay here now?

KUZOVKIN: No, I can't.

OLGA: Please, listen to me. I want to know what you think. I've learned to appreciate you, Mr Kuzovkin... Tell me, please – truthfully.

KUZOVKIN: I'm well aware of your kindness, Olga Petrovna, and believe me, I too know how to appreciate... (*He pauses, then continues with a sigh.*) No, I can't stay here – there's no way I can. They'll give me a beating yet, in my old age, there's no denying it. I've quietened down these days, of course – well, the master's been gone from the house a long time now – no call for that sort of thing. But the old people are still alive, and they haven't forgotten... how I was a kind of court jester to your late father. I used to play the fool, under compulsion, but sometimes I myself would...

(*OLGA turns away.*)

Don't be upset, Olga Petrovna... I mean, when all's said and done, I'm a stranger to you. I can't stay here.

OLGA: In that case... please... take this... (*Holds out a piece of paper to him.*)

KUZOVKIN: (*Accepts it doubtfully.*) What's this?

OLGA: It's... we've made over a sum of money... it's to redeem your property at Vetrovo... I hope you won't refuse it from us... from me...

(*KUZOVKIN lets the paper fall and covers his face with his hands.*)

KUZOVKIN: Olga Petrovna, why do you insult me – you of all people?

OLGA: In what way?

KUZOVKIN: You're trying to buy me off. But I've told you, I don't have any kind of proof. How do you know

I haven't made the whole thing up, that my intention all
along wasn't...?

OLGA: (*Interrupting him, agitated.*) If I didn't believe you, do
you think we would have agreed to...?

KUZOVKIN: You believe me – what more can I ask? What
do I want with this paper? I've never indulged myself,
not since childhood, and I'm not going to start now in
my old age. I don't need anything. A crust of bread,
that's all. And if you believe me... (*Stops short.*)

OLGA: Yes, yes, I believe you. You're not trying to trick
me, I know that. I do believe you... (*Suddenly embraces
him and lays her head against his chest.*)

KUZOVKIN: Oh, God... Olga Petrovna, please... please
don't... Olga...
(*Reeling, he slumps into the armchair at left. OLGA holds onto
him with one hand, and quickly retrieving the paper from the
floor with her free hand, hugs him tightly.*)

OLGA: You could refuse some stranger, some wealthy lady
– you could refuse my husband – but you can't refuse,
you mustn't refuse your very own daughter... (*Thrusts the
paper into his hand.*)

KUZOVKIN: (*Accepting it, tearfully.*) My dear lady... please...
whatever you want me to do, tell me... I'll do anything,
gladly. I'll go to the very ends of the earth. Now I can
die happy... I don't need anything now... (*OLGA wipes
away his tears with her handkerchief.*) Oh, Olya, Olya...

OLGA: Don't cry... please don't cry... We'll see each other
again... You'll come and see...

KUZOVKIN: Oh, Olga Petrovna, my Olya... I'm dreaming,
surely?

OLGA: Don't, don't...

KUZOVKIN: (*Hastily.*) Olya, get up – someone's coming...
(*OLGA, who has been almost sitting in his lap, springs to her
feet.*)
Give me your hand, that's all – just one last time...
(*He hurriedly kisses her hand, and OLGA moves apart.
KUZOVKIN tries to stand up, and is unable to. YELETSKY
and TROPACHEV, followed by KARPACHOV, enter through*

the doors at right. OLGA goes over to meet them, past KUZOVKIN, and stands between them and him.)

TROPACHEV: (*Bowing, and striking a pose.*) *Enfin* – we have the good fortune of seeing you, Olga Petrovna. How are you feeling?

OLGA: I'm very well, thank you.

TROPACHEV: Mm, your face... you look as if...

YELETSKY: (*Interrupting him.*) We're both a little out of sorts today.

TROPACHEV: This is delightful here. And your garden is extremely fine.

(*KUZOVKIN manages to rise, with an effort.*)

OLGA: I'm very pleased you like it.

TROPACHEV: (*As if offended.*) No, no, I'm telling you – it is the most charming garden – *mais c'est très beau, très beau...* The trees, the flowers – absolutely everything. Yes, indeed. Nature and poetry – my two weaknesses! But what's this I see? Albums? Why, it's just like a *salon* in St. Petersburg!

YELETSKY: (*Casually, with a meaningful look at his wife.*) So, did you manage to arrange everything?
(*OLGA nods. Out of courtesy, TROPACHEV turns away.*)
And he's accepted? Hm... good. (*Leads her a little way apart.*) You know, I must say again, I don't believe a word of that story, but it's up to you. It's worth ten thousand roubles, for a quiet life.

OLGA: (*Turns back to TROPACHEV, who has begun looking through the album on the table.*) Mr Tropachev, what's that you have there?

TROPACHEV: Oh, I'm sorry – it's your album, dear lady. This is all very nice. Tell me, are you acquainted with the Kovrinskys?

OLGA: No, I'm afraid not.

TROPACHEV: Really? You didn't know them before? Well, I advise you to do so. Their house is practically the finest in the district – or rather it was, up until yesterday, ha-ha!

YELETSKY: (*To KUZOVKIN, meanwhile.*) You're taking the money?

KUZOVKIN: Yes, sir.

YELETSKY: That means you lied?

KUZOVKIN: I lied.

YELETSKY: Hah! (*Turns to TROPACHEV, who is showing off before OLGA, striking an affected pose.*) Well now, Mr Tropachev, we were making fun of Mr Kuzovkin here yesterday, but it seems he's actually won that case of his. He's just had word. While we were walking in the garden.

TROPACHEV: You don't say?

YELETSKY: Yes, indeed. Olga's just told me. Ask him yourself.

TROPACHEV: Is this true, sir?

(*Until the end of this scene, KUZOVKIN is smiling like a contented child, but there is a tearful note in his voice.*)

KUZOVKIN: Yes, sir. Yes. I'm getting it back, sir.

TROPACHEV: Well, congratulations, Mr Kuzovkin, congratulations! (*In an undertone to YELETSKY.*) Hm, I understand... you're getting rid of him politely after yesterday's little...

(*YELETSKY attempts to assure him this is not the case.*) Yes, of course... and so refined, so magnanimous, so tactfully done... yes, very nice indeed. And I'm willing to bet that the idea... (*With a sweet smile at OLGA.*) ... was your dear wife's. Although you too, naturally...

(*YELETSKY smiles. TROPACHEV continues aloud.*) Good, good. So you'll have to go there now, Mr Kuzovkin, look after your estate for a while.

KUZOVKIN: Yes, of course, sir.

YELETSKY: Mr Kuzovkin has just been telling me he's actually going there today.

TROPACHEV: Oh, absolutely. I can well understand his impatience, ha-ha! Well, damn me – they've been leading the man by the nose for years, and now he's finally got his estate back! Why shouldn't he want to go and have a look at his property, eh? *N'est-ce pas,* my dear sir?

KUZOVKIN: Yes, indeed, sir.

TROPACHEV: And you'll have to go into town, of course.

KUZOVKIN: Most likely, sir. To get everything in order.

TROPACHEV: Well, we mustn't detain you.(*Winks at YELETSKY.*) This retired lawyer of yours, this Lychkov, must be quite something, eh? He fixed it all up? (*To KUZOVKIN.*) I take it you're pleased?

KUZOVKIN: Yes, indeed, sir – why shouldn't I be?

TROPACHEV: Well, you'll allow me to come to your housewarming, eh?

KUZOVKIN: I shall be honoured, Mr Tropachev.

TROPACHEV: (*Turning to YELETSKY.*) Now, my dear sir, what d'you say? We really should celebrate... wet this Vetrovo's head, so to speak.

YELETSKY: (*A little hesitantly.*) Mm... yes, perhaps. (*Goes over to the drawingroom door, calls.*) Send Trembinsky in here, please!

TREMBINSKY: (*Quickly leaps out from behind the door.*) Yes, sir?

YELETSKY: Oh! You're here. A bottle of champagne!

TREMBINSKY: (*As he exits.*) Right away, sir!

YELETSKY: Oh, and by the way...
(*TREMBINSKY appears in the doorway again.*)
I think I saw Mr Ivanov in the drawingroom – ask him to come in.

TREMBINSKY: Yes, sir. (*Exits.*)
(*TROPACHEV goes up to OLGA, who has been standing at the table all this time, now leafing through the albums, now gazing tenderly at KUZOVKIN.*)

TROPACHEV: Yes, Madame Kovrinskaya will be absolutely delighted to make your acquaintance – *enchantée, enchantée.* I do hope you'll like her. I'm a friend of the family there, it's like a second home... She's a clever lady, you know, and so... (*Gestures absurdly.*)

OLGA: (*Smiling.*) Really?

TROPACHEV: Oh yes, you'll see.
(*TREMBINSKY enters with the bottles and glasses on a tray.*)
Aha! Now then, Mr Kuzovkin – allow me to congratulate you, most heartily...
(*IVANOV enters, stops in the doorway and bows.*)

OLGA: (*To IVANOV, kindly.*) Good morning, I'm very
pleased to see you... Have you heard the news? Your
friend's got his property at Vetrovo back...
(*IVANOV bows again and goes over to KUZOVKIN.
TREMBINSKY hands everyone a glass of champagne.*)

IVANOV: (*To KUZOVKIN, sotto voce.*) Vasily, what lies are
they telling now?

KUZOVKIN: (*Also sotto voce.*) Vanya, be quiet. I'm happy...

TROPACHEV: (*Glass in hand.*) Here's to our new landowner!

ALL: (*Excluding IVANOV, who doesn't even drink.*) Your good
health! Your good health!

KARPACHOV: (*In a deep voice, alone.*) And long life!
(*TROPACHEV gives him a stern look; KARPACHOV is
embarrassed. KUZOVKIN thanks everyone, bowing and smiling.
YELETSKY appears reserved. OLGA feels uneasy, on the verge
of tears. IVANOV is bewildered, frowning.*)

KUZOVKIN: (*His voice trembling.*) If I may be permitted...
this is such a solemn day for me... I'd like to express my
gratitude for all your kindness...

YELETSKY: (*Interrupting him, sternly.*) Now then, Mr
Kuzovkin – why on earth are you thanking us?

KUZOVKIN: But surely, sir... After all, you are my
benefactor... And as far as my... what would you call it?...
as far as my conduct yesterday is concerned... well, I beg
you to forgive an old man. God knows why I took
offence yesterday, and said such...

YELETSKY: (*Again interrupting him.*) That's all right, that's
fine...

KUZOVKIN: After all, what was there to take offence at?
What harm were they doing? The gentlemen were just
having a little fun... (*Looking at OLGA.*) Anyway, I'm
beginning to ramble... Goodbye, my dear benefactors,
goodbye – may you be well, happy and joyful...

TROPACHEV: Why all the goodbyes, my dear sir? I mean,
it's not as if you were going to Siberia.

KUZOVKIN: (*Deeply moved, continues.*) May the good Lord give
you every blessing... as for me, I've nothing more to ask of
Him, I'm so happy, so... (*Stops short, fighting back tears.*)

YELETSKY: (*Aside, to himself.*) What a carry-on... When's he going to leave?

OLGA: (*To KUZOVKIN.*) Goodbye, Mr Kuzovkin... Once you've settled into your estate, don't forget us. I'll be very pleased to see you... (*Lowering her voice.*) ... to have a talk, just the two of us.

KUZOVKIN: (*Kisses her hand.*) Olga Petrovna... God will reward you.

YELETSKY: Well, then, that's fine, that's fine – goodbye, sir...

KUZOVKIN: Goodbye...

(*He bows, and goes towards the drawingroom door with IVANOV. The others accompany them. At the threshold, TROPACHEV exclaims: "Long live the new owner!" OLGA quickly exits to the study. TROPACHEV then turns to YELETSKY and claps him on the shoulder.*)

TROPACHEV: You know what I'm going to tell you? You're a most honourable man, sir.

YELETSKY: Oh, please! You're too kind...

(*End of the Play.*)

THE BACHELOR

Characters

MOSHKIN (MIKHAIL IVANOVICH)
a collegiate assessor, 50. A sprightly, somewhat fussy, kindhearted man. Trusting and affectionate, of a sanguine temperament

VILITSKY (PYOTR ILYICH – PETYA)
a collegiate secretary, 23. An indecisive, rather weak and selfish person

VON FONK (RODION KARLOVICH)
a titular councillor, 29. A dry, cold individual. Narrowminded and given to pedantry. Rigorously observes the proprieties. A man of determined character, as they say. Like many Russified Germans, enunciates every word rather too clearly and precisely

SHPUNDIK (FILIPP YEGOROVICH)
a landowner, 45. Some pretensions to an education

MASHA (MARYA VASILIEVNA BELOVA)
an orphan, 19, living with Moshkin. A simple Russian girl

PRYAZHKINA (YEKATERINA SAVISHNA)
Masha's aunt, 48. A gossipy woman, prone to tears. Deep down, extremely selfish

SOZOMENOS (ALKIVIAD MARTYNOVICH)
a friend of Von Fonk, 35. A Greek, with very coarse features and a low brow

MALANYA
Moshkin's cook, 40. A dullwitted Finnish woman

STRATILAT
A boy in Moshkin's service, 16. Naturally stupid, but even more so for his age

MITKA

Vilitsky's servant, 25. A smart young man, the product of domestic service in St. Petersburg

A POSTMAN

The action of the play takes place in St. Petersburg: Acts I and III in Moshkin's apartment, Act II in Vilitsky's. Between Acts I and II five days elapse, and between Acts II and III, a week

ACT ONE

The scene is the drawingroom of a government official who is neither rich nor poor: at right, two windows, with a mirror hung between them, and a table in front of the mirror. Upstage, a door leading to the hall, and at left, a door to an adjoining room. Also at left foreground a settee, a round table, and a few armchairs. In the right-hand corner a green baize screen. STRATILAT is lying on the settee. The wall clock strikes two.

STRATILAT: One... two... Two o'clock. Wonder what's keeping the master? I think I'll have a snooze. No, seems I'm feeling hungry again. (*Starts to whistle, picks up a book from the table and opens it.*) Ye gods, just look at these words! That's a long one and no mistake. (*Begins spelling it out.*) E... n... that's 'en'. L... i... g... enlig... eh? Oh, h... t... enlight... E... n..., that's 'en' again... 'Enlighten', right. M... e...
(*The outside doorbell rings. STRATILAT stands up, but keeps hold of the book.*)
En... light... en... me...
(*The bell rings again.*)
Oh, damn! How's a fellow ever going to learn to read in this place! (*Flings the book onto the table and hurries to open the door.*)
(*MOSHKIN enters. He is carrying a sugar-cone under his arm, in one hand a bottle, in the other, a lady's hatbox.*)

MOSHKIN: I suppose you were asleep, eh?

STRATILAT: Absolutely not, sir.

MOSHKIN: Yes, a likely story. (*Nods his head towards the sugar-cone.*) Here, take this. Give it to Malanya.
(*STRATILAT takes the sugar-cone and makes to exit.*)
Is Masha home?

STRATILAT: No, sir.

MOSHKIN: Where's she gone, do you know? (*Sets the hatbox and bottle down on the table and takes a small package out of his back pocket.*)

STRATILAT: I don't know, sir. Her aunt came for her.

MOSHKIN: How long ago?

STRATILAT: It'd be about an hour, sir.

MOSHKIN: Has Mr Vilitsky called while I've been out?

STRATILAT: No, sir.

MOSHKIN: (*After some thought.*) Well, off you go. Oh, and you can send Malanya in.

STRALILAT: Yes, sir. (*Exits.*)

MOSHKIN: (*Rummaging in his pockets.*) I don't think I've forgotten anything. I've bought everything, I'm sure. Yes, I've got the lot. (*Takes a small wrapped bottle from his pocket.*) That's the eau-de-cologne. (*Puts the bottle on the table.*) What's the time? (*Looks at his watch.*) A little after two. What on earth's keeping Petya? (*Looks at his watch again.*) Hm, just after two. (*Puts his hand into his breast pocket.*) And I've got the money ready for him. (*Begins pacing up and down the room.*) I've been running around like a mad thing. Well, it is a big occasion!

(*MALANYA and STRATILAT enter. MOSHKIN turns rapidly to them.*)

MOSHKIN: You're sure this is Friday?

STRATILAT: It's Friday, sir.

MOSHKIN: Yes, of course it is. (*To MALANYA.*) Will dinner be ready?

MALANYA: Yes, sir. Honestly!

MOSHKIN: A decent dinner?

MALANYA: Yes, sir. Honestly!

MOSHKIN: Well, make sure it's not late, my dear. Have you got everything?

MALANYA: Honestly! Yes, sir, I've got everything.

MOSHKIN: You're sure you don't need anything?

MALANYA: Nothing, sir. Just a little Madeira for the pudding.

MOSHKIN: (*Hands her the bottle from the table.*) There, there's your Madeira. Now then, Malanya, let's see you excel yourself. We're having guests to dinner this evening.

MALANYA: Yes, sir.

MOSHKIN: Well, I shan't keep you back. Off you go.
(*MALANYA exits.*)
Stratilat! Lay out my new frock coat and my bow tie,
d'you hear?
(*STRATILAT also exits, leaving MOSHKIN alone.*)
What on earth am I running around for? Am I mad?
(*Sits down and mops his brow with a handkerchief.*) Oh, I'm
so tired, I'm absolutely worn out.
(*The doorbell rings.*)
Who can that be? Must be Petya. (*Strains to listen.*) No,
it's not his voice.

STRATILAT: (*Enters.*) There's a gentleman to see you, sir.

MOSHKIN: Which gentleman?

STRATILAT: I don't know, sir. A stranger.

MOSHKIN: A stranger? You mean you didn't ask him who
he was?

STRATILAT: I did ask him, sir, but he said he wanted to
see you in person.

MOSHKIN: That's odd. Well, show him in.
(*STRATILAT exits. MOSHKIN looks at the door a little
anxiously. Enter SHPUNDIK, wearing a long pea-green coat.*)

SHPUNDIK: (*Goes up to MOSHKIN.*) What, don't you
recognise me?

MOSHKIN: Should I? I must confess, sir... I don't think
I've had the pleasure...

SHPUNDIK: Misha, Misha, surely you don't forget your
old friends?

MOSHKIN: (*Peering closely at him.*) Is it possible? No, it
can't be... is it Filipp?
(*SHPUNDIK flings wide his arms.*)
Shpundik!

SHPUNDIK: Yes, Misha, it's me!
(*They embrace warmly.*)

MOSHKIN: (*His voice breaking.*) My dear good friend... what
brings you here? Have you been here long? Sit down, sit
down. This is so unexpected... well, here's a turn-up...
(*They embrace again.*)
Sit down, please.

(They sit down and look at each other.)

SHPUNDIK: Ho-ho, my dear friend, we've not got any younger, have we!

MOSHKIN: That's true enough. We've grown old, we certainly have. It's the easiest thing in the world, right? Well, well, it must be all of twenty years since we last met.

SHPUNDIK: Yes, indeed, twenty years. How time flies, eh, Misha? D'you remember...

MOSHKIN: *(Interrupting him.)* You know, I'm looking at you, my dear chap, and I just can't believe my eyes. Filipp Shpundik, in my house in St. Petersburg! Welcome, my dear good friend! How on earth did you manage to find me?

SHPUNDIK: Oh, that's easy. It's no great trick to find a civil servant. After all, I knew which ministry you were working in. Ardalion Kuchin dropped in at my place in the country last summer... You surely remember old Kuchin?

MOSHKIN: Which Kuchin? You don't mean the one that married the Karavaev girl, the merchant's daughter – and didn't get any dowry, if memory serves?

SHPUNDIK: The very same.

MOSHKIN: Yes, of course I remember him. Is he still alive?

SHPUNDIK: Alive and kicking. Anyway, I found out from him where you were working... and oh yes, Lupinus sends his regards.

MOSHKIN: What, Ivan Lupinus?

SHPUNDIK: What d'you mean Ivan? No, Ivan Lupinus died ages ago – this is his son, Vasily. You remember him, don't you? Fellow with a limp.

MOSHKIN: Oh yes, of course.

SHPUNDIK: Anyway, that's the one. He's the local judge these days.

MOSHKIN: *(Shaking his head.)* You don't say! Goodness, how time flies. By the way, is Bundyukov still alive?

SHPUNDIK: He is. D'you want to know how's he doing? He married off his daughter last year to some German surveyor. How about that, eh? Bundyukov sends you his regards too. We think about you often, Misha.

MOSHKIN: Thank you, Filipp, thank you. Now, would you like something? Vodka, perhaps, or a bite to eat? Please say. Would you like a pipe? My goodness, we're old friends, eh?

(*Slaps him on the thigh and takes his cap from him.*)

SHPUNDIK: Thanks all the same, Misha, but I don't smoke.

MOSHKIN: Well, what about something to eat?

SHPUNDIK: No, thanks.

MOSHKIN: You must be tired from the journey, eh?

SHPUNDIK: No, not really. I actually slept the whole way from Moscow.

MOSHKIN: You'll have dinner with me, though?

SHPUNDIK: If you like.

MOSHKIN: Fine, that's a good chap. Well, well, my dear good friend – I didn't expect you, I must admit, no indeed. By the way, are you married?

SHPUNDIK: (*Sighs.*) Oh yes. What about you?

MOSHKIN: No no, my friend – not me. Have you any children?

SHPUNDIK: I certainly have. Five of them! It's on their account I've trailed all the way here.

MOSHKIN: Really?

SHPUNDIK: It's an impossible business, my dear chap. But I've got to find positions for them somewhere.

MOSHKIN: Yes, of course, of course. So where are you staying?

SHPUNDIK: Quite near here, actually. At the Europa Hotel, d'you know it? It's just behind Haymarket Square. Kuchin recommended it. By God, St. Petersburg is some city, I'll say that. I've still only managed to get as far as Palace Square, and I'll tell you... St. Isaac's Cathedral, well, St. Isaac's alone must've cost a fortune, eh? And those pavements – quite amazing.

MOSHKIN: Oh yes – and there's plenty more to see, just you wait. By the way, Filipp – d'you remember that old neighbour of ours?

SHPUNDIK: Tatyana Podolskaya, d'you mean?

MOSHKIN: Yes, yes, that's the one.

SHPUNDIK: She wished you a long life, Misha. Well, she's been dead now this past eight years.

MOSHKIN: (*After a moment's silence.*) God rest her soul. Anyway, how are things with you?

SHPUNDIK: Not too bad, thank goodness – can't complain. And yourself? I daresay you've gone up in the world, since you moved away from us.

MOSHKIN: No, not a chance. Gone up in the world? Hardly. Not too bad, though, likewise.

SHPUNDIK: You must've been promoted, surely?

MOSHKIN: Well, yes, I have... (*Glances towards the door.*)

SHPUNDIK: You look as if you're expecting somebody.

MOSHKIN: Yes, I am. (*Rubs his hands.*) Actually, I'm up to my neck in it just now.

SHPUNDIK: Oh, why?

MOSHKIN: Guess.

SHPUNDIK: Well, how am I supposed to...

MOSHKIN: No, go on – guess.

SHPUNDIK: (*Looking him straight in the eye.*) You're not... you're not thinking of getting married? Oh, Misha, take my advice – don't do it.

MOSHKIN: (*Laughing.*) No no, don't worry, my friend... Honestly, at my age! But you guessed right – there *is* going to be a wedding here.

SHPUNDIK: (*Pointing to the table.*) Yes, so I see. What's in the packages? Who's getting married?

MOSHKIN: You'll have to wait – I'll tell you, but not now, I haven't time. Wait till this evening, I've so many things I want to tell you. You'll be really surprised, my dear chap. Well, perhaps I can tell you now, very briefly. You see, Filipp, this is actually my drawingroom, and this is where I sleep... (*Points to the screen.*) My ward lives in the other rooms, a young orphan girl I've brought up. And it's her I'm giving away in marriage.

SHPUNDIK: Your ward?

MOSHKIN: Yes. In fact, she's an extremely refined young lady, the daughter of titular councillor Belov. I became

uainted with her late mother not long before she died
t was strange how things turned out. It's amazing,
nestly – there's no getting away from it, fate really is
inscrutable! Anyway, I should tell you, Filipp, that I've
only been in this apartment three years. And after the
death of her husband, Masha's mother rented two small
rooms on the fourth floor. He died quite a long time ago.
(*Sighs.*) They say he had frostbite in his feet – you can
imagine what a shock that was. Anyway, the old lady
lived in extreme poverty. She had a small pension, some
sort of charity, but no income to speak of, you
understand. Well, I was going up the stairs one day – it
was winter, in fact – and the caretaker had splashed some
water, without mopping it up, and the water had frozen
on the steps... (*Takes out his snuffbox.*) Will you have a
pinch of snuff?

SHPUNDIK: No, thanks.

MOSHKIN: (*Takes a large pinch of snuff.*) Anyway, I'm
going up the stairs, and this elderly lady comes towards
me, Masha's mother. I still didn't know her at that time.
She tried to step aside or something, and she suddenly
slipped backwards, and fell and broke her leg... Twisted
it underneath her, like this... (*Stands up to demonstrate to
SHPUNDIK, then sits down again.*) Well, you can
imagine, at her age, what sort of state she was in.
I picked her up immediately, of course, called for the
servants, and carried her up to her room, put her to
bed, and sent for a bone-setter. She suffered dreadfully,
the poor dear – and her daughter too, God knows. Well,
I started calling on them every day after that, yes, every
single day. I grew very fond of them, you wouldn't
believe it – as if they were my own family. Anyway, the
old lady was confined to bed for six months, until she
eventually recovered and got on her feet again. Then
she took a notion to go to the baths – some perverse fit
of cleanliness. So, off she went and caught a chill, was
sick for about four days and finally passed away. We
had to use the last remnant of her money to bury her.

Well, Filipp, can you imagine what her daughter's situation was now? Eh? No relatives. Well, to be honest, she does have one relative, a widow, a Mistress Pryazhkina – an aunt on her father's side. But she herself hasn't so much as a kopeck to her name. And she has an uncle, in fact, her mother's cousin, who was living on his estate at Konotop at that time, and still does, I think – Grach-Pekhter his name is, a landowner, with quite a few serfs, apparently. I wrote to him just after old Mrs Belova died, telling him how things were, asking him to help, and so forth, but the reply I got was: "I can't feed all these beggars – if you're so concerned about this girl, then you take her in, it's none of my business." What d'you make of that, eh? Well, I did take her in. She absolutely wouldn't hear of it at first, but I kept on at her. "What are you going to do?" I said, "I'm an old man, I've no children, I'll love you like my own daughter. What's going to become of you? You can't go onto the streets." Besides which, her late mother, on her deathbed, entrusted her into my care. Well, eventually she agreed, and she's been living here with me ever since. And she's a really fine young woman, Filipp, you wouldn't believe it. Wait till you see her. You'll fall in love with her at first sight...

SHPUNDIK: I believe you, Misha, I believe you. So who is she marrying?

MOSHKIN: Oh, he's a splendid chap too – a first-rate young man. And the whole thing has been arranged by your humble servant. Yes, my dear friend, I must say I can't complain – I'm a lucky man, thank God – far happier than I deserve.

SHPUNDIK: May I ask his name?

MOSHKIN: Of course, why not? The whole business is settled now – the wedding's in two weeks' time, God willing. Vilitsky, his name is, Petya Vilitsky. He works beside me in the Ministry. An absolutely splendid fellow. Collegiate secretary at the age of twenty-three, would you believe – and he'll be a titular councillor any day now. Yes, he'll go far. He has no money, but well, who cares? He has a good head on him, works hard, modest... knows all the best people. He's dining here today – actually, he dines here almost every day, but he wanted to bring a friend along with him, another young chap, quite high up – (*Makes a meaningful gesture.*) works alongside the Minister himself... So, you see how things are.

SHPUNDIK: Eh? (*Looks at himself.*) Good grief, I can't stay here like this... You must let me go home and put on my frock coat.

MOSHKIN: Oh, nonsense!

SHPUNDIK: (*Rising.*) No, not at all, Misha. Let me have my own way in this, please. Heaven knows what your guest might think – he'll take me for some country bumpkin straight in from the steppes. No no, my dear friend, I have ambitions of my own.

MOSHKIN: (*Also rising.*) Well, as you wish. Only please don't be late.

SHPUNDIK: I'll run like the wind. (*Takes his cap.*) Well, so this is the kind of people you're in with, eh? (*Shakes his hand.*) You know, I'm relying on you, Misha... on my boy's account. Besides which, my wife has given me a long list of demands, I'm at my wits' end. I'm supposed to buy ten roubles' worth of face cream alone, and bergamot oil, all the very best quality. You'll help me, won't you, my dear chap? I can see you're an old hand. (*Pointing at the packages.*)

MOSHKIN: It'll be my pleasure. I'll do a bit of chasing around myself, and I'll ask Petya. He's such an obliging chap – not the least hint of side about him. He hasn't been too well recently though – not quite himself.

SHPUNDIK: What, just before his wedding?

MOSHKIN: Well, I'm not exactly on top form myself. Oh, nothing serious – we've just been so busy, that's the whole problem. Still, I'm at your disposal, my dear friend, feel free to call on me, don't stand on ceremony...

SHPUNDIK: Thank you. I see you haven't changed a bit.

MOSHKIN: I hope not. You know, it was amazing how Petya and I got to know each other.

SHPUNDIK: (*About to leave.*) Oh, really?

MOSHKIN: Well, I'll tell you later. But he's an orphan too, would you believe. He lost his parents in childhood, and an uncle who was his guardian brought him to Petersburg, found him a place in the service, which resulted in the strangest circumstance... Anyway, I'll tell you everything later – but just as he finished his science course in high school, he lost his estate too; fortunately, I came along at that point... However, I mustn't detain you, it'll soon be three o'clock.

SHPUNDIK: And what time is dinner?

MOSHKIN: Four o'clock, my dear friend.

SHPUNDIK: So I've still time...

(*The outer doorbell rings.*)

Is that your guests already?

MOSHKIN: (*Listens.*) It could be. I wonder what's keeping Masha?

SHPUNDIK: (*Anxiously, looking round.*) Oh, dear... look, I can't... is there another way...

(*Enter MASHA and PRYAZHKINA in outdoor coats, which they do not remove.*)

MOSHKIN: Ah! Speak of the devil! Where on earth've you been?

PRYAZHKINA: Heavens, the things we've bought!

MOSHKIN: Well, that's fine. (*To MASHA.*) Masha, allow me to introduce my old friend and neighbour, Filipp Shpundik.

(*SHPUNDIK bows, MASHA curtseys. PRYAZHKINA looks at SHPUNDIK in wonderment.*)

He's just arrived from the country today, he's brought me some news from my village. I want you to be nice to him.

SHPUNDIK: Please excuse me, my dear young lady – I'm still in my travelling clothes, so to speak... I had no idea...

MOSHKIN: Good heavens, why should you excuse
yourself? Really, such affectation! (*To MASHA.*) Masha
dear, you're looking a bit pale today, are you tired?

MASHA: (*Feebly.*) Yes, I am.

MOSHKIN: (*To PRYAZHKINA.*) You've been running
around too much, dear lady – you're wearing her out.
Anyway, you'd better hurry – it's after three and
you're not dressed yet. What will our new guest think,
eh? He drops in on us, and this is what he sees? Now,
off you go...

PRYAZHKINA: We shan't be late, don't worry.

MOSHKIN: Good, good. Now take this hat, and the eau-de-
cologne, and these other things...
(*He gives her the purchases. MASHA and PRYAZHKINA exit
left.*)
Well, Filipp, how do you like Masha?

SHPUNDIK: I like her very much. Very much indeed.

MOSHKIN: I knew you would. Now, you'd better go, if
you have to.

SHPUNDIK: Yes, I really must... I felt absolutely terrible
in front of the ladies. But I'll be back presently. (*Exits to
the hall.*)

MOSHKIN: (*Calling after him.*) Don't be too long!
(*Begins pacing around the room.*) What a day! I'm so glad
Shpundik's come... he's such a nice chap. (*Comes to a halt.*)
Now, what was I thinking about? Oh yes – why is Masha
so pale today? Well, I suppose it's understandable...
I should be getting dressed, what am I doing? Stratilat!
Stratilat!
(*STRATILAT enters.*)
Bring me my frock-coat and my other tie.
(*MOSHKIN takes off his coat and scarf. STRATILAT goes behind
the screen, brings out his frock-coat and tie. MOSHKIN looks at
himself in the mirror.*)
I wonder why I'm looking so haggard? (*Runs a brush
through his hair, beginning at the back of his head.*) And why
hasn't Petya dropped in today? Let me have the tie.

(*With STRATILAT's help, puts on his tie.*) You're sure Mr
Vilitsky hasn't been here today?

STRATILAT: No, sir, he hasn't. I've already told you.

MOSHKIN: (*Irritated.*) Yes, yes, I know you did. I'm just
surprised. I wonder if he's feeling all right?

STRATILAT: I've no idea, sir.

MOSHKIN: Oh, tush! I wasn't talking to you!

MALANYA: (*Suddenly entering from the hall.*) Sir! Sir!

MOSHKIN: What is it?

MALANYA: I'll need some money for the cinnamon.

MOSHKIN: For cinnamon? (*Clutches his head.*) You're
determined to ruin me, I can see that! I thought you told
me you had everything you needed? (*Rummages in his
waistcoat pockets.*) Here's a quarter rouble. Now, look here
– if dinner isn't ready within... (*Looks at his watch.*) within
the next fifteen minutes, I'll... I'll... Well, go on, go on!
What're you waiting for?

STRATILAT: (*Sotto voce, to the departing MALANYA.*) Some
cook!

MALANYA: Oh, shut up, you silly creature!

MOSHKIN: Come on, don't stand there grinning – hand
me my coat.
(*Puts on his frock-coat. STRATILAT tugs it straight at the back.*)
Fine, that'll do, now off you go. Why don't you light the
lamps? Look, it's getting dark.
(*STRATILAT exits to the hall.*)
What a strange thing! I don't think I've been on my feet
all that much today – no more than yesterday, anyway,
yet my legs are starting to wobble. (*Sits down and looks at
his watch.*) Quarter past three... what's keeping them?
(*Looks round the room.*) Everything's in order, I think.
(*Stands up and wipes some dust off the table with his handkerchief.
The doorbell rings.*)
Ah! At last!

STRATILAT: (*Enters and announces.*) Mr Pyotr Vilitsky, and
Mr Von... (*Stammers.*) Von F-f-fonk...

MOSHKIN: (*To STRATILAT, sotto voce.*) Mr who? Is that
how he told you to announce him?

STRATILAT: (*Also sotto voce.*) Yes, sir.

MOSHKIN: Oh dear... (*Then aloud.*) Well, send them in.
(*STRATILAT exits. Enter VILITSKY and FONK, wearing frock-coats. VILITSKY is pale, and seems rather agitated. FONK bears himself with great dignity, a man with a strict sense of propriety.*)

VILITSKY: Mikhail Ivanych, allow me to introduce my good friend, Rodion Karlych von Fonk.
(*FONK makes a stiff bow.*)

MOSHKIN: (*Somewhat confused.*) I am extremely pleased and flattered... I've heard so much about your exceptional qualities... I'm most grateful to Petya for...

FONK: And I'm very pleased to meet you, sir. (*Bows.*)

MOSHKIN: Oh, not at all, sir...
(*An awkward silence.*)
Please, do sit down.
(*They all sit. Again, an awkward silence. FONK looks round the room appraisingly. MOSHKIN gives a little cough.*)
Well, what splendid weather we've had today! A little cold, perhaps, but very pleasant all the same.

FONK: Yes, it's been a cold day.

MOSHKIN: Yes, indeed. (*To VILITSKY, in an undertone.*) Why didn't you come today, Petya? Aren't you feeling well?
(*FONK raises his eyebrows almost imperceptibly at this show of intimacy.*)

VILITSKY: No, I'm fine, thank goodness. And how is Masha?

MOSHKIN: Masha's well... Ahem! (*To FONK.*) Have you been for a walk today, sir?

FONK: Yes, I took a stroll along the Nevsky Prospect once or twice.

MOSHKIN: That's a most agreeable walk. You find all the best people there, and there's sand too, spread on the pavements... all kinds of shops... extremely convenient.
(*A brief silence.*) Yes, St. Petersburg is the first capital of the world, one might say.

FONK: Indeed, it's a very fine city.

MOSHKIN: (*Tentatively.*) I don't suppose there's anything like it abroad?

FONK: I don't think so.

MOSHKIN: And especially once St. Isaac's Cathedral is completed – well, it'll have a significant advantage, wouldn't you say, sir?

FONK: St. Isaac's Cathedral is a splendid edifice in every respect.

MOSHKIN: I couldn't agree more, sir. May I enquire how His Excellency the Minister's health is these days?

FONK: He is well, praise the Lord!

MOSHKIN: Praise the Lord, indeed! (*Another silence.*) Ahem. (*With a smile.*) Well, my dear sir... I hope you will honour us... in two weeks' time... at his wedding... (*Indicates VILITSKY.*) I hope you'll grace us with your presence.

FONK: I should be extremely flattered...

MOSHKIN: No, on the contrary, sir, it's we who should... (*Falls silent again.*) My dear sir, you wouldn't believe how happy I am, just to see them, to see them both... (*Vaguely indicating VILITSKY, and the door to the left.*) For an old man, a bachelor – well, you can imagine what a surprise...

FONK: Yes, of course. Marriage, based on mutual affection and sound *judgement,* sir, is one of the greatest blessings of a man's life.

MOSHKIN: (*Listening to FONK with reverence.*) Yes, sir. Yes, indeed.

FONK: That is why, on my part, I wholeheartedly approve the intention of these two young people, who after due thought... will fulfil this... this sacred obligation.

MOSHKIN: (*Even more reverently.*) Yes, sir, yes. I'm in complete agreement with you, sir.

FONK: After all, what can be more agreeable than family life? However, one must exercise judgement over the choice of a spouse.

MOSHKIN: Of course, of course. You are absolutely right, my dear sir, in everything you say. I will confess, sir...

please excuse me... but I think Petya can count himself extremely fortunate in having merited your good offices.

FONK: (*A slight frown.*) Oh, not at all, sir.

MOSHKIN: No, I do assure you, I...

VILITSKY: (*Hastily interrupting him.*) Sir, I'd like to see Masha, if possible... I'd like a couple of words with her.

MOSHKIN: She's in her room... no doubt getting dressed now. You can knock the door, if you wish.

VILITSKY: Thank you. I'll be back in a minute. (*To FONK.*) If you'll excuse me...

FONK: Yes, of course.

(*VILITSKY exits left. MOSHKIN watches him go out, then crosses to FONK and takes his hand.*)

MOSHKIN: My dear sir, you must excuse me, I'm just a simple man... whatever I feel, I say it right out... Let me thank you again, most feelingly, from the bottom of my heart...

FONK: (*Coldly civil.*) What on earth for, sir?

MOSHKIN: Well, in the first place, for your visit. Secondly... I can see that you love my dear Petya. I have no children, sir, but I don't believe any man could be fonder of his own son, than I am of Petya. That's why I'm so touched, sir, I'm so deeply touched that I can't even say... (*His eyes fill with tears.*) Please, forgive me... (*Sotto voce, speaking to himself.*) What's the matter with you? Have you no shame? (*Laughs then, takes out his handkerchief, blows his nose and dries his eyes.*)

FONK: Believe me, sir, it gives me great pleasure to witness such emotion.

MOSHKIN: Sir, you will pardon an old man's frankness, but I have heard so much about you. Petya speaks of you with such respect. He values your opinion so highly. You'll see my Masha, sir, you'll see her... before God I swear to you, sir, she'll make him so happy. She's a truly splendid young woman.

FONK: I don't doubt that in the least. The very fact of my friend's attachment to her speaks strongly in her favour.

MOSHKIN: (*Again reverently.*) Oh, indeed, sir, yes...

FONK: As for myself, I wish him all the good in the world. (*A moment's silence.*) Sir, I believe you are in charge of one of the Chancellery departments?

MOSHKIN: That is correct, sir.

FONK: Might I ask whose section?

MOSHKIN: Kufnagel's section.

FONK: (*Impressed.*) Really? He's a fine man. I know him. A most excellent official.

MOSHKIN: He is indeed, sir. (*After a pause.*) Sir, if I may enquire – you've known my Petya for the last six months, I believe?

FONK: Yes.

(*PRYAZHKINA emerges from the side door. She is dressed to kill, with an enormous bow of yellow ribbons on her bonnet. She advances unheard towards the two men, sits down quietly behind them, and begins fiddling with the strings of her reticule.*)

What I find most pleasing about your friend is that he is a young man of fixed principles.

(*MOSHKIN listens attentively.*)

That's quite rare these days. He isn't... how shall I put it?... he isn't blown about by every wind...

(*Makes a 'weathercock' gesture. MOSHKIN does likewise, and nods in approval.*)

That's most important. I'm a young man myself...

(*MOSHKIN makes a deprecatory gesture.*)

I'm no Cato, but I do...

PRYAZHKINA: (*Discreetly, but quite audibly.*) Ahem!

(*FONK stops and looks round. So also does MOSHKIN. PRYAZHKINA curtseys.*)

MOSHKIN: (*Slightly irritated.*) What is it you wish, dear lady? (*FONK slowly rises. MOSHKIN stands up also.*)

PRYAZHKINA: (*Embarrassed.*) I... er... well, sir, I've come to see you...

(*FONK makes her a dignified bow. She curtseys to him, then falls silent.*)

MOSHKIN: Oh, look... (*Hesitates.*) My dear sir, allow me to present to you Mistress Pryazhkina – the widow of a staff officer. Mistress Pryazhkina is Masha's aunt...

FONK: (*Bowing stiffly.*) I'm pleased to meet you.
(*PRYAZHKINA curtseys again.*)

MOSHKIN: (*To PRYAZHKINA.*) Is there something you'd like?

PRYAZHKINA: Yes, sir. Masha asked me to... well, she didn't exactly ask me, but if you'd just come in for a minute...

MOSHKIN: (*Reproachfully.*) What is it? How can I go in now? (*Covertly points at FONK.*) Eh?

FONK: Sir, please don't stand on ceremony... go if you must.

MOSHKIN: You're so kind, sir. Honestly, I've no idea what they're calling me for. Anyway, I'll be back in a moment.

FONK: (*Waving his hand.*) Please...

MOSHKIN: I won't be a minute. (*Exits with PRYAZHKINA, expressing his displeasure to her.*)
(*Left alone, FONK watches them go, shrugs his shoulders, and begins pacing around the room. He goes up to the mirror, makes a few adjustments to his appearance. He picks up a hairbrush, then looks over the screen wonderingly.*)

FONK: What's going on? What's this all about? Why have I been brought here? What a ridiculous woman, and that old fellow too, chattering and crying – and such familiarity, besides. And the servant in some wretched Cossack livery – the whole place is filthy. And a bed, for heaven's sake, right here in the room. No doubt the dinner'll be absolutely disgusting, and the champagne to match... and I'll have to drink it.
(*STRATILAT enters and hangs the lighted lamps up on the wall. FONK stands looking at him with his arms folded. STRATILAT glances at him timidly and exits.*)
What on earth's going on? I just can't understand it. I'm absolutely lost. Well, anyway, we'll get a look at the bride.
(*VILITSKY emerges from the side door.*)
Ah, Vilitsky!

VILITSKY: Mikhail Ivanych told me you'd been left on your own here. Do forgive me, please – the old man's in such a dither.

FONK: Think nothing of it.

VILITSKY: (*Pressing his hand.*) You're so kind and understanding. I did try to warn you... Moshkin is a splendid old chap – indeed, I might call him my benefactor, but you can see for yourself, he's really rather simple...

(*VILITSKY waits for FONK to interrupt him, but FONK says nothing.*)

He is, isn't he.

FONK: Why so? No, I think Mr Moshkin is a thoroughly decent type. Of course, as far as I've been able to observe, he hasn't had much of an education, but that's of secondary importance. Incidentally, I've just seen a certain lady here... She's your fiancée's aunt, I believe?

VILITSKY: (*Flushing slightly, and giving a forced smile.*) Oh yes... she's not a wealthy woman. However, she's a goodhearted person too, and...

FONK: I don't doubt it. (*A pause.*) Have you known Mr Moshkin long?

VILITSKY: About three years.

FONK: And he's been in service here in Petersburg quite some time?

VILITSKY: Yes.

FONK: How old is he?

VILITSKY: Must be about fifty, I think.

FONK: So, he won't be a head of department much longer! Anyway, when can I expect the pleasure of seeing your fiancée?

VILITSKY: She'll be here presently.

FONK: Mr Moshkin spoke very highly about her.

VILITSKY: That's no surprise. He thinks the world of her. Masha's very nice, in fact, an extremely goodnatured girl. Of course, she was brought up in poverty, virtually in isolation, hardly ever saw anybody... Well, anyway, she's a trifle shy, even a little wild... She's rather awkward in company, but please don't judge her too harshly, not at first sight.

FONK: On the contrary, my dear Vilitsky I'm quite sure...

VILITSKY: Don't be too hard on her, please, that's all I ask.

FONK: You must forgive me, my dear friend, but your trust in me... I am genuinely flattered by your confidence in me, and that gives me a certain right, I believe. On the other hand, I'm not sure I should...

VILITSKY: No, tell me, please – speak out.

FONK: Your fiancée... she hasn't much of a fortune, has she.

VILITSKY: She hasn't anything.

FONK: (*After a pause.*) Yes, I see. Well, I can understand that... Love.

VILITSKY: (*Also after a pause.*) I love her very much.

FONK: Yes. In that case there's nothing else to be desired, and if this marriage can bring you happiness, then I congratulate you most sincerely. By the way, aren't you going to the theatre this evening? Rubini is singing in "Lucia di Lammermoor".

VILITSKY: This evening? No, I don't think so. I'm planning to go some time with my fiancée and Mr Moshkin. Actually, I got the feeling you were going to say something... something about my marriage.

FONK: Was I? No... Tell me, your fiancée is called Masha, isn't she? Marya?

VILITSKY: That's correct – Marya.

FONK: And her family name?

VILITSKY: Her name? (*Looking away.*) Belova.

FONK: (*After a pause.*) I see. Well, we're still going to see Baron Wiedehopf tomorrow?

VILITSKY: Yes, of course... if you're willing to introduce me to him.

FONK: With the greatest of pleasure. What time is it? (*Looks at his watch.*) A quarter to four.

VILITSKY: It's time for dinner... What's happened to Moshkin?

(*He looks round. Enter SHPUNDIK from the hall. He is wearing an old-fashioned black frock-coat, with a narrow waist and high collar, a tightly-knotted white tie, an extremely short striped velvet waistcoat with mother-of-pearl buttons, and light pea-green britches. He is carrying a soft velour hat in his hand. On seeing the two strangers, he attempts to bow, awkwardly thrusting forward his right leg and raising his left, at the same time pressing his hat to his stomach with both hands. He looks utterly bewildered. VILITSKY and FONK both bow to him in silence.)*

FONK: (*To VILITSKY, sotto voce.*) Who on earth is this gentleman?

VILITSKY: (*Also sotto voce.*) I really haven't a clue.
(*To SHPUNDIK.*) Sir, may I ask your business?

SHPUNDIK: Filipp Shpundik, sir, I'm a landowner from Tambov... please, don't concern yourselves about me.
(*Takes out a handkerchief and mops his brow.*)

VILITSKY: I'm pleased to meet you. Is it Mr Moshkin you wish to see, perhaps?

SHPUNDIK: Please don't go to any bother... I've already...
I've... (*Blushes, laughs, then sidles off to the right.*)

FONK: (*To VILITSKY.*) What a queer fellow.

VILITSKY: He must be some acquaintance of Mr Moshkin's. I've never seen him here before. (*Aloud to SHPUNDIK.*) Mr Moshkin will be here presently.
(*SHPUNDIK gestures vaguely, smiles, and turns away. VILITSKY turns to FONK, with an imploring expression.*)
Dear friend, please... you must forgive me...

FONK: (*Pressing his hand.*) Oh, nonsense, nonsense. Ah, I think this is Mr Moshkin now...
(*MOSHKIN and MASHA enter left. He is leading her by the hand, and PRYAZHKINA follows them in. MASHA is dressed in white, with a pale blue sash. She looks rather bewildered.*)

MOSHKIN: (*Triumphantly, but with a hint of nervousness.*)
Masha, allow me to present Mr von Fonk.
(*FONK bows, MASHA curtseys. PRYAZHKINA curtseys behind her.*)
Here she is, my dear sir – my Masha...

FONK: (*To MASHA.*) I'm deeply flattered... I consider myself most fortunate... I have long wished to have the pleasure...
(*MASHA makes no response to any of his phrases, simply bows her head.*)

VILITSKY: Masha, I do hope you will like my friend...

(*MASHA, her head bowed, looks up at VILITSKY. She is clearly uncomfortable. An awkward silence.*)

MOSHKIN: (*Catching sight of SHPUNDIK.*) Ah, Filipp – do come in! (*Takes him by the hand and introduces him to the assembled company.*) Filipp Shpundik, my old neighbour, a landowner in Tambov. He's just come from the country today – Filipp Yegorych Shpundik.

SHPUNDIK: (*Bows to everyone.*) I'm most grateful to you, my dear friend, I truly am...

MOSHKIN: (*Loudly, to the whole company.*) Do sit down, everyone, please.

(*MASHA sits down on the settee.*)

Mr Fonk, won't you sit here? (*Indicates a seat near MASHA. FONK sits.*)

Filipp! (*Points to an armchair opposite. SHPUNDIK sits.*) Mistress Pryazhkina! (*Points to the settee, beside MASHA. PRYAZHKINA sits down, tightly clutching her reticule. MOSHKIN himself sits in an armchair to the left.*)

Petya, please take a seat.

(*VILITSKY shakes his head and remains standing beside FONK. A silence.*)

Well, what splendid weather we've had today...

FONK: (*Smiles.*) Yes.

(*Another silence. FONK turns to MASHA.*)

Mr Vilitsky tells me you're planning to go to the opera some day soon.

MASHA: Yes, sir. Petya suggested we might... (*Her voice breaks down.*)

FONK: I'm sure you'll find it most pleasurable.

(*MOSHKIN, SHPUNDIK and PRYAZHKINA are listening to them with rapt attention.*)

Rubini's a wonderful performer. Quite extraordinary technique – the most amazing voice. I take it you're fond of music?

MASHA: Yes, sir. I like music very much.

FONK: Perhaps you play yourself?

MASHA: Oh no, sir, scarcely at all.

MOSHKIN: What nonsense – she plays the piano, sir. Variations and all sorts. Indeed she does.

FONK: That's splendid. I too play a little, on the violin.

MOSHKIN: And extremely well, I have no doubt.

FONK: No no, purely for my own pleasure. But I do wonder at parents who neglect the musical education, so to speak, of their children. I find that really incredible. (*Turns smilingly to PRYAZHKINA.*) Don't you agree? (*PRYAZHKINA's lips begin to quiver from sheer fright; she blinks one eye and emits a pained sound. MOSHKIN quickly comes to her aid.*)

MOSHKIN: Yes, you've hit the nail absolutely on the head, sir. I find that surprising too. You wouldn't credit the ignorance of some people!

SHPUNDIK: I quite agree, my dear friend. (*FONK then turns to SHPUNDIK, who coughs respectfully behind his hand.*)

FONK: Yes, I'm extremely pleased to note that here in Russia, even in the provinces, enthusiasm for the arts is becoming more widespread. That's an extremely good sign.

SHPUNDIK: (*In a quavering voice, emboldened by FONK's attention.*) It's just as you say, sir. I mean, I'm not a wealthy man – you can ask Mr Moshkin here about me – but I ordered up a piano from Moscow for my two daughters, I did indeed, sir. Only trouble is, it's quite difficult finding a teacher in our neck of the woods.

FONK: May I ask if you are from southern Russia?

SHPUNDIK: Yes, sir. From Tambov province, the county of Ostrogozhsk.

FONK: Ah yes, a grain-producing area.

SHPUNDIK: That's so, sir, but you couldn't say it's been all that satisfactory in recent years – not for us landowners, anyway.

FONK: Oh? Why not?

SHPUNDIK: Well, the harvests have been very poor... this is the third year in a row.

FONK: Really? That's terrible.

SHPUNDIK: There's not much good in it, sir. Still, you've got to keep trying, nothing else for it. We're simple country folks, of course, we can't keep running to Petersburg, that's where the best of everything goes, food and suchlike. Anyway, you do the best you can, as they say...

FONK: That's most praiseworthy.

SHPUNDIK: A man's duty comes first, sir. But there's a lot of inconveniences. Sometimes you just don't know where to turn. You try this and that... it's no use, sir. You just come to a dead end. You run out of ideas, your imagination flags. (*Assumes a weary expression.*)

FONK: What sort of inconveniences, for example?

SHPUNDIK: Ho, what not! Bad enough the dam suddenly bursts, but when the cattle, if I may say, just up and die on you... Well, it's all God's will. And we must bear it humbly, sir.

FONK: That's a great pity. (*Turns to face MASHA.*)

SHPUNDIK: Besides which, sir...

(*Realising FONK has turned his back on him, SHPUNDIK becomes confused and falls silent. During FONK's conversation with SHPUNDIK, VILITSKY has been whispering to MASHA.*)

FONK: (*To MASHA.*) So, I presume you're also fond of dancing?

MASHA: No, sir. Not very...

FONK: Really? How odd! (*To VILITSKY.*) The last ball at the Nobleman's Assembly was a truly dazzling affair – there must have been all of three thousand people there.

MOSHKIN: You don't say! (*Turning to SHPUNDIK.*) You see, Filipp? That's where you should go. You won't see that sort of thing back home, eh?

(*Laughs. SHPUNDIK apathetically averts his eyes.*)

FONK: (*To MASHA.*) You don't seriously mean you dislike dancing, and amusements in general? That's most peculiar...

MASHA: No, of course not... I do like...

FONK: (*Smiling in the direction of PRYAZHKINA.*) I presume your dear aunt attends to your dress. That can't be Mr Moshkin's responsibility, surely?

(*PRYAZHKINA again goes goggle-eyed with fright.*)

MASHA: No, sir, my aunt... of course...

(*FONK stares at her for some time, motionless. MASHA lowers her eyes.*)

VILITSKY: (*Goes up to MOSHKIN from behind: sotto voce.*) Mr Moshkin, what's keeping dinner? This is terrible, the conversation's ground to a halt.

MOSHKIN: (*Rises, whispers to VILITSKY with rare vehemence.*) What can you do with that damned cook? That creature'll have me in an early grave. Petya, for God's sake, go and tell her to serve the dinner right now, or I'll sack her tomorrow!

(*VILITSKY makes to exit.*)

And tell that idler Stratilat to bring in the starters – and on the new tray, mind – you can't trust him. The only thing he's good at is making a racket in the hall!

(*VILITSKY exits. MOSHKIN hurriedly turns to FONK.*)

MOSHKIN: (*Brightly.*) Yes indeed, sir, I couldn't agree more.

FONK: (*Looks at MOSHKIN, slightly surprised.*) Yes... So, tell me... (*At a loss what to say.*) Oh yes, where does Mr Kufnagel live?

MOSHKIN: The Blinnikov house on Great Podyachesky Street, sir – second floor, through the yard. There's a very interesting sign over the gate. Extremely curious, though you can't make head or tail of it. Must be a fine trade, though, whatever it is.

FONK: Well, I'm most grateful to you. I need to have a chat with Kufnagel. (*Laughs.*) You know, the most extraordinary event occurred once, when I was in his presence. We were walking along the Nevsky Prospect one day, and would you believe...

MOSHKIN: Yes, sir, indeed.

FONK: We're walking along Nevsky, and suddenly a very short man in a bearskin coat comes up to us, and this gentleman flings his arms round Kufnagel and tries to kiss him – can you imagine it? Kufnagel of course pushes him away, and says: "What's the matter with you, sir, are you out of your mind?" And this chap in the fur

coat hugs him again, and asks him how long it's been
since he arrived from Kharkov... and this is all
happening in the street, just imagine! Well, finally the
whole story came out – the man in the fur coat had
mistaken Kufnagel for one of his friends. The point is,
there really are people who look alike.
(*They all laugh.*)

MOSHKIN: (*Delightedly.*) Yes, a fascinating story, most
curious! People do often look alike. I mean, you
remember, Filipp, those two old neighbours of ours –
the Polugusov brothers – you could hardly tell them
apart. Like two peas in a pod, they were. Certainly, one
of them had a very wide nose, and a cataract in one eye
– he took to drink not long afterwards and went bald,
but the resemblance was amazing, just the same. Isn't
that so, Filipp?

SHPUNDIK: Oh yes, very much so. (*Pondering deeply.*)
You know, they say these things depend on all sorts of
causes. Science'll eventually get to the bottom of them,
of course.

MOSHKIN: (*Enthusiastically.*) It will indeed, nothing surer!

SHPUNDIK: (*Pompously.*) Well, I don't think you can say
that with absolute certainty, but it's possible. (*After a
pause.*) Yes, why not?

FONK: (*To MASHA.*) The vagaries of Nature are quite
remarkable in such cases.
(*MASHA is silent. STRATILAT enters from the hall bearing a
tray of hors d'oeuvres, followed by VILITSKY.*)

MOSHKIN: (*Fussing around.*) Now, would you care for a
little appetiser before dinner? (*Motions STRATILAT
towards FONK.*) Over there, over there. (*To FONK.*)
A little caviar, sir?
(*FONK politely declines.*)
No? As you wish, sir. Mistress Pryazhkina, please... help
yourself. And you, Masha...
(*PRYAZHKINA takes a piece of bread and caviar, and eats with
her mouth open. MASHA declines.*)
Filipp, wouldn't you like something?

(*SHPUNDIK stands up, leads STRATILAT a little way apart and pours himself a glass of vodka. VILITSKY goes up to FONK. At that point, MALANYA appears in the hall doorway.*)

MALANYA: Mr Moshkin, sir...

(*MOSHKIN is furious, rushes to prevent her entering, practically shoves her out of the room.*)

MOSHKIN: (*Sotto voce.*) Where on earth d'you think you're going, you idiot!

MALANYA: Sir, dinner is...

MOSHKIN: Fine, fine, now go! (*Hurriedly rejoins his guests.*) Would anyone like some more? No?

(*A silence. MOSHKIN whispers to STRATILAT.*)

Right, hurry up, go outside and announce that dinner is served.

(*STRATILAT exits. MOSHKIN turns to FONK.*)

May one ask, my dear sir, if you enjoy a game of cards?

FONK: Yes, I do. But I do believe dinner will be ready soon. And besides, I'm in such agreeable company...

(*Indicating MASHA. VILITSKY slightly purses his lips.*)

MOSHKIN: Yes, of course, we'll have dinner now. I was merely asking... We can play a hand or two after dinner, if you like.

FONK: With pleasure, sir. (*To MASHA.*) I imagine you'll be quite indifferent to cards?

MASHA: I am, sir. I don't play cards.

FONK: That's understandable. At your age you have other things on your mind. But perhaps your esteemed aunt plays?

MASHA: (*Turning slightly towards PRYAZHKINA.*) She does, sir.

FONK: Whist?

PRYAZHKINA: No, sir – hearts.

FONK: Ah. I don't know that game. Generally speaking, our dear ladies have a perfect right to complain about cards...

MASHA: (*Naively.*) Why so?

FONK: Why so? Your question surprises me.

VILITSKY: Honestly, Masha...

(*MASHA is extremely embarrassed.*)

STRATILAT: (*Enters from the hall.*) Dinner is served!

MOSHKIN: Thank heavens for that! Now, friends – let's sit down to whatever the good Lord has provided. Masha, take Mr Fonk's arm. Petya, take Mistress Pryazhkina's. (*To SHPUNDIK.*) We'll go in together, friend.
(*All make their way out to the hall, MOSHKIN and SHPUNDIK bringing up the rear.*)
We'll soon be setting out for the wedding like this, Filipp, eh? Why such a long face?

SHPUNDIK: (*Sighs.*) It's nothing, honestly, I'm feeling better now. It's just that... well, I can see Petersburg's not like home, not at all. I'm really puzzled by that!

MOSHKIN: Oh, it's all nonsense, don't worry. You wait, we'll crack a bottle of champagne to toast the newly-weds – that'll work wonders! Right, friends, let's go!
(*All exit. Curtain.*)
(*End of Act One.*)

ACT TWO

The scene is the poorly furnished room of a young bachelor clerk; a door upstage, another at right; a table, a settee, and a few chairs; some books on a shelf, tobacco pipes lying around in odd corners, a chest of drawers. VILITSKY is sitting fully-dressed, with a book opened on his lap.

VILITSKY: (*After a pause.*) Mitka!

MITKA: (*Entering from the hall.*) Yes, sir?

VILITSKY: Pipe.
(*MITKA goes over to the corner and fills a pipe with tobacco.*)
Hasn't anyone brought a note from Mr Fonk?

MITKA: No, sir, nothing. (*Hands VILITSKY the pipe and a match.*)

VILITSKY: (*Lights his pipe.*) Yes... Mr Moshkin might call today, so you can tell him again, I'm not at home. Do you understand?

MITKA: Yes, sir. (*Exits.*)
(*VILITSKY puffs at his pipe a few moments, then suddenly stands up and begins pacing up and down the room.*)

VILITSKY: Really, I've got to put an end to it, somehow or other! It's intolerable, absolutely intolerable. I've behaved like a pig, I know that, it's quite unforgivable. That's five whole days now I haven't seen them... not since that damned dinner. But what can I do, for God's sake? I'm no use at dissembling. But it's got to stop, no matter what. I can't keep on hiding, sitting around for days in other people's houses, staying overnight... I've really got to make up my mind! I mean, what'll they think in the office? It's an unpardonable weakness, absolute childishness! (*After a pause.*) Mitka!

MITKA: (*Enters from the hall.*) Yes, sir?

VILITSKY: Didn't you say Mr Moshkin was here yesterday too?

MITKA: Too true, sir! He's been dropping in every day since Sunday.

VILITSKY: Oh.

MITKA: Yes, he was very worried-looking when he ran up on Sunday, wanted to know was my master feeling all right, and why you hadn't been to see them the night before.

VILITSKY: Yes, yes, so you said. Anyway, you told him what?

MITKA: I told him you were out of town, sir. He's gone away on business, I said.

VILITSKY: So, what did he say to that?

MITKA: Well, he was very surprised, sir – what sort of business, he wanted to know, and why you'd taken off so sudden-like, without so much as a word. Then he says he's made enquiries at your office, sir, and it seems nobody there knows anything about it, so it can't be official business. Yes, he was very worried. Even wanted to know how you'd gone, had you taken a cab, or hired a coach, and how much clean linen you'd packed... Yes, very anxious, he was.

VILITSKY: And what did you say to all that?

MITKA: Well, I told him like you said: I don't know, I says, where the master's gone, except he went off with friends somewhere, maybe out of town. I'm expecting him back anytime, I says. So he had a bit of a think, and then left. Since then he's been back every day, asking after you. Day before yesterday, he even looked in twice, And yesterday he sat a whole hour and a half in your room, sir, just waiting for you. He left a note, too.

VILITSKY: Yes, I've read it. Right, now listen – if Mr Moshkin should appear, tell him I've come home, and had to go out again, but I'll definitely see him today. Without fail. Understood? Now get my uniform ready.

MITKA: (*Exits, smiling.*) He even asked the caretaker. My dear chap, he says, you don't happen to know where Mr Vilitsky's gone?

VILITSKY: Good God, what did the caretaker say?

MITKA: He said he didn't know, but he didn't think you'd spent the night at home.

VILITSKY: (*After a pause.*) Anyway, off you go.
(*MITKA exits, and VILITSKY resumes pacing the floor.*)
Oh, this is infantile! What a stupid idea, going into
hiding! It's just not possible – I'll have to lie my way
out of it now, invent some story. And I can't fool the
old man, it'll all come out in the open. Honestly, what
a rotten business! I don't know what on earth
possessed me. Why do I feel a chill up my spine, the
minute I think about having to go there? I'm her
fiancé, for God's sake, I'm getting married in a few
days' time! And I do love Masha, I do. I'm going to
marry her, it's all settled, I've given my word. And
really, I've no objections... (*Shrugs.*) It's astonishing –
I couldn't have foreseen this, I have to admit. (*Sits
down again.*) But that dinner! Oh, yes – that dinner.
I shan't forget that in a hurry. What in God's name
was wrong with Masha? I mean, she's not stupid – of
course she isn't. But she couldn't utter a word, not a
single damn word! There's Fonk going on about this
and that, one thing after another, and she just sits
there, as if she's carved out of stone. 'Yes, sir, no, sir,
is that so, sir?' Honestly, I couldn't help blushing for
her. I can't look Fonk in the eye now, so help me God,
I can't! It's as if he's laughing at me all the time. And
with good reason. Though of course he's too well-
mannered to say what he really thinks...
(*A pause.*)
Well, all right, she's shy... timid... she's never been in
society. Yes, of course. After all, who could she learn
from... how to behave, and all that? Not from old
Moshkin, that's for sure. But she's very kind, and she
does love me. Yes, and I love her. (*Heatedly.*) Have I ever
said I don't love her? It's just that...
(*Again, a pause. He picks up his book.*)
Fonk's right – education is so important, it's
absolutely crucial. However, I must go and see
them. Yes, I'll go there today... (*Flings the book aside.*)
Oh, this is all so awful!

(*MITKA enters.*)

What is it?

MITKA: (*Hands him a note.*) A letter, sir.

VILITSKY: (*Glancing at the handwriting.*) Oh... Right, then, off you go.

(*MITKA exits. VILITSKY hurriedly opens the letter, begins reading.*)

From Masha!... That's sheer exaggeration! What's the point of that? *'You no longer love me – that's clear to me now...'* Huh, how many times has *that* been written! *'Please don't feel constrained, we're both free agents. I began to notice your gradual cooling towards me quite some time ago...'* That's just not true! *'Although outwardly you haven't changed... I think you're now finding it difficult to keep up the pretence... So why bother? You were supposed to have left St Petersburg. Is that really true? Obviously, you're afraid to meet me. But in any event, I would like to come to an understanding with you... Yours devotedly...'* etc., etc. P.S..."When you return, you will find this letter. Please call on us, not for my sake, but for the sake of a poor old man, who is losing his mind because of all this. If I am mistaken, and have offended you without cause, then please forgive me... However, your last visit ... Goodbye...'* What's all this about? Why is Masha doing this? What's going on? Oh, this is shameful... these eternal misunderstandings! That bodes well for the future, I must say! All right, I suppose I am in the wrong – I haven't been there for five days now. But why should she suddenly jump to that conclusion? And such a pompous tone! (*Looks again at the letter, and solemnly shakes his head.*) No, no, there's more of pride than love there. That doesn't sound like love. (*A pause.*) Even so, I must see them today, without fail. Masha's right, I really am at fault. I'll look in on them now, before going into the office... That makes sense. Yes, yes, I'll definitely go... (*Stops.*) It'll be frightfully awkward, though, at the start... Still, it's got to be done!

(*A knock is heard outside in the hall. He strains to listen, and hides the letter in his pocket. MITKA enters.*)

What is it now?

MITKA: Mr Fonk has arrived, sir. He wants to see you.
He's got another gentleman with him.

VILITSKY: (*After a pause.*) Send them in.

(*MITKA exits. Enter FONK and SOZOMENOS. VILITSKY goes to meet them.*)

I'm so pleased...

FONK: (*Pressing his hand.*) Sir, allow me to introduce a good friend of mine...

(*VILITSKY and SOZOMENOS bow.*)

Perhaps you've heard of him... Mr Sozomenos.

VILITSKY: Indeed I have.

FONK: I'm sure you'll get on famously.

VILITSKY: I've no doubt we shall.

FONK: He's in the literary field, and extremely successful.

VILITSKY: (*Respectfully.*) Ah!

FONK: He hasn't had anything published yet, but he read me one of his stories a few days ago... a most exquisite piece! The style, especially – quite superb!

VILITSKY: (*To SOZOMENOS.*) May I enquire the title, sir?

SOZOMENOS: (*Curtly.*) "The Nobility of Judges on the Shores of the Volga."

VILITSKY: I see.

FONK: It's full of real feeling and warmth. There are even some elevated passages.

VILITSKY: I should be most flattered if Mr Sozomenos would read his story to me too.

FONK: I'm sure he would be delighted. Authors rarely refuse to do that.

(*SOZOMENOS responds with a restrained, hoarse laugh.*)

VILITSKY: Please be seated, gentlemen. Would you care for a pipe?

(*Offers them pipes and tobacco. FONK refuses. SOZOMENOS sits down, slowly fills the pipe and gazes round the room.*)

FONK: (*To VILITSKY meanwhile.*) Yes, it's the strangest thing, you wouldn't believe it. Up until now Mr Sozomenos had no inkling of any literary talent. And as you see, he's no longer in the first flush of youth. How old are you, Alkiviad?

SOZOMENOS: Thirty-five. May I have a light?

VILITSKY: (*Hands him some matches from the table.*) Here you are.

SOZOMENOS: Thank you. (*Lights up his pipe.*)

FONK: (*To VILITSKY.*) Besides which, he's not even Russian, though he left his native land at an early age and has occupied various posts here, mostly in the provinces. At any rate, he came to St Petersburg with the intention of dedicating himself to the soap-boiling industry – and suddenly he's begun to write! Now, that's what I call talent!

(*VILITSKY looks at SOZOMENOS with great interest.*)

I must confess I'm not all that keen on modern literature. They write such strange things these days. Moreover, although I regard myself as absolutely Russian, and acknowledge the Russian language, so to speak, as my native tongue, nonetheless, being of non-Russian origin, like Mr Sozomenos here, I don't have what one might call the authentic voice...

VILITSKY: Oh, nonsense! Good heavens, sir, you speak excellent Russian. I marvel constantly at the purity, the sheer beauty of your style. Really...

FONK: (*With a modest smile.*) Well, perhaps...

SOZOMENOS: A first-rate scholar.

FONK: Oh, hardly. Anyway, what was I going to say? Ah yes – I'm not a great enthusiast for contemporary literature...

(*Sits down. VILITSKY does likewise.*)

But I do love good Russian style, when it's correct and expressive. That's why I was so pleased with Sozomenos' story. Yes, I lost no time in acquainting him with my genuine satisfaction. However, I'm advising him not to publish, because unfortunately critics these days seem to have very little taste.

SOZOMENOS: (*Takes the pipe out of his mouth and stares at the floor.*) These critics know absolutely nothing.

VILITSKY: Yes, they're too smart for their own good.

SOZOMENOS: Nothing whatsoever.

VILITSKY: (*To FONK.*) You know, what you have told
me about Mr Sozomenos has greatly excited my
curiosity, and I'd very much like to become
acquainted with his work.

SOZOMENOS: (*Still staring at the floor, sotto voce.*) Not a
thing. (*He sticks his pipe back in his mouth.*)

FONK: He'll bring you his story in a day or two. (*Rises and
leads VILITSKY a little apart.*) Actually, he's a rather odd
individual, what one might call eccentric, but that's what
I like about him. All genuine writers are eccentric. I must
confess I'm delighted with my discovery. (*Self-importantly.*)
Je le protège. Well, how are you getting along, my dear
Petya? How are things?

VILITSKY: Oh, much the same.

FONK: You haven't been coming into the office these days.

VILITSKY: No, I haven't. (*After a pause.*) And you know why.

FONK: Hm. So, what are you planning to do now?

VILITSKY: I'll be honest with you, my dear Fonk... I was
meaning to go there today...

FONK: About time too.

VILITSKY: Things can't go on like this. I'm actually
ashamed, it's ridiculous. What's more, I'm not sure I'm
doing the right... Oh, look, I'd better explain, and
hopefully the whole business can be resolved.

FONK: Of course.

VILITSKY: (*Has a look round.*) To be honest, I've been
wanting to have a talk with you.

FONK: Well, why not? What's to hinder you now?

VILITSKY: I'd prefer if we could talk in private. This is a
rather delicate matter...

FONK: (*Sotto voce.*) Perhaps you're embarrassed by the
presence of Mr Sozomenos? Well, really – look at him.
(*Points at SOZOMENOS, who appears to be in a stupor, the
pipe-smoke barely issuing from his mouth.*) He doesn't even
see us. His imagination isn't like yours or mine: quite
possibly he's in the Orient now, or America, heaven only
knows. (*Takes VILITSKY's arm, and they begin pacing up and
down the room.*) Now, what did you want to say to me?

VILITSKY: (*Hesitantly.*) Well, you see, to tell you the truth, I hardly know where to begin. You've been so kindly disposed towards me. Your advice is always so practical, so wise.

FONK: Please, no compliments.

VILITSKY: (*Sotto voce.*) Please, you must help me. As you may have noted from our conversations this past while, I find myself in an extremely difficult position. You know I'm about to be married, I've made up my mind to it... I've given my word, and as an honourable man, I fully intend to keep it. I have nothing to reproach my fiancée with, she hasn't changed in the slightest. I love her, and yet... You won't believe it, but the very thought of my impending marriage has such an effect on me that... that I actually wonder if I have the right, in my present state of mind, to accept my fiancée's hand. After all, wouldn't it be deceit on my part? Tell me what you think. Is it simply the fear of losing my independence or is it some other feeling? I'm in a real quandary, I must confess.

FONK: My dear Petya, listen... May I be allowed to express my opinion with absolute frankness?

VILITSKY: Yes, yes, please do! (*Stops and looks round at SOZOMENOS.*) Well, to tell you the truth, I'm a little embarrassed in front of this gentleman... Ah! I think he's asleep.

FONK: Really? So he is.

(*He goes up to SOZOMENOS, who has fallen asleep, his head slumped on his chest, and he remains in that position throughout the conversation, except that now and again he gives a start, and as they say, 'catches fish'.*)

That's quite amusing. (*To himself.*) Eine allerliebste Geschichte. (*Aloud.*) Yes, that happens to him quite often. What strange fellows these authors are! (*Bends over him.*) Dead to the world. Actually, I rather like that. It's most original, don't you think?

VILITSKY: Yes, it is.

FONK: Anyway, you've nothing to worry about now. So, my dear Petya, you want to know my opinion concerning your marriage, right?

(*VILITSKY nods.*)

That's a very delicate matter. Let me start by saying... (*Stops.*) You see, Petya, a man, especially at our time of life, can't live without rules. I actually drew up some for myself, at a very early age, and I've never, under any circumstances, deviated from what one might call my 'laws'. And one of my most important rules goes as follows: 'A man must never lower himself; he must always keep his self-respect, and be prepared to account to himself, for all his actions.' I'll now turn to your own case. You became acquainted with Mr Moshkin two years ago. Mr Moshkin has done you a number of favours, perhaps quite important ones...

VILITSKY: Yes, that's true, I'm greatly in his debt, greatly.

FONK: I don't doubt that for an instant. And I also have no doubt of your gratitude. I know full well your honourable disposition. But the question which now arises demands the most careful consideration. Mr Moshkin is undoubtedly a most worthy person, but tell me honestly, my dear Vilitsky – do you and he really belong in the same company?

VILITSKY: Well, I'm as poor as he is – even poorer, in fact.

FONK: It's not a question of wealth, my dear sir. I'm talking about education, manners, way of life in general. You must excuse my frankness...

VILITSKY: Go on. I'm listening.

FONK: So... now to the matter of your fiancée. Tell me, Petya, do you love her?

VILITSKY: Yes. (*After a pause.*) Yes, I do.

FONK: You're in love with her?

(*VILITSKY is silent.*)

You see, my friend, love is... Well, of course, one can't say a word against love: it's a fire, a whirlwind, a whirlpool. In brief, it's a phenomenon. Love's very difficult to cope with, I know, but for my part, I think

that even here, reason doesn't abrogate its rights. However, my personal opinion in this matter can't serve as a general rule. If you truly do love your fiancée, then there's no point in discussing it: all our words will be, so to speak, absolutely in vain. But it seems to me that you're beginning to waver, that you're confused, that you're uncertain of your own feelings, indeed, and that's a very important point. At any rate, you're now in a position, as they say, to accept the advice of a friend. (*Takes him by the arm.*) So, let's cast a cold eye over your relationship with this young lady. Your fiancée is a most amiable, charming girl, there's no denying it. (*VILITSKY lowers his eyes.*) But you know, even the finest diamonds require a little polishing.
(*VILITSKY looks round hastily at SOZOMENOS.*) Don't worry, he's still asleep. Anyway, it isn't a question, my dear Petya, of whether or not you love your fiancée now, but of whether you are going to be happy with her. An educated man has certain requirements, which his wife cannot always appreciate; he is concerned with issues beyond her comprehension. Believe me, my friend, equality is essential in marriage. Let me explain: I will have no truck with that kind of specious equality between man and wife, which certain wild-eyed prophets... No, a wife owes her husband blind obedience – blind. I'm talking about a different sort of equality, you understand.

VILITSKY: That's true – I'm in complete agreement with you. But, my dear sir, put yourself in my place. Do you really want me to break my word? Good heavens! If I reject Masha now it'll be the end of her. I mean, she's like a child, she's put her trust in me. One might almost say I've brought her into the world. I sought her out, and I proposed to her! And now I have to see it through to the end. You surely don't want me to cast aside that responsibility? You would be the first to despise me for it.

FONK: No, wait – hear me out. I've no intention of acquitting you completely, but it's still possible to refute your arguments. You see, in my view, there are two sorts of duty: one's duty to others, and one's duty to oneself. What right have you to harm yourself, to ruin your own life? You're young, you're in the very flower of youth, as they say. You're in the public eye, with perhaps a glittering career before you. Why on earth should you throw all that away, when you've made such a good beginning?

VILITSKY: What do you mean, sir, throw it away? Surely I can continue my work...

FONK: Yes, of course you can, as a married man, there's no dispute about that. And you may achieve all things in time. But who wouldn't prefer the shortest route? Diligence, commitment, punctuality – such qualities don't go unrewarded, for sure. Shining ability is likewise always useful in a civil servant. It attracts the notice of one's superiors. But connections, my dear friend, connections, knowing the right people – that's vitally important in this world. I've already told you about my rule on avoiding close contact with the lower orders. And from that rule, there naturally flows another, and it's this: try to make the acquaintance of as many upper-class people as you can. It's not all that difficult. People in society will readily accept an energetic young official, modest, well-educated. And once he's accepted in society, with time he'll have the opportunity to make a decent match, especially if he's single, and has no inappropriate family ties.

VILITSKY: I'm in complete agreement with you, my dear sir. But I'm not that ambitious – I'm rather afraid of the *beau monde,* and I'd be quite happy to spend my life within the family circle. Besides which, I can't profess to having any shining abilities whatsoever, though commitment, as you yourself say, won't go unrewarded. No, it's other thoughts I find troubling. I keep thinking about the moral obligation I'm under... I'll go further, and say that I can't contemplate breaking off my engagement without a feeling of horror, yet at the same time the idea of marriage frightens me. So much so that I absolutely can't make up my mind what to do.

FONK: (*Pompously.*) I fully understand your state of mind. It's not as peculiar as you think. You see, my dear friend, you are at a point of transition. And this transitional state, so to speak, is a crisis. A crisis, d'you take my meaning? If you could only get away from here now, even for a month, I'm sure you would return a changed man. Then you'd be able to draw on all your resources, your strength of character, and come to a decision!

VILITSKY: You think so? But what about Masha, what about her? My conscience would torment me.

FONK: That's rather awkward, of course. You have my sympathy. But what's to be done?

VILITSKY: I'm a vile, pitiful creature!

FONK: (*Severely.*) What good does that do? Sir, allow me to observe – that's mere petulance. Forgive me, sir, but the sincere interest I take in your affairs...

(*VILITSKY presses his hand warmly.*)

It'll be hard for Marya Vasilievna at first, naturally. Indeed, it may be some time before she overcomes her grief. However, we must judge this matter dispassionately. You are in no way as guilty as you imagine. And as for your fiancée, she ought even to be grateful to you. You reached out to her, so to speak, you led her out of darkness, you awakened her dormant abilities – in a word, you began the process of her education. But you went further – you aroused hopes in her, which could not be fulfilled. You deceived her, yes, but you deceived yourself also. After all, sir, if I may say again – you didn't pretend to be in love with her, did you, you didn't deceive her on purpose?

VILITSKY: (*Heatedly.*) No, never, never!

FONK: Then why are you so worried? Why reproach yourself? Believe me, my dear Petya, so far you've done nothing but good to this young lady.

VILITSKY: Oh God, what am I going to do? Truly, you must despise me...

FONK: On the contrary, I feel sorry for you.

VILITSKY: However, I assure you, my dear friend, I can still find the strength to get out of this predicament. I am most sincerely grateful to you for your advice. I can't say I agree with you absolutely, I can't accept all your conclusions. I still don't see any necessity for changing my decision, but...

FONK: That's not at all what I'm asking, Petya. You must think over your situation yourself.

VILITSKY: Yes, of course, of course. I'm most grateful to you...

FONK: I'm a mere bystander in all this, of course.

VILITSKY: Heavens no, my dear sir.

(*MITKA enters from the hall.*)

Who's that? Oh, it's you. What do you want?

(*MITKA smiles.*)

Well, come on, what is it?

MITKA: There's a lady asking to see you, sir.

VILITSKY. Who?

MITKA: (*Smiles again.*) A lady, sir. Just a lady. Says she wants to see you alone, sir.

VILITSKY: (*Looks agitatedly at FONK, then turns to MITKA again.*) Why didn't you tell her I wasn't at home?

(*MITKA smiles.*)

Where is this lady?

MITKA: She's in the hall, sir.

FONK: (*Lowering his voice.*) You know, you don't need to stand on ceremony with us. He and I can leave. (*Tries to wake up SOZOMENOS.*) Sozomenos, wake up.

(*SOZOMENOS grunts.*)

Come on, wake up.

(*SOZOMENOS opens his eyes.*)

How can you sleep like that?

SOZOMENOS: I think I must've dozed off.

FONK: You did indeed, sir. It's time we were going.

(*SOZOMENOS slowly rises.*)

VILITSKY: (*Hurriedly.*) Gentlemen, gentlemen, why are you leaving?

FONK: Well, honestly...

VILITSKY: It might be nothing. It's just some person asking to see me.

SOZOMENOS: We'll stay if you like.

FONK: (*To SOZOMENOS.*) Ssshh! Sozomenos, you don't understand... there's a lady come to see him.

SOZOMENOS: (*Hoarsely, his eyes popping.*) A lady?

VILITSKY: That doesn't mean anything. It doesn't, I assure you. It's just one of those... oh, I don't know. It's nothing, really.

SOZOMENOS: Is she young?

VILITSKY: I don't know. Look, gentlemen, why don't you go into my bedroom for a few minutes – it might be a little awkward, you know, if you were to go into the hall... It's just for a minute or so.

FONK: As you wish. But please, don't concern yourself about us.

VILITSKY: No, truly, if you aren't in a hurry, if you're not going anywhere else, then do stay, please. We can talk some more.

FONK: It'll be my pleasure. Sozomenos, let's go.

(*They both head towards the door at right.*)

SOZOMENOS: (*To FONK.*) Is she young, then? Eh?

FONK: (*With a smile.*) I don't know.

(*They exit to the bedroom. MITKA has meanwhile been standing with his hands clasped behind his back, smiling.*)

MITKA: Well, sir, what shall I do?

VILITSKY: Send her in, of course.

(*MITKA exits. VILITSKY closes the door at right and returns to centre stage. Enter MASHA, wearing a hat, her face concealed by a veil. She stops a little way into the room, and VILITSKY approaches her.*)

VILITSKY: May I ask with whom I have the... Masha!

(*MASHA makes her way unsteadily to the settee and sits down and lifts up her veil. She is very pale.*)

Masha, it's you! Here, in my house!

(*Throughout the following scene VILITSKY frequently glances towards the bedroom door, and speaks in a half-whisper.*)

MASHA: You weren't expecting me, were you.

VILITSKY: How could I have imagined...

MASHA: You weren't expecting me. Well, don't worry, I won't keep you. Are you alone?

VILITSKY: Yes, I am... but...

MASHA: I thought I could hear voices.

VILITSKY: I had some friends here. They've left now.

MASHA: And I'll be leaving directly. Have you been back in town long?

VILITSKY: (*Embarrassed.*) Masha, I... I...

MASHA: So it's true. It's true, isn't it – you've been hiding from me. My God! Oh, don't worry – I didn't come here in order to make a scene.

VILITSKY: Masha, forgive me. I swear to you before God, I was coming to see you today.

MASHA: I'm honoured. However, I'm not here to reproach you. I've simply come to explain... I've written a letter to you today.

VILITSKY: Masha, calm down, please you're so pale. Are you feeling all right?

MASHA: I'm fine, thank you. I feel better than I should. I've simply come to...

VILITSKY: (*Sits down beside her.*) Masha, please, listen – this is my fault, it's all my fault, I truly am sorry. To be honest, no, I never left St. Petersburg. I've been trying to avoid meeting you. And you may well ask why. But I don't know, I swear. Sometimes I... Sometimes I do things I can't explain... the most stupid ideas come into my head, I'm just not myself at those times. But now you've instantly become suspicious. You're not very trusting, Masha.

MASHA: Not trusting? Five days, five whole days...

VILITSKY: Well, yes, all right – it's my fault, I'm sorry. Please forgive me, Masha, try and understand...

MASHA: And not a single word to me... (*She is on the verge of tears.*)

VILITSKY: Masha, for heaven's sake, calm down. This'll pass. And it'll all work out for the best, you'll see.

MASHA: No, Petya, it won't pass. Your love has passed, that's all. How could I have imagined, that two weeks before the wedding... What wedding! As if I can still believe...

VILITSKY: Masha, listen – we need to talk, we need to have a really serious discussion – not here and now, of course. We must put an end to all these misunderstandings...

MASHA: Put an end to what? It's already ended. As if I don't know that you're no longer in love with me, that you're bored with me, that I've become a burden to you! I'm well aware of that, Petya. Of course, I'm not worthy of you – I haven't had the right education. But it was you who first... Surely you remember? It wasn't I who begged for your friendship, was it. Anyway, I've only one request to make of you now – that you'll cease to torment me. Just tell me you've fallen out of love with me, that it's all over between us. Then at least I'll know where I stand.

VILITSKY: (*Aggrieved.*) Masha, why should you think...

MASHA: Why? D'you imagine I haven't noticed your coldness towards me? I don't need an education for that. Before, you hardly ever left my side, you used to bring me books, read them along with me. Sometimes you even called me... darling... (*Lowers her voice.*) You spoke to me as if we were lovers, but now... How could I possibly not notice the change, tell me? You're still my fiancé, you send me presents, but what does that matter? Oh, Petya, you don't love me any more, I know you don't.

VILITSKY: Masha, how can you say that? Yes, of course I'm at fault, but I'll say again, I can explain everything. We just need to have a talk, a little talk, that's all. I'm an honourable man, Masha, you know that. I've never tried to deceive you, and you've no reason to break my heart like this... Yes, I'm at fault, and I'm truly sorry.

MASHA: (*Lowering her head.*) You don't love me, you don't love me...

VILITSKY: Again! That's so cruel of you. You know perfectly well I love you. Look at me, Masha – don't you feel it? Calm down, please, and go home. I'll come this evening...

MASHA: Oh, I see – you want rid of me now?

VILITSKY: Masha, why do you say that? Why do you want to torture yourself and me? Well, I've no right to reproach you. It's my fault, and I'll say nothing. But listen to me, honestly...

MASHA: (*Her head still bowed.*) What could I have done to deserve such coldness, Petya, tell me? (*Begins crying.*) I haven't had the right education, it's true. Your friend must have had a good laugh at me. God only knows what he's said to you about me. You brought him in to inspect me, I know you did.
(*At the word 'inspect', VILITSKY winces slightly.*)
But at least I... (*Breaks down, weeping.*)

VILITSKY: (*Pleadingly.*) Don't, Masha, please. It won't help. There's no use tormenting yourself. Please don't cry.

MASHA: (*Tearfully.*) You don't love me.

VILITSKY: You've already said you wanted to have it out with me, and now you're in no state to listen to anything. How are we going to live together afterwards, if we're like this already, before the wedding?
(*MASHA sobs.*)
Masha, for God's sake... your tears are breaking my heart. For the love of God, calm down – it'll all turn out for the best, believe me. We must help one another – we'll have other difficulties to face in the future.

MASHA: (*Sobbing.*) You don't love me!

VILITSKY: (*Slightly irritated.*) Oh, for God's sake, stop it, that's enough! Have you lost every last shred of confidence in me? All right, I'm at fault – I'm sorry. Look, I'm getting down on my knees to you... (*Kneels down.*)

MASHA: (*Tearfully.*) Please, don't...

VILITSKY: (*Rather brusquely.*) For heaven's sake, Masha, if you love me, stop this at once. You have no idea what an absurd position you're putting me in... (*Almost in a whisper.*) Masha,

please, leave now. I'll visit you this evening, without fail,
I promise.

(*MASHA is still crying.*)

Masha, for the love of God!

MASHA: (*Tearfully.*) Goodbye forever, Petya! (*Begins loudly
sobbing.*)

VILITSKY: (*Jumps up.*) Oh, this is too much! Masha...
Masha... Masha!

(*She continues to sob. He is irritated.*)

Stop it, stop it, this minute! People can hear us!

MASHA: (*Removes her handkerchief from her face.*) What?

VILITSKY: (*Embarrassed and angry, points at the bedroom
door.*) There's a friend of mine – in there.

MASHA: (*Indignant.*) And you didn't tell me? Oh, how you
must despise me! (*Runs from the room.*)

VILITSKY: Masha, don't go, please! Masha!

(*He stands motionless a few moments, clutching his head in silence,
then recovering his composure, crosses to the bedroom door and
opens it. He is embarrassed, assumes a forced smile.*)

Gentlemen, forgive me! You may come in now.

(*FONK and SOZOMENOS enter. FONK is calm and blasé, as
if he had heard nothing, SOZOMENOS, however, is quite red
in the face from suppressed laughter.*)

Please, come in...

FONK: So, has your lady visitor gone?

VILITSKY: Yes... (*He looks at them askance, as if trying to
discover whether they have heard anything or not.*) Yes, she's
gone now. You must forgive me, I've detained you...

FONK: Not at all, sir, not at all. (*Makes a sign to
SOZOMENOS, who is about to burst out laughing.*) No, not
in the least. But what about you? Aren't you going out
for a walk today? It's a beautiful day.

VILITSKY: Yes, I'm going to the office. And where will
you be this evening?

FONK: Well, I was planning to...

(*SOZOMENOS suddenly explodes with laughter.*)

VILITSKY: (*After a pause, glumly.*) So, gentlemen, you
obviously heard everything.

SOZOMENOS: (*Giggling.*) And how!

FONK: (*To SOZOMENOS, sternly.*) Really, Sozomenos,
I must say – your laughter is quite uncalled for.
(*SOZOMENOS almost chokes, but carries on laughing. FONK
takes VILITSKY by the arm and leads him aside.*)
Petya, please, don't be angry with him. These writers are
all mad. Quite frankly, they shouldn't be allowed into a
respectable house. They've absolutely no idea how to
behave. But don't take it out on me, Petya, please...

VILITSKY: (*Bitterly.*) I'm not in the least angry, and I'm not
taking anything out on anybody. Mr Sozomenos is
absolutely right. The whole episode was farcical. Why
should I be angry? Please, feel free.
(*SOZOMENOS sits down, still chuckling, sighs, and wipes
his eyes.*)

FONK: (*To SOZOMENOS.*) That's quite enough,
Sozomenos! (*To VILITSKY, pressing his hand.*) Rest
assured, sir, no-one else will hear of this.

VILITSKY: Really? Why on earth not? It's a most amusing
anecdote.

FONK: (*Reproachfully*) Petya...

VILITSKY: No, truly.

FONK: Well, all right. Frankly, there's nothing surprising
about the whole business. You've brought it on yourself,
I must say. Your absence... I find that entirely natural,
even praiseworthy, from a certain standpoint.

VILITSKY: (*Smarting.*) You think so?

FONK: Yes, I do. And it's obvious that you're strongly
attached to her.

VILITSKY: Oh, undoubtedly!

FONK: (*After a pause.*) You see? A living commentary on
my words. Anyway, let's change the subject.

VILITSKY: (*Bitterly.*) Yes, let's. What shall we change it to?

FONK: (*To SOZOMENOS.*) Well, have you calmed down
at last?
(*SOZOMENOS nods.*)
Watch you don't feel asleep again.

SOZOMENOS: D'you think that's all I do?

FONK: Why don't you read us some poems? I'm sure you write poetry...

SOZOMENOS: No, I haven't so far, but I'll give it a try.

FONK: Do, I recommend it. (*To VILITSKY.*) Oh yes, I nearly forgot – did you manage to hear Rubini?

VILITSKY: No, I was planning to go to the theatre with my fiancée. Now I don't know when I'll have the chance.

FONK: I heard him again a couple of days ago in "Lucia di Lammermoor". He moved me to tears.

VILITSKY: (*Through gritted teeth.*) To tears, really...

FONK: I'll tell you something, Petya – you're a most upright and principled man.

VILITSKY: Me?

FONK: Yes, you.

VILITSKY: In what way?

(*The voices of MITKA and MOSHKIN are heard outside in the hall.*)

MITKA: He's not at home, sir. He's gone out of town again. (*VILITSKY falls silent and listens, as does FONK also.*)

MOSHKIN: Well, in that case I'll leave a message for him.

MITKA: Sir, he told me to say he'd be coming to see you this evening. You can write a note for him here, if you wish.

FONK: (*To VILITSKY.*) What's going on?

(*VILITSKY doesn't respond.*)

MOSHKIN: Why won't you let me come in?

MITKA: I can't, sir. The door's locked, and he's taken the key away with him.

MOSHKIN: But you were about to go in there for the inkstand, weren't you.

MITKA: No, sir, I can't. So help me, sir, I can't.

MOSHKIN: Mitka, I think your master's at home – indeed, I know he is. Let me come in.

MITKA: No, sir.

MOSHKIN: Mitka, that's enough – let me in. Your master hasn't left town at all. I've just been asking your caretaker, in the grocer's shop. (*Raising his voice.*) Petya! Petya, tell him to let me in! I know you're there.

(*VILITSKY, not daring to look at FONK and SOZOMENOS, who is again on the point of bursting out laughing, walks over to the door.*)

Come in, come in, Mr Moshkin, do, please. Mitka, have you gone mad?

(*MOSHKIN and MITKA enter. MOSHKIN is extremely agitated. On seeing FONK and SOZOMENOS, he begins to bow all around. VILITSKY shakes his hand, embarrassed.*)

Good morning, my dear sir, good morning. Please forgive me – there's been a misunderstanding...

(*To MITKA, who is trying to speak.*) Now, go away.

MITKA: Sir, you told me yourself...

VILITSKY: Clear off, I tell you.

(*MITKA exits.*)

MOSHKIN: Goodness, this is terrible. You must forgive me, on the contrary... it seems I have disturbed...

(*He bows again to FONK and SOZOMENOS, who acknowledge him. SOZOMENOS gets up from his chair. MOSHKIN goes up to FONK.*)

Mr Fonk, my most humble respects... I didn't recognise you at first. It's this sun, you see... (*Waves his hand in the air.*) So, how are you, my dear sir?

FONK: I'm well, thank God. And yourself?

MOSHKIN: Oh, not too bad, sir, thank you. (*Again bows to FONK and smiles.*) Very pleasant weather we're having, sir, don't you think?

(*He is obviously embarrassed. An awkward silence.*)

FONK: (*To VILITSKY.*) Well, goodbye, Petya. (*Picks up his hat.*) No doubt we'll see each other again later today.

MOSHKIN: (*To FONK.*) Sir, please, I hope I didn't disturb... I can come back another time. I just wanted to have a look at Petya here.

FONK: Not at all, sir – we were about to leave in any case. Sozomenos, come, let's go.

VILITSKY: (*Confused.*) You're not leaving?

FONK: Yes, but we can meet later. Where will you be dining?

VILITSKY: I don't know. Why?

FONK: Well, if you're not detained anywhere, why not come to me, around five o'clock, say? Meanwhile, goodbye. (*To MOSHKIN.*) Goodbye, sir. (*Bows.*)

VILITSKY: Goodbye, sir... Mr Sozomenos... By the way, sir, where do you live?

SOZOMENOS: In Gorokhovaya Street, Zhmukhin's house.

VILITSKY: If I might have the pleasure...
(*He accompanies them out into the hall. They exit, VILITSKY re-enters. MOSHKIN is standing motionless, and does not look at him. VILITSKY hesitantly approaches him.*)
I'm very glad to see you, Mr Moshkin.

MOSHKIN: And I... I'm very glad too, Petya, of course. Petya, I... I... (*Falls silent.*)

VILITSKY: I was meaning to call on you today, sir, and now I have to go out quite soon. Please, why don't you sit down?

MOSHKIN: (*Remains standing.*) I'm all right, thank you. So, how was your trip to the country? You're keeping well?

VILITSKY: (*Hastily.*) It was fine, very good, thanks. Er... what time is it now?

MOSHKIN: Must be going on two.

VILITSKY: Two o'clock already?

MOSHKIN: (*Quickly turns to look at VILITSKY.*) Petya... Petya, what's the matter with you?

VILITSKY: With me? Why, nothing.

MOSHKIN: (*Goes up to him.*) Why are you so angry with us, Petya?

VILITSKY: (*Without looking at him.*) Me?

MOSHKIN: You see, I know everything, Petya. You didn't leave town at all. And you haven't been near us for five whole days. You've been hiding from us. Petya, what's wrong, tell me. Has one of us offended you?

VILITSKY: No, please – on the contrary...

MOSHKIN: Then why this sudden change?

VILITSKY: Sir... Please, I'll explain everything later.

MOSHKIN: Petya, we're simple people, we love you with all our hearts. If we've done anything to offend

you, then please forgive us. All this time we haven't
known what to think, Petya, we've been so depressed
and exhausted. Try and imagine our situation, Petya.
People keep asking us: where's Petya? And I try to
say: oh, he's gone out of town for a few days, but
I can't get my tongue round the words. What can
I do? And so close to the wedding, just imagine it.
And as for poor Masha, well, I don't even want to talk
about it. I mean, Masha's your fiancée, Petya, she is
truly. The poor girl has absolutely nobody, except you
and me. If there was some reason, at least, but just
suddenly to... well, it's as if you've plunged a dagger
into our hearts.

VILITSKY: Honestly, sir, I...

MOSHKIN: Petya, Masha's been here today, I know she has.
(*VILITSKY gives a slight start.*)
She suddenly put on her hat this morning, and I asked
her where she was going. She seemed in a daze: "I'm
just going to the shops," she said. Well, that's hardly
likely, Petya, you know yourself Anyway, I said
nothing, and let her go, but I followed her. And I saw
that sweet child practically run through the streets and
come straight here. I stood at the corner, just by the
wineshop, and watched. And a quarter of an hour later,
I saw her come out, my dear little orphan, her face
white as a sheet. She got into a cab then, and hung her
head, obviously crying... (*Stops and wipes his eyes.*)
Petya, she looked so pitiful, truly!

VILITSKY: (*Agitatedly.*) It's my fault, sir. I've wronged both
her and you. I'm so sorry.

MOSHKIN: Oh, Petya, Petya, I didn't expect this of you!

VILITSKY: Please forgive me... I'll tell you everything. It'll
all come out right in the end, you'll see. It will, honestly.
I'll come and see you today and explain everything.
Forgive me, please.

MOSHKIN: Well, that's wonderful, Petya. Thank God for
that! I knew you wouldn't hurt us deliberately. Come, let

me embrace you, dear friend. Good heavens, I haven't
seen you for five days! (*Embraces him.*)

VILITSKY: (*Hurriedly.*) Sir, you mustn't think I said
anything disagreeable to Masha. On the contrary, I tried
everything I could to calm her down, but she was in such
a terrible state...

MOSHKIN: I believe you, Petya, but put yourself in
her place... Petya, you haven't taken a dislike to us,
have you?

VILITSKY: Sir, how can you even think...

MOSHKIN: And you haven't fallen out of love with her?
Petya, she loves you so much. If you abandon her,
she'll die.

VILITSKY: Mr Moshkin, how can you say that?

MOSHKIN: I mean, she is your fiancée, the wedding's all
been arranged, with your consent...

VILITSKY: And I'm not cancelling the wedding, am I?
Good heavens, sir, I love Masha.

MOSHKIN: Oh, thank God! Thank God for that! So, none
of this mattered – just something that didn't seem right
to you. Well, in future, Petya, it'd be better to speak up,
just point it out to us – I mean, really, these five days...

VILITSKY: Please, don't remind me. I feel so ashamed. It
won't ever happen again, believe me.

MOSHKIN: Well, it's all over now, Petya. Let bygones be
bygones, eh?

VILITSKY: (*Without looking at MOSHKIN.*) All I said to
Masha, and which I'm repeating to you now, is that she
and I need to have a little talk... you know, so that this
sort of misunderstanding doesn't arise in future.

MOSHKIN: What d'you mean, misunderstanding? What
sort of misunderstanding? I don't follow.

VILITSKY: Masha and I need to have a little talk, that's all.

MOSHKIN: Well, no-one's going to quarrel with that.
That's your right. She'll be your wife, and you'll be her
husband – who else but you will be her guide and
mentor, teach her how to live? After all, you'll have a
long life together, marriage isn't a bed of roses – you

need to be truthful with one another. You've already taken a great deal of interest in her, in her education, that is, since she is an orphan, and I'm not an educated man. You have a perfect right, Petya.

VILITSKY: No, sir, you just don't understand me. Anyway, it'll all be explained, and you'll see, very shortly, then everything'll turn out for the best. Poor, dear Mr Moshkin – even your appearance has changed.. and it's all my fault, it's quite unforgivable of me.

MOSHKIN: Nonsense! You've been a joy and a consolation to me these past three years – and now you've made me sad just once, what does that matter? It's not worth talking about. As for explanations, well, I'll leave that to you, you're a clever fellow, you'll do what's best, I know. Only don't be too hard on us, please. You know yourself, Masha gets so easily upset. She's a bit shy, a solitary creature, but don't pay any mind to that. She may not be *comme elle font,* as they say, but that's not where happiness in life lies, Petya, believe me. That comes from sound morals, from love, from goodness of heart. Your friends are educated people, of course, and they talk such high-flown stuff, whereas we... well, all we can do is love you with all our hearts. Nobody can argue with that, Petya.

VILITSKY: (*Pressing his hand.*) My dear, kind friend... What have I done to deserve such favour?

(*MOSHKIN smiles and waves his hand dismissively.*)

Honestly, I don't know.

(*A brief silence.*)

MOSHKIN: Petya, look me in the eye. There you are, you see, you're the same Petya again.

VILITSKY: You're so kind, so goodhearted.

(*Another brief silence.*)

Oh, what a nuisance! I've got to go the office.

MOSHKIN: To the office? Heavens! Well, I won't detain you. So, when will you come and see us, Petya?

VILITSKY: This evening, sir, without fail.

MOSHKIN: All right, then. Petya, why not now? Couldn't you just..?

VILITSKY: Sir, I honestly can't. Mitka!

MOSHKIN: Oh well, it can't be helped. But Masha and I would be so pleased...

MITKA: (*Entering.*) Yes, sir?

VILITSKY: My uniform.

MITKA: Right, sir. (*Exits.*)

MOSHKIN: I mean, after all the crying and worrying, think, Petya... Won't you come?

VILITSKY: No, honestly, sir, I can't. I'll come this evening, absolutely without fail.

MOSHKIN: (*Sighs.*) Oh, well.

VILITSKY: I haven't been at the office all this time either. And as you can imagine, they may have noticed.

MOSHKIN: Just a couple of minutes – before you go to the office.

VILITSKY: I haven't the strength to face up to the shame. Please, you'll have to prepare Masha – tell her to forgive me.

MOSHKIN: Oh, nonsense! She doesn't need any preparation – what an idea! I'll just take you in and say: "Here he is – here's our runaway!" And she'll run up and hug you, that's all the preparations we need!
(*MITKA enters with the uniform.*)
Put on your uniform, and we'll go.

VILITSKY: Well... only for a minute. (*Dons his uniform.*)

MOSHKIN: Yes, yes, we'll see. (*To MITKA.*) And as for you, sir, you're a shameless fellow!
(*MITKA smiles.*)
Still, I suppose I ought to praise you – a servant must do his master's bidding. Anyway, Petya, thank you, you've brought us all to life again. Now, let's go!

VILITSKY: Right. (*On the way out, to MITKA.*) If Mr Fonk should call, tell him I'll look in on him later...

MOSHKIN: Well, we'll see about that too. Now, put your hat on, sir, and let's go.

(*They exit. MITKA remains, watching them go, then slowly moves* .
downstage.)

MITKA: "Shameless fellow!" Honestly, you can't figure
them out. I mean, I was told not to let him in... Well, I'll
just lie down and have a snooze, I think. (*Flops out on the*
settee.) It's about time he bought himself a new couch,
these springs are worn out. Fat chance of that, though,
his mind's on other things. Chasing after women, yes!
Well, to hell with the lot of them. (*Lifts his feet up in the*
air, looks at them.) Yes, that rogue Kapiton makes a decent
pair of shoes! (*Falls asleep.*)
(*Curtain.*)
(*End of Act Two.*)

ACT THREE

The setting is the same as in Act I. MOSHKIN is wearing a dressing-gown. He looks sad and anxious, standing by the door at left, listening. After a few moments, PRYAZHKINA appears in the doorway.

MOSHKIN: (*Almost whispering.*) Well, how is she?

PRYAZHKINA: She's fallen asleep.

MOSHKIN: And she has no fever?

PRYAZHKINA: Not now.

MOSHKIN: Thank God!

(*A silence.*)

Listen, you'd better not leave her just the same.
Something might happen, you know.

PRYAZHKINA: Heavens, no, I certainly won't! Perhaps if you'd tell them to put on the samovar..?

MOSHKIN: Indeed I will, dear lady.

(*PRYAZHKINA exits. MOSHKIN slowly comes downstage, sits down, and stares motionless at the floor for a while. Then he passes his hand over his face and shouts.*)

Stratilat!

STRATILAT: (*Entering from the hall.*) Sir?

MOSHKIN: Put on the samovar for Mistress Pryazhkina.

STRATILAT: Yes, sir. (*Makes to exit.*)

MOSHKIN: (*Hesitantly.*) Has no-one come yet?

STRATILAT: Not a soul, sir.

MOSHKIN: And no-one... no-one's delivered anything?

STRATILAT: Not a thing, sir.

MOSHKIN: (*Sighs.*) Well, off you go.

(*STRATILAT exits. MOSHKIN looks round the room, is about to stand up, then slumps back in to his chair.*)

My God, my God, what does all this mean? Suddenly everything's in ruins again. It's all too clear now... (*Hangs his head.*) What can we do, what remedy is there? (*A brief silence.*) None at all, there's no remedy. It's all over... (*Waves his hand dismissively.*) Not unless... maybe it'll sort

itself out, maybe it'll all come right in the end. (*Sighs.*)
Oh, God in heaven!

(*Enter SHPUNDIK from the hall. MOSHKIN looks round.*)
Filipp, is that you? Thank goodness, at least you
didn't forget.

SHPUNDIK: (*Pressing his hand.*) Oh, come, sir – I'm not
one of these Petersburg types, am I. (*After a pause.*) Well,
has he been yet?

MOSHKIN: No, he hasn't.

SHPUNDIK: He hasn't? What's his reason?

MOSHKIN: God only knows. He keeps saying he's sorry,
says he's got no time...

SHPUNDIK: (*Sits down.*) No time? And how is Masha?

MOSHKIN: Masha's not very well. She hasn't slept the
whole night. She's resting now.

SHPUNDIK: (*Shaking his head.*) Fancy that! (*Sighs.*) Yes,
indeed.

MOSHKIN: So, what are you up to?

SHPUNDIK: Oh, I'm running around all over the place.
But I'll tell you this much, dear friend, the more I see of
these city people of yours, these Petersburgers, well, the
less I like them. The further away the better, that's my
view. No, sir, they're not for me, no way!

MOSHKIN: Why do you say that? There are some good
people here too.

SHPUNDIK: I'm not arguing with you, there may well be.
You've just got to keep your eyes skinned, that's all.
(*After a pause.*) So, Petya hasn't been yet?

MOSHKIN: Oh, Filipp, what's the point of trying to hide it
from you? Look at me, I'm a dead man.

SHPUNDIK: Good God!

MOSHKIN: It's true, I'm as good as dead, honestly. And
it's all happened so suddenly. You remember, Filipp,
when you came to see me a mere two weeks ago... you
remember how I greeted you, the plans I was making,
you remember, don't you? But now... now everything's in
ruins, dear friend, it's all gone to the devil, to hell itself –

gone right to the bottom, sir, and I'm left sitting here like a fool, racking my brains, and getting nowhere.

SHPUNDIK: Misha, you're exaggerating, surely?

MOSHKIN: Exaggerating? Filipp, you've been here almost every day, you can see for yourself. I mean, presumably there was something that upset him at that dinner, you remember the one, so he didn't come – he was being a bit silly, but never mind, I went to see him, had it out with him, and brought him back here. Masha cried a bit, but she forgave him, and that was fine. So, I thought everything was all right, didn't I? He didn't stay long, to tell you the truth – maybe feeling guilty, I don't know. Anyway, he reassured her, as you might expect – everything'll be back to the way it was, he says, the way a fiancé would. Fine. So, he arrives the following day, brings her a little present, turns round, and next minute he's gone! Business to attend to, he says. Next day he didn't come at all, then he turned up again, sat for about an hour, and said scarcely a word. I'm talking about the wedding, how it should be and when, it'll soon be time, I says. Yes, yes, he says, and that's about it. Since then he's disappeared again. We never manage to get him at home, and he doesn't answer our letters. Now, tell me, Filipp, what do *you* think all this means? It's as clear as daylight. It means he's jilting us! Doesn't it? He's jilting us! And you can imagine what sort of state I'm in now. After all, the responsibility, so to speak, lies on me. This was my doing... she hasn't another soul in the world, she's got nobody to take her part. But how could I have believed that Petya would... (*Stops short.*)

SHPUNDIK: (*Deep in thought.*) D'you know what I'm going to say to you, Misha, dear friend?

MOSHKIN: What?

SHPUNDIK: Don't you think he's just been a little silly? Sowing his wild oats, as they say? St. Petersburg's just the place for it, after all.

MOSHKIN: (*After a pause.*) No, it's not that. He's not that sort of man, he wouldn't do that.

SHPUNDIK: Maybe some other girl has caught his eye? That friend of his, he's an important man, maybe he's introduced him to some young lady...

MOSHKIN: That's more likely. However, it's not that, I'm sure. A change has come over him so suddenly, I just can't understand it, it's as if somebody's taken his place. He looks at me differently now, he doesn't laugh the way he used to – he even talks differently, and he avoids Masha altogether. Oh, Filipp, Filipp, I'm so depressed, you've no idea! It's terrible to think that just recently... and now... And what's it all for? How could this have happened?

SHPUNDIK: Yes, of course, Misha, you're right... it's not easy, as you say. Even so, I still think you've no reason to lose heart.

MOSHKIN: Oh, Filipp, Filipp – I loved him like a son, you know that. I shared everything with him, everything I had. And that's what upsets me – if he was even angry, it'd be easier to bear, I'd be more hopeful. But he's simply indifferent, he even feels sorry for us. That's what's killing me, Filipp. I mean, he hasn't come, and he won't come – he won't come tomorrow, and I actually find it strange to imagine he might come to see us at all.

SHPUNDIK: Yes, indeed, friend – as the poet says: "It's a wicked world we live in." Yes.

MOSHKIN: I might as well lie down and die.
(*Enter PRYAZHKINA.*)
How is she?

PRYAZHKINA: She's fine, dear sir – not to worry.
(*SHPUNDIK bows to her.*)
Good evening, Mr Shpundik.

SHPUNDIK: My respects, Mistress Pryazhkina. And how are you keeping?

PRYAZHKINA: Very well, sir, thank God. And you?

SHPUNDIK: Likewise, thank God. And how is your dear niece?

PRYAZHKINA: She's a little better now, sir. But she hardly slept a wink last night. (*A deep sigh, then to MOSHKIN.*) What about the tea, sir, did you order it?

MOSHKIN: Yes, I did indeed. Hasn't he brought it to you yet? Stratilat!

(*STRATILAT enters with the samovar.*)

What kept you?

STRATILAT: Sir, it's only just boiled up. (*Carries the samovar through into MASHA's room.*)

SHPUNDIK: (*To PRYAZHKINA.*) So, I imagine you won't be leaving your niece?

PRYAZHKINA: How can I? There's no-one else to look after her, you can see for yourself.

SHPUNDIK: Well, you're a great comfort to her, I'm sure – a model aunt.

PRYAZHKINA: Why, thank you, Mr Shpundik.

MOSHKIN: Splendid, splendid.

(*STRATILAT re-enters from MASHA's room and hands MOSHKIN a letter.*)

Who's this from?

STRATILAT: I don't know, sir.

MOSHKIN: (*Looking at the writing.*) This is Petya's handwriting!

(*He hurriedly unseals it and reads. SHPUNDIK and PRYAZHKINA watch him attentively. MOSHKIN turns quite pale as he reads it, and when he finishes, slumps into the armchair. SHPUNDIK and PRYAZHKINA are about to approach him, but he instantly leaps up and begins speaking, disjointedly.*)

Who... this... who brought... who... call...

STRATILAT: Sir, what is it?

MOSHKIN: Call him... whoever brought... call back...

(*Gestures wordlessly to SHPUNDIK and PRYAZHKINA. STRATILAT exits and returns almost immediately with the POSTMAN, wearing his official cap.*)

POSTMAN: Yes, sir, what can I do for you?

MOSHKIN: Tell me, friend – you brought this letter from Mr Vilitsky?

POSTMAN: No, sir. It came by ordinary post. We're strictly forbidden to carry private letters.

MOSHKIN: Yes, of course, I'm sorry. I just thought... (*He is quite bewildered.*)

SHPUNDIK: (*To MOSHKIN.*) Sir, calm yourself. Stratilat, pay the postman.

(*STRATILAT and the POSTMAN exit.*)

Misha, pull yourself together.

MOSHKIN: It's all over, my friends! Finished! I'm done for, Filipp, we're all done for. It's all over.

SHPUNDIK: What d'you mean?

MOSHKIN: (*Unfolds the letter.*) Here, listen! Mistress, you should hear this too. He's turning his back on us, my friends, he flatly rejects us. The wedding's off – it's all over, finished, gone to the dogs, absolutely! Look, this is what he writes to me:

(*SHPUNDIK and PRYAZHKINA stand alongside MOSHKIN.*)

"My dear Mr Moshkin, after a lengthy and protracted struggle with myself, I realise I owe you an explanation, so I shall be frank (*Looks up at SHPUNDIK.*)... I shall be frank with you. Believe me, this decision has cost me a very great deal. God knows, I couldn't have foreseen it, and I dearly wish I could avoid causing you any unpleasantness. However, even the slightest delay now would be unforgivable. I have hesitated too long as it is. Anyway, I confess I am incapable of making Masha happy, and beg her to release me from my promise." Release him. (*To SHPUNDIK.*) Look, you see what he's written? "Incapable", he says, "Release me." See?

(*SHPUNDIK looks at the letter. MOSHKIN continues.*)

"I dare not even ask her forgiveness. I feel so guilty before her and you both, and I hasten to assure you, sir, that I know of no young lady more worthy of the utmost respect..." D'you hear that? "Utmost respect", he says. "However, having foreseen the necessity of breaking off our engagement for a time, I now part from you with a heavy heart..." Eh? Eh? "I cannot but confess, my dear sir, that you have every right to consider me dishonourable (*MOSHKIN shakes his head.*) ... and I am not going to assure you and your ward of my devotion, my sincere commitment, and so on. Such words can now only arouse your just indignation, and I shall therefore keep silent. May you both be happy..." "Happy," he says, "Happy"! He can say that! Oh, oh! (*MOSHKIN covers his face with his hands.*)

SHPUNDIK: Misha, calm yourself – what can you do? (*After a pause.*) You haven't finished the letter.

MOSHKIN: It makes no sense! It can't be... I mean, he has no right – dammit, he hasn't! I'm going to see him this very minute! (*Begins pacing up and down the room.*) Stratilat! Bring me my hat! And my coat, be quick about it! Call me a cab – this instant, d'you hear!

SHPUNDIK: Misha, what are you doing? Where are you going?

MOSHKIN: Where? I'm going to his house. I'll show him! I'll... I'll... Oh, so this is your way, my dear sir? Well, that's just fine, that's really nice. I'll demand an answer from him, that's what I'll do!

SHPUNDIK: But how are you going to do that?

MOSHKIN: How? I'll tell you how. I'll say to him: 'I should like an answer, my dear sir, no more beating about the bush. Has Masha offended you in some way? Well, sir, has she? Has her conduct in some way displeased you, sir?'

SHPUNDIK: Yes, he'll...

MOSHKIN: 'No, answer me, sir, d'you hear? Isn't she a well-brought up young lady, sir? A young lady with principles, sir, eh?' (*Advancing on SHPUNDIK.*)

SHPUNDIK: Of course she is. I mean, he himself...

MOSHKIN: 'What? You've been coming to our house for two years, we've treated you like one of the family, shared our last kopeck with you, and finally, at your own importunate request, sir, yes – we've given you this treasure. The wedding day is set, and you... oh! No, I'm sorry, sir, you haven't heard the end of this, no no...' Stratilat, my hat!

(*STRATILAT enters.*)

'Suddenly you've changed your mind – you've picked up your pen, scrawled a few lines, and now you think it's all over? Well, I'm sorry, but it's not. I'll show you, sir, just

you wait. You're not going to make a mockery out of us!'
D'you know what he writes at the end? "I shall pay all
my debts to you in full." Well, I don't want a kopeck
from him! Why haven't I got my cap?
(*STRATILAT hands the cap to him, but he doesn't take it, continues
to pace the room.*)
To think he could do this! 'Petya, how could you...'
(*With an angry wave of his hand.*) Why the devil am
I calling him Petya? It's all over between us, finished!
Yes, he thinks Masha has no-one to stand up for her, so
he can do what he likes, just cast her aside. Where's
the harm in that, he says, I'll just ditch her. Well,
you're sadly mistaken, you've come up against the
wrong man, friend. I may be old, but I'm going to
challenge him to a duel!

PRYAZHKINA: (*Shrieks.*) Oh, my God!

SHPUNDIK: Misha, for heaven's sake! No, Misha!

MOSHKIN: Why not? You think I don't know how to
shoot a pistol? I'm as good as the next fellow. What's
going on? I keep asking for my cap, that's a dozen times
I've asked for it!

STRATILAT: Sir, it's here. I gave it to you already.

MOSHKIN: (*Snatches the cap from him.*) And you're as bad!
Get me my coat!
(*STRATILAT hurries to fetch the coat.*)
I'll show him, you see if I don't.

SHPUNDIK: Misha, wait, listen to the voice of reason!

MOSHKIN: And you can clear off with your voice and
your reason! You see a man here in despair, driven just
about crazy, and you're going on about reason! You can
all go to hell! (*Puts on his coat.*) Well, maybe I'll go down
on my knees to him. Maybe I'll kneel and say I'll die
right on this spot, if he doesn't come back to us. Yes,
have pity, I'll say, on a wretched orphan. I'll ask him
why he's killing her – tell me, please! Now, you stay here
a while, my friends – stay here, I beg you! I'll come
back, I won't be long – one way or another, I'll come
back. Only, for God's sake, don't let Masha know, while

I'm away, do you hear? I'll be back directly, I promise.
Just wait here for me.

SHPUNDIK: Well, with pleasure, my dear sir, but...

MOSHKIN: Don't say it! I don't want to hear another
word! I'll be back soon, I promise. Supposing I die, I'll
come back...

(*Hurries out. SHPUNDIK and STRATILAT are left bewildered.
PRYAZHKINA sighs and sits down. STRATILAT exchanges
glances with SHPUNDIK, then slowly exits.*)

PRYAZHKINA: (*Sighing and wringing her hands.*) Oh, Lord
in Heaven! Oh, Lord! Oh, Lord! I'm being punished for
my sins, that's what it is! Oh, merciful God, how is it all
going to end! Oh, Lord, dearest Lord, help me, help this
poor, luckless orphan!

SHPUNDIK: Dear lady, calm yourself. God willing, it
might still come out right in the end.

PRYAZHKINA: Oh, my dear, kind sir, I'm utterly lost.
How can it come out right? How can it? You see what a
tragedy has struck us! To think I've lived to see this day!
Oh, Lord Jesus Christ, have mercy on me, a poor sinner!

SHPUNDIK: (*Sits down beside her.*) Calm yourself, please,
dear lady. You'll do yourself an injury.

(*PRYAZHKINA blows her nose and recovers her composure a
little.*)

PRYAZHKINA: (*Tearfully.*) Oh, dear sir, try and put
yourself in my place. I mean, Masha is my niece –
imagine how I feel, having to bear this. And dear Mr
Moshkin – think how I feel about him. God only knows
what might happen to him.

SHPUNDIK: Yes, it's certainly all very unpleasant.

PRYAZHKINA: Oh, my dear sir, it couldn't be any worse!
And I foresaw all this, I did indeed... I knew this would
happen!

SHPUNDIK: Really?

PRYAZHKINA: I surely did, yes! But they took no notice
of me, Mr Shpundik, they wouldn't listen. I've said all
along no good would come of this wedding, but they just
wouldn't listen.

SHPUNDIK: Why wouldn't they?

PRYAZHKINA: (*Her tears quickly forgotten.*) Oh, God
knows why, Mr Shpundik. No doubt they thought, well,
she's an old woman, she must be talking nonsense. But
I tell you, dear sir, I'm a simple person, not out of the
top drawer, so to speak, there's no denying. Even so, my
husband, God rest him, was an officer in the Catering
Section – we mixed with the best people, we were
respected and admired by all sorts, and now our own
family take no notice of us. General Bondoidin's wife
used to receive us, my dear sir, and she had an
especially soft spot for myself, if I may say. I'd be
sitting alone with her in her bedroom, and she'd say to
me: "You know, Katerina my dear, I'm really surprised
– you have such good taste in everything." And
General Bondoidin's wife was acquainted with all the
very finest gentlemen. "I really do enjoy passing the
time with you," she'd say. She'd order tea for me,
honest to God she would. Why should I lie? And now
my own niece won't even listen to me! That's what all
the tears are about. But it's too late for that.

SHPUNDIK: Maybe it isn't too late.

PRYAZHKINA: What d'you mean, sir? How can you say
that? Of course it's too late. He won't come back. I'm
sorry, but it's all over.

SHPUNDIK. Well, perhaps. But tell me, dear lady –
I can see you're a sensible woman – why is it young
people these days never listen to us old folks? After
all, we only want what's best for them. Why don't they
listen, eh?

PRYAZHKINA: They're empty-headed, my dear sir,
that's why. General Bondoidin's wife was forever
saying that. "Oh, Katerina" she'd say, "When I look at
young people today – well, I feel like giving up, and
that's the truth!" I mean, that's what I told my niece.
You won't be marrying him, I said, he's a go-getter,
and that sort are too cagey. Don't even look at him,
I said, he's not for you. But her? "Leave me alone,

auntie!" – that's what she said. Well, do what you like, my girl. Now see where 'leave me alone' has got you! After all, I had a daughter of my own, dear sir – oh, I certainly had! A real beauty she was, such as you won't see the like of these days, no indeed, sir! Such lovely eyebrows she had, her nose – just wonderful. And her eyes – well, you just couldn't describe them. But empty-headed? Her eyes all over the place, absolutely all over the place. Anyway, I married her off – married her off well, too, a decent chap, an architect. So what if he was a bit too fond of the wine? We all have our faults. Anyway, I'd like to see how Mr Moshkin's going to settle Masha now. She'll wind up an old maid, you mark my words!

SHPUNDIK: So, is your daughter content with her husband? Is she happy?

PRYAZHKINA: Oh, Mr Shpundik, don't even mention her! She died last year, sir, and I'd had nothing to do with her for three years before her death.

SHPUNDIK: Why on earth not?

PRYAZHKINA: Because she was ungrateful, sir! You've married me off to a drunkard, mother, she said – he doesn't support me, and he curses me all the time. I mean, honestly, sir, how can you satisfy these young people? Her husband drinks, and it's a great tragedy! What man doesn't drink? My late husband, God rest him, got absolutely plastered at times – begging your pardon, sir – it was terrible, but I respected him just the same. She didn't have any money – well, of course, that's awkward, but poverty's no vice, as they say. And if he cursed her, most likely she deserved it. To my simple way of thinking, a husband's the head of the house, and there's nobody can tell him what to do. A wife's only a wife, after all, she shouldn't get above herself, right?

SHPUNDIK: I agree.

PRYAZHKINA: Anyway, I've forgiven her. She's dead now, God rest her. Maybe she's learnt the error of her ways.

I'm not a spiteful person, sir. What do I care? No, sir,
I just want to see out the rest of my days somehow.

SHPUNDIK: My dear lady, why do you say that? You're
not so old...

PRYAZHKINA: Oh, sir, really! Actually, the general's wife
was the same age as me, and she looked much older.
Even she was surprised. (*Listens.*) Oh dear... I think that's
Masha... no. No, it's nothing. I get this noise in my ears
at times. Just before dinner, I always get a noise in my
ears, or else my stomach rumbles so much I can scarcely
catch my breath. Why's that, I wonder, sir? An old
woman I know advised me to rub hempseed oil on my
stomach at night, what d'you think of that? She's very
good, actually an Arab woman – black as pitch, would
you believe, but such gentle hands.

SHPUNDIK: Well, why not try it? You know, these simple
remedies sometimes work wonders. I treat all my friends.
Something'll just come into my head, and I'll try it out
on them, and wouldn't you know, it works. I cured our
village headman of dropsy once, with tar. Just rub it in,
I told him, and that cured him, it did indeed!

PRYAZHKINA: Oh yes, for sure, these things happen. But
it's God's will, it's God's holy will in everything.

SHPUNDIK: Of course, I dare say you've got doctors
here in town, learned men, the very finest German
doctors. But we're stuck out in the steppe, at the back of
beyond, we've got to scrape along somehow. We can't
send out for doctors, no, we lead a simple life, and
that's a fact.

PRYAZHKINA: And that's the best sort of life, sir. You'll get
very little sense out of those learned doctors, I tell you.
They're as bad as that Petya of ours. And whose fault is it?
It's our own fault. You take Mr Moshkin here – what on
earth's he doing bringing up a girl that's not his own?
I mean, is it his business to find a husband for her? Is that
any job for a man? He wanted to do her a good turn –
well, good luck to him, sir, but it's none of his business, he
shouldn't have interfered, should he, sir. Eh?

SHPUNDIK: I suppose not. It's really a woman's place. All the same, it doesn't always work out for you women either. There's a neighbour of mine, for instance, Olimpiada her name is, she had three daughters, and they were all engaged, but not one of them got married. The last fellow ran out of the house in the middle of the night, freezing cold it was, too. And they say old Olimpiada was shouting after him, leaning out of the attic window in her nightie: "Stop, stop, please – let's talk things over!" But he shot off across the snow, like a frightened rabbit.

PRYAZHKINA: Well, you can't always control these things, worse luck. They do happen. Still, if they'd just listened to me... I had someone in mind, sir, a first-class gentleman, I'll tell you – a real treasure. (*Kisses her fingertips.*) Yes, indeed, sir. (*Sighs.*) Well, there's no sign of him now. I'll go and see how Masha's doing. Most likely she's still sleeping, the poor dear. I wonder what she'll say when she wakes up and finds out!(*Begins to whimper again.*) Oh, Lord, Lord, what's to become of us ! Why hasn't Mr Moshkin come back yet? Maybe something's happened to him. Maybe he's been killed, maybe they've done away with him, the poor dear man!

SHPUNDIK: No, no, it's not far away, but it still takes time to get there. I mean, he's got to get there and back, and he'll have sat down for a bit – to say his piece, like.

PRYAZHKINA: Yes, yes, you're right, sir. But I keep thinking – oh, there's no good'll come of this, sir, no good at all! He'll cripple him, sir, he will for sure!

SHPUNDIK: Oh, nonsense!

PRYAZHKINA: You wait and see. I'm never wrong about these things, sir, believe me, I know. That Petya looks as if butter wouldn't melt, but he's an absolute scoundrel!

SHPUNDIK: Surely not...

PRYAZHKINA: He'll give him a beating, sir, believe me – he'll draw blood for sure!

SHPUNDIK: Honestly, the way you talk, you'd think we were living in some sort of thieves' kitchen! People aren't allowed to fight here. We have a government, after all. Really! Cross yourself, mistress!

PRYAZHKINA: No no – he'll just say to him: "How dare you come here and bother me, sir! Devil take you and that Masha of yours both! What else did you expect, you old mongrel?" And then he'll punch him, sir, he will!

SHPUNDIK: Oh, nonsense! What are you saying? That can't be, surely?

PRYAZHKINA: He'll make his teeth rattle, sir – he'll punch that darling man.

SHPUNDIK: Good heavens, mistress!

PRYAZHKINA: (*Begins weeping.*) He'll strike him down, Mr Shpundik... like that wicked Cain in the Bible!

SHPUNDIK: And I took you for a sensible woman!

PRYAZHKINA: (*Sobbing.*) He'll hit him, I know he will.

SHPUNDIK: (*Irritated.*) Well, what if he does!

PRYAZHKINA: (*Wiping away her tears.*) And he won't care, either.

SHPUNDIK: Look, here's Mr Moshkin now.

(*PRYAZHKINA turns round to see MOSHKIN entering from the hall, still with his coat and hat on. He walks slowly towards centre stage, dejected, then stands motionless, looking down at the floor. STRATILAT follows him on.*)

PRYAZHKINA *and* SHPUNDIK: Well? What happened?

MOSHKIN: (*Without looking at them.*) He's gone away.

SHPUNDIK: Gone away?

MOSHKIN: Yes, gone away, and left orders not to say where. At least, not to tell me. That scoundrel of a caretaker laughed at me, no wonder. But I'll find out tomorrow, or today, even – I'll find out at his office. He won't get rid of me, by God he won't!

SHPUNDIK: Misha, take off your coat.

MOSHKIN: (*Flinging his hat on the floor.*) Here. take it, take anything you want. What do I want with all this?
(*STRATILAT removes his coat.*)
What's the point? What's it matter? Here, take it, take everything! (*Sits down and covers his face with his hands.*)
(*STRATILAT picks the cap off the floor, and exits with the coat.*)

SHPUNDIK: Misha, at least tell us what...

MOSHKIN: (*Suddenly looks up.*) What is there to tell?
I went there and asked, "Is he at home?" "No, sir, he isn't
– he's gone away." "Where to?" "I don't know." What
more d'you want me to say? It's perfectly clear. It's all
over, finished, end of story. And to think that just
recently, he and I were looking for an apartment for...
His own was too small, you see. Well, there's nothing left
now but to hang myself.

SHPUNDIK: Misha, what are you saying? Good God,
Misha!

MOSHKIN: Well, I'd like to see what you'd do in my
place! God, what am I going to do now, eh? How can
I look Masha in the eye?

PRYAZHKINA: And you wouldn't listen to me, no, you
wouldn't listen, would you.

MOSHKIN: Oh, for heaven's sake, mistress, I'm sick
listening to you! I've no time for you now. How is
Masha?

PRYAZHKINA: (*Her pride wounded.*) She's sleeping, sir.

MOSHKIN: I'm sorry – you must forgive me. You can see
the state I'm in. Anyway, you were always on his side –
that person... Petya. (*Places his hand on SHPUNDIK's
shoulder.*) You know, sir, this has been a real shock to
me... it's broken my heart, yes. Well, something needs to
be done, just the same. (*After a pause.*) I'll go to his office.
Find out where he's staying. Yes.

SHPUNDIK: Misha... dear friend, let me tell you something,
out of the fullness of my heart, as they say. Please, Misha.
You know, sometimes a word of advice... Please...

MOSHKIN: Go on – what is it?

SHPUNDIK: Misha, listen to me – don't go. Don't go,
d'you hear? Forget it. You'll only make things worse.
He's jilted her – well, there's nothing you can do about
that. You can't put that right, Misha, you can't. There's
absolutely nothing you can do. Believe me. And this
good lady here'll tell you the same thing. You'll only
make a fool of yourself.

MOSHKIN: That's easy for you to say!

SHPUNDIK: No, don't say that! I feel it too, Misha, just as painfully. But it's commonsense that's needed now. Think it over, Misha – what good'll come of it? You've got to consider the outcome, as they say. Who's likely to suffer, eh? Yourself, for a start, and Masha too. (*To PRYAZHKINA.*) Isn't that so? (*PRYAZHKINA nods.*) There, you see? Forget it, Misha, do. There's plenty of other fish in the sea. And Masha's a sensible girl.

MOSHKIN: Oh, you keep talking, and my head's spinning – it's as if somebody was whacking me across the head with a cudgel. There are other young men, that's for sure. But this business was settled, the wedding was practically upon us – it's a blot on her honour, sir, it's her honour that's suffered. Bear that in mind, sir. And will Masha want to marry somebody else? It's easy for you to talk, but what about me? She's my ward, she's in my care, sir, a poor orphan. And I've got to answer to God for her!

SHPUNDIK: But there's nothing you can do about it. He's jilted her. You'll only torture yourself.

MOSHKIN: I can put the fear of God into him.

SHPUNDIK: Frighten him? Oh, Misha, that's not for the likes of us. Forget it. Just put it out of your mind.

MOSHKIN: You think it's that easy? If it was you, every day for two years... Oh, what am I arguing about? I'll hang myself and that'll be an end to it!

SHPUNDIK: Misha, what are you saying? You ought to be ashamed of yourself, a man of your age...

MOSHKIN: What's my age got to do with it?

SHPUNDIK: Misha, that's enough, please. This is doing no good. Come to your senses, Misha, forget the whole thing.

PRYAZHKINA: Please, Mr Moshkin!

SHPUNDIK: Forget it, Misha, please! Take an old friend's advice. Just drop it.

PRYAZHKINA: That's right, Mr Moshkin – drop it.

MOSHKIN: (*Begins pacing the room again.*) No no, this is all wrong. You don't know what you're talking about. I must have a talk with Masha. I need to explain to her... and then let her decide. It's her business, after all. I'll go in and tell her: "Masha," I'll say, "It's all my fault. It was me that planned this whole thing, without thinking, like the old fool I am. Punish me however you see fit. And if you've set your heart on this man, well, I'll drag him back to you by the scruff of the neck, if I must. Just say the word, Masha, it's up to you..."

SHPUNDIK: No, no, friend, I can't approve of that either. That's no business for a girl, isn't that so, mistress?

PRYAZHKINA: It is indeed, my dear, kind sir.

SHPUNDIK: You see? You're going about this the wrong way. You'd do better to listen to the voice of reason. Things might turn out all right even yet. Remember what the poet said:

> Dearest, though it cause thee pain
> To lose thy love heart-sworn,
> All thy sorrow is in vain –
> Have faith, and cease to mourn...

MOSHKIN: (*Still pacing the room, as if to himself.*) Yes, that's a good idea. Fine, I'll do whatever she says. Yes.

SHPUNDIK: This is no business for a girl, sir, I'll say again. She won't even understand you – how could she? God knows what made you dream this up, sir – she'll burst out crying, that's what she'll do, and then what?

PRYAZHKINA: (*Whimpering.*) Oh, Mr Moshkin, don't talk like that. Have mercy on me, at least. Have pity on a old woman, dear sir!

MOSHKIN: (*Ignoring her.*) Yes, definitely, that's settled. (*To SHPUNDIK and PRYAZHKINA.*) Well, friends, thank you for having waited for me. However, now I'd like a half-hour or so to myself. It's a fine day, why don't you go out for a little stroll, my dears?

SHPUNDIK: What?

MOSHKIN: (*Hastily.*) Yes, do, please. Goodbye, goodbye... just for half an hour.

SHPUNDIK: Misha, where are we supposed to go?

MOSHKIN: Wherever you like. (*To SHPUNDIK.*) Filipp, take the good lady to Milyutin's shop – you'll see some wonderful pineapples there, as big as your fist. And there are all sorts of interesting sights, monuments and so on... (*Gently pushing them out.*)

SHPUNDIK: But I've seen all those already.

MOSHKIN: Well, have another look at them. Now, dear lady – you too...

PRYAZHKINA: But the tea's ready, sir – the samovar's boiling.

MOSHKIN: That doesn't matter – your samovar won't go missing. Goodbye...

SHPUNDIK: Really, Misha...

MOSHKIN: Filipp, for God's sake – here's your cap.

SHPUNDIK: Well, as you wish. Half an hour, then?

MOSHKIN: Yes, yes, half an hour. And here's your hat, dear lady. Your coat must be hanging up in the hall. Goodbye, goodbye... (*He ushers them out and then re-enters, walks rapidly to centre stage.*) Now, this is the moment of truth. I've sent them on their way, now I must act. What'll I say to her? I'll tell her, I'll say: "This is how things are, so what are we going to do now, my dearest?" I'll prepare as best I can, and then – well, then I'll show her the letter. Then I'll immediately go on to add that things can still be sorted out, I'll tell her we mustn't give up hope... (*After a pause.*) I'll have to be extremely careful. Oh yes. This calls for a bit of tact. Well, I'd better go and see her. (*Goes towards the door.*) Heavens, I'm scared stiff. My heart's in my mouth. God knows what I look like. (*Crosses hurriedly to the mirror.*) Ugh! What a face! (*Drags a brush through his hair.*) You're a handsome devil, sir, and no mistake. Well, there's no point in putting it off. Whew! (*Mops his brow.*) What a state I'm in! This is worse than going into battle, I'm sure. Well, what the hell... (*Buttons up his coat.*) Let's get it over with. (*Goes up to the door.*) What, is she asleep? She

can't be. Not with all the noise we've been making. Oh
dear, what if she's heard us? Well, so much the better.
Yes, surely. Come on, you coward, let's go... No, wait –
I must have a drink of water. (*Goes back to the table,
pours out a glass of water and drinks it.*)
(*MASHA emerges from the bedroom.*)
Now, with God's help... (*Turns round and catches sight of
MASHA, almost faints.*)
Oh! It's... it's... it's... how did... how did you...

MASHA: (*Bewildered.*) It's me, yes. What's wrong with you?

MOSHKIN: (*Hastily.*) Nothing, nothing – I'm fine... I just
wasn't expecting you... They said you were asleep.

MASHA: That's right – I've been asleep all this time. I've
only just got up.

MOSHKIN: And how do you feel?

MASHA: Not too bad. A slight headache.

MOSHKIN: No wonder after a night like that.
(*MASHA sits down.*)
So, you're feeling better? Thank God for that. It's a fine
day today. We'll go out for a sleigh ride later, if you like.
What d'you think?

MASHA: Yes, if you wish.

MOSHKIN: No no, it's what *you* wish. Since when have
I ever made you do anything? I'll do whatever you like.

MASHA: You're so good to me.

MOSHKIN: (*Sits down near her.*) Oh nonsense! Really, I'm
just... I mean, I'm... Oh, what's the difference. Masha,
turn round and look at me...
(*She does so.*)
Oh, Masha, Masha, you've been crying again. Masha,
I understand, I know what's been going on, but
honestly... Masha, there's no need... It might still work
out, honestly, Masha... (*Gesturing vaguely.*) He might
still.. Oh, you'll see...

MASHA: It's all right, I don't mind...

MOSHKIN: What do you mean, all right? You're not all
right, you're not. Good heavens, you're crying. And
for what reason? I'm not going to argue with you, but

even so... That goes without saying. Anyway, we'll see... (*Mops his brow.*) That idiot Stratilat has this room far too warm!

MASHA: You mustn't trouble yourself, dear sir, there's no need.

MOSHKIN: Who told you I was...

MASHA: Don't alarm yourself on my account, please. (*With a bitter smile.*) Believe me, I'm resigned to my fate.

MOSHKIN: Resigned to what, may I ask?

MASHA: I hope for nothing, and wish for nothing. I'm no longer willing to deceive myself. I know it's all over. Perhaps for the best, indeed.

MOSHKIN: No, no – how can you say that?

MASHA: Sir, now it's your turn to look at me.

MOSHKIN: What? Surely... (*Wants to look at her but can't.*)

MASHA: Oh, sir! Why go on pretending? What's the point of it? Who are we trying to deceive?

MOSHKIN: (*After a pause.*) Yes... you're right. Yes, of course. I just wouldn't have expected that sort of behaviour.

MASHA: (*Suddenly, intensely agitated.*) What do you mean?

MOSHKIN: (*Embarrassed.*) I... I... That is... I...

MASHA: You've been to see him again today, haven't you.

MOSHKIN: I... Yes.... Yes, I have.

MASHA: Well?

MOSHKIN: He wasn't at home.

MASHA: Then what are you talking about? What wouldn't you have expected?

MOSHKIN: Well, of course, he... And you yourself... Oh, he... he wrote me a letter.

MASHA: A letter?

MOSHKIN: (*Forcing a smile.*) Yes, a letter. You know the sort... Anyway, it was... I mean, I can't say exactly...

MASHA: Where is it?

MOSHKIN: Well, I have it...

MASHA: Give me that letter, please. Sir, for God's sake, let me have that letter!

MOSHKIN: Masha, I honestly don't know. I oughtn't to
have mentioned it. I don't know what I was thinking of.

MASHA: Give it to me, please, please!

MOSHKIN: (*Looks in his pockets.*) Actually, I don't know
where I've put it. Masha, this isn't a good idea. You're in
a terrible state...

MASHA: I'm perfectly calm. Please, the letter...

MOSHKIN: (*In despair.*) I can't, I just can't... oh, Lord! I've
got to prepare you, I was meaning to do that first...
Otherwise you might think... Oh, Lord! And look at me
now, I'm all at sixes and sevens!

MASHA: Sir, you're tormenting me...

MOSHKIN: Masha, at least promise me...

MASHA: I'll promise you anything, only for God's sake...
Oh, sir, can't you see?

MOSHKIN: Masha, please don't think... Look, it doesn't
mean anything. It was written in the heat of the moment,
obviously. Everything's fine still – there's nothing that
can't be put right. Quite easily, it'll be no trouble.

MASHA: For God's sake, let me have the letter!

MOSHKIN: (*Slowly takes it out of his pocket.*) Please, Masha...
(*MASHA snatches the letter from him and begins feverishly reading
it. MOSHKIN stands up, withdraws to one side and turns away.
MASHA reads the letter, remains motionless a moment, then
bursts into uncontrollable sobbing, covering her face with her
hands. MOSHKIN rushes up to her.*)
Masha, Masha, for God's sake! I told you it didn't
matter. Masha! Masha, for God's sake! (*To himself.*) Oh,
you dumb ox, you brainless old fool! All that talk
about being careful, tactful, huh! Oh, you ignoramus,
what do you know about tact, eh? You just pulled out
the letter and gave it to her! (*To MASHA again.*) Dearest
Masha, calm yourself, please! Don't cry. I'll take care of
everything. I'll sort it all out. Masha, you're killing me,
I can't bear to see you like this!
(*She holds out her hand to him.*)
Please, don't cry.

MASHA: (*Tearfully.*) I'm sorry. I'll get over it soon. It's just so sudden... (*Dries her eyes with her handkerchief.*)

MOSHKIN: (*Sits beside her again and takes back the letter.*) It's nothing, Masha, it's honestly nothing.

MASHA: It's not as if I hadn't expected it – as you know, I was prepared for anything. Of course, this letter, after all the promises... Still, I was under no illusions. I wish him every happiness... (*Begins crying again.*)

MOSHKIN: I'll have a word with him, Masha.

MASHA: No, sir, no – not for the world! He's cast me aside, well, good luck to him. I've no wish to bind him to anything. Sir, I beg you, not a word about me to Petya. I'm an orphan, I have no protection. He has insulted me, but what of it? I forgive him, I don't want to force myself on him. Please, my dear sir, not a word, not a single word, if you truly love me.

MOSHKIN: You say you have no protection, Masha – then what am I? Don't I love you as if you were my own daughter? This is killing me, Masha, and do you know why? It's the thought that I'm the cause of it all, it was my idea. He has cut me to the quick, Masha, there's no denying it, he has made a fool of me, but that's not the point. Do we simply forget the whole business, wave him goodbye, and walk away? No, I'm sorry, Masha, but that's not possible. Anyway, he might still change his mind. After all, I did bring him here the other day.

MASHA: And that was absolutely useless. What good did it do? You can see for yourself.

MOSHKIN: Masha dear, what else could I do? Put yourself in my place. Everything was going so well until recently, wasn't it? After all, if you yourself hadn't wanted to postpone the wedding, you'd have been a married woman by now. So how can you expect me to break everything off, just like that? This is a dream, surely, some sort of illusion, it's like a fog we're going through. You'll see, we'll wake up any minute. You'll look up, and everything'll be the way it was. Why on earth should he reject you, eh? Is it because you're not attractive? Surely not.

MASHA: (*Dejectedly.*) Sir, you're too kind. You love me, and because of that you like everything about me. But he... No, he doesn't want me. At first he found me amusing, but afterwards... I noticed it a long time ago, but I said nothing, because I was afraid you'd be annoyed. You see what kind of people his friends are. We can't compare with them! We're too ordinary for him, sir, too low. He despises us, and that's a fact.

MOSHKIN: Despises us? Well, he didn't despise the money he took from me. Just because he has some German friend, he's got above himself! No, sir, you're dealing with the wrong man...

MASHA: What's the point? It's no use. We can't bring back the past.

MOSHKIN: But, Masha, what'll people say? Think of that.

MASHA: I know, but what can we do?

MOSHKIN: What can we do? That's precisely what I'm thinking about.

MASHA: (*After a pause.*) Well, of course... I can't stay here any longer.

MOSHKIN: Wha-at?

MASHA: Sir, I must leave you.

MOSHKIN: What on earth for? What do you mean? Has your aunt been putting ideas into your head?

MASHA: Auntie did mention something about it, sir, but even if she hadn't, I'd still... Believe me, sir, my heart bleeds at the very thought of parting from you...

MOSHKIN: Good God, why don't you tell me just to jump out of the window! Oh, Masha, you must be out of your mind. Where on earth will you go, tell me that? Oh, that old witch! Yes, she's made up her mind to kill me, I can see that. But you, Masha – I can't believe it – why should you want to destroy me? Oh, dear Masha, what's the matter with you?

MASHA: Mr Moshkin, please – hear me out calmly, and you'll agree with me.

MOSHKIN: Indeed I won't, I won't agree, not ever!

MASHA: Listen, please – you took me into your house after my mother died. You were the only one who cared about me, and eventually you introduced me to Petya. Then, all this happened – he proposed to me, and now he's rejected me. That's my situation, sir. Now ask yourself, what are people going to think?

MOSHKIN: What d'you mean?

MASHA: (*Hastily.*) Sir, I am after all a stranger in your house. And people'll say: "Well, she's been jilted, so what? She's his ward, a foster-child, she's living on charity, anyway. She was engaged, and now she's been thrown over – who cares? It's not exactly a tragedy. She ought to be grateful somebody looked twice at her. Serves her right! If she'd stayed with her own relatives it'd never have happened. Unearned bread tastes sweeter, of course. Maybe she doesn't even want to work." That's what they'll say, sir – you see my position. I love you more than anybody else on this earth, but what can I do? Till this happened, I could live here with you, but now I can't remain here any longer, it's just not possible. I can't bear the thought of all that contempt. Surely you understand. And I'll manage to earn a living somehow.

MOSHKIN: Masha, I don't understand – I don't understand a word of this. Why are you saying these things? Earn a living? Contempt? Who would dare, eh? Good God, Masha! Who's responsible for you? I'm responsible for you! And I won't allow anybody to make a fool of me! I'll show the whole world, I'll show that damned milksop too!

MASHA: No, no! What are you saying!

MOSHKIN: You wait and see. You don't know me yet. You're living with me, you say? Masha, for heavens' sake, cross yourself! I'm an old man, a respectable person, everybody knows you're like a daughter to me. Honestly, I just don't understand you.

MASHA: No, sir, you do understand me, too well.

MOSHKIN: Masha, that's enough! You're joking, surely?
You can't mean what you've just said?

MASHA: (*Stands up.*) I'm not in the mood for joking.

MOSHKIN: And you're going to leave me?

MASHA: I must.

MOSHKIN: Where will you go?

MASHA: I don't know. I'll move in with my aunt to begin
with, then I'll see. Maybe I'll find a position somewhere.

MOSHKIN: (*Wringing his hands.*) I'm going mad, I swear,
I'm going mad. You'll move in with your aunt? You'd
better ask first where your aunt lives – she stays behind a
partition in the pantry, in a midwife's house, surrounded
by bath-brooms, dried mushrooms and filthy petticoats!

MASHA: (*A little offended.*) I'm not afraid of poverty.

MOSHKIN: (*Leaps to his feet.*) Oh, this is nonsense! I can't
stand any more of this! First him, then you... At least
show me you have a kind heart, Masha, not like his.
Are young people all like this these days? Masha,
please – I live only for you, and if you leave it'll kill
me. Have pity on a poor old man. What have I done to
deserve this?

MASHA: Mr Moshkin, put yourself in my place. I can't
stay here, I can't.

MOSHKIN: Oh, you women! God's sent you to punish
us. Once you get an idea into your heads, there's no
shifting it. No, Masha, I can't allow you to leave.
This is your nest, your home and hearth – everything
here is yours, it's all for you. I can't bear to be parted
from you. You're right, of course, Masha, I can see
that – people've got to respect you, and it's my job to
defend you, the way I would defend my own
daughter, because you live under my roof, because
I'm responsible for you before God and man.
Consequently, this is what I'm going to do. Now, just
keep calm, Masha, and I'll do what I intended – I'll
either get everything back the way it was, or else I'll
challenge him to a duel.

MASHA: A duel!

MOSHKIN: Yes, a duel! Swords or pistols, I don't care.

MASHA: (*Gasping for breath.*) No, no, listen! Unless you abandon this plan now, I'll take my own life, right this minute, I swear to God I will!

MOSHKIN: (*Almost shouting.*) Well, what am I going to do! Good God, Masha, I'm losing my mind! (*Suddenly stops.*) Listen, Masha... No, no, now I really *am* going crazy! Oh, who cares, anyway? Listen to me, Masha... You want people to respect you, right? You don't want anybody to think ill of you. And your present situation is extremely difficult, isn't it. Well, hear me out, Masha – just don't think I'm crazy... You see, it's like this... You can stay here... and nobody will... You understand me? I mean, absolutely nobody would dare to... Oh, Masha – in a word – will you marry me?

MASHA: (*Almost speechless.*) Mr Moshkin!

MOSHKIN: (*Hurriedly.*) Masha, don't interrupt me – I've no idea how this thought came into my head, but I've got to say it. It's a desperate measure, I agree, but so is our situation. And if I had any hope at all of Petya returning...

(*MASHA waves her hand dismissively.*)

Anyway, at least let me explain myself, otherwise you'll have every right to think me crazy, or even... No, you can't imagine me capable of insulting you.

MASHA: Heavens, no, but...

MOSHKIN: It's your own fault, Masha, frightening me like that, by threatening to leave. And all that talk about being despised, about earning a living, and so on – it just made my head spin. I mean, what am I afraid of, Masha? What do I want? I want people to respect you, to treat you like a queen. I want to prove to everybody, that to receive your hand in marriage, is the very height of bliss! One idiot, one silly boy, turned you down – turned down his own chance of happiness, yes, whereas here I am, a middle-aged civil servant, of irreproachable character, as they say, throwing myself

at your feet, asking you to consider me worthy. That's
what I want to prove to the whole world, Masha, and to
him as well, to Petya. If you can understand that... But
for heavens' sake, please don't think I'm...

MASHA: Mr Moshkin!

MOSHKIN: Wait, wait! I know what you're going to say, but
please, Masha, you must understand. I won't make much
of a husband, that goes without saying. But I realise you
can't live here with me as before, and you can't leave me.
Masha, I can offer you peace and quiet, respect, a roof
over your head – that's all I have to offer. I'm an honest
man, Masha, you know that. There's no stain on my
honour. And I'll cherish you, just as I have until now. I'll
be a father to you, that's what I'll be. Oh, Masha – they
were ready to fling you aside, to insult you – you're a
helpless orphan, you're living on charity, on the kindness
of strangers – no, absolutely not! You'll be mistress of this
house, Masha, a lady, and I... well, I'll be your protector,
don't you see? Your guardian, and that's all. Now, what do
you say to that?

MASHA: Sir, I'm astonished... and deeply moved. But you
can't wish me to answer right away.

MOSHKIN: Forgive me, Masha, I'm not forcing you. Take
your time, consider it at your leisure. It's for your
peace of mind – that's the only reason I've thought of
this. It's up to you. All you have to do today is tell me
you're staying. That'll make me so happy. I don't need
anything more.

MASHA: But I can't stay here if I... I can only stay if... Oh,
I can't give you an answer now.

MOSHKIN: As you wish. But please, think it over.

MASHA: Mr Moshkin, if I even... What right have I to take
advantage of you?

MOSHKIN: Oh, for heavens' sake! What earthly use am
I to anybody, d'you think? Eh? Tell me. Honestly, the
ideas you have! I mean, an old fool like me couldn't
even dream of such happiness. Good God, Masha, what
next? Just tell me now that you'll stay, and you can give

me your answer later – whenever, and whatever that
might be.

MASHA: (*After a pause.*) I am in your power.

MOSHKIN: (*Heatedly.*) Masha, if you say that once more,
I swear to God I'll march straight into the kitchen and
start cleaning Malanya's boots! You're in my power? God
in heaven, Masha!

MASHA: (*Looks at him for a moment, then, obviously moved.*)
I'll stay.

MOSHKIN: You'll stay? Oh, dearest Masha! (*About to
embrace her, stops.*) No, no, I don't dare...

MASHA: (*Embraces him.*) Oh, my dear, kind sir! Yes, yes,
you do love me, you care about me, I know that. You
won't deceive me, you won't ever betray me. I can
depend on you. But please let me go to my room now,
my head's spinning. I need to be alone.

MOSHKIN: Do as you please, Masha – whatever you wish.
There's no-one over you in this house. Have a rest, that's
the main thing. Everything else'll work out. (*Accompanies
her to the door.*) So, you will stay?

MASHA: Yes, I'll stay.

MOSHKIN: Oh, thank God, thank God! Just as long as
you're at peace and happy. And don't worry about
anything else. In cases like this, they say, one is
supposed to ask the beloved: "May I live in hope?" But
have no fear, I'm not going to ask you anything.

MASHA: (*After a pause.*) There's no need. Yes, you may
hope. (*After a moment's thought.*) Indeed you may, sir.
(*Quickly exits.*)

MOSHKIN: What was that she said? "You may hope"?
(*Jumps for joy.*) Stop, stop, you old fool. What are you
leaping around for? Surely you've got it wrong? Oh,
my God, who could have foreseen this? This is a
miracle, that's what it is, the like of which there's
never been! He jilts her, Masha stays, and here I am,
in all probability, getting married! Married? At my
age, and to whom? Why, to perfection itself, to an
angel! This is a dream, surely, an illusion. I must be

delirious, I'm in a fever, yes, a fever! Hah, Petya! You thought you'd play a dirty trick on us? No, sir, no! A fig for you, my dear sir! (*Looks round, then quietly to himself.*) That's why my heart sank when I made the match... (*Waves his hand dismissively.*) Oh, be quiet, you old fool, be quiet! Heavens, I can scarcely catch my breath! I think I'll go for a stroll...

(*Grabs his cap, and at the door, bumps into SHPUNDIK and PRYAZHKINA.*)

SHPUNDIK: Where on earth are you going?

MOSHKIN: Out for some air, Filipp, that's all – a short walk. I'll be back in a minute.

SHPUNDIK: What's wrong? Has something happened? How is Masha?

MOSHKIN: She's fine, fine. Don't disturb her. She's in her room, everything's fine. Filipp, my dear friend, let me embrace you! I've just this minute... Anyway, don't go in to see her, everything's fine, splendid. (*Hurries out.*)

SHPUNDIK: (*Turns to PRYAZHKINA, bewildered.*) What's going on? What's happened to him?

PRYAZHKINA: (*Gasping for breath, catches hold of the chair arm as if about to faint.*) Oh... it's a stroke, a stroke... God help us... a stroke...

SHPUNDIK: (*Alarmed, trying to support her.*) What is it? What's up? Are you having a stroke? (*Shouts.*) Stratilat! Stratilat, get a doctor, quickly!

PRYAZHKINA: Oh, sir... oh!

SHPUNDIK: Stratilat! Where *is* he! Stratilat!

STRATILAT: (*Running in from the hall.*) Yes, sir!

SHPUNDIK: Fetch the doctor! And hurry! Mistress Pryazhkina's ill, she's had a stroke – see...

PRYAZHKINA: (*Drawing herself erect, pushes SHPUNDIK away.*) What? Good Lord, sir, cross yourself this minute. What's the matter with you? Have you taken leave of your senses? What stroke?

SHPUNDIK: (*Astonished.*) But you yourself said...

PRYAZHKINA: It's not me that's had the stroke, it's him, dear Mr Moshkin – that's who's had the stroke.

SHPUNDIK: (*Annoyed.*) Well, really, dear lady – you frightened me half to death! (*To STRATILAT.*) Leave us, please. (*STRATILAT exits. To PRYAZHKINA.*) Honestly, you should be ashamed of yourself.

PRYAZHKINA: Why on earth should I? Are you blind, sir? Didn't you see him? His face was all twisted, and his lips too. He's had a stroke, sir, believe me. Our doctor had exactly the same a while back. Mind you, he was a drunkard, and he had dropsy besides, but their faces were just the same! Oh, I'm a poor, wretched woman – who's going to help me now?

SHPUNDIK: She's off again! Oh...
(*MOSHKIN hurries in from the hall.*)
Look, see for yourself – is he sick, or what? Silly woman! *To MOSHKIN.*) Just imagine, Misha Mistress Pryazhkina here is convinced you've had a stroke.

MOSHKIN: Eh? Well, in a certain sense that's true. Oh, I know, I know you're going to be surprised that I've... No, no, you'll just have to wait, I'll explain everything in due course.

SHPUNDIK: What on earth's the matter with you, my dear friend? Tell me, please – you really aren't yourself.

MOSHKIN: No, perhaps not. No, indeed! (*Draws SHPUNDIK to one side.*) You know, Filipp, there might still be a wedding.

SHPUNDIK: What? You've managed to sort everything out?

MOSHKIN: Oh yes, but not with him.

SHPUNDIK: What d'you mean, not with him? With whom, then?

MOSHKIN: Well, you'll find out, God willing. Anyway, give me a hug!

SHPUNDIK: All right. Only I must say...
(*They embrace.*)

MOSHKIN: (*Quietly.*) And congratulate me.

SHPUNDIK: Eh?

MOSHKIN: I'm sure you must have had your suspicions, Filipp...

SHPUNDIK: Suspicions? What about?

MOSHKIN: (*To PRYAZHKINA.*) And you too, dear lady –
(*Embraces her also.*) Now no more sadness, that's enough.
We're all going to be happy. Yes, you'll see we'll live
now. Filipp, when are you leaving for the country?

SHPUNDIK: In about three weeks' time. Why?

MOSHKIN: Well, some time before then we'll perhaps...
No, no – I'll say nothing, in case I spoil it.

PRYAZHKINA: Sir, what on earth are you talking about?

MOSHKIN: Don't ask me any more questions, dear friends
– just give me another hug! (*Embraces them both.*) Like
this! And Masha's going to be happy, I swear to God she
is! You hear that? You're my witnesses. She'll be happy!
She'll be happy!

(*End of the Play.*)

LUNCH AT HIS EXCELLENCY'S

Characters

BALAGALAEV (NIKOLAI IVANOVICH)
marshal of the nobility, 45

PEKHTEREV (PYOTR PETROVICH)
ex-marshal, 60

SUSLOV (YEVGENY TIKHONOVICH)
a judge

ALUPKIN (ANTON SEMYONOVICH)
a neighbouring landowner

MIRVOLIN
An impoverished landowner

BESPANDIN (FERAPONT ILYICH)
another landowner

KAUROVA (ANNA ILYINISHNA)
his widowed sister, 45

NAGLANOVICH (PORFIRY IGNATIEVICH)
district police inspector

VELVITSKY
The marshal's secretary

GERASIM
Balagalaev's valet

KARP
Kaurova's footman

The action takes place on Balagalaev's estate.

The scene is a dining-room; upstage centre, a door, and at left, another door leading to BALAGALAEV's study; windows at the rear, and a table set for lunch in the corner. GERASIM is busy at the table, and hearing the sound of an approaching carriage, he crosses to the window. MIRVOLIN enters.

MIRVOLIN: Good morning, Gerasim! How are you? What, hasn't he appeared yet?

GERASIM: Morning, sir. Where did you get hold of that horse?

MIRVOLIN: It's not a bad little beast, is it. I was offered two hundred roubles for it yesterday.

GERASIM: Who offered that?

MIRVOLIN: A merchant from Karachev.

GERASIM: Why didn't you sell it to him?

MIRVOLIN: Why do that? I need it myself. Be a good chap, and let me have a drink. I'm as dry as a bone, and it's so hot besides... (*Drinks, and eats something from the table.*) Are you setting this for lunch?

GERASIM: Well, it's hardly dinner-time.

MIRVOLIN: So many places! Must be expecting company, eh?

GERASIM: It would seem so.

MIRVOLIN: You don't know whom?

GERASIM: No. I hear they're trying to make peace between Mr Bespandin and his sister, though, so that might be the occasion.

MIRVOLIN: Eh? Really? Well, it's a good thing too. They should put an end to it, share out the property. Honestly, it's an absolute disgrace. But tell me, is it true His Excellency wants to buy Bespandin's woods?

GERASIM: God knows!

MIRVOLIN: (*Aside.*) I might just ask him for a little bit of timber.

BALAGALAEV: (*Off-stage.*) Filka! Tell Velvitsky I want to see him.

MIRVOLIN: I think the door from his study into the drawingroom's open... Now, Gerasim – what about another little drink?

315

GERASIM: What? You *must* be bone dry...

MIRVOLIN: Yes, it's something at the back of my throat... (*Drinks, and nibbles at some food. GERASIM exits. BALAGALAEV enters, followed by VELVITSKY.*)

BALAGALAEV: Yes, yes, yes – just do it that way, right? D'you understand? (*To MIRVOLIN.*) Oh, it's you – good morning.

MIRVOLIN: My most sincere respects, Nikolai Ivanych!

BALAGALAEV: (*To VELVITSKY.*) The way I told you, have you got that? Well, have you?

VELVITSKY: Yes, sir, of course.

BALAGALAEV: Right then, that'll be fine. Now, off you go... If I want you, I'll send somebody to fetch you. Well, go on...

VELVITSKY: Yes, sir. So... you want me to get the papers ready for the widow Kaurova's case?

BALAGALAEV: Yes, of course I do! Honestly, my dear sir, you amaze me – you've surely gathered that much?

VELVITSKY: But you didn't tell me anything about the...

BALAGALAEV: And why should I? I don't have to tell you everything, do I?

VELVITSKY: No, sir. (*Exits.*)

BALAGALAEV: That young man's none too quick on the uptake. (*To MIRVOLIN.*) Well, how are you? (*Sits down.*)

MIRVOLIN: I'm well, sir, thank goodness. And how are you keeping?

BALAGALAEV: Fine, fine. Have you been in town?

MIRVOLIN: Indeed I have, sir. Nothing new there, though. The merchant Selyodkin had a stroke a couple of days ago. Not that that's any surprise. And the lawyer's given his wife another...

BALAGALAEV: Really? The man doesn't know when to stop.

MIRVOLIN: I saw Dr Zhuravlyov, sir – he asked to be remembered to you. And I ran into Mr Pekhterev, in a new carriage – he looked as if he was going somewhere. He had a footman with him, and the footman had a new hat.

BALAGALAEV: He'll be here today. Was the carriage
quite nice?

MIRVOLIN: What can I say, sir? No, it wasn't up to much.
It was a nice enough shape, but when you get right down
to it – no, I didn't like it. It doesn't begin to compare
with yours!

BALAGALAEV: You think not? Did it have rubber tyres?

MIRVOLIN: Yes, it did, but so what? What use are they?
I mean, really – they're more for show than anything
else. He just likes showing off. They say he's planning to
put himself up for election again.

BALAGALAEV: What, for marshal of the nobility?

MIRVOLIN: Yes, looks like it. He's got his best black
horses in harness again anyway.

BALAGALAEV: Really? You know, I must say, Mr
Pekhterev's a thoroughly estimable chap, in every
respect, and he really does deserve... Of course, on the
other hand, if you want to win favour with the nobility...
Do have a vodka.

MIRVOLIN: Oh, thank you very much, sir.

BALAGALAEV: What, have you have been drinking already?

MIRVOLIN: No, absolutely not! Well, not drinking exactly
– it's my chest, you see... (*Coughs.*)

BALAGALAEV: Oh, nonsense – have a drink.

MIRVOLIN: (*Drinks.*) Your good health, sir! Actually, sir,
did you know – Pekhterev's real name isn't Pekhterev,
but Pekhteryov? Yes, it's Pekhteryov, and not Pekhterev.

BALAGALAEV: What makes you think that?

MIRVOLIN: I don't think, I know! Honestly. That's what
we used to call his father, yes, and all his uncles too.
They were all Pekhteryovs, from time immemorial, sir,
not Pekhterevs. We've never had any Pekhterevs in these
parts, what sort of name's that?

BALAGALAEV: Oh, well, what does it matter? As long as
a man has a good heart.

MIRVOLIN: You never spoke a truer word, sir. A good
heart, that's the thing. (*Looks out of the window.*)
Someone's coming, sir.

BALAGALAEV: And I'm still in my dressing-gown. That's because of chattering here with you. (*Stands up.*)

ALUPKIN: (*Off-stage.*) Tell him Mr A-a-alupkin's here. Alupkin, the nobleman.

GERASIM: (*Enters.*) Sir, a Mr Alupkin wishes to see you.

BALAGALAEV: Alupkin? Who's he? Show him in. (*To MIRVOLIN.*) Look after him, would you? I'll be out in a minute... (*Exits.*)

(*ALUPKIN enters.*)

MIRVOLIN: His Excellency'll be here directly, sir – won't you have a seat?

ALUPKIN: No, thank you, sir. I'll just stand. May I ask with whom I have the honour...?

MIRVOLIN: Mirvolin, sir – landowner, local resident... perhaps you've heard of me?

ALUPKIN: No, I haven't. No, sir. However, I'm very pleased to meet you. Tell me, sir – you wouldn't be related to a Mistress Baldashova? Tatyana Baldashova?

MIRVOLIN: No, not at all. Who is she?

ALUPKIN: She's a landowner from Tambov, sir, a widow.

MIRVOLIN: From Tambov?

ALUPKIN: Yes, sir – Tambov. A widow, sir. And may I ask if you're acquainted with the local police inspector?

MIRVOLIN: Naglanovich – Porfiry Naglanovich? Yes, indeed – he's an old friend.

ALUPKIN: He's the biggest swine that ever walked the earth – you'll forgive me, sir, but I'm a plain-spoken man, a soldier. I'm used to calling a spade a spade. And I'll tell you this, sir...

MIRVOLIN: Wouldn't you like something to eat, after your travels?

ALUPKIN: No, thank you. I'll tell you, sir – I moved to these parts quite recently. Before that, I lived in the Tambov district. But after my wife passed away I inherited fifty-two serfs here, in this area...

MIRVOLIN: Whereabouts exactly, may one ask?

ALUPKIN: The village of Trukhino, about three miles off the main road to Voronezh.

MIRVOLIN: Oh yes, I know it. Quite a nice little estate.

ALUPKIN: It's absolute rubbish. Nothing but sand.
Anyway, having inherited this from my deceased wife,
I thought it'd be a good idea to move here, the more so
since my house in Tambov, not to put too fine a point
on it, is falling apart. So, I moved here, sir, and what
d'you think? This police inspector of yours has already
managed to abuse me in the most shameful manner!

MIRVOLIN: You don't say? That's not very nice, is it.

ALUPKIN: No no, let me finish... It wouldn't matter to
anybody else, but I have a daughter, Katerina – this is
what I'm asking you to judge. Anyway, I'm relying on
Nikolai Ivanych. I've had the pleasure of meeting him
only twice, but I've heard a great deal about his fair-
mindedness...

MIRVOLIN: Ah, here he comes now, sir.

(*BALAGALAEV enters, wearing a frock-coat. ALUPKIN bows.*)

BALAGALAEV: Good day, sir. Please sit down. I... er...
I think I recall having seen you at Afanasy
Matveich's house.

ALUPKIN: That's correct, sir.

BALAGALAEV: And I believe you've only recently
become one of us – I mean, you've not long moved into
our district.

ALUPKIN: That's correct, sir.

BALAGALAEV: Well, I trust you won't regret your move.
(*A brief silence.*)
It's extremely hot today...

ALUPKIN: Nikolai Ivanych, will you permit an old soldier
to speak his mind?

BALAGALAEV: By all means. What is it about?

ALUPKIN: Nikolai Ivanych! You're our marshal of the
nobility, Nikolai Ivanych, our leader. You're like a second
father to us, but I'm a father myself, Nikolai Ivanych!

BALAGALAEV: Believe me, sir, I know that only too
well, I'm well aware of my duties. Besides which, the
flattering attention paid to me by the nobility... Tell me,
sir, what is it?

319

ALUPKIN: Nikolai Ivanych! That police chief of yours...
he's an absolute scoundrel!

BALAGALAEV: Hm! You're putting it a bit strong,
aren't you?

ALUPKIN: No, no, let me speak! Listen to me, please...
One of my peasants is supposed to have stolen a goat
from my neighbour's peasant Filipp... But you tell me,
sir, what does my peasant want with a goat? Eh? Just tell
me, what does he want with a goat? And why must it be
my peasant that steals a goat? Why not somebody else's?
What proof does he have? And even supposing it was
my peasant, what's that got to do with me? Why should
I be held responsible? Why bother me with it? Honestly,
what next? Am I to be called to account for every
missing goat? And will the police chief have the right to
come and insult me? The goat was found in your cattle-
yard, he says... well, he can go to hell, and his goat along
with him! It's not the goat that's the issue here, it's
common decency!

BALAGALAEV: I'm sorry, I'm not sure I quite understand.
You're saying one of your peasants stole a goat?

ALUPKIN: No, that's not what I'm saying – that's what the
police chief says.

BALAGALAEV: Well, there are legal procedures for this
sort of thing, surely – I really don't know why you're
bringing this to me.

ALUPKIN: And who else should I go to, then, Nikolai
Ivanych? You must understand my position. I'm an old
army man, and I've been insulted, my honour has been
impugned, sir. Your police chief told me – in the most
unseemly manner – you watch out, he says, or you'll...
I mean, really!

GERASIM: (*Enters.*) That's Mr Suslov arrived, sir.

BALAGALAEV: (*Stands up.*) I'm sorry, you must excuse
me... Yevgeny Tikhonych, my dear sir, do come in!
(*SUSLOV enters.*)
How are you keeping?

SUSLOV: Very well, thank you. Gentlemen! My best respects...

MIRVOLIN: And to you, Yevgeny Tikhonych.

SUSLOV: Good morning!

BALAGALAEV: And how is your dear lady?

SUSLOV: Well, sir, well... Oh, it's so hot! If I hadn't been coming here, Nikolai Ivanych, I swear to God I wouldn't have stirred from the house.

BALAGALAEV: Thank you. Would you like something? (*To ALUPKIN.*) I'm sorry, I didn't catch your name.

ALUPKIN: Anton Semyonovich.

BALAGALAEV: Well, my dear Anton Semyonych, you can tell me your troubles later, but for the moment... well, as you can see... Believe me, I'll give it my personal attention, you can rest assured of that. Are you acquainted with Mr Suslov here?

ALUPKIN: Not at all, sir.

BALAGALAEV: Then you must allow me to introduce you. He's our local judge, a most distinguished gentleman, in every respect, good-hearted, and greatly esteemed... Yevgeny Tikhonych!

SUSLOV: (*At the table, eating.*) Yes?

BALAGALAEV: Permit me to introduce a newcomer to our district – his name's Alupkin, Anton Semyonych, a new landowner.

SUSLOV: (*Continues eating.*) I'm delighted to meet you, sir. Where are you from?

ALUPKIN: From the Tambov area.

SUSLOV: Really? One of my relatives lives in Tambov, an extremely silly person. Still, Tambov's a nice enough place.

ALUPKIN: It's not a bad town.

SUSLOV: So – what's happened to our dear friends? Maybe they're not coming?

BALAGALAEV: No, I'm sure they are. I'm just surprised they haven't turned up yet. They were supposed to be here first.

SUSLOV: What d'you think – will we be able to reconcile them?

BALAGALAEV: I do hope so. I've invited Mr Pekhterev
too. Oh, by the way – there's something I want to ask
you, Mr Alupkin. You might be able to help us in this
matter – it's something that concerns all the gentry, so
to speak.

ALUPKIN: Ye-es, go on.

BALAGALAEV: Well, one of the landowners here –
Bespandin – he's a decent chap, but he's not right in the
head. Not crazy exactly, but, well... God knows. Anyway,
this Bespandin has a sister, Madame Kaurova, a widow,
and to tell you the truth, she's an extremely silly,
pigheaded woman, you won't get any sense out of her.
You'll see her soon, incidentally...

MIRVOLIN: It runs in the family, Nikolai Ivanych. Her
mother, Pelageya, God rest her, was even worse. People
say a brick fell on her head, when she was little, and
that's what caused it...

BALAGALAEV: Yes, maybe so. Maybe it's her nature...
Anyway, there's been a dispute between this Bespandin
and his sister, the widow Kaurova, over the division of
some property. Their aunt left them an estate in her
will, and for the life of them, they can't agree on how
to divide it. The sister in particular won't agree to
anything. They were going to take it to court, lay it
all out before the authorities, and well, you know the
trouble that would cause. Anyway, I eventually
decided to nip it in the bud, so to speak, take a firm
line and get to the bottom of the matter, knock some
sense into them. I've arranged to meet them here
today, but this is their last chance. If they don't agree
this time, I'll have to take other measures. Why should
I bother myself with it? Let the court sort it out.
Anyway, I've invited Mr Suslov here, and Mr
Pekhterev, the former marshal of nobility, to act as
arbiters, and witnesses. May I ask you to do the same?
Will you help us out in this matter?

ALUPKIN: I'd be glad to, sir. However, since I'm not
acquainted with them, I think...

BALAGALAEV: What of that? That doesn't matter. You're a landowner in these parts, you're a sensible person. In fact, that's even better, since they won't be able to question your impartiality.

ALUPKIN: All right, I'll do it.

GERASIM: (*Enters.*) Madame Kaurova's arrived, sir.

BALAGALAEV: Speak of the devil...

(*Enter MADAME KAUROVA, wearing a hat and carrying a reticule.*)

Ah, at last! Do come in, Madame Kaurova – this way, please.

KAUROVA: Hasn't my brother arrived yet?

BALAGALAEV: No, not yet, but he'll be here soon. Would you care for something to eat?

KAUROVA: No, thank you. I'm on a diet.

BALAGALAEV: Well, there's radishes, cucumber... Wouldn't you like some tea?

KAUROVA: Thank you, but no. I've already had lunch. You must excuse me, Nikolai Ivanych, for being late. (*Sits down.*) I thank God I got here in one piece – my coachman practically flung me out of the carriage

BALAGALAEV: You don't say? The road isn't that bad, is it?

KAUROVA: It wasn't the road, Nikolai Ivanych, nothing to do with the road. Anyway, here I am, but I don't expect much good to come of it. I know my brother's disposition too well.

BALAGALAEV: Well, we'll see, my dear lady. I'm actually hoping we can settle the matter today – and not before time, either.

KAUROVA: Let's hope so. I'll agree to anything, Nikolai Ivanych, you know that. I'm an easy-going person. I'm not one to quibble, it's not my style. I'm a defenceless widow, Nikolai Ivanych, I'm relying on you alone. But Ferapont wants to ruin me. Well, so be it, let him do what he likes, just as long as he doesn't destroy my dear little ones!

BALAGALAEV: Madame Kaurova, please! Look, let me introduce you to our new neighbour, Mr Alupkin – Anton Semyonych.

KAUROVA: I'm pleased to meet you, sir.

BALAGALAEV: If you like, he can take part in our
discussion too.

KAUROVA: Yes, yes, Nikolai Ivanych, I'll agree to
anything. You can invite the whole district if you want.
My conscience is clear, sir. They'll be on my side,
I know for sure. They won't see me abused. Anyway,
how are you these days, Mr Suslov?

SUSLOV: Fine, fine, can't complain, thank you very much.

MIRVOLIN: (*Kissing KAUROVA's hand.*) And how are your
children, dear lady?

KAUROVA: Alive and well, I thank God. But for how long,
eh? They'll be orphans soon enough, the poor little mites.

SUSLOV: Oh, come! Why are you saying these things?
Good heavens, you'll outlive us all.

KAUROVA: Why do I say these things? Well, just possibly
I have my reasons – maybe I can't keep silent any
longer. Yes, that's the whole point. Huh, you call yourself
a judge, and you think I'm going to speak without proof?

SUSLOV: What proof? What do you mean?

KAUROVA: Please, please... Nikolai Ivanych, ask my
coachman to come in.

BALAGALAEV: Who?

KAUROVA: My coachman, my coachman – Karp, his name
is. He's called Karp.

BALAGALAEV: What for?

KAUROVA: Please, just ask him to come in. Mr Suslov
here is demanding proof.

BALAGALAEV: But, my dear lady...

KAUROVA: Do as I ask, please.

BALAGALAEV: Oh, very well. (*To MIRVOLIN.*) Be a good
chap, run out and get him.

MIRVOLIN: Of course. (*Exits.*)

KAUROVA: You just won't believe me, Mr Suslov, and it's
not the first time! Well, that's up to you.

ALUPKIN: I'm sorry, but I can't understand why you have
to call in your coachman. What's he got to do with it?
I don't understand.

KAUROVA: You'll see.

ALUPKIN: It beats me.

(*Enter KARP and MIRVOLIN.*)

MIRVOLIN: Here he is.

KAUROVA: Karp, listen – look at me. These gentlemen won't believe that Ferapont tried to bribe you several times... Do you hear what I'm saying to you?

SUSLOV: Well, come on, my dear fellow, why don't you speak? Did Madame Kaurova's brother try to bribe you?

KARP: Bribe me how?

SUSLOV: I don't know. Madame Kaurova says...

KAUROVA: Karp! Now, you listen, and look at me! I'm sure you remember practically flinging me out of the carriage today, don't you?

KARP: When?

KAUROVA: When?! You idiot! At the bend in the road, obviously, just before the dam. One of the wheels almost came off.

KARP: Yes, ma'am.

KAUROVA: And do you remember what I said to you? I said: "Own up," I said, "Admit it – Ferapont has bribed you. You do her a mischief, Karp, old friend, he said, you get rid of your mistress, and I won't forget you." Now then, do you remember what you said to that? You said, "Forgive me, my lady, it's all my fault, I'm sorry."

SUSLOV: So he's sorry, it was his fault, that doesn't prove anything. What did he mean? What we need to establish is whether he was actually bribed, to do you an injury. Did you admit that? Eh? Did you confess?

KARP: Confess what?

KAUROVA: Karp! Listen to me, look at me! Right, Ferapont was going to bribe you, wasn't he. But naturally, you didn't agree... that's the truth, isn't it?

KARP: Ma'am, what are you saying?

KAUROVA: There you are, you see...

SUSLOV: No, hold on, hold on! Look here, friend – just tell me straight...

KAUROVA: No, let *me* ask him, Mr Suslov! I can't agree to this. You want to frighten him, I can't allow that. Karp, go away, just go away. And see you have a nap, you're asleep on your feet.
(*KARP exits.*)
Well, I must confess, Mr Suslov, I didn't expect this from you. What have I done to deserve this?

SUSLOV: You're pulling the wool over our eyes, dear lady!

BALAGALAEV: Please, please, that's enough. Madame Kaurova, sit down, please, calm yourself. We'll sort all this out.
(*Enter GERASIM.*)

GERASIM: Mr Bespandin's just arrived, sir.

BALAGALAEV: Aha! At last. Well, go on – show him in.
(*Enter BESPANDIN.*)

BALAGALAEV: Good day, sir! You've certainly kept us waiting.

BESPANDIN: I'm sorry, Nikolai Ivanych. Something came up, you wouldn't believe... Mr Suslov, our incorruptible judge, good day, sir, how are you?

SUSLOV: Good day.

BESPANDIN: You wouldn't believe what detained me...
(*Bows to his sister.*) Just imagine – somebody stole my saddle. I've no idea who stole it, either. So what could I do? I had to take the groom's saddle. (*Has a drink.*) Well, I go everywhere on horseback, as you know, but this confounded saddle, it's absolutely dreadful – you can't so much as trot on it, quite impossible...

BALAGALAEV: Mr Bespandin, my dear sir – allow me to introduce Mr... Alupkin – Anton Semyonych...

BESPANDIN: Pleased to meet you, sir. Tell me, are you a hunter?

ALUPKIN: A hunter? In what sense?

BESPANDIN: Eh? Well, the obvious sense – going after game, with hounds...

ALUPKIN: No, sir – I'm not fond of dogs, but I'll shoot at sitting ducks.

BESPANDIN: (*Laughs.*) Sitting ducks!

BALAGALAEV: Anyway, gentlemen, if you'll excuse me, I must interrupt your most interesting conversation. We can talk about dogs and sitting ducks another day, but for the moment I suggest we get down to the business we're all assembled for, without further ado. We can make a start without Mr Pekhterev, don't you think?

SUSLOV: Fair enough.

BALAGALAEV: Well then, my dear Bespandin, please be seated, and you too, Alupkin.

(*They all sit.*)

BESPANDIN: Nikolai Ivanych, I have the profoundest respect for you, I always have had, and it's at your wish that I'm here today. But let me tell you in advance, sir, if you're hoping to get any sense out of my most esteemed sister, then you'll be...

KAUROVA: (*Leaps up.*) You see, Nikolai Ivanych? You see what I mean?

BALAGALAEV: Mr Bespandin, please! And you too, Madame Kaurova! I must ask you to hear me out first. It's been my pleasure to invite you both here today, in order to settle this dispute once and for all. I mean, what kind of example are you giving, a brother and sister, from the same womb, so to speak...

BESPANDIN: Nikolai Ivanych, please...

ALUPKIN: Mr Bespandin, please don't interrupt.

BESPANDIN: What? Are you my teacher?

ALUPKIN: No, I'm not your teacher, but since I've been invited here by Nikolai Ivanych...

BALAGALAEV: That's right, my dear sir – I've invited him, along with our esteemed Mr Suslov here, to act as intermediaries. Now – Mr Bespandin, Madame Kaurova! I appeal to you... I mean, really, a brother and sister, from the same womb, as I said – that can't live in peace and harmony... My dear sir, my dear lady! Think what you're doing, I beseech you! Look, why am I saying all this? It's for your own good, that's all. This has got nothing to do with me, you must see that. I'm telling you for your own good!

BESPANDIN: But, Nikolai Ivanych, you don't know what she's like! Good God, you've only got to listen to her – you've no idea, I tell you!

KAUROVA: Oh yes, and what about you? You bribe my coachman, you egg my maids on to poison me – you want to see me dead, that's what! I'm only surprised I'm still in one piece!

BESPANDIN: Bribed what coachman? What are you talking about?

KAUROVA: Oh yes, sir! And he's ready to swear to it – these gentlemen here are witnesses.

BESPANDIN: (*Turns to the others.*) What's she raving about?

ALUPKIN: (*To KAUROVA.*) Madame, please! Don't bring me into this – I couldn't understand a word your coachman was saying. This is like my goat again.

KAUROVA: Your goat? My coachman looks like your goat? Yourself, more like, sir!

BALAGALAEV: Stop, stop, for God's sake! Madame Kaurova! Mr Bespandin! Why must you keep on insulting each other? Why not let bygones be bygones? Listen – do as I say: make peace now. Give each other a hug! You're not responding...

BESPANDIN: What? How can we? If I'd known this, sir, wild horses wouldn't have got me here!

KAUROVA: No, nor me neither!

BALAGALAEV: So why did you tell me just now you would agree to anything?

KAUROVA: To anything, yes, but not that.

SUSLOV: Nikolai Ivanych, if you don't mind my saying – you're going about this business the wrong way. You're talking about peace and harmony to them – don't you see what kind of people they are?

BALAGALAEV: So what would you do, Mr Suslov?

SUSLOV: Well, what did you invite them here for? To divide the property, wasn't it? I mean, that's at the root of their quarrel, and as long as they refuse to share, then neither you, nor I, nor anybody else will have any peace. And instead of staying home, in this hot weather, we'll

end up rattling along the roads. So let's get down to
dividing up the property, if we're to have any hope of
settling the matter... Where are the plans?

BALAGALAEV: Right, let's make a start. Gerasim!

GERASIM: (*Enters.*) Yes, sir?

BALAGALAEV: Ask Velvitsky to come in.

BESPANDIN: I'll tell you beforehand – I'll agree to anything.
Whatever Nikolai Ivanych says, that's fine with me.

KAUROVA: And me too.

SUSLOV: Hm – we'll see.

MIRVOLIN: Oh, give praise where it's due, sir.

(*Enter VELVITSKY, with the plans.*)

BALAGALAEV: Ah! Come over here... (*Unrolls the plans.*)
Bring that little table. There we are... now, let's have a
look. Yes... "The village of Kokushkino, along with
Rakovo – population, at the 8th Census, ninety-four serfs
of the male sex..." Look at this, look at all the pencil
marks – we've been over this plan more than once, that's
for sure... "Total land area, one thousand, nine hundred
and twenty-two acres, of which two hundred and nineteen
are uncultivated, and the manor-house and pasturage
occupy twenty-four acres; also some strip-farming, but
not much. "Now, gentlemen, please note – we have to
divide this estate equally between collegiate registrar
(retired) Ferapont Bespandin, and his sister Anna, widow
of the late lieutenant Kaurov – in equal parts, mind, as
prescribed by their aunt's will.

BESPANDIN: The old woman went out of her mind before
she died. If she'd left the whole thing to me, there
wouldn't have been any trouble...

KAUROVA: Huh! That's a good one.

BESPANDIN: Well, anyway, if she'd fixed your share by
law... But she'd no sense, what can you expect? Yes, and
people say you used to wash and comb her little dog
every morning!

KAUROVA: That's a damned lie! As if I would comb some
wretched dog – what sort of woman do you think I am?
As for you, well, that's a different story. You're dog-mad,

everybody knows that. That mongrel of yours – forgive me, sirs, if I overstep the mark – everybody knows you even kiss its ugly face!

BALAGALAEV: Please, please! I must ask you both to be quiet a moment. Right, this is how things stand – now, it's over three years since their aunt passed away, and would you believe, there's been no settlement yet. I've finally decided to act as arbiter between them, because it's my duty, you understand. Unfortunately, I've achieved nothing so far. And you can see the root of the difficulty: Mr Bespandin and his sister don't want to live in the same house, so that means the estate has to be divided, but it's quite impossible to split it up!

BESPANDIN: (*After a silence.*) Well... I'll give up my aunt's house, to hell with it!

BALAGALAEV: You'll give it up?

BESPANDIN: Yes, but I'll expect some compensation.

BALAGALAEV: Of course, of course, that's a just demand.

KAUROVA: Nikolai Ivanych, that's downright trickery! That's one of his crafty schemes. He's doing that in order to get his hands on the best land, the hemp-fields and so on. What does he want with the house? He's got his own place, and our aunt's house is a shambles anyway...

BESPANDIN: Well, if it's that bad...

KAUROVA: I'm not letting you have the hemp-fields. No way – I'm a widow, I've got children... how am I supposed to manage without the hemp-fields?

BESPANDIN: Look, if the house is no good...

KAUROVA: Do what you like...

ALUPKIN: Let him finish what he's saying!

BESPANDIN: If the house is so bad, let me have it, and they'll compensate you.

KAUROVA: Oh yes, they'll compensate me all right! A wretched half-acre of barren land, one stone piled on top of another, or worse, a piece of swamp, with nothing but reeds on it, that even the peasants' cows won't eat!

BALAGALAEV: There isn't any marsh-land on your estate...

KAUROVA: Well, if there isn't, you'll find something just as bad. Compensation? No, thanks – I know what that means!

ALUPKIN: (*To MIRVOLIN.*) Are all the women round here like this?

MIRVOLIN: Some of them are worse.

BALAGALAEV: Please, please! I must ask you again to be quiet a moment. And I'll tell you what I propose. We'll divide the whole estate right now into two parts. One part will include the house and its surrounds, and we can add some additional land to the other part, then let them make their choice.

BESPANDIN: I agree.

KAUROVA: And I don't.

BALAGALAEV: Why on earth not?

KAUROVA: So who gets first choice?

BALAGALAEV: You can draw lots.

KAUROVA: Never! God save us, sir, what do you think we are? D'you think we're heathens?

BESPANDIN: All right, then – *you* choose.

KAUROVA: No, I still don't agree!

ALUPKIN: Why not?

KAUROVA: How am I going to choose? Suppose I make a mistake?

BALAGALAEV: I'm sorry, but how can you make a mistake? There'll be two equal parts, and if one of them should turn out better, well, Mr Bespandin has offered you first choice.

KAUROVA: Yes, but who's going to tell me which is better? No no, Nikolai Ivanych – this is your affair, so you should do that. You tell me which to choose, and I'll take it, and be happy.

BALAGALAEV: Well, all right. So – the house with its surrounds and outbuildings can go to Madame Kaurova...

BESPANDIN: And the garden too?

KAUROVA: Of course the garden! What use is the house without the garden? The garden's a mess anyway, five or six apple trees, and the apples are disgustingly sour... the whole farm's not worth a light.

BESPANDIN: Well then, let me have it, for goodness' sake!

BALAGALAEV: Right, the house and garden, with all the outbuildings, and the manor-house, go to Madame Kaurova. Good. In which case, you'll want to see the agreement, yes? Velvitsky! Over here, please. Now, here's how I've made the division...

VELVITSKY: (*Reads from his notebook.*) "The project relating to the division between the landowner Ferapont Bespandin, and his sister, Madame Kaurova, widow of this..."

BALAGALAEV: Start at the dividing line.

VELVITSKY: "The dividing line runs from point A..."

BALAGALAEV: Have a look, please... from point A...

VELVITSKY: "From point A, at the boundary of the Volukhin estate, to point B, at the corner of the mill-dam..."

BALAGALAEV: To point B, at the corner of the mill-dam... Mr Suslov, what's the matter?

SUSLOV: (*Distantly.*) I can see.

VELVITSKY: "And from point B..."

KAUROVA: And may one inquire who's to have the pond?

BALAGALAEV: Well, that's to be held in common, obviously. That is, the right bank will be owned by one person, the left bank by the other.

KAUROVA: Oh. I see.

BALAGALAEV: Read on, read on.

VELVITSKY: "The infertile land will be shared equally: one hundred and thirty acres in the first lot, two hundred and seven in the second."

BALAGALAEV: So, what I'm now suggesting is that whoever doesn't get the farm, takes the whole of the first lot of infertile land; that is, they get sixty-five acres extra. See – here's the infertile land, the first and second lots.

VELVITSKY: "The owner of the first lot undertakes to transfer, at his or her own cost, two buildings into the second lot, and also to permit the re-settled peasants the use of the hemp-fields for two years..."

KAUROVA: Huh! I've no intention of transferring any peasants, or giving up the hemp-fields!

BALAGALAEV: Madame, please!

KAUROVA: Absolutely not, Nikolai Ivanych, not at any price!

ALUPKIN: Madame, please, don't interrupt!

KAUROVA: (*Crossing herself.*) What is this? What's happening? Am I dreaming, or what? Really, after this, I don't know what to say! The use of the hemp-fields for two years, the pond to be common property! No no, I'd be as well to give up the house...

BALAGALAEV: Madame, I must point out to you that Mr Bespandin...

KAUROVA: No, sir, no – don't trouble yourself. I'd just like to know what harm I've done you, to be treated...

BALAGALAEV: (*Interrupts her.*) Madame Kaurova, listen to me, please! You're going on about buildings, about hemp-fields, but your brother can simply add sixty-five acres to the other lot...

KAUROVA: (*Interrupts him.*) No, no, don't say another word, Nikolai Ivanych! Please! What kind of fool would I be, to give the hemp-fields away for nothing? Just remember one thing, Nikolai Ivanych – I'm a widow, I've nobody to stand up for me. And I've got young children, sir, you might at least take pity on me.

ALUPKIN: Oh, this is too much! No, it's too much!

BESPANDIN: So, you presumably think my land's better than yours?

KAUROVA: Sixty-five acres!

BESPANDIN: But is it better, tell me!

KAUROVA: Sixty-five acres! Who'd believe it?

ALUPKIN: Well, go on – answer. Is it better? Eh? Is it better?

KAUROVA: What are you shouting at me for, sir? Is that the custom in Tambov? You appear out of the blue, nobody knows who you are, or what you are, yet here you are shooting your mouth off!

ALUPKIN: Madame, I'd ask you not to forget yourself. You may well be a woman, for all I know, I'm not going to check, but I'm an old soldier, dammit!

BALAGALAEV: Stop, stop, please! Mr Alupkin! Calm down, I beg you! This is getting us nowhere.

ALUPKIN: I mean, really!

KAUROVA: You're a madman, sir! He's crazy!

BESPANDIN: Anyway, I'm asking you again: do you think my land's better?

KAUROVA: Well, of course it is – there's more of it, isn't there?

BESPANDIN: All right, then – let's swap.

(*A silence.*)

BALAGALAEV: Well? Why don't you answer?

KAUROVA: So how can I manage with no house? What use is the place without it?

BESPANDIN: Right, if my land's better, give me the house, and you take the extra sixty-five acres.

(*A silence.*)

BALAGALAEV: Madame Kaurova, at least be reasonable – follow your brother's example. He's made me a very happy man today, I tell you. Every possible concession has been made to you, you must see that. All you have to do is declare your wishes, with regard to the choice.

KAUROVA: I've already said I've no intention of choosing.

BALAGALAEV: So, you don't want to choose, but you won't agree to anything – that's priceless! Madame Kaurova, I must tell you my patience is wearing thin. If we fail to settle this today again, then I shall no longer act as arbiter between you. Let the courts deal with it. Will you please tell me what you actually want?

KAUROVA: I don't want anything, Nikolai Ivanych! I'm in your hands completely.

BALAGALAEV: Yes, but you won't trust me. My dear lady, we must bring this matter to a conclusion – good heavens, that's three years now! So, tell me, what have you decided?

KAUROVA: What do you want me to say, Nikolai Ivanych? You're all against me, I can see that. There are five of you, and only one of me... I'm a woman, so you can easily frighten me. I've no-one to defend me, apart from the good Lord. I'm in your power, sir – do with me as you will!

BALAGALAEV: That's unforgivable! You don't know what you're saying – five of us, and one of you? Do you honestly think we'd force you into anything?

KAUROVA: Absolutely!

BALAGALAEV: Oh, this is dreadful!

ALUPKIN: (*To BALAGALAEV.*) Just get rid of her!

BALAGALAEV: Hold on, Mr Alupkin. Madame Kaurova, please – listen to me. Tell us what it is you want: do you want us to leave the house with you, and reduce your brother's share, and if so, to reduce it by how much? Just tell us, what are your conditions?

KAUROVA: What can I tell you, Nikolai Ivanych? We're obviously not going to agree... but the Lord will judge us all, sir, indeed He will!

BALAGALAEV: Right, listen – I can see you're not happy with my suggestion...

ALUPKIN: Well, go on – answer him.

SUSLOV: (*To ALUPKIN.*) Leave her be – the woman's got a mind of her own.

KAUROVA: Very well. I'm not happy.

BALAGALAEV: Splendid! Now tell us, if you will, wherein your unhappiness lies.

KAUROVA: I can't say.

BALAGALAEV: Why can't you say?

KAUROVA: I just can't.

BALAGALAEV: Perhaps you don't understand me?

KAUROVA: I understand you only too well, Nikolai Ivanych!

BALAGALAEV: Right, for the last time, will you tell us, please, how we can satisfy your wishes, what conditions will you give your consent to?

KAUROVA: No, sir, I'm sorry. You can force me to do your bidding, I am only a weak woman, but as for my consent, no, that I shall not give, I'd rather die first!

ALUPKIN: What, you're a woman? A devil, more like! Yes, that's what you are – you're a troublemaker!

BALAGALAEV: Mr Alupkin!

KAUROVA: Oh, Lord, Lord!

SUSLOV *and* MIRVOLIN: Stop! Stop!

ALUPKIN: (*To KAUROVA.*) Now, you listen! I'm an old soldier, I don't make idle threats, so you can damn well stop playing the fool, or it'll be the worse for you! I'm not joking, do you hear me? If you'd talk sense, I wouldn't say a word, but you're as obstinate as a mule. You watch your step, woman, I'm telling you – watch your step!

BALAGALAEV: Mr Alupkin! Honestly, I must say...

BESPANDIN: Nikolai Ivanych, this is my business! (*To ALUPKIN.*) My dear sir, I'd like to know what right you have to...

ALUPKIN: You're taking your sister's side now?

BESPANDIN: Not at all. I don't care a fig for my sister, but this is about our family honour...

ALUPKIN: Your family honour? How have I insulted your family?

BESPANDIN: How have you insulted my family? Huh, that's a good one. No doubt, where you come from, any idiot can drop by and...

ALUPKIN: What! What did you say, sir?

BESPANDIN: (*Mocking.*) What did you say, sir?

ALUPKIN: Right, then. It's not the done thing to shout abuse in somebody else's house. But you're a gentleman, and so am I, sir, so if tomorrow isn't convenient for you...

BESPANDIN: Any time, sir! And with knives, if you like!

BALAGALAEV: Gentlemen, gentlemen! What are you doing? You should be ashamed of yourselves. For heaven's sake, and in my house!

BESPANDIN: You don't frighten me, sir!

ALUPKIN: And I'm not scared of you either, sir. And as for that sister of yours, well – decency forbids!

KAUROVA: All right, I agree! God in heaven, I'll consent to anything! Just let me sign, I'll sign anything you want me to!

SUSLOV: (*To MIRVOLIN.*) Now, where did I put my cap? You haven't seen it, have you?

BALAGALAEV: Gentlemen, gentlemen!

GERASIM: (*Enters and calls out.*) Mr Pekhterev, sir! (*PEKHTEREV enters.*)

PEKHTEREV: Good day, good day, my dear Nikolai Ivanych!

BALAGALAEV: Mr Pekhterev, how do you do! How is your dear wife?

PEKHTEREV: (*Bows to all.*) Gentlemen, dear lady... My wife is well, I thank God. *Ah, mon cher,* I'm late, I'm so sorry. You've begun without me, I see, and done rather well. So, how are you, my dear Suslov, Mr Bespandin, Madame Kaurova? (*To MIRVOLIN.*) What, you're here too, you poor soul? Well, then, are we making progress?

BALAGALAEV: No, I can't say we are.

PEKHTEREV: Really? But I thought... Oh, friends, friends, that's very bad. If an old man might be permitted to scold you a little... You must settle this, you must.

BALAGALAEV: Will you have something to eat?

PEKHTEREV: No, thank you. (*Takes BALAGALAEV to one side, and points to ALUPKIN.*) *Qui est ça?*

BALAGALAEV: He's a newcomer – his name's Alupkin. I'll introduce you to him... Mr Alupkin! Allow me to present our greatly esteemed former marshal, Mr Pekhterev... Mr Alupkin comes from Tambov.

ALUPKIN: Pleased to meet you.

PEKHTEREV: You're most welcome, sir, to these parts. Your name's Alupkin, you say? I used to know an Alupkin in St. Petersburg. Tall chap, good-looking, with a cataract in one eye – played a mean hand of cards, and built houses... he wasn't a relative of yours?

ALUPKIN: No, not at all. I haven't any relatives.

PEKHTEREV: No relatives? Really? (*To KAUROVA.*) So, my dear lady, how are your little ones?

KAUROVA: They're very well, sir, thanks be to God.

PEKHTEREV: Anyway, friends, let's get down to business, we can have a chat afterwards. Where did I interrupt you?

BALAGALAEV: You haven't interrupted us at all, my dear sir. On the contrary, you've arrived in the nick of time. This is where we are...

PEKHTEREV: What's this? Are these plans?

BALAGALAEV: Yes, indeed. The thing is, you see, we can't reach any sort of understanding, we simply can't get Mr Bespandin and his sister to agree. And frankly, I'm beginning to doubt we'll ever succeed, I'm about ready to give up.

PEKHTEREV: Oh no, no, never, Nikolai Ivanych! A little patience, sir... What, marshal of the nobility? You should be patience personified.

BALAGALAEV: Well, the trouble is, my dear sir – the farmstead isn't to be split up, both parties are agreed about that, so something has to be added to one person's share. And that's where the difficulty lies – what sort of compensation to make for the farmstead? I've suggested all this uncultivated land here, to be given to...

PEKHTEREV: This land... yes, let me see, yes...

BALAGALAEV: And that's where we're stuck now. He agrees, but his sister not only won't agree to anything, she won't even tell us what she wants.

ALUPKIN: As they say, we're getting nowhere fast.

PEKHTEREV: I see, I see. Hm... I'll tell you what, Nikolai Ivanych... of course, you know better than me, but that's not how I would divide it.

BALAGALAEV: Oh, and how would you do it?

PEKHTEREV: Well, I'm talking nonsense, perhaps, but if you'll indulge an old man... *Savez-vous, cher ami?* I think I'd divide it up like this... let's have a pencil.

MIRVOLIN: Here you are, sir.

PEKHTEREV: Thank you. Now, Nikolai Ivanych, let's see... mm, yes... if we draw a line from here, to here... and from here, to here, you see? And finally, from here to here...

BALAGALAEV: No, I'm sorry, my dear sir – in the first place, these plots don't work out evenly...

PEKHTEREV: Well, what of it?

BALAGALAEV: And in the second place, there's no grass for hay in this section.

PEKHTEREV: That doesn't matter – you can grow grass anywhere.

BALAGALAEV: Besides which, you're surely not handing over all the woodland to one owner?

KAUROVA: That's my share, I'll take that with pleasure!

BALAGALAEV: And the peasants, sir – how will they get from here to wherever they're going?

PEKHTEREV: Well, of course, it would be easy to answer all your objections – however, you know best, obviously. I'm sorry, sir.

KAUROVA: But I like this, very much.

ALUPKIN: Like what?

KAUROVA: The way Mr Pekhterev has divided it.

BESPANDIN: Let's have a look at it.

KAUROVA: Do as you please, but I'm in complete agreement with Mr Pekhterev.

ALUPKIN: This is frightful! She hasn't even seen it, and she's agreed to it!

KAUROVA: How do you know, sirs, whether I've seen it or not?

ALUPKIN: All right, then – if you have seen it, tell us which plot you're taking.

KAUROVA: Which one? The one with all the woods, and the hay-meadow, and the extra land.

ALUPKIN: Oh yes, we'll hand over everything to you!

SUSLOV: (*To ALUPKIN.*) Leave her alone.

PEKHTEREV: (*To BESPANDIN.*) Well, sir – what do you think?

BESPANDIN: To be quite frank, I don't think it'll work. However, I'm prepared to accept it, if I'm given this piece here.

KAUROVA: And I'll accept it, if I get this piece.

ALUPKIN: Which?

KAUROVA: The one my dear brother's just asked for.

SUSLOV: There you are, you see? And you're saying she'll agree to nothing!

PEKHTEREV: Hold on hold on... you can't give the same land to two people. One of you will have to make a sacrifice, show a little magnanimity, and take the slightly inferior plot.

BESPANDIN: And may I make so bold as to ask, sir, why the hell I should be the one to show magnanimity?

PEKHTEREV: Why the hell... really, sir, what an uncouth expression! For your dear sister's sake, that's why.

BESPANDIN: Huh, that's rich!

PEKHTEREV: Never forget, sir, your sister belongs to the weaker sex. She is a woman, you are a man – yes, she is a woman, Mr Bespandin!

BESPANDIN: Oh yes, this is pure sophistry now!

PEKHTEREV: What do you mean, sophistry?

BESPANDIN: What I say, damn it!

PEKHTEREV: Well, I'm surprised at you, sir... What about you, gentlemen?

ALUPKIN: Me? After today, I'm surprised at nothing in this entire situation. You could tell me you'd devoured your own father, the pair of you, and I wouldn't be in the least surprised, I'd believe it.

BALAGALAEV: Gentlemen, gentlemen! Please, let me speak. I think this renewed obstinacy should prove to you, my dear sir, that your division isn't exactly a success...

PEKHTEREV: Not a success? Well, that's still to be proved, hasn't it. I won't argue with you – your proposal was no doubt excellent, but mine can't be judged at first sight either. I've drawn the line *en gros,* so to speak, and naturally I may have erred on a few minor details. Both parts must be equal, that goes without saying, we'll have to study them more closely, but that doesn't mean it's a failure, surely?

ALUPKIN: (*To SUSLOV.*) How did he draw the line?

SUSLOV: *En gros.*

ALUPKIN: What does that mean?

SUSLOV: God knows. Must be a German word.

BALAGALAEV: Sir, I have no doubt your idea is splendid, first-rate, but the main thing is to share out the property equally. That's the tricky part.

PEKHTEREV: Yes, indeed. Anyway, you know best. And naturally, I can't dispute with you in this matter. My proposal, as you say, won't work...

BALAGALAEV: No no, my dear sir...

KAUROVA: Oh yes, I can see why Nikolai Ivanych wants it his way.

BALAGALAEV: What do you mean, dear lady? Explain yourself...

KAUROVA: Huh, you think I don't know?

BALAGALAEV: Please, explain.

KAUROVA: Nikolai Ivanych thinks he'll be able to buy the woods from my brother for a song... that's why he's making sure they go to him!

BALAGALAEV: What? Madame Kaurova, please, I think you forget yourself! Mr Bespandin isn't a child. And you'll get your half-share, won't you? Anyway, who told you I intended to buy the woods? You can't seriously prevent your brother selling his own property.

KAUROVA: No, I can't prevent him, but that's not the point – the point is you're not dealing with us fairly, and above board, sir, but just as it suits you.

BALAGALAEV: Oh, this is too much!

ALUPKIN: You see, you're saying the same yourself now!

PEKHTEREV: Well, I must confess this is all a bit of a mix-up, very mysterious.

BALAGALAEV: This is enough to make anybody lose patience... What's mixed up about it? What's so mysterious? All right, then – yes, I intend to buy Mr Bespandin's woods – I might even want to get my hands on his entire estate, so what? What of it, eh? I'm not dealing above board? How can you say such a thing! Madame Kaurova is a woman, I can excuse her, but you, sir... mixed up?! You should have had a proper look first, to see if the estate was divided fairly... You'd see it was, all they had to do was make their choice.

PEKHTEREV: Nikolai Ivanych, there's no need to lose your temper.

BALAGALAEV: No, I'm sorry, but if people are suspecting me of God knows what – me, the marshal of the nobility, considered worthy of the respect and esteem of his peers! No no, why shouldn't I lose my temper, sir, when my honour is impugned!

PEKHTEREV: No-one's impugning your honour, my dear sir, and in any case, why shouldn't a man make a little personal profit from someone else's good fortune, if it can be done without causing offence, as they say? And as far as your being the marshal is concerned, believe me, sir, people don't always choose the most worthy, and just because someone loses an election, it doesn't mean they're unworthy. I'm not talking about you, my dear sir, of course, but...

BALAGALAEV: Oh, I understand you, sir. You're talking about yourself, but it's me you have in mind. Well, you can have another go! The elections are coming up soon. Maybe the nobility will open their eyes this time – maybe they'll finally appreciate your sterling qualities.

PEKHTEREV: If the nobility feel like placing their confidence in me, well, I shan't refuse, you may rest assured.

KAUROVA: Yes, and then we'll have a proper marshal!

BALAGALAEV: Oh, I don't doubt it! But understand this right now, that after all these insulting remarks, it would be positively indecent for me to involve myself further in this business of yours, and accordingly...

BESPANDIN: Nikolai Ivanych, in heaven's name, why?

PEKHTEREV: My dear sir, I honestly didn't...

BALAGALAEV: No, I'm sorry. Velvitsky, bring me all their papers. Now, here are your letters, here are your plans. Divide it up however you like, or get Mr Pekhterev to do it.

KAUROVA: With pleasure, sir, with pleasure!

PEKHTEREV: And I categorically refuse. I have no
intention of... good heavens, sir!

BESPANDIN: Nikolai Ivanych, please, do the honours.
And forgive us, sir – at least, this stupid woman. I mean,
she's the cause of it all.

BALAGALAEV: I don't want to hear another word! I'll tell
you again, divide it however you want, it's nothing to do
with me. I'm sick and tired of it!

BESPANDIN: It's all your fault, you brainless woman!
Why did you mess everything up? Honest to God! You
think I'm going to let you have the woods, and the hay-
meadows, and the manor-house, just like that? Huh!
You'll have a long wait!

ALUPKIN: Good for you, sir! That's what she needs!

KAUROVA: Mr Pekhterev, for goodness' sake, speak up for
me! You don't know what he's like – he'll kill me on the
spot, he's a monster, an assassin! God almighty, sir, he's
tried to poison me several times already!

BESPANDIN: Oh, shut up, you crazy woman! Nikolai
Ivanych, please, oblige us!

KAUROVA: (*To PEKHTEREV.*) Sir, help me, please!

PEKHTEREV: Hold on, hold on! What on earth's going on?
(*Enter NAGLANOVICH.*)

NAGLANOVICH: Nikolai Ivanych, sir! I've come to see
you... If Your Excellency will permit...

ALUPKIN: What, you again? Are you still after me about
that goat? Eh? Eh?

NAGLANOVICH: What are you on about? What's the
matter with you? Who is this person?

ALUPKIN: Oh, I suppose you didn't recognise me?
Alupkin's the name, sir – Alupkin the landowner.

NAGLANOVICH: Leave me alone. Your goat's had his day
in court, sir. I didn't come to see you, it's Nikolai
Ivanych I want.

PEKHTEREV: (*To KAUROVA.*) Madame, will you let me go!

KAUROVA: Defend me, sir! You make the division!

ALUPKIN: (*To NAGLANOVICH.*) Sir, I don't give a damn what you want! You've insulted me, sir! You can go to hell, but you're not taking me for a goat, and that's a fact!

NAGLANOVICH: The man's mad, he's off his rocker!

BESPANDIN: Nikolai Ivanych, take these papers back.

BALAGALAEV: Gentlemen, gentlemen, wait – listen! I feel as if my head's going round in circles. Divisions, goats, pigheaded females, landowners from Tambov, police out of the blue, pistols at dawn, guilty consciences, woods going for a song, lunch, noise, argument – no, no, it's too much! I'm sorry, but I'm in no state – I don't understand a word you're saying, I'm worn out, I can't go on, I just can't! (*Exits.*)

PEKHTEREV: Nikolai Ivanych! Nikolai Ivanych! Oh, this is very nice – our host has just walked out, now what are we going to do?

NAGLANOVICH: What a shambles! (*To VELVITSKY.*) Look, run along and tell him I have to speak to him, it's official business.
(*VELVITSKY exits.*)

KAUROVA: Oh, good riddance. So, when are you going to divide our property, sir?

PEKHTEREV: Who? Me? Your humble servant, ma'am, but you must be mistaking me for someone else.

BESPANDIN: Well, that's us stuck now! Honestly, you! A curse on all women, now and forever more! (*Exits.*)

KAUROVA: Well, at least none of this is my fault.
(*VELVITSKY enters.*)

VELVITSKY: Nikolai Ivanych bids me say that he can't receive anybody. He's taken to his bed.

NAGLANOVICH: Well, his guests have certainly taken care of him. There's nothing for it but to leave a note... My respects to all the company. (*Exits.*)

PEKHTEREV: Wait, hold on – where are you going? I'll come with you. I must admit, I've never seen anything like it. (*Exits.*)

KAUROVA: Mr Pekhterev, sir! Please, judge for yourself...
(*Follows PEKHTEREV out.*)

MIRVOLIN: Well, Mr Suslov, what about you? We can't stay here on our own. Let's go.

SUSLOV: Wait a bit. He'll soon come round, and we can have a game of whist.

MIRVOLIN: Fair enough. And under the circumstances, where's the harm in a little drink?

SUSLOV: Yes, why not, dear sir, why not? That's some woman, eh? She could even run rings round my wife Glafira. Anyway, I suppose that's what you'd call an amicable settlement!
(*End of the Play.*)

A PROVINCIAL LADY

Characters

STUPENDIEV ALEKSEI IVANOVICH
a provincial official, 48

DARYA IVANOVNA
His wife, 28

MISHA
A distant relative of Darya Ivanovna, 19

LYUBIN
Count Valerian Nikolaevich, 49
Valet
The Count's manservant, 30

VASILIEVNA
Stupendiev's cook, 50

APOLLON
A boy in Stupendiev's service, 17

*The scene is the drawingroom of a minor civil servant; upstage, a
door leading to the hall; at right, a door to the study, and at left, two
windows and a door off to a small garden; in the upstage left corner,
a low screen, and in the foreground a settee, two chairs, a table, and
a lace-making frame; at right, in the background, a small piano, in
front of which is a table and chair. DARYA IVANOVNA is at the
lace-making frame. She is simply and tastefully dressed. MISHA is
sitting on the settee, quietly reading.*

DARYA IVANOVNA: (*Without looking up, and continuing to
  sew.*) Misha!
MISHA: (*Lets fall his book.*) What is it?
DARYA IVANOVNA: Have you been to see Popov?
MISHA: Yes, I have.
DARYA IVANOVNA: And what did he say?
MISHA: He said he'll send it, everything'll be fine. I made
  a point of asking him about the red wine. He says you're
  not to worry. (*A pause.*) May I inquire, ma'am, if you're
  expecting somebody?
DARYA IVANOVNA: Yes, I am.
MISHA: May I ask whom?
DARYA IVANOVNA: You're very curious. Still, I know
  you won't gossip, so I can tell you – I'm expecting
  Count Lyubin.
MISHA: What, that rich gentleman who came back to his
  estate a while ago?
DARYA IVANOVNA: Yes.
MISHA: He's supposed to be dining at Kuleshkin's
  restaurant today. Is he really a friend of yours, ma'am?
DARYA IVANOVNA: Well, not these days.
MISHA: I see. So he used to be?
DARYA IVANOVNA: What is this, an interrogation?
MISHA: I'm sorry, ma'am. (*After a pause.*) Oh, of course,
  I'm so stupid – isn't he the son of Katerina Dmitrievna,
  the lady who brought you up?
DARYA IVANOVNA: (*Looks at him.*) My benefactress, yes.
  (*The voice of STUPENDIEV is heard off-stage: "She told you
  not to? Why did she say that?".*)

What's going on?

(*STUPENDIEV and VASILIEVNA enter from the study. STUPENDIEV is in his waistcoat, and VASILIEVNA is carrying a frock-coat.*)

STUPENDIEV: (*To DARYA IVANOVNA.*) Darya, my dear, is it true you told her...

(*MISHA stands up and bows.*)

Oh, good morning, Misha, good morning... Is it true you told this woman not to let me have my old coat today, eh?

DARYA IVANOVNA: No, I didn't.

STUPENDIEV: (*Triumphantly, to VASILIEVNA.*) There you are – you see?

DARYA IVANOVNA: I told her to ask you not to wear it today, that's all.

STUPENDIEV: And what on earth's up with it? I like it, I like the colours and the pattern – good heavens, you gave it to me yourself.

DARYA IVANOVNA: Yes, and how many years ago was that!

VASILIEVNA: You see? Now, come on, put on your frock-coat, sir. Oh yes, it's a lovely colour all right – the elbows are worn clean through, and the back shines something awful.

STUPENDIEV: (*Putting on the frock-coat.*) And who told you to look at the back? Hold on, hold on, take it easy – you might at least have asked me.

VASILIEVNA: Oh, you, you're just... oh! (*Exits.*)

STUPENDIEV: (*Calling after her.*) And don't answer back, woman. Dammit, this is dreadful, it's so tight under the arms! You know, there are some really rotten tailors... it's as if I'm being jerked up on the end of a rope. Honestly, Darya, I can't imagine what's got into you, to have me dressed up in a frock-coat. It'll be twelve o'clock soon, I'm due in at the office, and I'll have to put my uniform on, anyway.

DARYA IVANOVNA: Well, we might be having visitors.

STUPENDIEV: Visitors? What do you mean, visitors?

DARYA IVANOVNA: Count Lyubin. You know him, don't you?

STUPENDIEV: Lyubin? Really? You're expecting Count Lyubin?

DARYA IVANOVNA: Yes, I am. (*Looks at him.*) What's so surprising about that?

STUPENDIEV: Nothing, nothing at all. I agree absolutely. But allow me to point out, my dear, that it's quite impossible.

DARYA IVANOVNA: Why?

STUPENDIEV: It's just not possible, that's all. Anyway, why would he be coming here?

DARYA IVANOVNA: He wants to have a chat with you.

STUPENDIEV: Yes, I dare say he does, but that doesn't prove anything – not a thing. He'll want me to call on him. He'll summon me to his place.

DARYA IVANOVNA: He and I are old friends. He used to see me at his mother's house.

STUPENDIEV: And that doesn't prove anything either. What do you think, Misha?

MISHA: Me, sir? I don't think anything.

STUPENDIEV: (*To his wife.*) There, you see? He won't come. Honestly, how could you...

DARYA IVANOVNA: Well, maybe – maybe not. But don't take off your coat, anyway.

STUPENDIEV: (*After a pause.*) Yes, yes, absolutely. (*Begins pacing around the room.*) So, that's why there's been so much dust raised in here since morning. All this cleaning carry-on. And you're looking rather smart.

DARYA IVANOVNA: Aleksei, please – don't pass remarks.

STUPENDIEV: All right, I won't. No remarks, of course... You know, this Count of yours has lost all his money, that's why he's come back here. Is he young?

DARYA IVANOVNA: Younger than you.

STUPENDIEV: Hm... Yes, absolutely. And that's why you were playing the piano all day yesterday... (*Gestures with his hands.*) Yes... (*Begins humming a tune.*)

MISHA: I looked in at Kuleshkin's today. They're waiting for him there.

STUPENDIEV: Really? Oh well, let them wait. (*To his wife.*) So how come I never saw him at Katerina Dmitrievna's house?

DARYA IVANOVNA: He was working in St Petersburg then.

STUPENDIEV: Hm... They say he's one of the top brass now. Do you really think he'll come? All right, all right, I'm sorry...

(APOLLON enters from the hall, wearing pale blue livery with white buttons, extremely ill-fitting. An expression of dumb bewilderment on his face.)

APOLLON: (*To STUPENDIEV, conspiratorially.*) There's a gentleman asking to see you, sir.

STUPENDIEV: (*Panicked.*) What gentleman?

APOLLON: I don't know, sir, but he's got a hat, and side-whiskers.

STUPENDIEV: (*Agitated.*) Send him in.

(APOLLON gives STUPENDIEV a mysterious look and exits.) Can it be the Count?

(The Count's VALET enters from the hall. He is dressed for travelling, but very fashionably, and he does not remove his hat. VASILIEVNA and APOLLON peep round the doorway, out of curiosity.)

VALET: (*With a German accent.*) Is this where a certain Mr Stupendiev lives?

STUPENDIEV: Yes. What can I do for you?

VALET: You're Mr Stupendiev?

DARYA IVANOVNA: Aleksei!

VALET: Count Lyubin has arrived, and wishes you to call upon him.

STUPENDIEV: You've come from the Count?

DARYA IVANOVNA: Aleksei, come here, please.

STUPENDIEV: (*Goes over to her.*) What is it?

DARYA IVANOVNA: Tell him to remove his hat.

STUPENDIEV: You think I should? Hm... Yes, yes... (*Goes up to the VALET.*) I say, don't you find it a little warm indoors? (*Pointing to the hat.*)

VALET: Not especially. Anyway, I assume you'll come?

STUPENDIEV: Well, I... er...
(*DARYA IVANOVNA signals to him.*)
Actually, may I ask who you are?

VALET: I'm His Highness' servant – his *valet-de-chambre.*

STUPENDIEV: (*Suddenly flaring up.*) Well, take off your
hat, dammit! Take it off, do you hear!
(*The VALET complies, slowly and with dignity.*)
And tell His Highness that I'll...

DARYA IVANOVNA: (*Stands up.*) Tell the Count that my
husband is busy at the moment, and can't leave the
house. However, if the Count wishes to see him, he's
very welcome to do so here. Now, off you go.
(*The VALET exits.*)

STUPENDIEV: (*To DARYA IVANOVNA.*) Well, really, Darya
my dear, you might've... I mean, honestly...
(*DARYA IVANOVNA is silently pacing to and fro.*)
Anyway, I quite agree. But I sorted that fellow out, didn't
I? Gave him what for, as they say. Damn cheek of him!
(*To MISHA.*) Not bad, eh?

MISHA: Indeed, sir. Not bad at all.

STUPENDIEV: Yes, exactly.

DARYA IVANOVNA: Apollon!
(*APOLLON enters, followed by VASILIEVNA. DARYA
IVANOVNA looks at APOLLON a few moments.*)
No, you're just too ridiculous in that outfit. You'd better
keep out of sight.

VASILIEVNA: Why is he ridiculous, ma'am? He's a man,
same as anybody else, and he's my nephew, besides...

STUPENDIEV: Don't argue, woman!

DARYA IVANOVNA: (*To APOLLON.*) Turn round!
(*APOLLON does so.*)
No, definitely not – the Count mustn't clap eyes on you.
Go and hide yourself somewhere... And you, Vasilievna,
go and sit in the hall, please.

VASILIEVNA: Ma'am, I've got work to do in the kitchen.

STUPENDIEV: And who is it tells you to work, you
spoilt creature?

VASILIEVNA: Yes, all right, but...

STUPENDIEV: Don't argue, woman! Shame on you! Now get out, both of you!

(*VASILIEVNA and APOLLON exit.*)

STUPENDIEV: (*To DARYA IVANOVNA.*) So, you really think the Count will come now?

DARYA IVANOVNA: I think so.

STUPENDIEV: (*Pacing the floor.*) I'm in a state of nerves. He'll be furious when he comes. I'm really very nervous.

DARYA IVANOVNA: Please, don't get excited – just keep calm.

STUPENDIEV: Yes. But I'm still nervous. Misha, aren't you nervous?

MISHA: Not in the least, sir.

STUPENDIEV: Well, I certainly am. (*To DARYA IVANOVNA.*) Why didn't you let me go to his place?

DARYA IVANOVNA: That's my business. Just remember he needs you, that's all.

STUPENDIEV: He needs me, yes. But I'm still nervous. What's that?

(*APOLLON enters, panic-stricken.*)

APOLLON: Ma'am, I didn't have time to hide – the gentleman's here! I didn't have time, honestly!

STUPENDIEV: (*Hisses.*) Well, get in here, quickly! (*Shoves APOLLON into his study.*)

APOLLON: I didn't have time, and Vasilievna's gone off to the kitchen. (*Vanishes.*)

(*The voice of COUNT LYUBIN is heard off-stage.*)

LYUBIN: What's going on? Isn't there anyone here? Why did that fellow run off?

STUPENDIEV: (*To DARYA IVANOVNA, despairingly.*) Vasilievna's gone into the kitchen!

LYUBIN: I say! You there!

DARYA IVANOVNA: Misha, go and open the door.

(*MISHA does so, and COUNT LYUBIN enters. He is stylishly and somewhat exquisitely dressed, in the customary fashion of an ageing man-about-town.*)

MISHA: Come in, please.

LYUBIN: Is Mr Stupendiev here?

STUPENDIEV: (*Bowing, rather confused.*) I... er... I'm
Stupendiev, yes.

LYUBIN: Pleased to meet you, sir. I am Count Lyubin.
I sent my man to you, but it seems you declined to call
on me.

STUPENDIEV: Your Highness, I do apologise... I...
(*LYUBIN turns and bows rather stiffly to DARYA IVANOVNA,
who has moved a little way apart.*)

LYUBIN: My respects, ma'am. Yes, I must confess I'm a
little surprised, but I dare say you're an extremely busy
man.

STUPENDIEV: That's true, Your Highness – I am very
busy.

LYUBIN: Perhaps so, I won't dispute that, but I do think
there are certain people for whom one might set aside
one's business, especially when... when...
(*VASILIEVNA enters from the hall. STUPENDIEV motions
her to go away. LYUBIN looks round in amazement.
VASILIEVNA stares hard at him, then hurries out. LYUBIN
turns again to STUPENDIEV, with a smile.*)
... when one is asked...

STUPENDIEV: Oh, that's nothing, Your Highness. It's
just... er, it's just a woman, who came in and went out.
Unfortunately, she came in, but fortunately, she went out
again. Now, if you'll permit me, I'd like to introduce you
to my wife.
(*COUNT LYUBIN barely glances at her, makes a formal bow.*)

LYUBIN: Oh yes... delighted to meet you...

STUPENDIEV: Darya Ivanovna, Your Highness, this is
Darya Ivanovna...

LYUBIN: (*Again, coldly.*) Yes, yes, delighted, I'm sure, but
I've come here to...

DARYA IVANOVNA: (*Modestly.*) Why, Count, don't you
recognise me?

LYUBIN: (*Peering at her.*) Good Lord! Let me see... yes,
it's Darya Ivanovna! Well, well, this *is* an unexpected
meeting! Heavens, it must be ages... It's really you?
Tell me, is it?

DARYA IVANOVNA: It is indeed, sir. Obviously, I must have changed a great deal since then.

LYUBIN: No, forgive me, you're looking even better. As for myself, well, that's a different story!

DARYA IVANOVNA: (*Innocently.*) Not at all – you haven't changed a bit.

LYUBIN: Oh, come, come... Anyway, I'm truly delighted now that your husband was unable to call on me. That's given me the opportunity to renew our acquaintance. After all, we're very old friends, are we not?

STUPENDIEV: Actually, Your Highness, it was my wife's...

DARYA IVANOVNA: (*Hurriedly interrupting him.*) Yes, yes, very old friends indeed. Still, I dare say you haven't given much thought to your old friends all this time...

LYUBIN: I haven't? On the contrary, I assure you. I must admit I couldn't quite recall who it was you married – my late mother wrote me something about it not long before she died, but...

DARYA IVANOVNA: Really, what else would you do in St Petersburg, in the big city, except forget old friends? But us poor provincials, well, we don't forget... (*A gentle sigh.*) No, we don't forget anything.

LYUBIN: No no, I assure you. (*After a pause.*) Believe me, I've always taken the most lively interest in your welfare, and I truly am delighted to see you now, so... so... (*Searching for the right words.*) ... so happily settled.

STUPENDIEV: (*Bowing in gratitude.*) Yes, yes, very happily settled, Your Highness. Poverty, lack of means, that's our only trouble.

LYUBIN: Ah well, yes, I suppose so. (*A pause, then to STUPENDIEV.*) Incidentally, I don't believe I caught your full name...

STUPENDIEV: (*Bowing.*) It's Aleksei Ivanych, Your Highness – Aleksei Ivanych Stupendiev.

LYUBIN: Well, my dear Aleksei Ivanych, you and I need to talk over a little business. I don't think it'll be of interest to your good lady, so it'd probably be better if we were to withdraw. If you'd leave us alone for a little while, perhaps? You and I can have a chat...

STUPENDIEV: As Your Highness wishes. Darya, my dear...
(*DARYA IVANOVNA makes to exit.*)

LYUBIN: No no, please, stay here. Aleksei Ivanych and I can go out. We can go into your room, sir, if you don't mind.

STUPENDIEV: Into my room? Hm... yes, into my study...

LYUBIN: Yes, your study...

STUPENDIEV: Well, if that's what Your Highness wishes, but...

LYUBIN: (*To DARYA IVANOVNA.*) And I trust we shall see each other again, dear lady...
(*DARYA IVANOVNA curtseys.*)
Farewell... (*To STUPENDIEV.*) Now, which way, sir? In here? (*Points with his hat at the study door.*)

STUPENDIEV: Yes, in there. But really, Your Highness...

LYUBIN: (*Not heeding him.*) Good, good, that's fine...
(*Exits to the study, followed by STUPENDIEV, who makes a sign to his wife as he goes. DARYA IVANOVNA remains, deep in thought, watching them go out. After a few moments, APOLLON shoots out of the study, and runs into the hall. DARYA IVANOVNA shrugs, smiles, and resumes her reflections.*)

MISHA: (*Approaches her.*) Darya Ivanovna!

DARYA IVANOVNA: (*Startled.*) Yes?

MISHA: May I ask how long it is since you last saw His Highness?

DARYA IVANOVNA: A long time – twelve years.

MISHA: Twelve years! Really? And you've had no news from him all that time?

DARYA IVANOVNA: Me? No, not a word. He'll have given as much thought to me as to the Emperor of China.

MISHA: You don't say? So why on earth did he say he'd taken the most lively interest in your welfare?

DARYA IVANOVNA: What, you find that surprising? Well, if that surprises you, you really are a very young man.
(*After a pause.*) How old he's got.

MISHA: Old?

DARYA IVANOVNA: Yes, he paints and powders. And he dyes his hair, but those wrinkles, well...

MISHA: He dyes his hair? Dear me, that's shameful. (*After a pause.*) I think he'll be leaving soon.

DARYA IVANOVNA: (*Turns round quickly to MISHA.*) What makes you think that?

MISHA: (*Modestly lowers his eyes.*) I don't know, I just do.

DARYA IVANOVNA: No no, he'll be staying to dinner.

MISHA: (*Sighs.*) Really? Now, that *would* be nice.

DARYA IVANOVNA: Why?

MISHA: Well, all that food'll be wasted, ma'am... and the wine. I mean, if he doesn't stay.

DARYA IVANOVNA: (*Thoughtfully.*) Ye-e-es. Anyway, Misha, let's get down to business. They'll be coming out soon...

MISHA: Yes, ma'am?

DARYA IVANOVNA: So... I want you to leave me here on my own now, you understand?

MISHA: Yes, ma'am.

DARYA IVANOVNA: I'll invite the Count to stay for dinner, and send my husband...

MISHA: I understand, ma'am.

DARYA IVANOVNA: (*Raising her eyebrows.*) You understand what? I'll send my husband out to you...

MISHA: Right, ma'am.

DARYA IVANOVNA: And you can keep him busy – not too long, mind. Tell him I want to discuss something with the Count, which will be to his advantage. Now do you understand?

MISHA: Yes, ma'am.

DARYA IVANOVNA: Right, then. I'm relying on you. You can go for a walk with him, if you like.

MISHA: Yes, ma'am, of course. Yes, why not go for a walk?

DARYA IVANOVNA: Indeed. Now off you go, leave me alone.

MISHA: Yes, ma'am. (*On his way out, stops.*) Ma'am, you won't forget me, will you. I mean, you know how devoted I am to you, body and soul, ma'am.

DARYA IVANOVNA: What are you trying to say?

MISHA: Oh, ma'am, I'm so desperate to get away to St. Petersburg! What would I do here without you? Please, ma'am, do me this favour – I'll pay you back some day!

DARYA IVANOVNA: (*After a pause.*) I don't know what you mean. Really, I don't even know myself... Well, all right. Now, off you go.

MISHA: Yes, ma'am! (*Raising his eyes to the heavens.*) I'll pay you back, ma'am, I promise! (*Exits to the hall.*)
(*DARYA IVANOVNA stands motionless a few moments.*)

DARYA IVANOVNA: He isn't taking the least notice of me, that's obvious. He's forgotten me. So it seems I've been relying on his coming in vain. And the hopes I've placed on that coming! (*Looks round the room.*) Surely I won't have to stay here forever? Well, it can't be helped. (*After a pause.*) Still, nothing's been decided yet. And he's hardly even seen me... (*Looks in the mirror.*) At least I don't dye my hair. Hm, we'll see, we'll see... (*Paces the room briefly, then crosses to the piano and plays a few chords.*) They won't be out for a while yet. This waiting is killing me. (*Sits down on the settee.*) Maybe I've grown rusty in this godforsaken town. How do I know I haven't? Who's going to tell me here what's become of me? Who, in a society like this, can give me any sense of what's happened to me? I'm superior to all of them, unfortunately, but as far as he's concerned, I'm still a provincial, a district official's wife, brought up by a wealthy lady. I've got myself comfortably settled somehow, while he's a famous person, titled, rich... Well, not exactly rich – his business in St. Petersburg has gone to pieces, and I don't think he's come here just for the good of his health. He's a handsome man – or at least he was. These days he uses make-up and dyes his hair. They do say that people in his situation hold their youthful memories particularly dear, and after all he did know me twelve years ago, pursued me, indeed. Oh, to be sure, he chased after me because he'd nothing better to do, but even so... (*Sighs.*) And at that time, I remember, I used to dream of... Well, at sixteen, what *don't* we dream of! (*Suddenly sits up.*) Good Lord! I think I've saved one of his letters! Yes, I'm sure I have. But where is it? Why on earth didn't I think of it before? With any luck... (*After a pause.*) Now, let's see. These notes and books have turned up at just the right time. This is funny – I feel like a general on the eve of battle, preparing to confront the enemy. I've changed a great deal recently. Is this really me, so cool and calm, planning my next move? Well, necessity is the mother of invention; it also breaks us of bad habits. No, I'm not particularly calm, I'm excited now, but only because I don't know whether or not I'll succeed. Oh, nonsense. After all, I'm not a baby, I've started to cherish my own memories, no matter what they are. After all, I won't have any others, and that's half my life – no, more than half – gone already. (*Smiles.*) Meanwhile, they still haven't emerged. And what am I asking for? What is it I'm after? The merest trifle. As far as he's concerned, giving us the chance to move to St. Petersburg is a mere bagatelle. And my husband'll be delighted with any sort of position... can I really not achieve that? If that's the case, I ought to stay in this provincial mudhole, I don't deserve a better fate. (*Putting her hand to her cheek.*) All this uncertainty, these thoughts, have thrown me into a fever – my cheeks are burning. (*After a pause.*) Well, so much the better. (*Hears a noise in the study.*) They're coming out. Now let battle commence! Oh, my timidity, this is no place for you now – leave me! (*Picks up a book and leans back on the settee.*) (*STUPENDIEV and COUNT LYUBIN enter.*)

LYUBIN: So, my dear sir, I can rely on you, can I?

STUPENDIEV: For my part, Your Highness, I am ready to do whatever lies in my power.

LYUBIN: I'm extremely obliged to you, sir. I'll send you the papers shortly. I'll return home today, and either tomorrow or the day after...

STUPENDIEV: Yes, sir, of course.

LYUBIN: (*Going up to DARYA IVANOVNA.*) Darya Ivanovna, you must excuse me, please. Unfortunately, I can't stay longer today, but I do hope, at another time...

DARYA IVANOVNA: Aren't you going to dine with us, Count? (*Stands up.*)

LYUBIN: I'm much obliged to you for the invitation, but...

DARYA IVANOVNA: Oh, and I'd been so delighted... I'd hoped you would spend even a little while with us. But of course we wouldn't dare detain you...

LYUBIN: You're too kind, but honestly... if you knew how much business I must attend to.

DARYA IVANOVNA: But think how long it is since we last met, and heaven only knows when we'll see each other again! You're such a rare visitor here.

STUPENDIEV: That's true, Your Highness – you're like a phoenix, one might say.

DARYA IVANOVNA: (*Interrupting him.*) Besides which, you won't be able to get home now in time for dinner, and I can assure you, you'll dine better here than anywhere in town.

STUPENDIEV: Yes, indeed   after all, we did know Your Highness was coming.

DARYA IVANOVNA: So you'll stay to dinner, won't you?

LYUBIN: (*Under compulsion.*) Well... you're asking me so kindly, I can scarcely refuse.

DARYA IVANOVNA: Aha! (*Takes his hat from his hand and puts it on the piano.*)

LYUBIN: (*To DARYA IVANOVNA.*) I must confess that when I left home this morning, I didn't expect to have the pleasure of meeting you... (*After a pause.*) This is quite a nice town you have here, from what I've seen of it.

STUPENDIEV: Yes, for a provincial town it's quite lively, Your Highness.

DARYA IVANOVNA: (*Sitting down.*) Do sit down, Count, please. (*He does so.*) You can't imagine how happy I am, how delighted to see you in my home. (*To her husband.*) Oh, by the way, *Alexis,* Misha was asking for you.

STUPENDIEV: What does he want?

DARYA IVANOVNA: I've no idea, but it seemed quite urgent. You'd better go and see him.

STUPENDIEV: Now, how am I supposed to... I mean, His Highness is here, I can't go now.

LYUBIN: Oh, please, don't stand on ceremony, sir. I shall be in very pleasant company. (*Casually runs his hand through his hair.*)

STUPENDIEV: What on earth is he in such a flap about?

DARYA IVANOVNA: He needs to speak to you, you'd better go, *mon ami.*

STUPENDIEV: (*After a pause.*) All right. I'll be back in a moment, Your Highness...

(*They exchange bows and STUPENDIEV exits to the hall, talking to himself.*)

What does he want all of a sudden?

(*A brief silence. The Count glances sidelong at Darya, smiles and shakes his head.*)

DARYA IVANOVNA: (*Lowering her eyes.*) Will Your Highness be staying here long?

LYUBIN: A couple of months, I think. I shall leave as soon as my affairs are straightened out a little.

DARYA IVANOVNA: And you're staying at Spassk?

LYUBIN: Yes, on my mother's estate.

DARYA IVANOVNA: In the same house?

LYUBIN: The very same. Though I must confess it's not so pleasant living there now. It's quite dilapidated now, practically in ruins. I think I'll demolish it next year.

DARYA IVANOVNA: You say it isn't very pleasant living there now, Count... Well, I don't know, but my recollections of it are extremely pleasant. You're surely not going to demolish it?

LYUBIN: What, you feel sorry for it?

DARYA IVANOVNA: Indeed! I spent the best years of my life in that house. Besides which, the memory of my benefactress, your dear late mother... You understand...

LYUBIN: Yes, yes, I do. (*After a pause.*) Yes, we certainly had some good times there in the old days.

DARYA IVANOVNA: And you haven't forgotten them?

LYUBIN: What?

DARYA IVANOVNA: (*Again lowering her eyes.*) The old days. (*The Count gradually turns round, and begins looking at DARYA IVANOVNA intently.*)

LYUBIN: I've forgotten nothing, believe me. Darya Ivanovna, tell me, please – how old were you then? No, wait, wait – you know you won't be able to conceal your age from me?

DARYA IVANOVNA: I'm not going to conceal it. I'm the same age now, Count, as you were then – twenty-eight.

LYUBIN: Twenty-eight? Was I really as old as that? No, I think you've made a mistake...

DARYA IVANOVNA: No, Count – no mistake. I remember all too well everything that concerns you.

LYUBIN: (*With a forced smile.*) That must make me an old man, I guess!

DARYA IVANOVNA: You, an old man? Nonsense!

LYUBIN: Well, as you wish – I'm not going to argue with you. (*After a pause.*) Yes, indeed, those were good times. D'you remember our morning walks in the garden, a stroll under the lime trees before breakfast?
(*DARYA IVANOVNA lowers her eyes.*)
No, tell me – do you remember?

DARYA IVANOVNA: I've already told you, Count – we simple country folk can't forget the past, especially since nothing like that ever happened again. But as for you, well, that's a different matter.

LYUBIN: (*Growing more animated.*) No, listen, Darya Ivanovna, you mustn't think like that. Seriously, I mean it. Yes, of course there are many distractions in a big city, especially for a young man; of course it's an extremely varied, busy life... But I can assure you,

Darya Ivanovna, a man's first impressions are never effaced, and sometimes, in the very midst of the whirlwind, the heart cries out for... You understand me, the heart grows weary of all that frivolity, and there's a kind of yearning...

DARYA IVANOVNA: Oh yes, Count, I agree – first impressions never leave one. I've experienced that too.

LYUBIN: Ah! (*After a pause.*) Now admit it, Darya Ivanovna – don't you find life here rather boring?

DARYA IVANOVNA: (*Thoughtfully.*) No-o-o, I can't say that. To be sure, it was hard getting used to this way of life at first. But afterwards... my husband is such a wonderful, kind man!

LYUBIN: Oh, I quite agree – he's a very worthy chap, yes. But...

DARYA IVANOVNA: Anyway, I got used to it. You don't need much to be happy: a good home, a family... (*Lowering her voice.*) ... and a few pleasant memories.

LYUBIN: You have memories like that?

DARYA IVANOVNA: I do, same as everyone else. They make it easier to put up with boredom.

LYUBIN: So, it seems you're bored at times nonetheless?

DARYA IVANOVNA: Does that surprise you, Count? You must remember I had the good fortune to be brought up in your dear mother's house. And just compare what I was accustomed to in my youth, with what surrounds me now. Of course, neither my birth, nor my condition – nothing, in a word – gave me any right to hope that I should continue to live as I had begun. But as you yourself said: first impressions can never be effaced. We can't forcibly erase from the memory even what our reason would counsel us to forget. I shall be frank with you, Count. Do you really think I don't know how wretched, and comical, yes, everything here must seem to you? That lackey who ran away from you like a scared rabbit – that cook... yes, and I dare say even myself...

LYUBIN: You, Darya Ivanovna? Good heavens, you must be joking! No no, I do assure you... On the contrary, I'm surprised...

DARYA IVANOVNA: (*Quickly.*) I'll tell you what surprises you, Count. You're surprised I haven't yet lost all the accomplishments of my youth, that I haven't yet turned into the complete provincial wife. And do you think I find your surprise flattering?

LYUBIN: Darya Ivanovna, you're misinterpreting my words!

DARYA IVANOVNA: Well, perhaps I am. Anyway, let's drop the subject, please. Some wounds remain painful to the touch, even after they're healed. In any case I'm resigned to my fate, living alone in my little dark corner. If your coming here hadn't awakened so many memories, none of this would have entered my head. I'd certainly never have mentioned it. I feel ashamed as it is, speaking like this, instead of trying to entertain you more fittingly.

LYUBIN: Now what sort of person do you take me for, may I ask? Do you think I don't value your trust in me, that I don't appreciate it? Anyway, you're doing yourself a disservice. I just can't believe – I *won't* believe that you, with your intelligence, your education, can have remained unnoticed here.

DARYA IVANOVNA: Oh, absolutely, Count, I assure you. And it doesn't bother me in the slightest. You must understand – I'm a proud woman, but that's all I have left from my past. I have no desire to be liked by people I dislike. Then again, we're poor, and dependent on others – all of which is an obstacle to the sort of acquaintance I might not find offensive. However, that's not possible, so I have preferred solitude. Anyway, I don't mind being on my own – I read, study, and fortunately, I've found a good man in my husband.

LYUBIN: Yes, that's quite obvious.

DARYA IVANOVNA: My husband, of course, has his little oddities... I can say this quite freely, since I'm sure, with that piercing gaze of yours, you can't have missed them,

but he's a fine man. And I would have nothing to
complain of, I'd be perfectly content, if only...

LYUBIN: If?

DARYA IVANOVNA: If only... if sometimes... if certain
unforeseen occurrences didn't disturb my peace of mind.

LYUBIN: Darya Ivanovna, I don't dare understand you...
What occurrences? You spoke of memories at first...

DARYA IVANOVNA: (*Looking straight into his eyes, innocently.*)
Count, listen to me. I won't try to deceive you. I don't
know how to in any case, and with you, that would be just
laughable. Do you really think it means nothing to a
woman, to meet a man she knew in her youth, a man she
knew in a totally different world, under quite different
circumstances – and to see him, as I see you now...
(*The Count covertly fixes his hair.*)
To speak with him, to recall the past..?

LYUBIN: (*Interrupting her.*) And surely you don't think it
means nothing to a man, whom Fate, so to speak, has
hurled to the very ends of the earth... that it means
nothing to him to meet a woman who, like yourself, has
retained that... that first blush of youth, that intelligence,
that charm – *cette grâce?*

DARYA IVANOVNA: (*With a smile.*) Yet that woman could
barely persuade that man to stay for dinner!

LYUBIN: Ah, *touché!* But seriously, tell me – do you think
it means nothing to him?

DARYA IVANOVNA: No, I don't. You see how frank I have
been with you. It is always pleasant to reminisce about
one's youth, especially when there is nothing which
might serve as a reproach.

LYUBIN: So tell me, what answer would that woman give,
if he, that man, were to assure her that he has never,
never forgotten her, and that meeting her has, so to
speak, affected him deeply?

DARYA IVANOVNA: What would she say?

LYUBIN: Yes, yes, what would she say?

DARYA IVANOVNA: She would say that she too was
moved by his tender words, and... (*Offers him her hand.*)

would offer him her hand in renewal of a very old and sincere friendship.

LYUBIN: *Vous êtes charmante.* (*About to kiss her hand, but she withdraws it.*) You are charming, absolutely charming!

DARYA IVANOVNA: (*Stands up, gaily.*) Oh, I'm so happy! I'm so glad! I was so afraid you wouldn't want to remember me, that you'd feel awkward and ill at ease here, that you'd even find us uncultured.

LYUBIN: (*Remains seated, but observes her closely.*) Darya Ivanovna, tell me...

DARYA IVANOVNA: Yes?

LYUBIN: Was it you who advised your husband not to come to me?(*DARYA IVANOVNA cunningly shakes her head.*) Was it you? (*Stands up.*) On my word of honour, I promise you won't regret it.

DARYA IVANOVNA: Why should I? I've seen you, haven't I?

LYUBIN: No no, I didn't mean in that sense.

DARYA IVANOVNA: (*Innocently.*) No? In what sense, then?

LYUBIN: In the sense that you're being stuck here is a crime. I won't stand for it. I won't permit such a pearl to be lost out here in the backwoods. And I'll see to it that you... that your husband obtains a position in St. Petersburg.

DARYA IVANOVNA: Oh, nonsense!

LYUBIN: No no, you'll see.

DARYA IVANOVNA: I don't believe a word of it.

LYUBIN: Darya Ivanovna, perhaps you don't believe I have sufficient... er... er... (*Searching for the word.*) influence?

DARYA IVANOVNA: *Oh, j'en suis parfaitement persuadée!*

LYUBIN: (*Without thinking.*) *Tiens!*

DARYA IVANOVNA: (*Laughing.*) Didn't you say '*tiens*', Count? Surely you don't think I've forgotten my French?

LYUBIN: No, indeed I don't... *mais quel accent!*

DARYA IVANOVNA: Oh, stuff!

LYUBIN: Nonetheless, I can promise you a position.

DARYA IVANOVNA: Really? You're not joking?

LYUBIN: No, no, absolutely not.

DARYA IVANOVNA: Well, so much the better. My husband will be extremely grateful. (*After a pause.*) Only please don't imagine...

LYUBIN: What?

DARYA IVANOVNA: Oh, nothing, nothing. The thought couldn't have entered your head, therefore it shouldn't have entered mine. So, perhaps we'll be living in Petersburg? What joy! My husband will be delighted!

LYUBIN: And we'll see one another quite often, *n'est-ce pas?* You know, I look at you, at your eyes, at your curls, and really, it's as if you were still sixteen, and we were strolling together as we used to in the garden, *sous ces magnifiques tilleuls...* Your smile hasn't changed in the slightest, your laughter has the same merry ring, *aussi jeune qu'alors.*

DARYA IVANOVNA: How do you know that?

LYUBIN: How? D'you think I don't remember?

DARYA IVANOVNA: I didn't laugh much in those days. I wasn't in the mood. I was sad and thoughtful, silent – can you really have forgotten?

LYUBIN: Still, sometimes...

DARYA IVANOVNA: You should be the last person to forget that, *monsieur le comte.* Oh, we were so young in those days, myself especially! When you came to us, you were already a brilliant young officer. D'you remember how overjoyed your mother was? How she never tired of looking at you? Remember your old aunt, Countess Liza – how you even turned her head? (*After a pause.*) No, I didn't laugh much in those days.

LYUBIN: *Vous êtes adorable... plus adorable que jamais.*

DARYA IVANOVNA: *En vérité?* Memory is a wonderful thing! You didn't say that to me then.

LYUBIN: I didn't? I, who...

DARYA IVANOVNA: Anyway, enough. Otherwise I might think you're flirting with me, and that's not the done thing between old friends.

LYUBIN: Flirting with you?

DARYA IVANOVNA: Yes, indeed. You don't think you've changed all that much, since I last saw you? Anyway, let's change the subject. Tell me what you're doing in St. Petersburg – how you live there – that's far more interesting. I presume you've still keen on music?

LYUBIN: Yes, among other things.

DARYA IVANOVNA: Still in excellent voice?

LYUBIN: Well, I've never possessed an excellent voice, but I still sing, yes.

DARYA IVANOVNA: Come now, I remember you had a superb voice, so rich and warm... And didn't you also compose?

LYUBIN: Yes, I still dash off the odd piece, now and again.

DARYA IVANOVNA: In what style?

LYUBIN: Oh, the Italian style. I don't acknowledge any other. *Pour moi – je fais peu, mais ce que je fais est bien.* You used to enjoy music too, as I recall. You sang very sweetly, and played the piano extremely well. I trust you haven't given it up?

DARYA IVANOVNA: (*Pointing to the piano, and the music lying on it.*) There is my answer.

LYUBIN: Ah! (*Goes up to the piano.*)

DARYA IVANOVNA: Unfortunately, it's not a very good piano, but at least it's in tune. It jangles a little, but it keeps me from getting bored.

LYUBIN: (*Plays a few chords.*) Mm, not a bad tone. Now there's a thought! You can sight read, of course?

DARYA IVANOVNA: Yes, I can, if it's not too difficult.

LYUBIN: Oh, it's not at all difficult. I actually have a little piece with me, *une bagatelle que j'ai composée,* a duet from my opera, for tenor and soprano. You may have heard, I've been writing an opera – just for amusement, of course... *sans aucune prétention.*

DARYA IVANOVNA: Really?

LYUBIN: Yes, indeed, and if you'll permit me, I'll send for this little duet... no, better still, I'll go and get it myself. Then we'll try it out, shall we?

DARYA IVANOVNA: You have it here?

LYUBIN: Yes, in my apartment.

DARYA IVANOVNA: Well, for goodness' sake, Count, bring it here, quickly. I shall be most grateful. Go now, please.

LYUBIN: (*Picks up his hat.*) I'll be right back. *Vous verrez, cela n'est pas mal.* I hope you'll like my little trifle.

DARYA IVANOVNA: Could I do otherwise? Only, I must crave your indulgence beforehand...

LYUBIN: Oh, nonsense! On the contrary, I... (*On his way out, stops at the door.*) So – you didn't feel like laughing in those days?

DARYA IVANOVNA: I think you're laughing at me now. However, there is something I could show you...

LYUBIN: Yes? What is it?

DARYA IVANOVNA: Something I've kept. I'd like to see whether you recognise it.

LYUBIN: What on earth are you talking about?

DARYA IVANOVNA: Oh, I know what I'm talking about. Now, run along and fetch your duet, and we'll see later.

LYUBIN: *Vous êtes un ange.* I'll be back in a moment. *Vous êtes un ange!* (*With a wave of his hand, exits to the hall. DARYA IVANOVNA watches him go.*)

DARYA IVANOVNA: (*After a pause.*) Yes! Victory! Is it possible? And so suddenly? Ah! *Je suis un ange – je suis adorable!* Maybe I haven't grown completely rusty. I'm still attractive even to people like him... (*Smiles.*) Oh, my dear Count! There's no concealing the fact that you're really rather comical, and quite old. Yet he didn't so much as blush when I told him he was twenty-eight in those days, and not thirty-nine! Well, I lied through my teeth, quite calmly. Off you go for your little duet, as you call it. Rest assured I shall find it utterly charming. (*Stops in front of a mirror, and admires her figure, passes both hands over her waist.*) Oh, my poor little country dress – I'll soon be parting company with you, goodbye! So I didn't waste my time on you, begging the pattern from the mayor's wife. You've done me good service. I shan't ever throw you away, but I'm not going to wear you in St.

Petersburg. (*Titivating herself.*) Mm, I think even velvet might grace these shoulders...

(*The hall door is opened a little way and MISHA pops his head round. He looks at DARYA IVANOVNA a few moments, and without entering, calls sotto voce.*)

MISHA: Darya Ivanovna!

DARYA IVANOVNA: Oh, it's you, Misha! What do you want? I've no time now...

MISHA: I know, I know – I won't come in, ma'am. I just wanted to warn you that Aleksei Ivanych'll be back any minute.

DARYA IVANOVNA: Why didn't you take him for a walk?

MISHA: I did, ma'am, but he said he wanted to go to the office, and I couldn't stop him.

DARYA IVANOVNA: Well, and did he go to his office?

MISHA: Yes, ma'am, he did, but after a while he came out again.

DARYA IVANOVNA: How do you know he came out?

MISHA: I was watching from around the corner, ma'am. (*Listens.*) I think that's him coming now. (*Disappears, then reappears a moment later.*) Ma'am, you won't forget me, will you?

DARYA IVANOVNA: No, of course not.

MISHA: Thank you, ma'am. (*Exits.*)

DARYA IVANOVNA: Is it possible Aleksei's just a little jealous? Now, that *would* be useful!

(*She sits down. STUPENDIEV enters from the hall, rather confused. DARYA IVANOVNA looks round.*)

Is that you, *Alexis?*

STUPENDIEV: It is, my dear, yes. Has the Count left already?

DARYA IVANOVNA: I thought you were at the office?

STUPENDIEV: I just popped in to tell them not to expect me. I mean, I could hardly go in today, with such a distinguished guest. Where on earth has he gone?

DARYA IVANOVNA: (*Stands up.*) My dear, listen! How would you like a fine position in St. Petersburg, with a good salary?

STUPENDIEV: Me? You're joking.

DARYA IVANOVNA: Well, would you?

STUPENDIEV: Of course I would. Honestly, what a question!

DARYA IVANOVNA: Then leave me alone.

STUPENDIEV: What do you mean, alone?

DARYA IVANOVNA: Alone with the Count. He'll be back any second. He's gone to his apartment to fetch a duet.

STUPENDIEV: A duet?

DARYA IVANOVNA: Yes, a duet. He's composed a duet. We're going to try it out together.

STUPENDIEV: So why have I got to leave? I'd like to hear it too.

DARYA IVANOVNA: Oh, Aleksei! You know how terribly sensitive these composers are, and a third party – well, they just hate that.

STUPENDIEV: Composers do? Hm... I see, a third party. You know, I'm not sure it would be proper... I mean, if I were to leave the house. The Count might feel insulted.

DARYA IVANOVNA: Not in the least, I do assure you. He knows you're a busy man, a government official, and besides, you'll be home for dinner.

STUPENDIEV: For dinner? Yes, of course.

DARYA IVANOVNA: At three o'clock.

STUPENDIEV: Three o'clock? Hm... Yes, absolutely. For dinner. Yes, at three o'clock. (*Turns to leave, pauses.*)

DARYA IVANOVNA: Well? What's the matter?

STUPENDIEV: I don't know... I've got a sort of headache – a pain, just here, at the left side.

DARYA IVANOVNA: Really? At the left?

STUPENDIEV: Yes, I swear – the whole side of my head, right here. I think I'd better stay at home.

DARYA IVANOVNA: Oh, come – you're jealous of the Count, that's what's the matter.

STUPENDIEV: Me? Where'd you get that idea? That'd be just too silly...

DARYA IVANOVNA: Yes, it would be extremely silly, there's no doubt about that. Nevertheless, you *are* jealous.

STUPENDIEV: I am?

DARYA IVANOVNA: And you're jealous of a man who dyes his hair.

STUPENDIEV: The Count dyes his hair? Well, so what? I wear a wig.

DARYA IVANOVNA: That's true. All right, then – since your peace of mind matters more than anything else you'd better stay. But you can forget about St. Petersburg.

STUPENDIEV: What do you mean? Does this position in St. Petersburg... does this depend on my absence?

DARYA IVANOVNA: It does indeed.

STUPENDIEV: Hm... Most peculiar. Well, I won't argue with you, but you must agree, it's a bit odd.

DARYA IVANOVNA: I daresay.

STUPENDIEV: I mean, really odd – distinctly odd! (*Pacing around the room.*) Hm!

DARYA IVANOVNA: You'd better make your mind up quickly. The Count'll be back any minute.

STUPENDIEV: Extremely odd! (*After a pause.*) You know, Darya my dear, I think I'll stay.

DARYA IVANOVNA: As you wish.

STUPENDIEV: Did the Count tell you anything about this position?

DARYA IVANOVNA: I can't add anything to what I've already told you. Stay or go, it's up to you.

STUPENDIEV: And it's a good position?

DARYA IVANOVNA: Yes.

STUPENDIEV: Well, I agree, absolutely. I'll stay. Yes, my dear, I'll definitely stay.
(*The COUNT is heard in the hall, singing a practice scale.*) That's him now. (*After a slight hesitation.*) Right, three o'clock! Goodbye! (*Exits hurriedly to his study.*)

DARYA IVANOVNA: Thank God!
(*Enter LYUBIN, holding a package of music.*)
My dear Count, you're here at last.

LYUBIN: *Me voilà, me voilà, ma toute belle!* I was a little
    delayed.

DARYA IVANOVNA: Show me, show me the music! You
    can't imagine how impatient I am to see it. (*Takes the
    music from his hand and eagerly peruses it.*)

LYUBIN: Please don't expect anything out of the ordinary.
    As I said, it's a trifle, a mere nothing.

DARYA IVANOVNA: (*Her eyes glued to the paper.*) On the
    contrary, sir, on the contrary... *Oh! mais c'est charmant!*
    And this transition is quite charming! Oh, and I simply
    adore this one!

LYUBIN: (*Smiling modestly.*) Yes, it is slightly unusual.

DARYA IVANOVNA: And this *rentrée!*

LYUBIN: You like it?

DARYA IVANOVNA: It's absolutely divine! Oh, let's try it,
    now – why waste time?
    (*She crosses to the piano, and places the music on the stand.
    LYUBIN positions himself behind her.*)
    This is *andante,* right?

LYUBIN: *Andante, andante amoroso, quasi cantando.* (*Clears his
    throat.*) Ahem! Ahem! You must excuse me, I'm not in
    good voice today. *Une voix de compositeur, vous savez.*

DARYA IVANOVNA: Oh, that's an old excuse. Poor me,
    what can I say after that? Anyway, I'll begin... (*She plays
    the ritornello.*) This is quite hard.

LYUBIN: No, not for you.

DARYA IVANOVNA: The words are quite charming.

LYUBIN: Yes, I found them, I think, *dans Metastase.* I don't
    know if they've been accurately transcribed. This is what
    he sings to her:
        La dolce tua immagine,
        O vergine amata,
        Dell'alma inamorata...
    So, anyway, here's how it goes...
    (*He sings the lyric in the Italian style, while DARYA IVANOVNA
    accompanies him.*)

DARYA IVANOVNA: That's so beautiful! *Oh, que c'est joli!*

LYUBIN: You really think so?

DARYA IVANOVNA: Yes, it's wonderful, truly!

LYUBIN: Well, I didn't sing it properly. But the way you accompanied me, good heavens! I assure you, no-one's ever accompanied me like that – absolutely no-one!

DARYA IVANOVNA: Oh, come, you're flattering me.

LYUBIN: Me? No no, it's not in my nature, Darya Ivanovna. Believe me, *c'est moi qui vous le dis* – you are a superb musician.

DARYA IVANOVNA: (*As if she is still totally wrapped up in the music.*) I really love this passage – this is so original!

LYUBIN: Yes, it is, isn't it.

DARYA IVANOVNA: And is the whole opera really as good as this?

LYUBIN: Well, the composer can't be the judge of that, but the rest is no worse, I would say, if not better.

DARYA IVANOVNA: Gracious! Oh, please, won't you play me something from the opera?

LYUBIN: I should be only too delighted to accede to your request, Darya Ivanovna, but unfortunately I don't play the piano, and I haven't brought the music with me either.

DARYA IVANOVNA: Oh, what a pity! (*Standing up.*) Well, another time, perhaps. Anyway, I do hope you'll come and see us, Count, before your departure.

LYUBIN: Really? Why, with your permission, I shall willingly visit you every day. As to the promise I made, you may rest assured on that score, absolutely.

DARYA IVANOVNA: (*Innocently.*) What promise?

LYUBIN: I shall obtain a position for your husband in St. Petersburg, I give you my word. You mustn't stay here. Seriously, that would be a crying shame. *Vous n'êtes pas faites pour végéter ici,* and that's a fact. You ought to be one of the most brilliant ornaments of our society, and I wish... I shall be proud that I was the first... However, it seems to me that you are deep in thought. Might I ask, about what?

DARYA IVANOVNA: (*Singing softly, as if to herself.*) La dolce tua immagine...

LYUBIN: Ah! I knew it, I knew that phrase would stay in your mind! In fact, everything I do is *très chantant*.

DARYA IVANOVNA: It's a beautiful line, quite extraordinary. Forgive me, Count, I didn't hear what you were saying – your music is so enchanting.

LYUBIN: I was saying, Darya Ivanovna, you really must move to St. Petersburg – firstly, for your own and your husband's sake, but secondly, for mine. I make so bold as to mention myself, because... well, because our connection of yore, one might say, gives me a certain right to do so. I have never forgotten you, Darya Ivanovna, and now more than ever I can assure you of my sincere devotion... that this meeting with you...

DARYA IVANOVNA: (*Sadly.*) Count, why do you say these things?

LYUBIN: Why shouldn't I say what I feel?

DARYA IVANOVNA: Because you mustn't awaken in me...

LYUBIN: Awaken? Awaken what? Tell me...

(*STUPENDIEV appears in the doorway of his study.*)

DARYA IVANOVNA: Vain hopes.

LYUBIN: Why vain? What kind of hopes?

DARYA IVANOVNA: Why? Oh, Valerian, I'll try to be frank with you.

LYUBIN: You remember my name!

DARYA IVANOVNA: You see, here, in this place... well, you've paid me some attention, but in St. Petersburg I shall perhaps seem such a nonentity that you'll regret what you're now planning to do for us.

LYUBIN: Oh, that's nonsense! You simply don't know your own worth. Surely you can see... *mais vous êtes une femme charmante*... How could I possibly regret what I'm going to do for you, Darya Ivanovna?

DARYA IVANOVNA: (*Catching sight of STUPENDIEV.*) For my husband, you mean.

LYUBIN: Yes, yes, for your husband, of course. Regret? No, you still don't know my true feelings. And I shall be frank with you, in turn.

DARYA IVANOVNA: (*Flustered.*) Count...

LYUBIN: I say again, you don't know my true feelings, you have no idea.

(*STUPENDIEV rushes into the room, goes up to LYUBIN, who has his back turned to him, and bows.*)

STUPENDIEV: Your Highness, Your Highness!

LYUBIN: No, you don't know how I feel, Darya Ivanovna...

STUPENDIEV: (*Loudly.*) Your Highness! Your Highness!

(*LYUBIN whirls round, stares at him a moment, then regains his composure.*)

LYUBIN: Ah, it's you, my dear Stupendiev. Where did you spring from?

STUPENDIEV: From my study... from my study, Your Highness. I was right here, in my study.

LYUBIN: I thought you were at your office. Your dear wife and I have been making music here. Mr Stupendiev, you're extremely fortunate. I can tell you that quite openly, man to man, because I've known your dear wife since childhood.

STUPENDIEV: You're too kind, Your Highness.

LYUBIN: Yes, indeed – you're a lucky man.

DARYA IVANOVNA: And, darling, you'll be able to thank the Count for...

LYUBIN: (*Quickly interrupts.*) *Permettez... je lui dirai moi-même... plus tard... quand nous serons plus d'accord.* (*Then aloud to STUPENDIEV.*) Yes, you're a lucky man, sir! Do you like music?

STUPENDIEV: Why, of course, Your Highness. I...

LYUBIN: (*Turning to DARYA IVANOVNA.*) By the way, you were going to show me something – have you forgotten?

DARYA IVANOVNA: I was?

LYUBIN: Yes, indeed. *Vous avez déjà oublié?*

DARYA IVANOVNA: (*Hurriedly, sotto voce.*) *Il est jaloux, et il comprend le français.* Oh yes, of course. I remember now – I was going to... I was going to show you the garden. We still have time before dinner.

LYUBIN: Ah! (*After a pause.*) So, you have a garden?

DARYA IVANOVNA: It's quite small, but there are lots of flowers.

LYUBIN: Oh yes, I remember. You've always been very keen on flowers. Yes, do show me your garden, please. (*Crosses to the piano to collect his hat.*)

STUPENDIEV: (*Sotto voce, to DARYA IVANOVNA.*) What's this all about? What's going on?

DARYA IVANOVNA: (*Hisses.*) Three o'clock, or forget St. Petersburg! (*Collects her parasol from the table.*)

LYUBIN: (*Returning.*) Will you give me your arm, please? (*Sotto voce.*) I understand you now.

DARYA IVANOVNA: (*With a faint smile.*) Do you think so?

STUPENDIEV: (*As understanding dawns.*) Yes, yes, by all means... And I'll come with you!

DARYA IVANOVNA: So, you want to come too, *mon ami?* All right, let's go. Come on.
(*LYUBIN and she walk towards the door.*)

STUPENDIEV: I'm just coming. (*Snatches up his hat and moves a few steps.*)

DARYA IVANOVNA: Well, come on, get a move on. (*She exits with LYUBIN.*)
(*STUPENDIEV takes a few more steps, then crumples up his hat and flings it on the floor.*)

STUPENDIEV: Oh, to hell with it, I'll stay! I'll stay here, I'm not going! (*Begins pacing the room.*) I'm a decisive man, I don't like half-measures. I want to see just how far... I want to see this through to the end. I'll be convinced by the evidence of my own eyes, that's what I want. Really, this is absolutely unheard of! All right, let's say she did know him in childhood. Let's say she's an educated woman, an extremely educated woman – why does she need to make a fool of me? Is it because I haven't been brought up like that? In the first place, that's not my fault. She's talking about a position in St. Petersburg – what nonsense! I'm supposed to believe that? Fat chance! This Count of hers'll find me a position just like that – oh yes, of course, he's such an important person. Huh, his own affairs are a shambles. Anyway, even if he can somehow find me a position, why has she got to spend all day with him, *tête-à-tête?* It's not decent! Well, I've given my word, so there's an end to it. Three o'clock. That's what she says – three o'clock. (*Looks at his watch.*) And it's only quarter past two! Right, I'm going out to the garden! (*Looks out.*) You see? They're nowhere to be seen. (*Picks up his hat and straightens it out.*) I'm going, I swear to God I'm going. She told me herself, didn't she? (*Mimics his wife.*) Come on, *mon ami!* (*After a pause.*) No, not a chance! No, sir, I know you too well – you won't go. And what if you did, eh? (*Annoyed, flings his hat on the floor again. Enter MISHA from the hall.*)

MISHA: Sir, is anything wrong? You seem out of sorts. (*Picks up the hat, straightens it out and puts it on the table.*) Are you feeling all right?

STUPENDIEV: Just leave me alone, boy. Don't bother me.

MISHA: Sir, please don't speak to me like that. Have I done something to upset you?

STUPENDIEV: (*After a pause.*) No, you haven't upset me. *He* has! (*Pointing in the direction of the garden.*)

MISHA: (*Innocently.*) Sir, if I may be so bold – who exactly is 'he'?

STUPENDIEV: Who? Him, of course.

MISHA: Sir, who...

STUPENDIEV: As if you don't know! That Count person!

MISHA: And how has he managed to upset you, sir?

STUPENDIEV: How? Why, he's never left Darya Ivanovna's side since morning, singing with her, going for walks with her... I mean, d'you think that's nice? Eh? For her husband, eh?

MISHA: It doesn't matter, sir.

STUPENDIEV: Doesn't matter? Didn't you hear what I said? Singing, going for walks together?

MISHA: Is that all? Really, sir, it's a shame to get so worked up over something like that. After all, it's for your own good, so to speak. The Count's an important man, sir, with a lot of influence, and he's known Darya Ivanovna since childhood – why not take advantage, eh?

Good heavens, sir, after this you'd be ashamed to show
yourself to any right-thinking person. I know I'm putting
it a bit strong, sir, perhaps too strong, but my devotion
to you...

STUPENDIEV: Clear off! And take your devotion with
you! (*Sits down, and turns his back on MISHA.*)

MISHA: Sir... (*After a pause.*) Mr Stupendiev!

STUPENDIEV: (*Without moving.*) Well?

MISHA: Why are you sitting there like that? You'd be
better going for a walk.

STUPENDIEV: I don't want to.

MISHA: Come on, sir, let's go. For heavens' sake, sir...

STUPENDIEV: (*Quickly turns round, and folds his arms.*)
Right, just what is it you're after, eh? Why have you
been dogging my heels all day? Why do you keep
trailing after me, like some sort of nursemaid?

MISHA: (*Lowering his eyes.*) Sir, I was told to.

STUPENDIEV: By whom, might I ask?

MISHA: Mr Stupendiev, it's for your own good!

STUPENDIEV: Please, my dear young sir, I want to know
– who told you to follow me?

MISHA: (*With a groan.*) Mr Stupendiev, please, for God's
sake, hear me out. Two words, that's all, just two words,
I can't explain it all in detail. Oh, look, I think there's a
shower on the way – they'll be coming back in now...

STUPENDIEV: There's a shower on the way, and you want
me to go for a walk?

MISHA: Well, we can't go outside like this. Sir, don't be
alarmed, please. Honestly, what have you got to fear?
We're right here, we can keep an eye on them. Anyway,
it's still the same arrangement, I think. You've to come
back at three o'clock, and...

STUPENDIEV: What business is it of yours? Why are you
fussing around? What has she told you?

MISHA: She didn't tell me anything, sir, believe me. But, after
all, sir, you're my benefactors. You are, and so is Darya
Ivanovna – besides which, we're related. So, obviously, I'm
delighted that you'll be going to... (*Takes his arm.*)

STUPENDIEV: I'm staying here, dammit! I have a position here! Where I'm master in my own house! And I'll put a stop to their little scheme!

MISHA: Well, of course you're the master, sir. But I'm only telling you what I know.

STUPENDIEV: Hah! You don't think she's put one over on you? You'd better watch out, boy, you're still young and foolish. You don't know women, do you.

MISHA: Sir, you can hardly expect me to. Even so...

STUPENDIEV: Listen, I found the Count in here, and with my own ears I heard him making advances: 'My dear lady, you don't know my feelings. I'll show you my true feelings...' And you want me to go for a stroll!

MISHA: (*Glumly.*) I think it's starting to drizzle... Oh, Mr Stupendiev, please!

STUPENDIEV: Good God, he was flirting with her! (*After a pause.*) Hm... it actually is starting to rain.

MISHA: They're coming this way, they're coming back in... (*Again takes STUPENDIEV by the arm.*)

STUPENDIEV: (*Stubbornly.*) No, leave go, I tell you! (*After a pause.*) Oh, what the hell, let's go for a walk!

MISHA: I'll fetch your hat, sir.

STUPENDIEV: Oh, what do I want a hat for? Leave it! (*They both exit hurriedly to the hall. DARYA IVANOVNA and LYUBIN enter.*)

LYUBIN: *Charmant, charmant!*

DARYA IVANOVNA: You think so?

LYUBIN: Your garden is utterly charming, like everything in this place. (*After a pause.*) Darya Ivanovna, I must confess... I didn't expect this at all. I'm enchanted, absolutely enchanted.

DARYA IVANOVNA: What didn't you expect, Count?

LYUBIN: You know what I mean. Now, when are you going to show me this letter?

DARYA IVANOVNA: What do you want it for?

LYUBIN: What for? I'd like to know if I felt the same way in those days, those wonderful days when we were both so young.

DARYA IVANOVNA: Count, I think we'd better not concern ourselves with those days.

LYUBIN: But why not? Darya Ivanovna, can't you see what an impression you've made on me?

DARYA IVANOVNA: (*Embarrassed.*) Really, Count...

LYUBIN: No, no, hear me out. I'll tell you the truth now. When I arrived here, when I first saw you, I must admit I thought – please forgive me – I thought you only wanted to renew our acquaintance...

DARYA IVANOVNA: And you weren't mistaken.

LYUBIN: And that was why I... I...

DARYA IVANOVNA: (*With a smile.*) Go on, Count, go on.

LYUBIN: Well, then I suddenly realised I was dealing with an extremely attractive woman, and now I'll freely confess that you've quite turned my head.

DARYA IVANOVNA: Come, sir, you're laughing at me.

LYUBIN: Me? Laughing at you?

DARYA IVANOVNA: Of course you are! Let's sit down, Count, please. I have a few words to say to you. (*They sit.*)

LYUBIN: You still don't believe me!

DARYA IVANOVNA: What, you really want me to believe you? Oh, nonsense. You think I don't know what sort of impression I'm making on you? Today, for some reason or other, you like me – tomorrow, you'll forget all about me.

(*He is about to speak, but she forestalls him.*)

Put yourself in my place, sir. You're still a young man, a celebrity, you move in the highest circles, and you're a visitor here quite by chance.

LYUBIN: But...

DARYA IVANOVNA: (*Cuts him off.*) In passing, you happen to have noticed me. You know how our paths in life will diverge, so it means little to you to assure me of your... of your friendship. But for myself, Count – I have been fated to live out my days here in seclusion, and I must guard my peace of mind, I must keep a strict watch over my feelings, if I don't want eventually to...

LYUBIN: (*Interrupts her.*) Feelings? *Vous dîtes* feelings? You think I have no feelings? What makes you so sure that those feelings haven't at long last been awakened? And you say seclusion – in heavens' name why?

DARYA IVANOVNA: I've expressed myself badly, Count. I'm not alone – I have no right to talk about seclusion.

LYUBIN: I know, I know – your husband... But honestly... don't you see... I mean, this is between ourselves... alone in that sense, cut off... *de la sympathie.*

(*A brief silence.*)

What really pains me, I must confess, is that you do me an injustice, that you see me as some kind of – oh, I don't know – some kind of false, shallow person, that you don't actually trust me.

DARYA IVANOVNA: (*After a pause, with a sly look at him.*) And should I trust you, Count?

LYUBIN: *Oh, vous êtes charmante!*

(*He takes her hand. She makes to withdraw it at first, then leaves it in his. LYUBIN kisses it passionately.*)

Oh, trust me, Darya Ivanovna, have faith in me – I won't deceive you! I'll keep every single one of my promises. You want to live in St. Petersburg... Well, you'll... you'll see... And not in seclusion either – I can guarantee that. You say I'll forget you? I only hope you won't forget me!

DARYA IVANOVNA: Oh, Valerian!

LYUBIN: Ah, now you see how disagreeable, how hurtful is your mistrust of me. After all, I might think the same, that you're only pretending, *que ce n'est pas pour mes beaux yeux.*

DARYA IVANOVNA: Valerian!

LYUBIN: (*More and more animated.*) Anyway, I don't care – people can think what they like about me! I... I've got to tell you, I'm utterly devoted to you, I'm in love with you, passionately in love, I'm ready to swear it on my bended knees.

DARYA IVANOVNA: On your knees, Count? (*Rises.*)

LYUBIN: Yes, yes, on my knees – it's not the accepted thing, of course – a bit melodramatic.

DARYA IVANOVNA: Why so? On the contrary, I'd say it's really quite acceptable, to a woman. All right – down on your knees, Count – to prove you're not making fun of me!

LYUBIN: With pleasure, Darya Ivanovna – anything to make you believe me... (*Gets down on his knees with some difficulty.*)

DARYA IVANOVNA: Good heavens, Count, what are you doing? I was only joking.

LYUBIN: (*Tries to stand and can't.*) It's all right – I'll manage. *Je vous aime, Dorothée... Et vous?*

DARYA IVANOVNA: Please get up.

(*STUPENDIEV appears from the hall, followed by MISHA, vainly trying to hold him back.*)

Get up, please. (*She makes frantic signs to her husband, scarcely able to restrain her laughter.*) Count, stand up, please!

LYUBIN: Who are you signalling to?

DARYA IVANOVNA: Count, for heaven's sake, get up!

LYUBIN: Give me your hand.

(*STUPENDIEV meanwhile approaches LYUBIN, and MISHA remains in the doorway. DARYA IVANOVNA looks at the Count, then her husband, and slumps into a chair, helpless with laughter. LYUBIN looks round bewildered, and sees STUPENDIEV, who bows to him in greeting. LYUBIN, exasperated, turns to STUPENDIEV for assistance.*)

Lend me a hand, dear sir, I can't get up... I've... I've fallen onto my knees somehow. Help me up, please.

STUPENDIEV: (*Tries to raise him by the arms.*) Yes, sir – yes, Your Highness! Excuse me, I'll have to...

LYUBIN: (*Thrusts him aside and leaps to his feet.*) It's all right, it's all right – I can manage. (*Crosses to DARYA IVANOVNA.*) Well, that's just wonderful, Darya Ivanovna – thank you very much.

DARYA IVANOVNA: (*Pleadingly.*) Why is it my fault, Valerian?

LYUBIN: Oh no, of course it's not your fault! After all, you can't help laughing if something's funny. I'm not reproaching you, believe me, but it looks to me as if this was all fixed up in advance with your husband.

DARYA IVANOVNA: What makes you think that, Count?

LYUBIN: Eh? Because in situations like this, people don't normally laugh, and make signs.

STUPENDIEV: I beg your pardon, Your Highness, but there was nothing fixed up between us. Believe me, Your Highness, it's the truth.

(*MISHA tugs at his coat-tails.*)

LYUBIN: (*With a bitter laugh, to DARYA IVANOVNA.*) After this it's going to be very difficult to deny... (*Stops, then after a pause.*) Well, you don't have to deny anything. I thoroughly deserved it.

DARYA IVANOVNA: Count...

LYUBIN: No, don't apologise, please. (*After a pause, to himself.*) What a disgrace! There's only one way out of this absurd situation. (*Aloud.*) Darya Ivanovna?

DARYA IVANOVNA: Count?

LYUBIN: No doubt you think I won't keep my word now, that I'll simply leave, without forgiving you for your trickery. And no doubt I have every right, since you shouldn't have made fun of a respectable man in that fashion. However, I should like you to know what kind of person you're dealing with... *Madame, je suis un galant homme.* Accordingly, I have the utmost reverence for the fair sex, even when they make a fool of me. I shall stay to dinner – that's if Mr Stupendiev has no objections – and I say again, I shall keep my promises, now even more than ever.

DARYA IVANOVNA: My dear Count, I too hope you will not have a poor opinion of me – that you surely won't think I don't know how to appreciate... that I am not deeply touched by your magnanimity. I am to blame, but you will come to know me, sir, as I now know you.

LYUBIN: Oh, please – what's the point of all these words. It's not even worth your gratitude... But you're giving an excellent performance!

DARYA IVANOVNA: Count, you know you can only give a good performance when you feel what you're saying...

LYUBIN: Aha! There you go again... No, I'm sorry, I'm not going to be caught twice. (*To STUPENDIEV.*) I must look very funny to you, my dear sir, but I shall indeed prove my desire to be of use to you.

STUPENDIEV: Your Highness, believe me, I... (*Aside.*) I don't understand any of this.

DARYA IVANOVNA: That's not necessary. Just thank His Highness.

STUPENDIEV: Your Highness, believe me...

LYUBIN: Enough, enough.

DARYA IVANOVNA: I shall thank you, my dear Count, in St. Petersburg.

LYUBIN: And you'll show me the letter?

DARYA IVANOVNA: I shall indeed, and perhaps also the reply.

LYUBIN: *Eh bien! il n'y a pas à dire, vous êtes charmante après tout...* and I don't regret a thing.

DARYA IVANOVNA: Whereas I, perhaps, may not be in a position to say that.

(*LYUBIN preens himself; she smiles.*)

STUPENDIEV: (*Aside, looking at his watch.*) Hm, and I came in at a quarter to three – not three o'clock!

MISHA: (*Timidly.*) Darya Ivanovna, what about me? I think you've forgotten. And I tried very hard, honestly!

DARYA IVANOVNA: (*Sotto voce.*) I haven't forgotten you. (*Aloud.*) Count, permit me to introduce a certain young man... (*MISHA bows.*) I've taken quite an interest in him, and if you...

LYUBIN: You're interested in him? Say no more... Young man, you may rest assured we shall not forget you.

MISHA: (*Ingratiatingly.*) Your Highness!

(*Enter APOLLON from the hall, followed by VASILIEVNA.*)

APOLLON: Dinner is...

VASILIEVNA: Grub's up!

STUPENDIEV: Ah! Your Highness, may we have the pleasure?

LYUBIN: (*Taking DARYA IVANOVNA's arm, to STUPENDIEV.*) And may I..?

STUPENDIEV: Be my guest.

(*LYUBIN and DARYA IVANOVNA walk towards the door.*)

But I didn't come at three, I came at a quarter *to* three...
So, what's the difference? I don't understand any of this,
but my wife's a wonderful woman!

MISHA: Let's go in, sir.

DARYA IVANOVNA: Count, I must ask your pardon in
advance for our provincial dinner.

LYUBIN: Not at all, not at all... And I'll see you in St.
Petersburg, my provincial lady!

(*End of the Play.*)